Diabetic Cookbook for Beginners

607 Simple and healthy Diabetic Diet Recipes
for Newly Diagnosed
30-day selected meal plan for you,
with 5 meals per day included.

SUZANNE SCARRETT

Table of Contents

The Author

Hi, I'm Suzanne. Thank you for purchasing my book.

I invite you immediately to visit my website, which I manage every day:

www.suzannescarrett.com

Every day I receive dozens of emails and many more personal requests for help.

I am genuinely happy and proud of everything my team and I can do and deliver to our customers.

You will find several recipes with images and articles about nutrition and health. Furthermore, I am at your complete disposal to receive any advice or request you want to write privately.

If you wish, you can also subscribe for free to my mailing list. I do not send spam, and your contact remains private.

To subscribe follow scan the QR code on the next page with your smartphone.

Finally, you will also find a section to contact me privately if you wish.

All that remains is to wish you much joy and serenity by reading this book.

Thank you for purchasing my book.

Suzanne Scarrett

SCAN ME

Introduction

What is Diabetes?

Diabetes and its complications affect millions of people around the world. The most common form is type 2 diabetes which afflicts over 30 million people in the United States alone.

If your blood glucose level is too high, your body can destroy cells in your kidneys and eyes. As a result, you can develop cataracts and lose vision. If it stays too low, you can suffer diabetic ketoacidosis and coma.

During prediabetes, you may experience high blood sugar levels, but they do not cause long-term effects on your health. Because prediabetes is not a serious illness, it does not require a medical diagnosis. You should talk to your doctor if you have blood glucose levels higher than normal for your age and gender (200 mg./dl. for women and 140 mg./dl. for men).

Once you are diagnosed with diabetes, the best way to lower your blood glucose level is to eat healthy foods that are low in sugar and high in fiber, such as whole grains and vegetables.

Diabetes is a disease that can threaten your life. It is a primary cause of heart attack, stroke, kidney failure, neuropathy, blindness, and poor circulation. Although it can be manageable in terms of symptoms and signs, it cannot be cured or prevented. This is why you need to learn how to control it first.

A balanced diet is a very important part of maintaining a healthy lifestyle. For a diabetic, there is a very high risk of becoming obese due to poor nutrition alone. In addition to this, diabetes can cause many complications such as heart disease and kidney

The cornerstone of a diabetic diet is plenty of fresh vegetables, fruit, whole grains, legumes, and other low glycemic index food that will keep blood sugar stable and won’t trigger cravings for unhealthy refined carbohydrates.

It’s so important to remember when cooking for diabetics to emulate the same dietary plan. Most doctors today recommend that all diabetics who have been managing their disease for at least a year or so, begin eliminating refined carbohydrates (white flour products) and sugar, and gradually boost the number of high-fiber foods (vegetables, grains, beans) in the diet.

Types of Diabetes

Based on the order of blood sugar levels in the human body, diabetes can be categorized into three basic kinds: type 1 diabetes, type 2 diabetes, and gestational diabetes.

Type 1 Diabetes

Once diagnosed with type 1 diabetes, the patient is dependent on a strict medical prescription all their life. The doctors in this case provide insulin to the patient's body either by injections or by using an insulin pump. About 10% of diabetes patients worldwide are affected by type 1 diabetes. The only way out for the person is to alter their lifestyle. The person is required to follow a strict diet and exercise routine along with administering insulin shots to maintain a functional body. As the disease advances, type 1 diabetes can led to other medical complications, like hyperosmolar coma, ketoacidosis, heart stroke. Even excessive administration of insulin leads to various malfunctions in the human body. Abdominal pain, frequent urination, thirst, weakness, extreme fatigue, ulcers, vision loss and unpleasant breathing are some of the most common symptoms of type 1 diabetes.

Type 2 Diabetes

The most common type of diabetes, type 2, is also known as lifestyle diabetes. About 90% of diabetic cases worldwide suffer from this type. In this case, the human body can produce insulin through the pancreas to break down food for energy; however, the insulin is not enough to break down blood glucose completely. When ignored for some time, the blood has enough sugar deposited to start showing signs of diabetes. In this case, the doctors do not need to administer insulin to the body through artificial methods; rather, they rely on medicines to do this. Along with the medicines, the patient is required to engage in lifestyle changes to promote a healthy body. The patient needs to work on their weight, change their eating habits, and exercise regularly to prevent the diabetes from moving to an acute state. The symptoms of type 1 diabetes are barely noticeable, though one should be attentive if they develop bad breath, are overweight, or start losing their eyesight. In certain cases, type 2 diabetes has been found to carry from one generation to another.

Gestational Diabetes

Restricted to women, gestational diabetes is a state that is found mostly in cases of women delivering a child. Some women, during the course of pregnancy, show signs of a shooting blood sugar level. This state is called gestational diabetes. The doctor in this case will monitor the mother and child for any long-term sign of the disease. This is done in certain cases after the child has been delivered; both mother and child show signs of completely fighting diabetes until it vanishes. The doctors also call this false diabetes, as the pregnant mother who undergoes a plethora of metabolic activities inside her body can, for a while, show symptoms similar to those of diabetes. The women with this condition do not have to be a pre-diabetic patient. Any pregnant woman can be diagnosed with gestational diabetes. In certain cases, if the problem persists, both mother and child might be contenders for type 2 diabetes. The treatment involves healthy food, mild exercise, and a stress-free life.

How Can Diabetes Be Prevented and Controlled?

Although, medically, diabetes has no cure, minor lifestyle changes will go a long way in preventing or controlling the disease. While type 1 diabetes requires regular monitoring by a doctor, type 2 diabetes can be controlled by following a healthy lifestyle. The idea behind this effort is to identify the factors leading to the pre-diabetes phase, which is just before the onset of diabetes. While a person cannot change the genes leading to diabetes, all of us can put the disease in check when it starts to build up excessive blood sugar levels.

Simple Remedies to Prevent Hunger Pangs for Diabetics

There are also some 'tricks' you can use to entice meal flavors and enhance your eating experience, while lessening your risk of diabetes.

Be realistic

Remember to be realistic with your diet and recognize that really; you can enjoy most things in moderation, so long as you are mindful of what you are consuming. If you want to make sure that you are on track to good health, you can do so by making sure that you are realistic about your goals. If you are new to this diet, instead of cutting out all sweets, for example, you may choose to instead start to sub in healthier food options. Instead of ice cream, you could freeze and blend bananas with some chocolate powder to create a similar effect, for example.

Avoid buying temptation foods

By simply not buying foods that would otherwise be tempting to you that you can't have on your diet, you can actually make sticking to your diet much easier on a technicality.

Keep healthy snacks around you

Make sure that you also set a good example by making sure that you always have healthy snacks on you. If you are going to be working, make sure that you've got some healthy snacks around you so that when you are eventually hungry, you can enjoy your snack and move on without feeling tempted to cheat or get something out of a vending machine.

Cravings List

The infamous 'craving' - oh how it can topple an otherwise well-structured week. By knowing what you need, physically, you can stay one step ahead of the game to out-play those binges. Keep a few of each food substitute at hand, so when you feel the urge to splurge, you're giving your body what it actually needs. By always having options for your 'munchies,' you will teach your body it will always receive exactly the nutritious food it needs, thereby satisfying the immediate craving as well as slowly suppressing the urges.

You Want	What You Need	What to Eat Instead
Chocolate	Magnesium	Raw cacao, nuts, seeds, veggies, fruits
Sugary foods	Chromium	Broccoli, grapes, cheese, chicken
	Carbon	Fresh fruit (berries, apples)
	Phosphorus	Chicken, fish, eggs, dairy, nuts, veggies
	Sulphur	Cranberries, cabbage, cauliflower
	Tryptophan	Cheese, raisins, sweet potato, spinach
Bread, pasta & other carbs	Nitrogen	High protein foods, meat, fish, nuts, beans, chia seeds
Oily Foods	Calcium	Organic milk, cheese, leafy greens
Salty Foods	Chloride	Fatty fish, goat milk, radishes

Effective Tips for Improving Health

We're all here for one thing: to live fuller, healthier lives. And for those living with diabetes, that often means balancing the demands of a challenging disease with a demanding lifestyle. Being a good caregiver is tough. But, armed with the right facts and the right tools, any diabetic can handle the daily challenges of diabetes better—things like counting carbs and measuring blood glucose levels. And that's when you can move forward. How diabetes affects your life it's easy to get frustrated with the disease and its challenges. But any diabetic who has been living with the condition for any time knows that some of this frustration is a waste of precious energy and adds nothing to managing the condition. It's important to keep the focus on the big picture—your lifelong quest to enjoy all life has to offer, even as you live with diabetes every day. Living with diabetes is a long-term process, not a short-term condition. You can be in control of the disease, but you have to get on board and take care of yourself first.

Living successfully with diabetes (type 1 or type 2) also means making the right lifestyle changes—like eating a diet that balances calories, carbs, fat, and nutrients. In short, for any diabetic diet to be effective, it must be:

1. *Diet-Adapted:* the right foods for you.
2. *Well-Balanced:* enough of the right foods to keep you healthy and satisfied.
3. *Nutritious:* plenty of vitamins, minerals, and fiber, in the form of fruits, vegetables, whole grains, and healthy fats.

For diabetics, that means relying on food that's good for you—not just to make you thinner or healthier—but to help keep your blood sugar levels stable. A diabetic diet focuses on maximizing your healthy eating and minimizing the unhealthy. Here's a list of the right foods for the type of diabetic you are:

- For Type 1 diabetes, the right foods include low-fat dairy products and meats and whole grains.
- For Type 2 diabetes, try unrefined carbohydrates including potatoes, sweet potatoes, yams, and black beans.
- For both types of diabetes, legumes like beans (black or pinto), lentils, and peanuts are great sources of protein.

To meet your fiber needs, enjoy plenty of fruits and vegetables—they're the best sources of fiber.

For either type of diabetes, the right fat foods are fish like salmon or tuna, and cold-water fish oil supplements.

If you or your loved ones are committed to a diabetic diet, it's time for you to get healthy, too:

- Control sugar and carbohydrate intake: One of the basic steps that your doctor will advise you to take is to limit your intake of sugar, carbs, and processed food items. Elevating your sugar intake will lead to extra pressure on the pancreas to produce insulin from which to derive energy for cells by breaking down the sugars in food.

- Exercise regularly: With everything being handed to us on a platter thanks to the bane of the technologically enabled lifestyle, most of us underutilize our bodies. Lack of physical movement, along with excessive intake of food, has made obesity a household ailment. When a person regularly exercises, the process activates the cells in the body to function even in a condition of low insulin. This allows the insulin to easily break down the sugar into energy for the cells—and, in turn, for the body. A person diagnosed with type 2 diabetes can keep the ailment at bay without taking medication, provided they exercise regularly.
- Drink water: Water is one of the main elements of the human body and a great caretaker for people diagnosed with diabetes. Drinking water more frequently rather than relying on other beverages helps you avoid the non-essential carbs and sugar that one can intake by drinking aerated drinks. People who consume soda or aerated drinks as their first choice of beverage are more likely to develop LADA, a type 1 diabetes.
- Lose weight: Being overweight is one of the precursors to type 2 diabetes. Therefore, a person should be careful to ensure that they are not becoming obese. One of the easiest methods is to regularly check your body mass index. The reading will give you a fair idea of whether you are starting to grow extra fat in your body. Even a small amount of fat gain greatly affects your chances of attracting diabetes. Follow a healthy diet plan and start working out as soon as possible.
- Do not smoke: Other than causing life-threatening cancer, smoking wildly affects a diabetic patient. Not just smoking, but also second-hand smoke, has been shown to have signs of aggravating type 2 diabetes. Get counseling, if necessary, but quit smoking.

Breakfast

Reduced Carb Berry Parfaits

Preparation Time: 7minutes |Cooking Time: 23 minutes |Servings: 4

Ingredients:

For the nut granola

- Two cups of mixed nuts
- One tablespoon of flax seed
- One tablespoon of sesame seeds
- One tablespoon of chia seeds
- Two tablespoons of pumpkin seeds
- Two tablespoon of coconut oil melted
- Two tablespoons of honey or low carb sweetener to taste (optional)
- Pinch of salt

For the blueberry sauce

- Two cups of frozen blueberries
- Three tablespoon of Xylitol or (sugar alternative)
- One tablespoon of water

For the parfait

- Plain Greek yoghurt
- Fresh raspberries or other fruit of your choice

Direction

1. To prepare the granola, heat the oven to about 175°c and cover a baking tray with baking parchment.
2. Mix all the granola ingredients and put them in the oven, then drop them onto the baking tray.
3. Leave it to bake until the nuts are golden brown for 5-10 minutes. Regularly inspect the granola since it will quickly melt.
4. Allow to cool after you have removed from the oven.
5. Combine all the ingredients in a shallow saucepan to make the blueberry sauce and get it to a boil. Allow the berries to cook for 5-10 minutes until their juice is released. Remove from the oven and allow for few minutes to cool.
6. Lay the yoghurt with the granola, fresh fruit and sauce in your preference bowl to make the parfaits. If the parfait is 30 made in a pot, close the lid and place it overnight in the fridge before serving.

Nutrition *Calories: 2171 |Protein: 65g |Fat: 168g*

Healthy Avocado Toast

Preparation Time: 5minutes |Cooking Time: 13 minutes |Servings: 4

Ingredients

- One avocado peeled and seeded
- Two tablespoon chopped cilantro
- Juice of half lime
- Half tablespoon of red pepper flakes optional
- Salt & pepper to taste
- Two slices of whole grain bread or bread of your choice
- Two eggs fried, scrambled, optional

Direction

1. Toast 2 whole grain slices in an oven until they are crispy and golden.
2. Mix and crush the avocado, lime, cilantro and salt and pepper in a shallow bowl to taste.
3. Spread on all the toasted bread slice with half of the combination.
4. Top with fried poached or scrambled egg, if wished.

Nutrition: *Calories: 501|Fat: 28g |Protein: 16g*

Whole Egg Baked Sweet Potatoes

Preparation Time: 30minutes |Cooking Time: 60 minutes |Servings: 4

Ingredients

For the Potatoes:

- Four medium Sweet Potatoes
- Two heads of Garlic
- Two teaspoons of Extra Virgin Olive Oil
- Half tablespoon of Taco Seasoning
- One quarter cup of Fresh Cilantro, plus additional for garnish
- Salt and Pepper
- Four Eggs

For the Sauce:

- Half cup Avocado, about 1 medium avocado
- One tablespoon of Fresh Lime Juice
- One teaspoon Of Lime Zest
- Salt and Pepper
- Two tablespoons of Water

Direction

1. Preheat the oven to 395°F, cover with baking sheet and tinfoil then place the potatoes on it.
2. Rip off the garlic tips, keep the head intact, and softly rub in the olive oil on top of the uncovered cloves. Create 2 layers of tinfoil in a small packet and wrapping the garlic in it, then put it in the pan. Bake the garlic for about 40 minutes, until it is tender. Remove from the pan and proceed to cook the potatoes for 35 additional 25-35 minutes, until fork tender and soft. When the potatoes are tender, set them aside for about 10 minutes until they're cool enough to treat. In addition, decrease the temperature of the oven to 375 degrees.
3. Break the potatoes down the middle and softly peel the skin back, leaving the skin intact on the sides. In a wide cup, carefully scoop out the skin, leaving a little amount on the sides of the potato to help maintain its form.
4. Mash the flesh of the sweet potato and then cut half of it from the bowl (you will not use this flesh, so use it at a later date in another meal!) Add in the taco seasoning, cilantro and season with salt and pepper to taste into the mashed flesh. Finally, from the roasted heads, squeeze in all the fluffy garlic. Blend well.
5. Divide the flesh between the four sweet potatoes, spreading it softly to fill the meat, leaving a large hole in the middle of each potato.
6. Back on the baking sheet, put the sweet potatoes and crack an egg into each hole and spray it with pepper and salt. Bake to your taste until the egg is well fried. For a good runny yolk, it normally takes about 10-15 minutes and blend until smooth. Then, with the food processor running, pour in the water and combine until well mixed. Sprinkle with salt and pepper to taste.
7. Break the avocado sauce between them until the potatoes are cooked, spreading it out on top.
8. Garnish with sliced tomatoes and cilantro in addition. And enjoy!

Nutrition: *Calories: 399|Fat: 32g|Protein: 18g*

Berry Avocado Smoothie

Preparation Time: 7minutes |Cooking Time: 0 minutes |Servings: 2

Ingredients

- Half of an avocado
- One cup of strawberries
- One quarter cup of blueberries
- Half cup of low-fat milk
- Half cup of 2% Greek yogurt
- One teaspoon of raw honey, optional

Direction

1. Fill the blender with avocado, strawberries, blueberries and milk.
2. Blend until perfectly smooth.
3. Taste, then, if using honey, you can add.
4. Serve or put in a refrigerator for up to two days.

Nutrition :|*Calories: 350|Fat: 17g|Protein: 24g*

Bagel Hummus Toast

Preparation Time: 30minutes |Cooking Time: 4 hours |Servings: 2

Ingredients

- One soft boiled egg, halved
- Six tbsp. of plain hummus
- Two pieces gluten-free bread, toasted
- Pinch of paprika
- Two tsp. of Everything Bagel Spice
- Drizzle of olive oil

Directions

1. Spread each bread piece with 3 tablespoons of hummus.
2. Attach of slice of halved egg and finish with 1 teaspoon of 'Bagel' spice each.
3. Sprinkle small amount of paprika, muzzle with olive oil and serve at once.

Nutrition: *Calories 213|Fat 11.6g |Protein 6.5g*

Black Bean Tacos Breakfast

Preparation Time: 9minutes |Cooking Time: 13 minutes |Servings: 4

Ingredients

- Half cup of red onion, diced
- 86-inch soft white corn tortillas, warmed
- One clove of garlic, minced
- One tsp avocado oil
- One quarter cup of chopped fresh cilantro
- Four eggs
- One 15 ounce can of black beans, rinsed and drained
- One small avocado, diced

- One quarter teaspoon of ground chipotle powder
- Half cup fresh or your favorite jarred salsa

Direction

1. Scramble Eggs. You know how it can be done. Make them as you would usually make them. Here's a guide if you need a reminder, maybe!
2. Sauté the beans: Heat the avocado oil over moderate heat in a large skillet. Sauté the onion for about 3 minutes until it is tender.
3. Add the garlic and beans and heat until fully cooked, about 2-5 minutes.
4. Blister the tortillas or heat them in a dry skillet over an open fire on the range. Put aside, wrapped to keep them warm, in a cloth napkin.
5. Layer the beans, then slice each tortilla with the eggs. Maintain to only 1/4 cup of beans per taco. You may be tempted but try not to overstuff the tortillas. Top up as needed with salsa, avocado and cilantro.

Nutrition: *Calories: 349|Protein: 11.5g|Fat: 15g*

Strawberry Coconut Bake

Preparation Time: 11minutes |Cooking Time: 23 41minutes |Servings: 2

Ingredients

- Half cup of chopped walnuts
- Two cups of unsweetened coconut flakes
- One tsp. Of cinnamon
- One quarter cup of chia seeds
- Two cups of diced strawberries
- One ripe banana mashed
- One tsp baking soda
- Four large eggs
- One quarter tsp of salt
- One cup of unsweetened nut milk
- Two tbsp of coconut oil, melted

Direction

1. Preheat to 375 degrees in your oven. Grease a square 8-inch pan and set aside.
2. Combine the dried ingredients in a big bowl: walnuts, chia seeds, cinnamon, salt and baking soda.
3. Whisk the eggs and milk together in a smaller dish. Now, add mashed banana and coconut oil to the mixture. To dry, add the wet ingredients and blend properly. Fold the strawberries in.
4. Bake for about 40 minutes, or until the top is golden and solid.
5. And serve hot!

Nutrition:|*Calories 395 |Fat 40g|Protein 7.5g*

Paleo Breakfast Hash

Preparation Time: 7minutes |Cooking Time: 33 minutes |Servings: 5

Ingredients

- Eight oz white mushroom, quartered
- 1lb brussels sprout, quartered
- Everything bagel seasoning
- One tbsp olive oil or avocado oil
- Three cloves of garlic, minced
- One small onion diced
- Crushed red pepper, optional
- Eight slices of nitrate free bacon sugar free, for Whole30, cut into pieces
- Sea salt and pepper to taste
- Six large eggs

Direction

1. Preheat to 425 degrees F in your oven. Arrange the mushrooms and Brussels sprouts in a single layer on a sheet tray, drizzle with the olive oil and add salt and pepper. Sprinkle the onions on the end and place the strips of bacon equally over the vegetables.
2. Roast for 15 mins in the preheated oven, then sprinkle with the garlic and stir gently. Roast for another 10 minutes or until the bacon and vegetables are crisp and fluffy, then extract from the oven.
3. For each egg, make tiny gaps in the hash, gently smash one at a time into a space, careful not to 'split' the yolk. Sprinkle all the bagel seasoning and crushed red pepper over the bacon, eggs and vegetables as you wished.
4. Return the baking tray to the oven and bake for another 5-10 minutes or until the eggs are ideally fried. For me, for solid whites and light yolks, it was 7 minutes. Remove from the oven and quickly serve. Enjoy! Enjoy!

Nutrition: *Calories: 250 |Protein: 14g |Fat: 18g*

Omelet with Chickpea Flour*

Preparation Time: 10minutes |Cooking Time: 20 minutes |Servings: 1

Ingredients:

- 1 cup, chickpea flour
- 1/3 cup, nutritional yeast
- 3 finely chopped green onions
- 4 ounces, sautéed mushrooms
- ½ teaspoon, onion powder
- ¼ teaspoon, black pepper
- ½ teaspoon, garlic powder
- ½ teaspoon, baking soda
- ¼ teaspoon, white pepper

Directions:

1. Combine the onion powder, white pepper, chickpea flour, garlic powder, black and white pepper, baking soda, and nutritional yeast.
2. Add 1 cup of water and create a smooth batter. On medium heat, put a frying pan and add the batter just like the way you would cook pancakes.
3. On the batter, sprinkle some green onion and mushrooms. Flip the omelet and cook evenly on both sides. Once both sides are cooked, serve the omelet with spinach, tomatoes, hot sauce, and salsa.

Nutrition:*150 Calorie|2g Fat|2g Carb|10gvProteins*

White Sandwich Bread *

Preparation Time: 10minutes |Cooking Time: 20 minutes |Servings: 1

Ingredients:

- 1 cup warm water
- 1 cup warm almond milk or any other nondairy milk of your choice
- 2 tablespoons active dry yeast
- 4 tablespoons oil
- 2 ½ teaspoons salt
- 2 tablespoons raw sugar or 4 tablespoons maple syrup /agave nectar
- 6 cups all-purpose flour

Directions:

4. Add warm water, yeast and sugar into a bowl and stir. Set aside for 5 minutes or until lots of tiny bubbles are formed, sort of frothy.
5. Add flour and salt into a mixing bowl and stir. Pour the oil, yeast mix and milk and mix into dough. If the dough is too hard, add a little water, a tablespoon at a time and mix well each time. If the dough is too sticky, add more flour, a tablespoon at a time. Knead the dough until soft and supple. Use hands or hook attachment of the stand mixer.
6. Now spray some water on top of the dough. Keep the bowl covered with a towel. Let it rest until it doubles in size.
7. Remove the dough from the bowl and place on your countertop. Punch the dough.
8. Line a loaf pan with parchment paper. You can also grease with some oil if you prefer.
9. Place the dough in the loaf pan. Now spray some more water on top of the dough. Keep the loaf pan covered with a towel. Let it rest until the dough doubles in size.
10. Bake in a preheated oven at 370 degrees for about 40 – 50 minutes.
11. Let it cool to room temperature. Cut into 16 equal slices and use as required. Store in a breadbox at room temperature.

Nutrition: *209 Calories |4g Fat |3.5g Carb*

Sprouted Toast with Creamy Avocado and Sprouts

Preparation Time: 10minutes |Cooking Time: 15 minutes |Servings: 3

Ingredients:

- 2 small sized bread sprouts
- 1 cup of finely cut tomatoes
- 2 moderate size avocados
- 1 small cup of alfalfa
- Pure sea salt and bell pepper

Directions:

1. Add the avocado, alfalfa, and tomatoes to the bread and season to taste with pure sea salt and pepper. Have a sumptuous breakfast with any freshly extracted juice of your choice.

Nutrition:*82 calories |15g fiber|30g protein*

Scrambled Turmeric Tofu

Preparation Time: 5minutes |Cooking Time: 15 minutes |Servings: 4

Ingredients:

- 1 crumbled serve of tofu
- 1 small cup of finely chopped onions
- 1 teaspoon of the fresh parsley
- 1 teaspoon of coconut oil
- 1 cup of soft spinach
- 1 small teaspoon of Turmeric
- 2 avocado serves

- 75g of tomatoes
- One small spoon of roasted paprika

Directions:

1. Make tofu crumbs with your hands and keep it separately. Sauté diced onions in oil till it softens.
2. Put your tofu, tomatoes, and other seasonings and combine till tofu is well prepared. Add veggies and stir. Serve in a bowl alongside some avocado.

Nutrition:*91 calories|12g fiber|8g sugar*

Breakfast Salad

Preparation Time: 5minutes |Cooking Time: 15 minutes |Servings: 3

Ingredients:

- 1 cup of finely diced kale
- 1 cup of cabbage, red and Chinese
- 2 tablespoons of coconut oil
- 1 cup of spinach
- 2 moderate avocados
- 1.2kg of chickpeas sprout
- 2 tablespoons of sunflower seed sprouts
- Pure sea salt (seasoning)
- Bell pepper (seasoning)
- Lemon juice (seasoning)

Directions:

1. Add spinach, Chinese and red cabbage, kale, coconut oil, in a container.
2. Add seasoning to taste and mix adequately. Add other ingredients and mix.

Nutrition:*112 calories|28g protein|10g fiber*

Green Goddess Bowl with Avocado Cumin Dressing

Preparation Time: 10minutes |Cooking Time: 20 minutes |Servings: 4

Ingredients:

- 3 heaping cups of finely sliced kale
- 1 small cup of diced broccoli florets
- ½ cup of zucchini spiralized noodles
- ½ cup of soaked Kelp noodles
- 3 cups of tomatoes
- 2 tablespoon of hemp seeds
- Tahini dressing ingredients:
- 1 small cup of sesame butter
- 1 cup of alkaline water
- 1 cup of freshly extracted lemon
- 1 garlic, finely chopped clove
- ¾ tablespoon of pure sea salt
- 1 spoon of olive oil
- Bell pepper
- Avocado dressing ingredients:
- 1 big avocado
- 2 freshly extracted lime
- 1 cup of alkaline water
- 1 tablespoon of olive oil
- Bell pepper
- 1 tablespoon of powdered cumin

Directions:

1. Simmer veggies — kale and broccoli for about four minutes.
2. Combine noodles and add avocado cumin dressing. Toss for a while. Add tomatoes and combine well. Put the cooked kale and broccoli in a plate, add Tahini dressing, add noodles and tomatoes.
3. Add a couple of hemp seeds to the whole dish and enjoy it.

Nutrition:*109 Calories |17g fiber|8g sugar*

Quinoa Burrito*

Preparation Time: 15minutes |Cooking Time: 10 minutes |Servings: 1

Ingredients:

- 1 cup of quinoa - 2 cups of black beans
- 4 finely chopped onions, green
- 4 finely chopped garlic
- Two freshly cut limes
- 1 big tablespoon of cumin
- 2 beautifully diced avocado
- 1 small cup of beautifully diced cilantro

Directions:

- Boil quinoa. During this process, put the beans in low heat. Add other ingredients to the beans pot and let it mix well for about 15 minutes. Serve quinoa and add the prepared beans.

Nutrition:*117 Calories|27g protein|10g fiber*

Baked Banana-Nut Oatmeal Cups

Preparation Time: 17minutes |Cooking Time: 40 minutes |Servings: 4

Ingredients

- Three cups of rolled oats.
- One and half cups of low-fat milk

- Two ripe bananas
- One-quarter cup of packed brown sugar
- Two larges lightly beaten eggs.
- One teaspoon of baking powder
- One teaspoon of ground cinnamon
- One teaspoon of vanilla extract
- Half teaspoon of salt
- Half cup of toasted chopped pecans

Directions

1. Preheat Cooking appliance to 375 degrees F. Coat a gem tin with change of state spray.
2. Combine oats, milk, bananas, refined sugar, eggs, leaven, cinnamon, vanilla and salt during a giant bowl. Fold in pecans. Divide the mixture among the gem cups (about 1/3 cup each). Bake till a pick inserted within the center comes out clean, regarding twenty-five minutes.
3. Cool within the pan for ten minutes, then end up onto a wire rack.
4. Serve heat or at temperature.

Nutrition: *Calories 178|Protein 5.3g |Fat 6.3g*

Veggie Breakfast Wrap

Preparation Time: 12minutes |Cooking Time: 13 minutes |Servings: 2

Ingredients

- Two teaspoon of olive oil or other
- One cup of sliced mushrooms
- Two eggs
- Half cup of egg white or egg replacement
- One cup of firmly packed spinach or other greens
- Two tablespoons of sliced scallions.
- One cooking nonstick spray
- Two whole wheat and low-carb flour tortillas
- Two tablespoons of salsa

Directions

1. Add oil to the frying pan over medium heat. Add mushrooms and sauté till nicely brown at edges (about three minutes), set aside.
2. Beat eggs with egg whites or egg substitute in medium sized bowl, employing a mixer or by hand, till emulsified. Stir in cut spinach, and scallions. you'll additionally further recent or dried herbs like basil or parsley for Moe flavor.
3. Begin heating medium/large frying pan over medium-low heat. Coat pan munificently with change of state spray. Pour in egg mixture and still scramble the mixture because it cooks employing a spatula. once eggs area unit broiled to your feeling, close up the warmth and stir in mushrooms.
4. Unfold 1/2 the egg mixture down the 36 middle of every battercake. high every with one tablespoon recent condiment or alternative e sauce of your alternative. Garnish with further toppings like avocado slices, bell pepper or tomato if desired, then roll it up to form a wrap.

Nutrition: *Calories 220 |Fat 11g |Protein 19g*

Breakfast Egg and Ham Burrito

Preparation Time: 21minutes |Cooking Time: 13 minutes |Servings: 3

Ingredients

- Four eggs
- egg whites
- one dash hot pepper sauce
- one quarter teaspoon of black pepper
- two tablespoon of cheddar cheese
- two tablespoons of margarine
- four slices of deli
- one quarter cup of sliced onion
- one quarter cup of diced green pepper.
- Four heated corn tortilla
- Salsa

Directions

1. Using a medium bowl, whisk along the eggs, egg whites, hot Poivrade, black pepper, and cheese.
2. Heat the spread during a medium non-stick pan over medium heat. Add the ham and sauté for 2-3 minutes. Take away the ham from the pan.
3. Add the onions and fresh peppers to the recent pan and cook for regarding five minutes. Add the ham back to pan.
4. Scale back the warmth to low and add the eggs to pan. Gently stir the eggs with a spoon or spatula and continue gently change of state over low heat till the eggs area unit broiled and set.
5. Equally divide the egg mixture into four servings. Spoon every portion of the egg mixture into a battercake and high every with one tsp. Salsa. Fold the battercake to shut.

Nutrition: *Calories 210 |Fat 9g |Carbohydrate 16g*

Breakfast Cups for Meat Lover

Preparation Time: 12minutes |Cooking Time: 13 minutes |Servings: 4

Ingredients

- One tablespoon of light sour cream
- Two pre-cooked defrosted and diced turkey breakfast sausage patties
- One clove of minced garlic
- Two tablespoons of thinly sliced onion
- One and half cup of frozen hash browns
- One teaspoon of canola oil
- One-quarter teaspoon of salt
- A pinch of black pepper
- One cup of egg substitute
- Two tablespoon of turkey bacon
- Two tablespoon of Monterey jack cheese

Directions

1. Heat up the kitchen appliance to four hundred F. Coat a six-cup quick bread tin with sloppy preparation spray. Equally di vide the hash browns among the quick bread cups and press firmly into the lowest and up the perimeters of every cup.
2. In an exceedingly giant frying pan, heat the oil over medium heat. Sauté the onion till tender. Add the garlic and sausage; cook for one minute additional. Take away the frying pan from the heat; stir within the soured cream.
3. In an exceedingly medium bowl, beat the egg substitute with the salt and black pepper, then pour it equally into the potato-lined quick bread cups. High every cup with a number of the sausage mixture, bacon, and cheese.
4. Bake fifteen to eighteen minutes, or till the eggs area unit set. Serve instantly or freeze for later.

Nutrition: Calories *120 |Fat 4g |Carbohydrate 10g*

Breakfast Quesadilla

Preparation Time: 13minutes |Cooking Time: 16 minutes |Servings: 4

Ingredients

- One cooking spray
- One quarter cup of canned green chiles
- Four beaten eggs
- One quarter teaspoon of black pepper
- Two 10-inch of whole wheat flour tortillas
- One and half cup of cheddar cheese (reduced fat)
- four slices of turkey bacon (cooked crisp and crumbled)

Directions:

1. Lightly brush a small skillet with a cooking oil.
2. Sauté the green chilies over medium-low heat for 1-2 minutes. Attach beaten eggs and cook until scrambled and set, stirring. Season with some pepper.
3. Lightly brush a second large skillet with cooking oil. Place one tortilla in the skillet and cook over medium heat for about 1 minute, until the air bubbles begin to form. Flip the tortilla and cook for another 1 minute (don't let the tortilla get crispy).
4. Layer half of the cheese thinly over the tortilla, protecting the corners.
5. Reduce heat to minimum temperatures. Arrange half of the fried bacon and half of the egg mixture over the cheese easily. Cook until the cheese begins to melt for about 1 minute.
6. To make a half-moon shape, fold the tortilla in half. Flip the folded tortilla over and cook for 1-2minutes, until lightly toasted and the cheese filling is fully melted.

Nutrition: Calories *160 |Fat 19g |Carbohydrate 8g*

Toasts with Egg and Avocado

Preparation Time: 17minutes |Cooking Time: 0 minutes |Servings: 4

Ingredients

- Four eggs
- Four slices of hearty whole grain bread
- One avocado (mashed)
- Half teaspoon of salt (optional)
- One quarter teaspoon of black pepper
- One quarter cup of Greek yogurt (non-fat)

Direction

1. To poach each egg, fill 1/2 cup of water with a 1-cup microwaveable bowl or teacup. Crack an egg into the water 48 softly, make sure it's fully submerged. Cover on high for around 1 minute with a saucer and microwave, or before the white is set and the yolk starts to set, but still fluffy (not runny).
2. Toast the bread and use 1/4 of the mashed avocado to scatter each slice.

3. Sprinkle the salt with avocado (optional) and pepper. Top with a poached egg on each piece. Top the egg with one tablespoon of Greek yogurt.

Nutrition

Calories 230 |Fat 13g |Carbohydrate 26g

Turkey Sausages and Egg Casserole

Preparation Time: 13minutes |Cooking Time: 13 minutes |Servings: 5

Ingredients

- Half cup of green chopped onions
- Two cups of nonfat milk
- One nonstick cooking spray
- Half teaspoon of mustard powder
- One quarter teaspoon of salt
- One quarter teaspoon of black pepper
- egg substitute
- Four slices of whole wheat bread (cut into 1/2–inch cubes)
- Three precooked (diced turkey breakfast sausage patties
- One quarter cup of cheddar cheese (reduced fat, shredded)

Directions

1. Preheat oven to 350-degree F. Coat a 9x13 baking dish with cooking spray.
2. In a medium bowl, whisk together nonfat milk, green onions, dry mustard, salt (optional), pepper, and egg substitute.
3. Place bread cubes and sausage on the bottom of the baking dish, pour egg mixture evenly over bread and sausage. Top with cheddar cheese.
4. Cover pan with aluminum foil and bake for 20 minutes. Remove foil and bake for an additional 40 minutes.

Nutrition: *Calories 120 |Fat 3g | Carbohydrate 9g*

Huevos Rancheros

Preparation Time: 12minutes |Cooking Time: 33 minutes |Servings: 2

Ingredients

- Four corn tortillas
- One can of tomato(es) (14.5-ounce, no-salt-added, diced, drained)
- One teaspoon of ground cumin
- One eight teaspoon of cayenne pepper (optional)
- Half teaspoon of salt
- Four large eggs
- One oz. part-skim mozzarella cheese or reduced-fat feta (shredded)
- One quarter cup of cilantro (chopped)

Directions

1. Preheat the oven to 425 degrees F.
2. Position the tortillas on the baking sheet and bake them on each side for 3 minutes.
3. Meanwhile, in a medium nonstick skillet, place the tomatoes, cumin, cayenne, and salt, and bring to a boil over medium-high heat. Decrease heat to medium-low and cook, covered, until lightly thickened, or 3 minutes. Split one egg into a cup for calculation. Slide the egg gently over the tomato mixture. Repeat for the eggs that remain. Simmer gently, covered, over medium heat, 2 1/2 to 3 minutes or until the whites are fully set and the yolks start to thicken slightly.
4. Put a tortilla on each of the four plates for dinner. Cover with the eggs and the tomato mixture. Using cheese and cilantro to scatter.

Nutrition: *Calories 162 |Fat 8g | Carbohydrate 14.6g*

Apple-Walnut French Toast

Preparation Time: 12minutes |Cooking Time: 14 minutes |Servings: 4

Ingredients

- Four slices of multi-grain Italian bread6 oz
- One cup of egg substitute
- Four teaspoon of pure maple syrup
- One cup of diced apple
- walnuts (chopped)

Directions

1. Preheat your oven to 450 degrees F. Meanwhile, put the bread in a baking pan of 13 to 9 inches, pour over all the egg substitute, and turn several times until the bread slices are thoroughly coated and egg mixture is used. (Stand in the baking pan when preheating the oven.) Put bread slices coated with cooking spray on the baking sheet.
2. Bake for 6 minutes, turn, and bake for 5 minutes or until the bottom is golden. Serve with similar proportions of syrup, apples and nuts in the mixture.

Nutrition: *Calories 276 |Fat 12g | Carbohydrate 3.5g*

Summer Smoothie Fruit

Preparation Time: 12minutes |Cooking Time: 0 minutes |Servings: 4

Ingredients
- One cup of fresh blueberries
- One cup of fresh strawberries (chopped)
- Two peaches (peeled, seeded and chopped)
- Peach flavored Greek style yogurt (non-fat)
- One cup of unsweetened almond milk
- Two tablespoon of ground flax seed
- Half cup of ice

Directions
1. Combine in a blender and puree all ingredients until creamy.

Nutrition: *Calories 130 |Fat 4g | Carbohydrate 23g*

Chicken and Egg Salad

Preparation Time: 5minutes |Cooking Time: 25 minutes |Servings: 2

Ingredients
- Two cooked chicken breasts
- Three hard-boiled eggs
- Two tablespoons of fat-free mayo
- One tablespoon of curry powder
- Chives or basil (optional)
- Salt (optional)

Direction
1. Bake the chicken for maybe 15 minutes in the oven around 360 F (confirm with just a knife that now the meat is cooked all the through).
2. For 8 minutes, cook the eggs. Cut the eggs and chicken into a small-sized piece.
3. Combine the cream cheese with curry powder
4. In a large bowl, combine everything and mix.
5. Allow a minimum of 10 minutes to chill in the refrigerator (it gets even better if 59 you leave it overnight in the refrigerator).
6. Serve with chives on toast or muffins and a bit of salt on top.

Nutrition: *Calories 139 |Fat 9g |Carbohydrate 23g*

Niçoise Salad Tuna *

Preparation Time: 12minutes |Cooking Time: 5

Ingredients
- Four oz. ahi tuna steak
- One whole egg
- Two cups of baby spinach (3oz)
- Two oz. green beans2
- One and half oz. broccoli1
- Half red bell peppers
- Three and half oz. cucumber
- One radish
- Three large black olives
- Handful of parsley
- One teaspoon of olive oil
- One teaspoon of balsamic vinegar
- Half teaspoon of Dijon mustard
- Half teaspoon of pepper

Direction
1. Cook the egg and place it aside to cool.
2. Steam beans and broccoli, then set aside. 2-3 mins of a little water in the microwave or 3 minutes in a kettle of hot water does the trick.
3. In a tub, heat a bit of oil over high heat.
4. On all sides, season the seafood using pepper, then place it there in the heat and stir on each edge for about two minutes.
5. To the salad bowl or pan, add the spinach.
6. Chopped the red pepper, grapefruit as well as egg into pieces that are bitesize. Add the spinach on top.
7. Cut the radish into slices and mix the broccoli, beans and olives together. Add the spinach salad on top.
8. Break the tuna into strips and add it to the salad.
9. Toss the olive oil, balsamic vinegar, mustard, salt and pepper together.
10. The parsley is chopped and added to the vinaigrette.
11. For drizzling the vinaigrette over a salad, use a spoon

Nutrition: *Calories 149 |Fat 6g |Carbohydrate 21g*

Rolls with Spinach

Preparation Time: 15minutes |Cooking Time: 40 minutes |Servings: 4

Ingredients
- Sixteen ounces of frozen spinach leaves
- Three eggs
- Two and half ounce of onion
- Two ounces of carrot
- One ounce of low-fat mozzarella cheese

- Four ounce of fat-free cottage cheese
- Half cup of parsley
- One clove of garlic
- One teaspoon of curry powder
- One quarter teaspoon of chili flakes
- Teaspoon of salt
- One teaspoon of pepper
- Cooking spray

Direction

1. Preheat the furnace to 200 degrees C (400 degrees F).
2. Thaw the spinach and squeeze the water out (you can use a strainer). In order to accelerate the thawing process, you can microwave the spinach for a few minutes.
3. Mix the spinach, 2 eggs, mozzarella, ginger, half the salt and pepper together in a baking bowl.
4. Place parchment paper on a baking sheet and coat it with cooking spray. Move the spinach mixture, about half an inch thick and about 10 to 12 inches in height, to the sheet and press it down.
5. Bake for 15 minutes and then set aside to cool on a rack. Don't turn the oven off.
6. Finely chop the onion and parsley. Grate the carrots.
7. In a pan with a bit of cooking oil, fry the onions for about a minute. Add the carrots and parsley to the pan and let it cook for about 2 minutes.
8. Add cottage cheese, curry, chili, salt and pepper to the other half. Briefly mix.
9. Remove the fire from the pan, add an egg, and mix it all together.
10. Spread the filling over the spinach that has been cooled. Do not stretch it 65 all the way to the corners or as you fold it out, it will fall out.
11. Roll the spinach mat carefully and fill it, then bake for 25 minutes.
12. Take out the roll once the time is up, and let it cool for 5-10 minutes before cutting it into slices and serving.

Nutrition: *Calories 149 |Fat 11g |Carbohydrate 26g*

Balanced Turkey Meatballs

Preparation Time: 12minutes |Cooking Time: 26 minutes |Servings: 2

Ingredients

- Twenty ounces ground of turkey
- Three and half ounce of fresh or frozen spinach
- One quarter cup of oats
- Two egg whites
- Celery sticks
- Three cloves' garlic
- Half green bell peppers
- Half red onion
- Half cup parsley
- Half teaspoon of cumin
- One teaspoon mustard powder
- One teaspoon thyme
- Half teaspoon turmeric
- Half teaspoon of chipotle pepper
- One teaspoon of salt
- A pinch of pepper

Direction

1. Preheat the oven to 350 F (175 C).
2. Chop the onion, garlic, and celery very finely (or use a food processor) and add to a large mixing cup.
3. In the dish, add the ham, egg whites, oats, and spices and combine well. Make sure the mix contains no pockets of spices or oats.
4. Spinach, green peppers (stalked and seeded), and parsley are chopped. The bits need to be about a dime 's size.
5. To the tub, add the vegetables and mix it until well-combined.
6. Line the parchment paper with a baking sheet.
7. Roll the turkey mixture (about the size of golf balls) into 15 balls and put them on the baking sheet.
8. Bake for 25 minutes, until fully baked.

Nutrition: *Calories 129 |Fat 9g |Carbohydrate 16g*

Curried Chicken with Apples

Preparation Time: 12minutes |Cooking Time: 13 minutes |Servings: 3

Ingredients

- 1lbs of cooked, diced chicken breast.
- One Granny Smith diced apple.
- Two celery stalks, (diced)
- Two green onions, (diced)
- Half cup of sliced cashew.
- One cup of plain Greek yogurt

- One tablespoon of tahini
- Four teaspoon of curry powder
- One teaspoon of ground cinnamon

Direction

1. In a big mixing cup, add the milk, tahini, curry powder, and cinnamon.
2. Add the chicken, apple, celery, cashews and green onions. Stir to blend.
3. To offer it ever something of a tropical feel, this salad can be eaten on its own, as a snack, or in a plucked-out papaya.

Nutrition: *Calories 139 |Fat 8g |Carbohydrate 19g*

Homemade Chicken Nuggets

Preparation Time: 15minutes |Cooking Time: 23 minutes |Servings: 2

Ingredients

- Half cup almond flour
- One tablespoon of Italian seasoning
- Two tablespoon of extra virgin olive oil
- Half teaspoon of salt
- Half teaspoon of pepper

Direction

1. Preheat the furnace to 200 C (400 F). Using parchment paper to arrange a large baking dish.
2. Whisk the Italian seasoning, almond flour, pepper and salt together in a dish.
3. Start cutting and remove any fat from the chicken breasts, after which slice into 1-inch-thick bits.
4. Sprinkle the extra virgin olive oil to the chicken.
5. Place each chicken piece in the flour bowl and toss until thoroughly covered, then move the chicken to the baking sheet that has been prepared.
6. For 20 minutes, roast.
7. To get exterior crispy, toggle the broiler on and put the chicken nuggets underneath the broiler for 3-4 minutes.

Nutrition: *Calories 149|Fat 9g|Carbohydrate 29g*

Beef Fajitas

Preparation Time: 6minutes |Cooking Time: 19 minutes |Servings: 4

Ingredients

- 1 lbs. beef stir-fry strips
- One medium red onion
- One red bell pepper
- One yellow bell pepper
- Half teaspoon of cumin
- Half teaspoon of chili powder
- Splash of oil
- Salt
- Pepper
- Half juice of lime
- Freshly chopped cilantro (also called coriander)
- One avocado

Direction

1. Over medium fire, steam a cast-iron pan.
2. Clean and dress bell peppers and cut them to long strips of 0.5cm thick and then Set aside.
3. Clean and cut the red onion into strips. Set aside.
4. add a little bit of oil once the skillet is heated.
5. Add 2-3 packets of stir-fry strips while the oil is hot. please ensure the strips wouldn't hit one another.
6. Inside the pan, stir-fry each beef batch thoroughly with salt and pepper. Cook on each side for around 1 minute and set aside on a plate and covered to stay warm.
7. introduce chopped onion as well as ringer peppers to the residual meat juice 76 when all the beef is finished cooking and set aside. Sweetened with chili powder and cumin, then simmer-fry till the preferred consistency is achieved.
8. Move the stir-fry strips of vegetables and beef to just a plate and eat alongside a chopped avocado, a sprinkling of lemon juice, and a spray of fresh cilantro.

Nutrition: *Calories 151 |Fat 6g |Carbohydrate 27g*

Keto Salad

Preparation Time: 11minutes |Cooking Time: 0 minutes |Servings: 2

Ingredients

- Four cherry tomatoes
- Half avocado
- One hardboiled egg
- Two cups of mixed green salad
- Two ounce of chicken breast, shredded
- One ounce of feta cheese(crumbled)

- One quarter cup of cooked bacon, (crumbled)

Direction

1. Slice the avocado and tomatoes. Slice the egg that is hard-boiled.
2. 2.In a large plate, put the mixed greens.
3. Quantify the pulverized chicken breast, crushed bacon, and feta cheese.
4. Position the tomatoes, egg, chicken, avocado, feta, and bacon on top of the greens in horizontal rows.

Nutrition: *Calories 152 |Fat 9g |Carbohydrate 24g*

Instant Pot Chicken Chili

Preparation Time: 6minutes |Cooking Time: 21 minutes |Servings: 2

Ingredients

- One tablespoon of vegetable oil
- One yellow diced onion
- Four minced garlic cloves
- One teaspoon of ground cumin
- One teaspoon of oregano
- Two and halls' chicken breasts,
- Sixteen ounce of salsa Verde

For Toppings

- Two packages of queso fresco or sour cream
- Two diced avocados
- Finely chopped radishes
- Eight springs cilantro (optional)

Direction

1. Set the Instant Pot to a medium sauté setting.
2. Add the oil to the vegetables.
3. Attach the onion and simmer for 3mins till the onion starts to melt, stirring regularly.
4. Apply the garlic, then stir for a minute.
5. Add the oregano and cumin and simmer for the next minute.
6. Through the pot, add 1/2 of the salsa Verde. Finish only with breasts of chicken and spill over the chicken mostly with left over salsa Verde.
7. Position the cover on the Instant Pot, switch the nozzle to "seal," and choose "manual." set the timer to 10 minutes.
8. Then let pressure release naturally when the timer is up.
9. Lift the cover, move the chicken to a small bowl just after pressure has dropped, and slice it with a fork.
10. To mix mostly with remaining ingredients, transfer the meat to the pot and stir.

Nutrition

Calories 144 |Fat 7g |Carbohydrate 20g

Smoked Cheese Wraps with Salmon and Cream

Preparation Time: 12minutes |Cooking Time: 15 minutes |Servings: 2

Ingredients

- One 8-inch low carb flour tortilla
- Two ounces of smoked salmon
- Two teaspoons of low-fat cream cheese
- One and half ounce of red onion
- Handful of arugulas
- Half teaspoon of fresh or dried basil
- A pinch of pepper

Direction

1. In the oven or microwave, warm the tortilla (pro tip: to prevent it from drying out, warm it between 2 pieces of moist paper towel).
2. The cream cheese, basil, and pepper are mixed together and then scattered over the tortilla.
3. With the salmon, arugula, and finely sliced onion, finish it off. Roll it up and enjoy the wrap!

Nutrition: *Calories 138 |Fat 6g |Carbohydrate 19g*

Cheese Yogurt

Preparation Time: 12minutes |Cooking Time: 15 minutes |Servings: 2

Ingredients

- One thick and Creamy Yogurt or store-bought yogurt
- Half tsp. of kosher salt

Directions

4. Line a strainer of twice the normal or plastic cheesecloth thickness.
5. Place the strainer on top of a bowl and apply the yogurt.
6. Cover and refrigerate for 2 hours. Stir in the salt and continue to drip for another 22 hours until the yoghurt cheese is ready to spread.

Nutrition: *83 Calories |5g protein|5.4g fat*

Muffins of Savory Egg

Preparation Time: 12minutes |Cooking Time: 33 minutes |Servings: 6

Ingredients

- One and half cups of water
- Two tbsp. of unsalted butter
- One (6-ounce) package Stove, Top lower-sodium Stuffing Mix for chicken
- Three ounces of bulk pork sausage
- Cooking spray
- Six eggs, beaten
- Half cup of (1.5 ounces) Monterey Jack cheese, shredded
- Half cup of finely chopped red bell pepper
- One quarter cup of sliced green onions

Direction

1. Preheat oven to 400°.
2. In a medium saucepan, put 1 1/2 cups of water and butter to a boil. Stir in the blend of stuffing. Cover, detach from heat and leave to stand for 5 minutes; use a fork to fluff. Let stand 10 minutes or before cool enough to hold, uncovered.
3. Cook the sausage in a small skillet over medium-high heat until browned while the stuffing is cooling; stir to crumble.
4. Coat the fingers with a mist for frying.
5. Press approximately 1/4 cup of stuffing into the bottom and sides of each of the 12 deeply coated muffin cups with cooking oil. Pour the egg uniformly into 18the cups of stuffing. Layer cheese, ham, bell pepper, and green onions equally over the egg if desired.
6. Bake for 18 to 20 minutes at 400F or until the centers are centered. Let it stand before serving for 5 minutes. Run a thin, sharp knife along the edges to loosen the muffin cups. Delete from the casseroles. Immediately serve.

Nutrition: *292 calories|16.7g fat|14.6g protein*

Parfaits of Yogurt, Honey and Walnut

Preparation Time: 25minutes |Cooking Time: 15 minutes |Servings: 6

Ingredients

- Three tbsp. of unsalted butter, melted
- Four sheets of phyllo, thawed if frozen One-third cup of sugar
- One cup of walnuts, toasted and chopped
- Three cups of Greek-style plain yogurt (don't use nonfat)
- Halt tsp. of vanilla extract
- Half cup of honey

Directions

1. Preheat the furnace to 375oF. Brush with the molten butter on a rimmed baking dish. Lay a tray of pastry on top.
2. Sprinkle with more honey, then add sugar and nuts. Repeat with the remaining sheets of pastry, butter, sugar and nuts, then apply the sugar and nuts.
3. Bake 10 to 15 minutes until golden brown and crisp. Enable it to cool on a wire rack on a baking sheet. Break the pastry into chunks.
4. Mix the yogurt and vanilla together in a tub. There are alternating layers of yogurt, honey and phyllo bits in 4 glasses. Immediately serve.

Nutrition: *420 calories|22g fat|14g protein*

Greek-Yogurt Style

Preparation Time: 12minutes |Cooking Time: 15 minutes |Servings: 2

Ingredients

- One thick and Creamy Yogurt or store-bought yogurt

Directions

1. Line a double thickness strainer with standard or synthetic cheesecloth (like reusable Ply ban; getculture.com).
2. Place the strainer on top of a bowl and apply the yogurt. Chill and cover. Depending about how dense you want it, let it drain for 1 to 2 1/2 hours.

Nutrition: *240 calories|14g protein |14g fat*

Shrimp and Grits Cajun-Style

Preparation Time: 12minutes |Cooking Time: 20 minutes |Servings: 6

Ingredients

- One tbsp. of olive oil
- Half cups (two ounces) of Tasso ham, minced
- One cup of chopped onion One garlic clove, minced
- Thirty-six medium shrimp, peeled (about 1 1/4 pounds)

- One tsp. of Cajun seasoning
- Two and half cups of water, divided
- One tbsp. of unsalted butter
- One cup of fat-free milk
- One quarter tsp. of salt
- One cup of uncooked quick-cooking grits
- One cup (4 ounces) of sharp cheddar cheese, shredded
- Half cup of sliced green onions

Directions

1. Heat the olive oil over a medium-high heat in a large skillet. Add Tasso; sauté for 2 minutes or until golden on the edges. Stir in the onion; sauté for 2 minutes. Stir in garlic; sauté for 1 minute.
2. Sprinkle with Cajun seasoning, add the shrimp to the grill, and cook for 3 minutes, rotating once. Apply ¼ cup water to loosen the browned pieces, scratching the pan. Remove from heat; mix with butter, stirring until melted. Cover yourself and stay warm.
3. On a medium-high heat, put milk, salt, and 2 cups of water to a boil. Heat elimination. Add the grits steadily and cook until thick and sparkling (about 5minutes), stirring continuously with a whisk. Drop the grits from the high temperatures; add the cheese and stir until the cheese melts, with a whisk.
4. On 6 plates, the spoon grates evenly. Using seafood, ham combination, and green onions to finish uniformly.

Nutrition: *346 calories|14g fat|24g protein*

Scramble for Lox, Eggs and Onion

Preparation Time: 12minutes |Cooking Time: 15 minutes |Servings: 4

Ingredients

- Six eggs
- Four egg whites
- One tsp. of canola oil
- One-third cup of sliced green onions
- Four ounces of smoked salmon, cut into 1/2-inch pieces
- One quarter cup of reduced-fat cream
- cheese, cut into 12 pieces
- One quarter tsp. of freshly ground black pepper
- Four slices pumpernickel bread, toasted

Direction

1. Place the eggs and egg whites in a bowl; stir until mixed with a whisk.
2. Over medium-high prepare, heat a medium nonstick skillet. In a bath, apply oil, swirl to coat. In the pan, add the green onions; sauté for 2 minutes or until tender. Attach a tray of egg mixture. Until the mixture settles on the rim, cook without stirring.
3. Draw a spatula to form curds over the bottom of the tub.
4. Add the cream cheese and salmon. Continue to draw the spatula across the bottom of the pan until the egg mixture is somewhat thick but still moist; do not continuously stir.
5. Remove directly from the pan. Sprinkle the pepper with the egg mixture. Serve the toast of pumpernickel.

Nutrition: *297 calories|14.5g fat|22.8g protein*

Peach and Pancakes with Blueberry

Preparation Time: 12minutes |Cooking Time: 16 minutes |Servings: 6

Ingredients

- One and half cups of all-purpose flour 2 tablespoons sugar
- Two tbsp. of flaxseed (optional) One tbsp. of baking powder
- Half tsp. of kosher salt
- One and half cups of nonfat buttermilk One tsp. of grated lemon rind
- Two eggs
- One cup of fresh or frozen blueberries, thawed
- One cup of chopped fresh or frozen peaches, thawed
- Two tbsp. of unsalted butter
- Fresh blueberries (optional)

Directions

1. Weigh or spoon the flour gently into dry measuring cups; level it with a knife. In a large cup, mix the flour, sugar, flaxseed, baking powder and salt if necessary, and stir with a fork.
2. In a medium cup, mix the buttermilk, lemon rind, and eggs and stir with a fork. To the flour mixture, apply the buttermilk mixture, stirring only so it is moist. Fold in the blueberries and peaches kindly.
3. Heat a nonstick griddle or nonstick skillet over medium heat. Pour 1/3 of a cup of flour into the pan per pancake. Cook for 2 to 3 minutes over medium heat or until bubbles cover the tops and the edges appear fried.

Switch the cakes over gently; cook for 2 - 3 mins or until the bottoms become golden brown.

Nutrition: *Calories 238|Fat 2.8g|Protein 8.1g*

Omelet with Turmeric, Tomato, and Onions

Preparation Time: 8minutes |Cooking Time: 15 minutes |Servings: 2

Ingredients

- Four large eggs
- Kosher salt
- One tbsp. of olive oil
- One quarter tsp. of brown mustard seeds Turmeric powder
- Two green onions, finely chopped
- One quarter cup of diced plum tomato
- Dash of black pepper

Directions

4. Whisk the eggs and salt together.
5. Heat oil over medium-high heat in a large cast-iron skillet. Apply the mustard and turmeric seeds; simmer for 30 seconds or until the seeds pop up, stirring regularly. Add onions; simmer for 30 seconds or until tender, stirring regularly. Add the tomato; simmer for 1 minute or until very tender, stirring regularly.
6. Pour the plate with the egg mixture, scatter uniformly. Cook until the edges are set (about 2 minutes). Slide the spatula's front edge between the omelet edge and the plate. Raise the omelet edge softly, tilting the pan to allow the pan to come into contact with any uncooked egg mixture.
7. Procedure to replicate on the opposite edge. Continue to cook till center is really just set (about two minutes). Loosen the omelet and fold it in half with a spatula. Slide the omelet carefully onto a platter. Halve the omelet and dust it with black pepper.

Nutrition: *216 calories|16.9g fat|13.3g protein*

Breakfast Bowl of Yogurt

Preparation Time: 8minutes |Cooking Time: 15 minutes |Servings: 4

Ingredients

- One tsp. of tandoori spice or curry powder
- One quarter cup of honey
- Two cups of 2% plain Greek yogurt
- Half cup of all-natural granola
- One cup of fresh berries
- One cup of freeze-dried mango, pineapple and/or berries
- Small sprigs fresh cilantro

Directions

1. Toast the spices on low in a small skillet, stirring, until very fragrant, for about 2 minutes. Take it out of the oven, add honey and stir.
2. Break the yogurt into 4 cups. Drizzle with spiced honey; finish with cilantro, granola and mango. Just serve.

Nutrition: *227 calories|3.1g fat|11g protein*

Tex-Mex Migas

Preparation Time: 9minutes |Cooking Time: 15 minutes |Servings: 4

Ingredients

- Three large eggs
- Three egg whites
- One tbsp. of canola oil
- Four corn tortillas, cut into 1/2-inch-wide strips
- Half cup of chopped onion
- Two large, seeded jalapeño peppers
- Two-third cup of lower-sodium salsa
- Half cup of Monterey Jack cheese, shredded
- Half cup of sliced green onions
- Hot sauce (optional)
- Lower-sodium red salsa (optional)
- Lower-sodium green salsa (optional)

Direction

1. Place the eggs and egg whites in a bowl; stir until mixed with a whisk.
2. Over medium-high prepare, heat a medium nonstick skillet. In a bath, apply oil, swirl to coat. Apply tortilla strips to the skillet and cook, stirring constantly, for 3 minutes or until brown.
3. In a sauce, add the onion and jalapeño peppers; sauté for 2 minutes or until tender. Stir in 2/3 of a cup of salsa, and simmer for 1 minute, stirring continuously.
4. Add the mixture of eggs; simmer for 2 minutes or until the eggs are tender, stirring periodically. Sprinkle the cheese with the egg mixture. Cook for thirty seconds or until the cheese is molten.

5. Cover with the green onions, then serve right away. If preferred, serve with hot sauce, red salsa, or green salsa.

Nutrition: *193 calories |10.4g fat |10.2g protein*

Barley Breakfast with Banana & Sunflower Seeds *

Preparation Time: 5minutes |Cooking Time: 11 minutes |Servings: 1

Ingredients

- Two-third cup of water
- One third cup of uncooked quick-
- cooking pearl barley
- One banana, sliced
- One tsp. of honey
- One tbsp. of unsalted sunflower seeds

Directions

1. In a shallow microwave-safe cup, mix water and barley a high 6-minute microwave.
2. Delete and leave to stand for 2 minutes.
3. Cover with slices of banana, sunflower seeds, and honey.

Nutrition: *410 calories|6g fat|10g protein*

Banana Smoothie for Breakfast

Preparation Time: 12minutes |Cooking Time: 0 minutes |Servings: 2

Ingredients

- Half cup of 1% low-fat milk
- Half cup of crushed ice
- One tbsp. of honey
- Half teaspoon ground nutmeg
- One frozen sliced ripe large banana
- One cup of plain 2% reduced-fat Greek yogurt

Directions

1. In a blender, combine the first 5 ingredients; mix for 2 minutes or until smooth. Add the yogurt; just process until it's blended. Immediately serve.

Nutrition: *212 calories|3.6g fat|14.2g protein*

Blackberry-Mango Shake

Preparation Time: 12minutes |Cooking Time: 0 minutes |Servings: 4

Ingredients

- One cup of orange juice
- One cup of refrigerated bottled mango slices
- One quarter cup of light firm silken tofu Three tbsp. of honey
- One and half cups of frozen blackberries

Direction

1. In a blender, place all ingredients in the order given, process until smooth.

Nutrition: *162 calories|0.6g fat|3.7g protein*

Bulgur Porridge Breakfast

Preparation Time: 5minutes |Cooking Time: 15 minutes |Servings: 4

Ingredients

- Four cups of 1% low-fat milk
- One cup of bulgur
- One-*-third cup of dried cherries
- One quarter tbsp. of salt
- One-third cup of dried apricots, coarsely chopped
- Half cup of sliced almonds

Directions

1. Combine the milk, bulgur, dried cherries, and salt in a medium saucepan; bring it to a boil. Reduce heat to low and simmer, stirring regularly, until tender and the oatmeal consistency of the bulgur is tender (10-15 minutes).
2. Divide into 4 bowls of hot porridge: top with the apricots and almonds.

Nutrition: *340 calories |6.7g fat|15g protein*

Turkey Meatballs

Preparation Time: 16minutes |Cooking Time: 25 minutes |Servings: 5

- Twenty ounces of ground turkey
- Four ounces of fresh or frozen spinach One quarter cup of oats
- Two egg whites
- Two celery sticks
- Three cloves' garlic
- Half green bell peppers
- Half red onion
- Half cup of parsley
- Half teaspoon of cumin
- One teaspoon of mustard powder
- One teaspoon of thyme
- Half tablespoon of turmeric
- Half teaspoon of chipotle pepper
- One teaspoon of salt - Pinch of pepper

Direction

1. Preheat the oven to 350 F Celsius (175 C).
2. Chop very finely (or use a food processor) the

onion, garlic, and celery, and add to a large mixing cup.

3. In the dish, add the ham, egg whites, oats, and spices and combine well. Make sure the blend has no pockets of spices or oats.
4. Spinach, green peppers (stalked and seeded), and parsley are chopped. The bits need to be about a dime's size.
5. To the tub, add the vegetables and mix it until well-combined.
6. Line the parchment paper with a baking sheet.
7. Roll the turkey mixture (about the size of golf balls) into 15 balls and put them on the baking sheet.
8. Bake for 25 minutes, until fully baked.

Nutrition: *349 calories |7g fat|19g protein*

Lunch

Gazpacho

Preparation Time: 15minutes |Cooking Time: 0 minutes |Servings: 4

Ingredients:

- 3 pounds ripe tomatoes
- 1 cup low-sodium tomato juice
- ½ red onion, chopped
- 1 cucumber
- 1 red bell pepper
- 2 celery stalks
- 2 tablespoons parsley
- 2 garlic cloves
- 2 tablespoons extra-virgin olive oil
- 2 tablespoons red wine vinegar
- 1 teaspoon honey
- ½ teaspoon salt
- ¼ teaspoon freshly ground black pepper

Direction

1. In a blender jar, combine the tomatoes, tomato juice, onion, cucumber, bell pepper, celery, parsley, garlic, olive oil, vinegar, honey, salt, and pepper. Pulse until blended but still slightly chunky.
2. Adjust the seasonings as needed and serve.

Nutrition: 170 Calories|24g Carbs|16g Sugars

Tomato and Kale Soup

Preparation Time: 10minutes |Cooking Time: 15 minutes |Servings: 4

Ingredients:

- 1 tablespoon extra-virgin olive oil
- 1 medium onion
- 2 carrots
- 3 garlic cloves
- 4 cups low-sodium vegetable broth
- 1 (28-ounce) can crushed tomatoes
- ½ teaspoon dried oregano
- ¼ teaspoon dried basil
- 4 cups chopped baby kale leaves
- ¼ teaspoon salt

Direction

1. In a huge pot, heat up oil over medium heat. Sauté onion and carrots for 3 to 5 minutes. Add the garlic and sauté for 30 seconds more, until fragrant.
2. Add the vegetable broth, tomatoes, oregano, and basil to the pot and boil. Decrease the heat to low and simmer for 5 minutes.
3. Using an immersion blender, purée the soup.
4. Add the kale and simmer for 3 more minutes. Season with the salt. Serve immediately.

Nutrition: 170 Calories|31g Carbs|13g Sugars

Comforting Summer Squash Soup with Crispy Chickpeas

Preparation Time: 10minutes |Cooking Time: 20 minutes |Servings: 4

Ingredients:

- 1 (15-ounce) can low-sodium chickpeas
- 1 teaspoon extra-virgin olive oil
- ¼ teaspoon smoked paprika
- Pinch salt, plus ½ teaspoon
- 3 medium zucchinis
- 3 cups low-sodium vegetable broth
- ½ onion
- 3 garlic cloves
- 2 tablespoons plain low-fat Greek yogurt
- Freshly ground black pepper

Direction:

1. Preheat the oven to 425°F. Line a baking sheet with parchment paper.
2. In a medium mixing bowl, toss the chickpeas with 1 teaspoon of olive oil, the smoked paprika, and a pinch salt. Transfer to the prepared baking sheet and roast until crispy, about 20 minutes, stirring once. Set aside.
3. Meanwhile, in a medium pot, heat the

remaining 1 tablespoon of oil over medium heat.
4. Add the zucchini, broth, onion, and garlic to the pot, and boil. Simmer, and cook for 20 minutes.
5. In a blender jar, purée the soup. Return to the pot.
6. Add the yogurt, remaining ½ teaspoon of salt, and pepper, and stir well. Serve topped with the roasted chickpeas.

Nutrition: 188 Calories|24g Carbs|7g Sugars

Curried Carrot Soup

Preparation Time: 10minutes |Cooking Time: 5 minutes |Servings: 6

Ingredients:

- 1 tablespoon extra-virgin olive oil
- 1 small onion
- 2 celery stalks
- 1½ teaspoons curry powder
- 1 teaspoon ground cumin
- 1 teaspoon minced fresh ginger
- 6 medium carrots
- 4 cups low-sodium vegetable broth
- ¼ teaspoon salt
- 1 cup canned coconut milk
- ¼ teaspoon freshly ground black pepper
- 1 tablespoon chopped fresh cilantro

Direction:

1. Heat an Instant Pot to high and add the olive oil.
2. Sauté the onion and celery for 2 to 3 minutes. Add the curry powder, cumin, and ginger to the pot and cook until fragrant, about 30 seconds.
3. Add the carrots, vegetable broth, and salt to the pot. Close and seal and set for 5 minutes on high. Allow the pressure to release naturally.
4. In a blender jar, carefully purée the soup in batches and transfer back to the pot.
5. Stir in the coconut milk and pepper, and heat through. Top with the cilantro and serve.

Nutrition: 145 Calories|13g Carbs|4g Sugars

Thai Peanut, Carrot, and Shrimp Soup

Preparation Time: 10minutes |Cooking Time: 10 minutes |Servings: 4

Ingredients:

- 1 tablespoon coconut oil
- 1 tablespoon Thai red curry paste
- ½ onion
- 3 garlic cloves
- 2 cups chopped carrots
- ½ cup whole unsalted peanuts
- 4 cups low-sodium vegetable broth
- ½ cup unsweetened plain almond milk
- ½ pound shrimp,
- Minced fresh cilantro, for garnish

Direction:

1. In a big pan, heat up oil over medium-high heat until shimmering.
2. Cook curry paste, stirring continuously, for 1 minute. Add the onion, garlic, carrots, and peanuts to the pan, and continue to cook for 2 to 3 minutes.
3. Boil broth. Reduce the heat to low and simmer for 5 to 6 minutes.
4. Purée the soup until smooth and return it to the pot. Over low heat, pour almond milk and stir to combine. Cook shrimp in the pot for 2 to 3 minutes.
5. Garnish with cilantro and serve.

Nutrition: 237 Calories|17g Carbs|6g Sugars

Chicken Tortilla Soup

Preparation Time: 10minutes |Cooking Time: 35 minutes |Servings: 4

Ingredients:

- 1 tablespoon extra-virgin olive oil
- 1 onion, thinly sliced
- 1 garlic clove, minced
- 1 jalapeño pepper, diced
- 2 boneless, skinless chicken breasts
- 4 cups low-sodium chicken broth

- 1 roma tomato, diced
- ½ teaspoon salt
- 2 (6-inch) corn tortillas
- Juice of 1 lime
- Minced fresh cilantro, for garnish
- ¼ cup shredded cheddar cheese, for garnish

Direction

1. In a medium pot, cook oil over medium-high heat. Add the onion and cook for 3 to 5 minutes until it begins to soften. Add the garlic and jalapeño, and cook until fragrant, about 1 minute more.
2. Add the chicken, chicken broth, tomato, and salt to the pot and boil. Lower heat to medium and simmer mildly for 20 to 25 minutes. Remove the chicken from the pot and set aside.
3. Preheat a broiler to high.
4. Spray the tortilla strips with nonstick cooking spray and toss to coat. Spread in a single layer on a baking sheet and broil for 3 to 5 minutes, flipping once, until crisp.
5. Once chicken is cooked, shred it with two forks and return to the pot.
6. Season the soup with the lime juice. Serve hot, garnished with cilantro, cheese, and tortilla strips.

Nutrition:
191 Calories|13g Carbohydrates|2g Sugars

Beef and Mushroom Barley Soup

Preparation Time: 10minutes |Cooking Time: 80 minutes |Servings: 6

Ingredients:

- 1-pound beef stew meat, cubed
- ¼ teaspoon salt
- ¼ teaspoon freshly ground black pepper
- 1 tablespoon extra-virgin olive oil
- 8 ounces sliced mushrooms
- 1 onion, chopped
- 2 carrots, chopped
- 3 celery stalks, chopped
- 6 garlic cloves, minced
- ½ teaspoon dried thyme
- 4 cups low-sodium beef broth
- 1 cup water
- ½ cup pearl barley

Direction:

1. Season the meat well.
2. In an Instant Pot, heat the oil over high heat. Cook meat on all sides. Remove from the pot and set aside.
3. Add the mushrooms to the pot and cook for 1 to 2 minutes. Remove the mushrooms and set aside with the meat.
4. Sauté onion, carrots, and celery for 3 to 4 minutes. Add the garlic and continue to cook until fragrant, about 30 seconds longer.
5. Return the meat and mushrooms to the pot, then add the thyme, beef broth, and water. Adjust the pressure on high and cook for 15 minutes. Let the pressure release naturally.
6. Open the Instant Pot and add the barley. Use the slow cooker function on the Instant Pot, affix the lid (vent open), and continue to cook for 1 hour. Serve.

Nutrition: 245 Calories|19g Carbs|3g Sugars

Tomato and Guaca Salad

Preparation Time: 10minutes |Cooking Time: 0 minutes |Servings: 4

Ingredients:

- 1 cup cherry tomatoes
- 1 large cucumber
- 1 small red onion
- 1 avocado
- 2 tablespoons chopped fresh dill
- 2 tablespoons extra-virgin olive oil
- Juice of 1 lemon
- ¼ teaspoon salt
- ¼ teaspoon freshly ground black pepper

Direction:
1. In a big mixing bowl, mix the tomatoes, cucumber, onion, avocado, and dill.
2. In a small bowl, combine the oil, lemon juice, salt, and pepper, and mix well.
3. Drizzle the dressing over the vegetables and toss to combine. Serve.

Nutrition: 151 Calories|11g Carbs|4g Sugars

Coleslaw

Preparation Time: 15minutes |Cooking Time: 0 minutes |Servings: 4

Ingredients:
- 2 cups green cabbage
- 2 cups red cabbage
- 2 cups grated carrots
- 3 scallions
- 2 tablespoons extra-virgin olive oil
- 2 tablespoons rice vinegar
- 1 teaspoon honey
- 1 garlic clove
- ¼ teaspoon salt

Direction
1. Throw together the green and red cabbage, carrots, and scallions.
2. In a small bowl, whisk together the oil, vinegar, honey, garlic, and salt.
3. Pour the dressing over the veggies and mix to thoroughly combine.
4. Serve immediately or cover and chill for several hours before serving.

Nutrition: |80 Calories|10g Carbs|6g Sugars

Green Salad with Berries and Sweet Potatoes

Preparation Time: 15minutes |Cooking Time: 20 minutes |Servings: 4

Ingredients:

For the vinaigrette
- 1-pint blackberries
- 2 tablespoons red wine vinegar
- 1 tablespoon honey
- 3 tablespoons extra-virgin olive oil
- ¼ teaspoon salt
- Freshly ground black pepper

For the salad
- 1 sweet potato, cubed
- 1 teaspoon extra-virgin olive oil
- 8 cups salad greens (baby spinach, spicy greens, romaine)
- ½ red onion, sliced
- ¼ cup crumbled goat cheese

Direction:

For vinaigrette
1. In a blender jar, combine the blackberries, vinegar, honey, oil, salt, and pepper, and process until smooth. Set aside.

For salad

2. Preheat the oven to 425°F. Line a baking sheet with parchment paper.
3. Mix the sweet potato with the olive oil. Transfer to the prepared baking sheet and roast for 20 minutes, stirring once halfway through, until tender. Remove and cool for a few minutes.
4. In a large bowl, toss the greens with the red onion and cooled sweet potato, and drizzle with the vinaigrette. Serve topped with 1 tablespoon of goat cheese per serving.

Nutrition: 196 Calories|21g Carbs|10g Sugars

Three Bean and Scallion Salad

Preparation Time: 10minutes |Cooking Time: 0 minutes |Servings: 4

Ingredients:
- 1 (15-ounce) can low-sodium chickpeas
- 1 (15-ounce) can low-sodium kidney beans
- 1 (15-ounce) can low-sodium white beans
- 1 red bell pepper
- ¼ cup chopped scallions
- ¼ cup finely chopped fresh basil
- 3 garlic cloves, minced
- 2 tablespoons extra-virgin olive oil
- 1 tablespoon red wine vinegar

- 1 teaspoon Dijon mustard
- ¼ teaspoon freshly ground black pepper

Direction:

1. Toss chickpeas, kidney beans, white beans, bell pepper, scallions, basil, and garlic gently.
2. Blend together olive oil, vinegar, mustard, and pepper. Toss with the salad.
3. Wrap and chill for 1 hour.

Nutrition: 193 Calories|29g Carbs|3g Sugars

Chicken cauliflower rice bowl

Preparation Time: 40 minutes |Cooking Time: 10 minutes |Servings: 4

Ingredients:

- 1 fresh pineapple, peeled, cored and cubed (about 3 cups), divided
- 1/2 cup coconut Greek yogurt
- 2 tablespoons plus 1/2 cup chopped fresh cilantro, divided
- 3 tablespoons lime juice, divided
- 3/4 teaspoon salt, divided
- 1/4 teaspoon crushed red pepper flakes
- 1/8 teaspoon chili powder
- 4 boneless skinless chicken breast halves (6 ounces each)
- 3 cups fresh cauliflower florets (about 1/2 small cauliflower)
- 1 tablespoon canola oil
- 1 small red onion, finely chopped
- Optional: Toasted sweetened shredded coconut or lime wedges

Directions:

1. For marinade, place 1 cup pineapple, yogurt, 2 tablespoons each cilantro and lime juice, 1/4 teaspoon salt, pepper flakes and chili powder in a food processor; process until blended. In a large bowl, toss chicken with marinade; refrigerate, covered, 1-3 hours.
2. In a clean food processor, pulse cauliflower until it resembles rice (do not overprocess). In a large skillet, heat oil over medium-high heat; sauté onion until lightly browned, 3-5 minutes. Add cauliflower; cook and stir until lightly browned, 5-7 minutes. Stir in 1 cup pineapple and the remaining lime juice and salt; cook, covered, over medium heat until cauliflower is tender, 3-5 minutes. Stir in remaining cilantro. Keep warm.
3. Preheat grill or broiler. Drain chicken, discarding marinade. Place chicken on an oiled grill rack over medium heat or in a greased foil-lined 15x10x1-in. pan. Grill, covered, or broil 4 in. from heat until a thermometer reads 165°, 4-6 minutes per side. Let stand 5 minutes before slicing.
4. To serve, divide cauliflower mixture among 4 bowls. Top with chicken, remaining pineapple and, if desired, coconut and lime wedges.

Nutrition: 318 Calories|9g Fat|1g Carb

Rainbow Bean Salad

Preparation Time: 15minutes |Cooking Time: 0 minutes |Servings: 5

Ingredients:

- 1 (15-ounce) can low-sodium black beans
- 1 avocado, diced
- 1 cup cherry
- 3 tomatoes, halved
- 1 cup chopped baby spinach
- ½ cup red bell pepper
- ¼ cup jicama
- ½ cup scallions
- ¼ cup fresh cilantro
- 2 tablespoons lime juice
- 1 tablespoon extra-virgin olive oil
- 2 garlic cloves, minced
- 1 teaspoon honey
- ¼ teaspoon salt
- ¼ teaspoon freshly ground black pepper

Direction:

1. Mix black beans, avocado, tomatoes, spinach, bell pepper, jicama, scallions, and cilantro.

2. Blend lime juice, oil, garlic, honey, salt, and pepper. Add to the salad and toss.
3. Chill for 1 hour before serving.

Nutrition: 169 Calories|22g Carbs|3g Sugars

Warm Barley and Squash Salad

Preparation Time: 20 minutes |Cooking Time: 40 minutes |Servings: 2

Ingredients:

- 1 small butternut squash
- 3 tablespoons extra-virgin olive oil
- 2 cups broccoli florets
- 1 cup pearl barley
- 1 cup toasted chopped walnuts
- 2 cups baby kale
- ½ red onion, sliced
- 2 tablespoons balsamic vinegar
- 2 garlic cloves, minced
- ½ teaspoon salt
- ¼ teaspoon black pepper

Direction:

1. Preheat the oven to 400°F. Line a baking sheet with parchment paper.
2. Peel off the squash, and slice into dice. In a large bowl, toss the squash with 2 teaspoons of olive oil. Transfer to the prepared baking sheet and roast for 20 minutes.
3. While the squash is roasting, toss the broccoli in the same bowl with 1 teaspoon of olive oil. After 20 minutes, flip the squash and push it to one side of the baking sheet. Add the broccoli to the other side and continue to roast for 20 more minutes until tender.
4. While the veggies are roasting, in a medium pot, cover the barley with several inches of water. Boil, then adjust heat, cover, and simmer for 30 minutes until tender. Drain and rinse.
5. Transfer the barley to a large bowl, and toss with the cooked squash and broccoli, walnuts, kale, and onion.
6. In a small bowl, mix the remaining 2 tablespoons of olive oil, balsamic vinegar, garlic, salt, and pepper. Drizzle dressing over the salad and toss.

Nutrition: 274 Calories|32g Carbs|3g Sugars

Citrus and Chicken Salad

Preparation Time: 10 minutes |Cooking Time: 0 minutes |Servings: 4

Ingredients:

- 4 cups baby spinach
- 2 tablespoons extra-virgin olive oil
- 1 tablespoon lemon juice
- 1/8 teaspoon salt
- 2 cups chopped cooked chicken
- 2 mandarin oranges
- ½ peeled grapefruit, sectioned
- ¼ cup sliced almonds

Direction:

1. Toss spinach with the olive oil, lemon juice, salt, and pepper.
2. Add the chicken, oranges, grapefruit, and almonds to the bowl. Toss gently.
3. Arrange on 4 plates and serve.

Nutrition: |249 Calories|11g Carbs|7g Sugars

Blueberry and Chicken Salad

Preparation Time: 10 minutes |Cooking Time: 0 minutes |Servings: 4

Ingredients:

- 2 cups chopped cooked chicken
- 1 cup fresh blueberries
- ¼ cup almonds
- 1 celery stalk
- ¼ cup red onion
- 1 tablespoon fresh basil
- 1 tablespoon fresh cilantro
- ½ cup plain, vegan mayonnaise
- ¼ teaspoon salt
- ¼ teaspoon freshly ground black pepper

- 8 cups salad greens

Direction:
1. Toss chicken, blueberries, almonds, celery, onion, basil, and cilantro.
2. Blend yogurt, salt, and pepper. Stir chicken salad to combine.
3. Situate 2 cups of salad greens on each of 4 plates and divide the chicken salad among the plates to serve.

Nutrition: 207 Calories|11g Carbs|6g Sugars

Crunchy Strawberry Salad

Preparation Time: 10 minutes |Cooking Time: 0 minutes |Servings: 3

Ingredients:
- 0.6 lb. romaine lettuce leaves, roughly torn
- 0.6 lb. strawberries, sliced
- 0.2 lb. nuts of choice

Directions:
1. In a large mixing bowl add strawberry slices, lettuce, and nuts; toss to combine.
2. Add to a serving bowl.

Nutrition: 94 Calories |0.3g Fat |11g Protein

Zucchini Noodle Salad with Almonds

Preparation Time: 35 minutes |Cooking Time: 10 minutes |Servings: 4

Ingredients:
- 2-3 zucchini, noodled
- 2 tbsp. olive oil
- 1 carrot, peeled, noodled
- 0.2 lb. red cabbage, thinly sliced
- 2 tbsp. lime juice
- Kosher salt and pepper, to taste
- 0.3 lb. toasted almonds, chopped
- 3-4 tbsp. cilantro leaves

Directions:
1. Combine zucchini, carrots, cabbage, and almonds. Season with salt, pepper, lemon juice, and olive oil then toss it well.
2. Add to a serving platter.

Nutrition: 264 Calories |2g Fat |6g Protein

Carrot and Spinach Salad

Preparation Time: 60 minutes |Cooking Time: 4 minutes |Servings: 4

Ingredients:
- 0.8 lb. baby spinach leaves
- 2 carrots, peeled, grated
- 5 tbsp. olive oil
- 4 tbsp. lemon juice
- Salt and black pepper, to taste
- 1 tsp. thyme
- 1-2 garlic cloves, minced
- ¼ tsp. olive powder

Directions:
1. Stir in lemon juice, olive oil, salt, pepper, onion powder, and garlic. Mix well.
2. Add carrots and spinach leaves to mixture. Toss to combine.
3. Cover the bowl with a plastic wrapper. Place it in the refrigerator for about 50 minutes before serving.

Nutrition: 215 Calories |4.5g Fat |14g Protein

Red Cabbage Salad

Preparation Time: 15 minutes |Cooking Time: 0 minutes |Servings: 4

Ingredients:
- 1 lb. red cabbage, thinly sliced
- 2 carrots, peeled, thinly sliced
- 2 tbsp. olive oil
- Salt and black pepper, to taste
- 2 tbsp. lemon juice
- 2 tbsp. coriander leaves, chopped
- 1 tbsp. mint leaves, chopped

Directions:
1. Combine cabbage, carrots, mint, and coriander.
2. Mix in salt, pepper, lemon juice, and olive oil then toss it well. Transfer salad onto a serving platter.

Nutrition: 226 Calories |5g Fat |12g Protein

Quinoa Fruit Salad

Preparation Time: 15 minutes |Cooking Time: 0 minutes |Servings: 3

Ingredients:

- 1 lb. cooked quinoa
- 1 mango, peeled and diced
- ½ lb. strawberries, quartered
- ½ lb. blueberries
- 2 tbsp. pine nuts
- Chopped mint leaves, for garnish
- 4 tbsp. olive oil
- Zest of 1 lemon, as required
- 3 tbsp. freshly squeezed lemon juice
- 1 tbsp. date sugar

Directions:

1. For the vinaigrette, beat the olive oil, lemon zest, juice, and sugar in a small bowl. Set aside.
2. Mix quinoa, mango, strawberries, blueberries, and pine nuts in a large bowl. Add the lemon vinaigrette.

Nutrition: 490 Calories |7.2g Fat |9.8g Protein

Power Sicilian lasagna

Preparation Time: 30 minutes |Cooking Time: 40 minutes |Servings: 8

Ingredients:

- 9 whole wheat lasagna noodles
- 1-pound lean ground beef (90% lean)
- 1 medium zucchini, finely chopped
- 1 medium onion, finely chopped
- 1 medium green pepper, finely chopped
- 3 garlic cloves, minced
- 1 jar (24 ounces) meatless pasta sauce
- 1 can (14-1/2 ounces) no-salt-added diced tomatoes, drained
- 1/2 cup loosely packed basil leaves, chopped
- 2 tablespoons ground flaxseed
- 5 teaspoons Italian seasoning
- 1/4 teaspoon pepper
- 1 carton (15 ounces) fat-free ricotta cheese
- 1 package (10 ounces) frozen chopped spinach, thawed and squeezed dry
- 1 large egg, lightly beaten
- 2 tablespoons white balsamic vinegar
- 2 cups shredded part-skim mozzarella cheese
- 1/4 cup grated Parmesan cheese

Directions:

1. Preheat oven to 350°. Cook noodles according to package directions. Meanwhile, in a 6-qt. stockpot, cook beef, zucchini, onion and green pepper over medium heat until beef is no longer pink, breaking up beef into crumbles. Add garlic; cook 1 minute longer. Drain.
2. Stir in pasta sauce, diced tomatoes, basil, flax, Italian seasoning and pepper, heat through. Drain noodles and rinse in cold water.
3. In a small bowl, mix ricotta cheese, spinach, egg and vinegar. Spread 1 cup meat mixture into a 13x9-in. baking dish coated with cooking spray. Layer with three noodles, 2 cups meat mixture, 1-1/4 cups ricotta cheese mixture and 2/3 cup mozzarella cheese. Repeat layers. Top with remaining noodles, meat mixture and mozzarella cheese; sprinkle with Parmesan cheese.
4. Bake, covered, 30 minutes. Bake, uncovered, 10-15 minutes longer or until cheese is melted. Let stand 10 minutes before serving.

Nutrition: 386 Calories | 8g Fat | 32g Carb

Beef and Red Bean Chili

Preparation Time: 10 minutes |Cooking Time: 6 hours |Servings: 4

Ingredients

- 1 cup dry red beans
- 1 tablespoon olive oil
- 2 pounds boneless beef chuck
- 1 large onion, coarsely chopped
- 1 (14 ounce) can beef broth
- 2 chipotle chili peppers in adobo sauce
- 2 teaspoons dried oregano, crushed
- 1 teaspoon ground cumin
- ½ teaspoon salt
- 1 (14.5 ounce) can tomatoes with mild green chilis
- 1 (15 ounce) can tomato sauce
- ¼ cup snipped fresh cilantro
- 1 medium red sweet pepper

Direction

1. Rinse out the beans and place them into a Dutch oven or big saucepan, then add in water enough to cover them. Allow the beans to boil then drop the heat down. Simmer the beans without a cover for 10 minutes. Take off the heat and keep covered for an hour.
2. In a big frypan, heat up the oil upon medium-high heat, then cook onion and half the beef until they brown a bit over medium-high heat. Move into a 3 1/2- or 4-quart crockery cooker. Do this again with what's left of the beef. Add in tomato sauce, tomatoes (not drained), salt, cumin, oregano, adobo sauce, chipotle peppers, and broth, stirring to blend. Strain out and rinse beans and stir in the cooker.
3. Cook while covered on a low setting for around 10-12 hours or on high setting for 5-6 hours. Spoon the chili into bowls or mugs and top with sweet pepper and cilantro.

Nutrition 288 Calories|24g Carbs |5g Sugar

Berry Apple Cider

Preparation Time: 15 minutes |Cooking Time: 3 hours Servings: 3

Ingredients

- 4 cinnamon sticks, cut into 1-inch pieces
- 1½ teaspoons whole cloves
- 4 cups apple cider
- 4 cups low-calorie cranberry-raspberry juice drink
- 1 medium apple

Direction

1. To make the spice bag, cut out a 6-inch square from double thick, pure cotton cheesecloth. Put in the cloves and cinnamon, then bring the corners up, tie it closed using a clean kitchen string that is pure cotton.
2. In a 3 1/2- 5-quart slow cooker, combine cranberry-raspberry juice, apple cider, and the spice bag.
3. Cook while covered over low heat setting for around 4-6 hours or on a high heat setting for 2-2 1/2 hours.
4. Throw out the spice bag. Serve right away or keep it warm while covered on warm or low heat setting up to 2 hours, occasionally stirring. Garnish each serving with apples (thinly sliced).

Nutrition 89 Calories |22g Carbs |19g Sugar

Brunswick Stew

Preparation Time: 10 minutes |Cooking Time: 10 minutes |Servings: 3

Ingredients

- 4 ounces diced salt pork
- 2 pounds chicken parts
- 8 cups water
- 3 potatoes, cubed
- 3 onions, chopped
- 1 (28 ounce) can whole peeled tomatoes
- 2 cups canned whole kernel corn
- 1 (10 ounce) package frozen lima beans
- 1 tablespoon Worcestershire sauce

- 1/2 teaspoon salt
- 1/4 teaspoon ground black pepper

Direction

1. Mix and boil water, chicken and salt pork in a big pot on high heat. Lower heat to low. Cover then simmer until chicken is tender for 45 minutes.
2. Take out chicken. Let cool until easily handled. Take meat out. Throw out bones and skin. Chop meat to bite-sized pieces. Put back in the soup.
3. Add ground black pepper, salt, Worcestershire sauce, lima beans, corn, tomatoes, onions and potatoes.
4. Mix well. Stir well and simmer for 1 hour, uncovered.

Nutrition
368 Calories |25.9g Carbs |27.9g Protein

Buffalo Chicken Salads

Preparation Time: 7 minutes |Cooking Time: 3 hours |Servings: 3

Ingredients

- 1½ pounds chicken breast halves
- ½ cup Wing Time® Buffalo chicken sauce
- 4 teaspoons cider vinegar
- 1 teaspoon Worcestershire sauce
- 1 teaspoon paprika
- 1/3 cup light mayonnaise
- 2 tablespoons fat-free milk
- 2 tablespoons crumbled blue cheese
- 2 romaine hearts, chopped
- 1 cup whole grain croutons
- ½ cup very thinly sliced red onion

Direction

1. Place chicken in a 2-quarts slow cooker. Mix together Worcestershire sauce, 2 teaspoons of vinegar and Buffalo sauce in a small bowl; pour over chicken. Dust with paprika. Close and cook for 3 hours on low-heat setting.
2. Mix the leftover 2 teaspoons of vinegar with milk and light mayonnaise together in a small bowl at serving time; mix in blue cheese. While chicken is still in the slow cooker, pull meat into bite-sized pieces using two forks.
3. Split the romaine among 6 dishes. Spoon sauce and chicken over lettuce. Pour with blue cheese dressing then add red onion slices and croutons on top.

Nutrition: 274 Calories|11g Carbs |2g Fiber

Cacciatore Style Chicken

Preparation Time: 10 minutes |Cooking Time: 4 hours Servings: 6

Ingredients

- 2 cups sliced fresh mushrooms
- 1 cup sliced celery
- 1 cup chopped carrot
- 2 medium onions, cut into wedges
- 1 green, yellow, or red sweet peppers
- 4 cloves garlic, minced
- 12 chicken drumsticks
- ½ cup chicken broth
- ¼ cup dry white wine
- 2 tablespoons quick-cooking tapioca
- 2 bay leaves
- 1 teaspoon dried oregano, crushed
- 1 teaspoon sugar
- ½ teaspoon salt
- ¼ teaspoon pepper
- 1 (14.5 ounce) can diced tomatoes
- 1/3 cup tomato paste
- Hot cooked pasta or rice

Direction

1. Mix garlic, sweet pepper, onions, carrot, celery and mushrooms in a 5- or 6-qt. slow cooker. Cover veggies with the chicken. Add pepper, salt, sugar, oregano, bay leaves, tapioca, wine and broth.
2. Cover. Cook for 3–3 1/2 hours on high-heat setting.
3. Take chicken out; keep warm. Discard bay leaves. Turn to high-heat setting if

using low-heat setting. Mix tomato paste and undrained tomatoes in. Cover. Cook on high heat setting for 15 more minutes. Serving: Put veggie mixture on top of pasta and chicken.

Nutrition: 324 Calories |7g Sugar |35g Carbs

Carnitas Tacos

Preparation Time: 10 minutes |Cooking Time: 5 hours Servings: 4

Ingredients

- 3 to 3½-pound bone-in pork shoulder roast
- ½ cup chopped onion
- 1/3 cup orange juice
- 1 tablespoon ground cumin
- 1½ teaspoons kosher salt
- 1 teaspoon dried oregano, crushed
- ¼ teaspoon cayenne pepper
- 1 lime
- 2 (5.3 ounce) containers plain low-fat Greek yogurt
- 1 pinch kosher salt
- 16 (6 inch) soft yellow corn tortillas, such as Mission® brand
- 4 leaves green cabbage, quartered
- 1 cup very thinly sliced red onion
- 1 cup salsa (optional)

Direction

1. Take off meat from the bone; throw away bone. Trim meat fat. Slice meat into 2 to 3-inch pieces; put in a slow cooker of 3 1/2 or 4-quart in size. Mix in cayenne, oregano, salt, cumin, orange juice and onion.
2. Cover and cook for 4 to 5 hours on high. Take out meat from the cooker. Shred meat with two forks. Mix in enough cooking liquid to moisten.
3. Take out 1 teaspoon zest (put aside) for lime crema, then squeeze 2 tablespoons lime juice. Mix dash salt, yogurt, and lime juice in a small bowl.
4. Serve lime crema, salsa (if wished), red onion and cabbage with meat in tortillas. Scatter with lime zest.

Nutrition: 301 Calories|28g Carbs|7g Sugar

Chicken Chili

Preparation Time: 6 minutes |Cooking Time: 1 hour |Servings: 4

Ingredients

- 3 tablespoons vegetable oil
- 2 cloves garlic, minced
- 1 green bell pepper, chopped
- 1 onion, chopped
- 1 stalk celery, sliced
- 1/4-pound mushrooms, chopped
- 1-pound chicken breast
- 1 tablespoon chili powder
- 1 teaspoon dried oregano
- 1 teaspoon ground cumin
- 1/2 teaspoon paprika
- 1/2 teaspoon cocoa powder
- 1/4 teaspoon salt
- 1 pinch crushed red pepper flakes
- 1 pinch ground black pepper
- 1 (14.5 oz) can tomatoes with juice
- 1 (19 oz) can kidney beans

Direction

1. Fill 2 tablespoons of oil into a big skillet and heat it at moderate heat. Add mushrooms, celery, onion, bell pepper and garlic, sautéing for 5 minutes. Put it to one side.
2. Insert the leftover 1 tablespoon of oil into the skillet. At high heat, cook the chicken until browned and its exterior turns firm. Transfer the vegetable mixture back into skillet.
3. Stir in ground black pepper, hot pepper flakes, salt, cocoa powder, paprika, oregano, cumin and chili powder. Continue stirring for several minutes to avoid burning. Pour in the beans and tomatoes and lead the entire mixture to

boiling point then adjust the setting to low heat. Place a lid on the skillet and leave it simmering for 15 minutes.

4. Uncover the skillet and leave it simmering for another 15 minutes.

Nutrition: 308 Calories|25g Carbs|29g Protein

Chicken Vera Cruz

Preparation Time: 7 minutes |Cooking Time: 10 hours |Servings: 5

Ingredients

- 1 medium onion, cut into wedges
- 1-pound yellow-skin potatoes
- 6 skinless, boneless chicken thighs
- 2 (14.5 oz.) cans no-salt-added diced tomatoes
- 1 fresh jalapeño chili pepper
- 2 tablespoons Worcestershire sauce
- 1 tablespoon chopped garlic
- 1 teaspoon dried oregano, crushed
- ¼ teaspoon ground cinnamon
- 1/8 teaspoon ground cloves
- ½ cup snipped fresh parsley
- ¼ cup chopped pimiento-stuffed green olives

Direction

1. Put onion in a 3 1/2- or 4-quart slow cooker. Place chicken thighs and potatoes on top. Drain and discard juices from a can of tomatoes. Stir undrained and drained tomatoes, cloves, cinnamon, oregano, garlic, Worcestershire sauce and jalapeño pepper together in a bowl. Pour over all in the cooker.
2. Cook with a cover for 10 hours on low-heat setting.
3. To make the topping: Stir chopped pimiento-stuffed green olives and snipped fresh parsley together in a small bowl. Drizzle the topping over each serving of chicken.

Nutrition: 228 Calories |9g Sugar |25g Carbs

Chicken and Cornmeal Dumplings

Preparation Time: 8 minutes |Cooking Time: 8 hours |Servings: 4

Ingredients

Chicken and Vegetable Filling

- 2 medium carrots, thinly sliced
- 1 stalk celery, thinly sliced
- 1/3 cup corn kernels
- ½ of a medium onion, thinly sliced
- 2 cloves garlic, minced
- 1 teaspoon snipped fresh rosemary
- ¼ teaspoon ground black pepper
- 2 chicken thighs, skinned
- 1 cup reduced sodium chicken broth
- ½ cup fat-free milk
- 1 tablespoon all-purpose flour

Cornmeal Dumplings

- ¼ cup flour
- ¼ cup cornmeal
- ½ teaspoon baking powder
- 1 egg white
- 1 tablespoon fat-free milk
- 1 tablespoon canola oil

Direction

1. Mix 1/4 teaspoon pepper, carrots, garlic, celery, rosemary, corn, and onion in a 1 1/2 or 2-quart slow cooker. Place chicken on top. Pour the broth atop mixture in the cooker.
2. Close and cook on low heat for 7 to 8 hours.
3. If cooking with the low-heat setting, switch to high-heat setting (or if heat setting is not available, continue to cook). Place the chicken onto a cutting board and let to cool slightly. Once cool enough to handle, chop off chicken from bones and get rid of the bones. Chop the chicken and place back into the mixture in cooker. Mix flour and milk in a small bowl until smooth. Stir into the mixture in cooker.
4. Drop the Cornmeal Dumplings dough into 4 mounds atop hot chicken mixture using two spoons. Cover and cook for 20 to 25 minutes more or until a toothpick come

out clean when inserted into a dumpling. (Avoid lifting lid when cooking.) Sprinkle each of the serving with coarse pepper if desired.

5. Mix together 1/2 teaspoon baking powder, 1/4 cup flour, a dash of salt and 1/4 cup cornmeal in a medium bowl. Mix 1 tablespoon canola oil, 1 egg white and 1 tablespoon fat-free milk in a small bowl. Pour the egg mixture into the flour mixture.
6. Mix just until moistened.

Nutrition: 369 Calories|9g Sugar 47g Carbs

Chicken and Pepperoni *

Preparation Time: 4 minutes |Cooking Time: 4 hours Servings: 1

Ingredients

- 3½ to 4 pounds meaty chicken pieces
- 1/8 teaspoon salt
- 1/8 teaspoon black pepper
- 2 ounces sliced turkey pepperoni
- ¼ cup sliced pitted ripe olives
- ½ cup reduced-sodium chicken broth
- 1 tablespoon tomato paste
- 1 teaspoon dried Italian seasoning, crushed
- ½ cup shredded part-skim mozzarella cheese (2 ounces)

Direction

1. Put chicken into a 3 1/2 to 5-qt. slow cooker. Sprinkle pepper and salt on the chicken. Slice pepperoni slices in half. Put olives and pepperoni into the slow cooker. In a small bowl, blend Italian seasoning, tomato paste and chicken broth together. Transfer the mixture into the slow cooker.
2. Cook with a cover for 3-3 1/2 hours on high.
3. Transfer the olives, pepperoni and chicken onto a serving platter with a slotted spoon. Discard the cooking liquid. Sprinkle cheese over the chicken. Use foil to loosely cover and allow to sit for 5 minutes to melt the cheese.

Nutrition: 243 Calories |1g Carbs |41g Protein

Chicken and Sausage Gumbo

Preparation Time: 6 minutes |Cooking Time: 4 hours Servings: 5

Ingredients

- 1/3 cup all-purpose flour
- 1 (14 ounce) can reduced-sodium chicken broth
- 2 cups chicken breast
- 8 ounces smoked turkey sausage links
- 2 cups sliced fresh okra
- 1 cup water
- 1 cup coarsely chopped onion
- 1 cup sweet pepper
- ½ cup sliced celery
- 4 cloves garlic, minced
- 1 teaspoon dried thyme
- ½ teaspoon ground black pepper
- ¼ teaspoon cayenne pepper
- 3 cups hot cooked brown rice

Direction

1. To make the roux: Cook the flour upon a medium heat in a heavy medium-sized saucepan, stirring periodically, for roughly 6 minutes or until the flour browns. Take off the heat and slightly cool, then slowly stir in the broth. Cook the roux until it bubbles and thickens up.
2. Pour the roux in a 3 1/2- or 4-quart slow cooker, then add in cayenne pepper, black pepper, thyme, garlic, celery, sweet pepper, onion, water, okra, sausage, and chicken.
3. Cook the soup covered on a high setting for 3 - 3 1/2 hours. Take the fat off the top and serve atop hot cooked brown rice.

Nutrition :230 Calories |3g Sugar |19g Protein

Chicken, Barley, and Leek Stew *

Preparation Time: 10 minutes |Cooking Time: 3 hours |Servings: 1

Ingredients

- 1-pound chicken thighs
- 1 tablespoon olive oil
- 1 (49 ounce) can reduced-sodium chicken broth
- 1 cup regular barley (not quick cooking)
- 2 medium leeks, halved lengthwise and sliced
- 2 medium carrots, thinly sliced
- 1½ teaspoons dried basil or Italian seasoning, crushed
- ¼ teaspoon cracked black pepper

Direction

1. In the big skillet, cook the chicken in hot oil till becoming brown on all sides. In the 4-5-qt. slow cooker, whisk the pepper, dried basil, carrots, leeks, barley, chicken broth and chicken.
2. Keep covered and cooked over high heat setting for 2 – 2.5 hours or till the barley softens. As you wish, drizzle with the parsley or fresh basil prior to serving.

Nutrition:248 Calories |6g Fiber|27g Carbs

Cider Pork Stew

Preparation Time: 35 minutes |Cooking Time: 12 hours Servings: 4

Ingredients

- 2 pounds pork shoulder roast
- 3 medium cubed potatoes
- 3 medium carrots
- 2 medium onions, sliced
- 1 cup coarsely chopped apple
- ½ cup coarsely chopped celery
- 3 tablespoons quick-cooking tapioca
- 2 cups apple juice
- 1 teaspoon salt
- 1 teaspoon caraway seeds
- ¼ teaspoon black pepper

Direction

1. Chop the meat into 1-in. cubes. In the 3.5-5.5 qt. slow cooker, mix the tapioca, celery, apple, onions, carrots, potatoes and meat. Whisk in pepper, caraway seeds, salt and apple juice.
2. Keep covered and cook over low heat setting for 10-12 hours. If you want, use the celery leaves to decorate each of the servings.

Nutrition: 244 Calories |5g Fiber|33g Carbs

Creamy Chicken Noodle Soup

Preparation Time: 7 minutes |Cooking Time: 8 hours Servings: 4

Ingredients

- 1 (32 fluid ounce) container reduced-sodium chicken broth
- 3 cups water
- 2½ cups chopped cooked chicken
- 3 medium carrots, sliced
- 3 stalks celery
- 1½ cups sliced fresh mushrooms
- ¼ cup chopped onion
- 1½ teaspoons dried thyme, crushed
- ¾ teaspoon garlic-pepper seasoning
- 3 ounces reduced-fat cream cheese (Neufchâtel), cut up
- 2 cups dried egg noodles

Direction

1. Mix together the garlic-pepper seasoning, thyme, onion, mushrooms, celery, carrots, chicken, water and broth in a 5 to 6-quart slow cooker.
2. Put cover and let it cook for 6-8 hours on low-heat setting.
3. Increase to high-heat setting if you are using low-heat setting. Mix in the cream cheese until blended. Mix in uncooked noodles. Put cover and let it cook for an additional 20-30 minutes or just until the noodles become tender.

Nutrition :170 Calories |3g Sugar |2g Fiber

Cuban Pulled Pork Sandwich*

Preparation Time: 6 minutes |Cooking Time: 5 hours |Servings: 1

Ingredients

- 1 teaspoon dried oregano, crushed
- ¾ teaspoon ground cumin
- ½ teaspoon ground coriander
- ¼ teaspoon salt
- ¼ teaspoon black pepper
- ¼ teaspoon ground allspice
- 1 2 to 2½-pound boneless pork shoulder roast
- 1 tablespoon olive oil
- Nonstick cooking spray
- 2 cups sliced onions
- 2 green sweet peppers, cut into bite-size strips
- ½ to 1 fresh jalapeño pepper
- 4 cloves garlic, minced
- ¼ cup orange juice
- ¼ cup lime juice
- 6 heart-healthy wheat hamburger buns, toasted
- 2 tablespoons jalapeño mustard

Direction

1. Mix allspice, oregano, black pepper, cumin, salt, and coriander together in a small bowl. Press each side of the roast into the spice mixture.
2. On medium-high heat, heat oil in a big non-stick pan; put in roast. Cook for 5mins until both sides of the roast is light brown, turn the roast one time.
3. Using a cooking spray, grease a 3 1/2 or 4qt slow cooker; arrange the garlic, onions, jalapeno, and green peppers in a layer. Pour in lime juice and orange juice. Slice the roast if needed to fit inside the cooker; put on top of the vegetables covered or 4 1/2-5hrs on high heat setting.
4. Move roast to a cutting board using a slotted spoon. Drain the cooking liquid and keep the jalapeno, green peppers, and onions. Shred the roast with 2 forks then place it back in the cooker. Remove fat from the liquid. Mix half cup of cooking liquid and reserved vegetables into the cooker. Pour in more cooking liquid if desired. Discard the remaining cooking liquid.
5. Slather mustard on rolls. Split the meat between the bottom roll halves. Add avocado on top if desired. Place the roll tops to sandwiches.

Nutrition:379 Calories|32g Carbs |4g Fiber

Lemon-Tarragon Soup

Preparation Time: 10 minutes |Cooking Time: 10 minutes |Servings: 2

Ingredients

- 1 tablespoon avocado oil
- ½ cup diced onion
- 3 garlic cloves, crushed
- ¼ plus 1/8 teaspoon sea salt
- ¼ plus 1/8 teaspoon freshly ground black pepper
- 1 (13.5-ounce) can full-fat coconut milk
- 1 tablespoon freshly squeezed lemon juice
- ½ cup raw cashews
- 1 celery stalk
- 2 tablespoons chopped fresh tarragon

Directions:

1. In a medium skillet over medium-high heat, heat up avocado oil. Sauté onion, garlic, salt, and pepper for 4 minutes.
2. In a high-speed blender, blend together the coconut milk, lemon juice, cashews, celery, and tarragon with the onion mixture until smooth. Adjust seasonings, if necessary.
3. Pour into 1 large or 2 small bowls and enjoy immediately, or transfer to a medium saucepan and warm on low heat for 3 to 5 minutes before serving.

Nutrition: 264 calories |11g fiber|10g fats

Chilled Cucumber and Lime Soup

Preparation Time: 25 minutes |Cooking Time: 20 minutes |Servings: 2

Ingredients:

- 1 cucumber, peeled
- ½ zucchini, peeled
- 1 tablespoon freshly squeezed lime juice
- 1 tablespoon fresh cilantro leaves
- 1 garlic clove, crushed
- ¼ teaspoon sea salt

Directions:

1. In a blender, blend together the cucumber, zucchini, lime juice, cilantro, garlic, and salt until well combined. Add more salt, if necessary.
2. Pour into 1 large or 2 small bowls and enjoy immediately or refrigerate for 15 to 20 minutes to chill before serving.

Nutrition: 254 calories|30g protein|8g fat

Coconut, Cilantro, and Jalapeño Soup

Preparation Time: 5 minutes |Cooking Time: 5 minutes |Servings: 2

Ingredients:

- 2 tablespoons avocado oil
- ½ cup diced onions
- 3 garlic cloves, crushed
- ¼ teaspoon sea salt
- 1 (13.5-ounce) can full-fat coconut milk
- 1 tablespoon freshly squeezed lime juice
- ½ to 1 jalapeño
- 2 tablespoons fresh cilantro leaves

Directions:

1. Using medium skillet over medium-high heat, heat up avocado oil. Sauté onion, garlic, and salt for 4 minutes.
2. In a blender, blend together the coconut milk, lime juice, jalapeño, and cilantro with the onion mixture until creamy.
3. Pour into 1 large or 2 small bowls and enjoy.

Nutrition:159 calories|11g fat|37g protein

Spicy Watermelon Gazpacho

Preparation Time: 5 minutes |Cooking Time: 0 minutes |Servings: 2

Ingredients:

- 2 cups cubed watermelon
- ¼ cup diced onion
- ¼ cup packed cilantro leaves
- ½ to 1 jalapeño
- 2 tablespoons freshly squeezed lime juice

Directions:

1. In a blender or food processor, pulse to combine the watermelon, onion, cilantro, jalapeño, and lime juice only long enough to break down the ingredients, leaving them very finely diced and taking care to not over process.
2. Pour into 1 large or 2 small bowls and enjoy.

Nutrition: 207 calories|5g fat|36g protein

Roasted Carrot and Leek Soup

Preparation Time: 35 minutes |Cooking Time: 30 minutes |Servings: 1 to 4

Ingredients:

- 6 carrots
- 1 cup chopped onion
- 1 fennel bulb, cubed
- 2 garlic cloves, crushed
- 2 tablespoons avocado oil
- 1 teaspoon sea salt
- 1 teaspoon freshly ground black pepper
- 2 cups almond milk, plus more if desired

Directions:

1. Preheat the oven to 400°F. Line a baking sheet with parchment paper. Cut the carrots into thirds, and then cut each third in half. Transfer to a medium bowl.
2. Add the onion, fennel, garlic, and avocado oil, and toss to coat. Season with the salt and pepper and toss again.
3. Transfer the vegetables to the prepared baking sheet, and roast for 30 minutes.

Remove from the oven and allow the vegetables to cool.

4. In a high-speed blender, blend together the almond milk and roasted vegetables until creamy and smooth. Adjust the seasonings, if necessary, and add additional milk if you prefer a thinner consistency.
5. Pour into 2 large or 4 small bowls and enjoy.

Nutrition: 220 calories|15g fiber|28g protein

Lemon Cauliflower & Pine Nuts

Preparation Time: 5 minutes |Cooking Time: 20 minutes |Servings: 4

Ingredients:

- 1 teaspoon lemon zest
- ¼ teaspoon sea salt
- 1 (10 ounces) package cauliflower florets
- 2 tablespoons extra virgin olive oil
- 2 tablespoons pine nuts
- 1 tablespoon parsley, fresh flat leaf
- 1 ½ teaspoons lemon juice
- ¼ teaspoon fresh ground black pepper

Directions:

1. Preheat your oven to 400° Fahrenheit.
2. In a large bowl, combine all of your ingredients. Then set onto a baking sheet.
3. Bake for 20 minutes, serve and enjoy!

Nutrition: 60 Calories | 4g Protein | 0,1 g Fat

Beef Tenderloin & Avocado Cream

Preparation Time: 10 minutes |Cooking Time: 8 minutes |Servings: 2

Ingredients:

- 1 teaspoon mustard
- 2 (6 ounces) beef steaks
- ¼ cup sour cream
- 2 teaspoons lemon juice, fresh
- 1/3 avocado
- 1 tablespoon olive oil-slicked
- sea salt along with fresh ground black pepper as needed

Directions:

1. Preheat your oven to 450° Fahrenheit.
2. Sprinkle the beef steaks with some salt and pepper.
3. Mix the mustard and oil and spread the mixture over the meat.
4. Place the steaks into a skillet over medium-high heat for 3 minutes.
5. Transfer the steaks to a baking sheet and place in the oven, then bake for 6 minutes.
6. Blend the avocado with lemon juice and sour cream.
7. Serve steaks with avocado cream and enjoy!

Nutrition: 205 Calories | 20g Protein | 15g Fat

Salmon & Citrus Sauce

Preparation Time: 10 minutes |Cooking Time: 15 minutes |Servings: 2

Ingredients:

- ¾ lb. salmon fillets
- 1/3 cup fresh orange juice
- 1 tablespoon fresh lime juice
- 1 tablespoon fresh lemon juice
- 1 tablespoon honey
- 1 tablespoon olive oil
- 1 ½ tablespoons mustard
- sea salt along with fresh ground black pepper as needed
- ¼ teaspoon smoked paprika

Directions:

1. Sprinkle fillets with paprika, salt and pepper. Then, cook in a skillet over medium-high heat for 5 minutes per side.
2. While fillets are cooking, mix the lemon, orange, lime juices, and honey, then add to a small saucepan. Add the mustard and stir to combine—Cook over low heat for 10 minutes.
3. Add the salmon fillets to serving dishes, then pour the sauce over the fillets. Serve and enjoy!

Nutrition: 210 Calories |20g Protein | 222 g Fat

Orange-Avocado Salad *

Preparation Time: 10 minutes |Cooking Time: 0 minutes |Servings: 1

Ingredients:

- ½ teaspoon arugula
- 1 avocado
- 1 navel orange
- 1 tablespoon fresh lime juice
- 1 tablespoon extra-virgin olive oil

Directions:

1. Mix your lime juice, arugula and oil in a bowl.
2. Add the peeled and sectioned pieces of orange, then toss.
3. Add the diced avocado just before serving, then enjoy!

Nutrition: 30 Calories |2g Protein | 2g Fat

Avocados with Walnut-Herb

Preparation Time: 7 minutes |Cooking Time: 5 minutes |Servings: 2

Ingredients:

- 1 avocado
- ¼ cup walnuts
- 1 ½ teaspoons virgin olive oil
- 1 ½ teaspoons lemon juice (fresh)
- 1 tablespoon fresh basil
- sea salt and black pepper to taste

Directions:

1. Fry the chopped nuts for about 5 minutes over medium-low heat in a pan.
2. In a small bowl, mix the chopped basil, lemon juice, oil, sea salt and pepper.
3. Slice avocado in half, then top slices with the walnut mixture, serve and enjoy!

Nutrition: 200 Calories | 2g Protein | 17 g Fat

Barbecue Brisket

Preparation Time: 15 minutes |Cooking Time: 5 hours Servings: 4

Ingredients:

- 1 cup beef broth
- 2 lb. beef brisket
- 1 sweet onion, diced
- ½ cup barbecue sauce
- ½ tablespoon steak seasoning

Directions:

1. Add the prepared onion to your slow cooker. Rub the trimmed brisket with seasoning.
2. Cut the brisket into pieces and add to your slow cooker.
3. Pour the beef broth and barbecue sauce over the brisket.
4. Cook on low for 5 hours, slice brisket. Serve and enjoy!

Nutrition: 188 Calories | 13g Protein | 8g Fat

Broccoli & Hot Sauce

Preparation Time: 5 minutes |Cooking Time: 5 minutes |Servings: 2

Ingredients:

- 4 cups broccoli florets
- 1 tablespoon extra-virgin olive oil
- ½ teaspoon hot sauce
- sea salt along with black ground pepper as needed

Directions:

1. Arrange your broccoli in a steamer basket. Steam your broccoli for about 5 minutes or until tender.
2. Drizzle with the oil and sprinkle with hot sauce, sea salt and black pepper. Serve and enjoy!

Nutrition: 30 Calories | 4g Protein | 0,1g Fat

Chicken Thighs

Preparation Time: 10 minutes |Cooking Time: 40 minutes |Servings: 4

Ingredients:

- 4 bone-in skinless chicken thighs
- ½ teaspoon ginger
- 1 tablespoon olive oil
- 2 tablespoons soy sauce
- ¼ teaspoon dry mustard
- 1 garlic clove
- ¼ teaspoon red pepper
- ¼ teaspoon all-spice

Directions:

1. Preheat the oven to 400° Fahrenheit and sauté the minced garlic, ground allspice, ground ginger, crushed red pepper and mustard in hot oil for 5 minutes. Remove from heat.
2. Whisk in soy sauce, then place the chicken thighs on a baking sheet. Add the garlic mixture over the chicken, and toss.

Nutrition: 120 Calories | 8g Protein | 5g Fat

Creamy Bell Pepper-Corn Salad & Seared Zucchini *

Preparation Time: 10 minutes |Cooking Time: 20 minutes |Servings: 1

Ingredients:

- 2 zucchinis
- ½ cup celery
- 1 green bell pepper, sliced and seeded
- 1 dozen cherry tomatoes
- 2 cups kernel corn
- 4 tablespoons sour cream
- ½ cup mayonnaise
- 2 teaspoons sweetener
- sea salt along with ground black pepper as needed

Directions:

1. Cook your corn by following package instructions.
2. Mix the chopped celery, sliced bell pepper, whole cherry tomatoes, mayonnaise, sour cream, sweetener, salt and pepper in a large salad bowl.
3. Heat a skillet over medium-high heat. Cook the zucchini sliced lengthwise for about 10 minutes. Turn occasionally, then add salt to zucchini.
4. Once zucchini is cooked, add it to the corn mixture.
5. You can serve this dish alongside your favorite meat dish!

Nutrition: 100 Calories | 6g Protein | 3g Fat

Corn Tortillas & Spinach Salad

Preparation Time: 3 minutes |Cooking Time: 5 minutes |Servings: 4

Ingredients:

- 2 cups baby spinach, chopped
- 4 corn tortillas
- 2 tablespoons red onion, chopped
- 4 cherry tomatoes, whole
- 2 teaspoons balsamic vinegar
- 8 olives, ripe and pitted
- 1 tablespoon extra-virgin olive oil
- salt and pepper to taste

Directions:

1. Heat your tortillas according to their package instructions.
2. Mix the remaining ingredients in a bowl.
3. Serve the tortillas along with your salad and enjoy!

Nutrition: 2200 Calories | 10g Protein | 3g Fat

Smoky Carrot & Black Bean Stew

Preparation Time: 15 minutes |Cooking Time: 25 minutes |Servings: 2

Ingredients:

- 1 (15 ounces) can salt-free black beans
- 1 cup carrots, chopped
- 1 (15 ounces) can diced tomatoes
- 1 carton chicken broth
- 2 teaspoons smoked paprika
- ¾ cup onion, chopped
- 1 ½ teaspoons extra virgin olive oil
- 2 garlic cloves, minced
- 1 avocado, pitted and chopped

Directions:

1. Add your extra virgin olive oil to a pan placed over medium-high heat.
2. Add your onion and carrots, then fry for 5 minutes.
3. Stir in the minced garlic, paprika, and cook for one minute.
4. Add the beans, broth and diced tomatoes, then bring to a boil.
5. Reduce the pan heat, simmer until carrots are tender.
6. Top each serving with chopped avocado, then serve and enjoy!

Nutrition: 100 Calories | 15g Proteins | 7g Fat

Oven-Baked Potatoes & Green Beans

Preparation Time: 10 minutes |Cooking Time: 20 minutes |Servings: 4

Ingredients:

- ½ lb. green beans
- ½ lb. potatoes, peeled and sliced into chunks
- 2 teaspoons extra virgin olive oil
- ½ teaspoon garlic powder
- 2 teaspoons Dijon mustard
- sea salt along with fresh ground black pepper as needed

Directions:

1. Preheat oven to 375° Fahrenheit.
2. Mix your chunks of potatoes with oil and mustard. Spread prepared potato chunks over a baking sheet. Bake for 15 minutes to make the first layer.
3. Add your green beans, garlic powder, sea salt and black pepper to your potatoes and toss—Bake for an additional 15 minutes. Serve and enjoy!

Nutrition: 35 Calories | 1.3g Protein | 0.3g Fat

Hummus & Salad Pita Flats

Preparation Time: 15 minutes |Cooking Time: 0 minutes |Servings: 2

Ingredients:

- 2 ounces whole-wheat pitas
- 8 black olives, pitted
- ¼ cup sweet roasted red pepper hummus
- 2 large eggs
- 2 teaspoons spring mix
- 1 teaspoon dried oregano
- 2 teaspoons extra-virgin olive oil

Directions:

1. Heat your pitas according to the package instructions.
2. Spread the hummus over the pitas.
3. Top pitas with hard-boiled eggs, dried oregano, and olives.
4. Add the spring mix and extra-virgin olive oil. Serve and enjoy!

Nutrition: 250 Calories | 8g protein |2g Fat

Lettuce Salad with Lemon

Preparation Time: 5 minutes |Cooking Time: 5 minutes |Servings: 2

Ingredients:

- 2 ounces arugula
- ½ head Romaine lettuce, chopped
- 1 avocado, pitted and sliced
- 2 teaspoons extra-virgin olive oil
- 1 tablespoon lemon juice
- ¼ teaspoon mustard
- sea salt along with fresh ground black pepper as needed

Directions:

1. Whisk your torn arugula, lemon juice, chopped avocado, olive oil, sea salt and pepper.
2. Add the chopped lettuce and toss to coat. Serve and enjoy!

Nutrition: 15 Calories | 2g protein | 2g Fat

Pork Chops & Butternut Squash Salad

Preparation Time: 20 minutes |Cooking Time: 25 minutes |Servings: 4

Ingredients:

- 4 boneless pork chops
- 1 ½ tablespoons fresh lemon juice

- 1 pkg. pomegranate seeds
- 1 pkg. baby arugula
- 3 cups butternut squash, peeled and cubed
- ½ cup pine nuts
- 2 tablespoons extra-virgin olive oil (divided)
- 2 garlic cloves, minced
- 6 tablespoons balsamic vinaigrette
- sea salt along with fresh ground black pepper as needed

Directions:

1. Preheat your oven to 475° Fahrenheit.
2. Combine a tablespoon of olive oil, minced garlic and lemon juice.
3. Mix your pork chops with oil mixture, sprinkle the top of chops with sea salt and pepper.
4. Mix squash and 1 tablespoon of oil, sprinkle with salt and pepper.
5. Place your pork chops onto a baking sheet, add place cubed squash around the chops. Bake for 25 minutes, then turn chops.
6. Toast your pine nuts for about 5 minutes in a small pan over medium-high heat.
7. Combine your squash, nuts, arugula and pomegranate seeds. Drizzle with balsamic vinaigrette and toss. Serve and enjoy!

Nutrition: 310 Calories | 20g protein | 14g Fat

Low Carb Stuffed Peppers

Preparation Time: 15 minutes |Cooking Time: 30 minutes |Servings: 4

Ingredients:

- 1 onion, diced
- 2 lb. Ground steak
- 4 green bell peppers, seeds removed and cut in half
- sea salt along with black ground pepper
- 1 tablespoon Worcestershire sauce
- 2 teaspoons garlic, minced

Directions:

1. Heat your oil, add diced onions and minced garlic along with some salt and pepper in the pan over medium-high heat.
2. Add diced steak pieces into the pan along with Worcestershire sauce and cook for 5 minutes.
3. Add cooked steak and other ingredients into a bowl and combine (except cheese slices and pepper halves).
4. Fill the pepper halves with steak mixture and top with a thin piece of mozzarella cheese on top of each half pepper.
5. Place the peppers into a baking pan and bake for 3o minutes. Serve and enjoy!

Nutrition: 320 Calories |40g Protein | 19g Fat

Chicken Cordon Bleu

Preparation Time: 20 minutes |Cooking Time: 10 minutes |Servings: 8

Ingredients:

- 8 chicken breasts, boneless and skinless
- ½ cup fat-free sour cream
- 2/3 cup skim milk
- 1 ½ cups mozzarella cheese, grated
- 8 slices ham
- 1 cup corn flakes, crushed
- 1 can low-fat condensed cream of chicken soup
- 1 teaspoon lemon juice
- 1 teaspoon paprika
- ½ teaspoon garlic powder
- ½ teaspoon black pepper
- ¼ teaspoon sea salt
- nonstick cooking spray as needed

Directions:

1. Heat your oven to 350° Fahrenheit. Spray a 13×9 baking dish lightly with cooking spray.
2. Flatten the chicken breasts to 1/4-inch thick. Sprinkle with pepper and top with a slice of ham and 3 tablespoons of cheese down the middle. Roll up, and tuck ends under and secure with toothpicks.

3. Pour the milk into a shallow bowl. In another bowl, combine corn flakes and seasoning. Dip the chicken into milk, roll in the cornflake mixture, and then place on a prepared baking dish.
4. Bake for 30 minutes or until your chicken is cooked through.
5. In a small pan, whisk the soup, lemon juice, and sour cream until well combined. Cook over medium heat until hot.
6. Remove the toothpicks from your chicken and place onto serving plates. Top with sauce, serve and enjoy!

Nutrition: 382 Calories | 50 g Protein | 14g Fats

Beef Goulash

Preparation Time: 15 minutes |Cooking Time: 60 minutes |Servings: 2

Ingredients:

- 2 lb. chuck steak, trim the fat and cut into bite-sized pieces
- 1 orange pepper, chopped
- 1 red pepper, chopped
- 1 green pepper, chopped
- 3 onions, quartered
- 3 garlic cloves, diced fine
- 1 cup low-sodium beef broth
- 1 can tomatoes, chopped
- 2 tablespoons tomato paste
- 3 cups water
- 2 bay leaves
- 1 tablespoon paprika
- 1 tablespoon olive oil
- 2 teaspoons hot smoked paprika
- sea salt and black pepper to taste

Directions:

1. Heat your oil in a soup pot over medium-high heat. Add the steak and cook until browned, stirring often.
2. Add your onions and continue to cook for another 5 minutes or until soft. Add the garlic and cook for another minute, stirring often.
3. Add your remaining ingredients, then bring to a boil. Reduce the heat to a low simmer for 50 minutes, stirring occasionally. The Goulash is done when the steak is tender.
4. Stir well, then add to serving bowls and enjoy!

Nutrition: 413 Calories | 53g Proteins | 15g Fat

Cajun Beef & Rice Skillet

Preparation Time: 10 minutes |Cooking Time: 25 minutes |Servings: 4

Ingredients:

- 2 cups cauliflower rice, cooked
- ¾ lb. lean ground beef
- 1 red bell pepper, sliced thin
- 1 jalapeno pepper, with seeds removed and diced fine
- 1 celery stalk, sliced thin
- ½ yellow onion, diced
- ¼ cup parsley, fresh diced
- 4 teaspoons Cajun seasoning
- ½ cup low-sodium beef broth

Directions:

1. Place the beef along with 1 ½ teaspoon of Cajun seasoning into a large skillet over medium-high heat.
2. Add the vegetables, except cauliflower and remaining Cajun seasoning. Cook, occasionally stirring, for about 8 minutes or until vegetables are tender.
3. Add the broth and stir and cook for 3 minutes or until the mixture has thickened. Stir in your cauliflower rice and cook until heated through. Remove from heat and add to serving bowls, then top with parsley, serve and enjoy!

Nutrition: 198 Calories | 28g Proteins | 6g Fats

Cheesy Beef & Noodles

Preparation Time: 10 minutes |Cooking Time: 15 minutes |Servings: 4

Ingredients:

- 1 lb. lean ground beef
- 2 cups mozzarella cheese, grated
- 1 onion, diced
- ½ cup + 2 tablespoons fresh parsley, diced
- 1 package fettuccine noodles
- 2 tablespoons tomato paste
- 1 tablespoon Worcestershire sauce
- 1 tablespoon extra-virgin olive oil
- 3 garlic cloves, minced
- 1 teaspoon red pepper flakes
- sea salt and black pepper to taste

Directions:

1. Heat your oil in a large skillet placed over medium-high heat. Add the beef and cook while breaking up with the spatula for about 2 minutes.
2. Cook the noodles according to package instructions.
3. Lower the heat of your skillet to medium, then season with salt and pepper. Stir in your garlic, pepper flakes, onion, tomato paste, ½ cup parsley, Worcestershire sauce, and ½ cup of water. Bring to a simmer while occasionally stirring for about 8 minutes.
4. Stir in the cooked noodles and continue to cook for another 2 minutes. Stir in 1 cup of cheese over the top and cover with a lid until cheese melts. Serve garnishing with remaining parsley and enjoy!

Nutrition: 372 Calories | 18g Fats|44g Proteins

Bistro Steak Salad with Horseradish Dressing *

Preparation Time: 8 minutes |Cooking Time: 30 minutes |Servings: 1

Ingredients:

- 1 (12 oz.) rib-eye steak
- ¼ t. of each:
- -Pepper
- -Salt
- 1 (2.1 oz.) small red onion
- 1 (7 oz.) bag romaine salad greens
- 4 slices uncured bacon
- ½ cup (2 oz.) sliced radishes
- 4.2 oz. cherry tomatoes

for the Dressing:

- 2 tbsp. prepared horseradish
- ¼ c. mayonnaise
- Pepper and salt

Direction

1. Thinly slice the onion and radishes.
2. Place parchment paper on a baking tin. Set the oven temperature to 350ºF. Arrange the bacon in a single layer in the pan. Bake for 15 minutes. Drain and break into small pieces.
3. Pat the steak with paper towels. Season with the pepper and salt. Grill for four minutes and flip. Continue cooking another 12-15 minutes (medium is approximately 12 minutes or an internal temperature of 155ºF.).
4. Let it cool down five minutes, and slice against the grain into small slices.
5. Prepare the dressing (below) and enjoy it.

Nutrition: Calories:736|Protein:41.4g|Fat: 59.4g

Caprese Salad with Horseradish Dressing

Preparation Time: 10 minutes |Cooking Time: 19 minutes |Servings: 4

Ingredients:

- 3 c. grape tomatoes
- 4 peeled garlic cloves
- 2 tbsp. avocado oil
- 10 pearl-sized mozzarella balls
- 4 c. baby spinach leaves
- ¼ c. fresh basil leaves
- 1 tbsp. of each:
- -Brine reserved from the cheese
- -Pesto

For Dressing

- 1 egg yolk

- 1-2 t. white vinegar/lemon juice
- 1 tbsp. Dijon mustard
- 1 c. light olive oil

Direction

1. Use aluminum foil to cover a baking tray. Program the oven to 400ºF. Arrange the cloves and tomatoes on the baking pan and drizzle with the oil.
2. Bake 20-30 minutes until the tops are slightly browned.
3. Drain the liquid (saving one tablespoon) from the mozzarella. Mix the pesto with the brine.
4. Arrange the spinach in a large serving bowl.
5. Transfer the tomatoes to the dish along with the roasted garlic. Drizzle with the pesto sauce.
6. Garnish with the mozzarella balls, and freshly torn basil leaves.

For Dressing

7. Ahead of time, take out the egg and mustard to become room temperature.
8. Mix the mustard and egg. Slowly, pour the oil until the mixture thickens.
9. Pour in the lemon juice/vinegar. Stir well. Add a pinch of salt and pepper for additional flavoring.

Nutrition: 736 Calories | 41g Protein | 59g Fat

Egg Salad Stuffed Avocado

Preparation Time: 10 minutes |Cooking Time: 28 minutes |Servings: 6

Ingredients:

- 6 large, hard-boiled eggs
- 3 celery ribs
- 1/3 med. red onion
- 4 tbsp. mayonnaise
- 2 tbsp. fresh lime juice
- 2 t. brown mustard
- Pepper & salt to taste
- ½ t. cumin
- 1 t. hot sauce
- 3 med. avocados

Direction

1. Begin by chopping the onions, celery, and eggs. Discard the pit and slice the avocado in half.
2. Combine with all of the other fixings except for the avocado.
3. Scoop the salad into the avocado and serve!

Nutrition: 281 Calories| 24g Fat | 8g Protein

Thai Pork Salad

Preparation Time: 9 minutes |Cooking Time: 30 minutes |Servings: 2

Ingredients

for the Salad:

- 2 c. romaine lettuce
- 10 oz. pulled pork
- ¼ medium chopped red bell pepper
- ¼ c. chopped cilantro

for the Sauce:

- 2 tbsp. of each:
- -Tomato paste
- -Chopped cilantro
- Juice & zest of 1 lime
- 2 tbsp. (+) 2 t. soy sauce
- 1 t. of each:
- -Red curry paste
- -Five Spice
- -Fish sauce
- ¼ t. red pepper flakes
- 1 tbsp. (+) 1 t. rice wine vinegar
- ½ t. mango extract
- 10 drops liquid stevia

Direction

1. Zest half of the lime and chop the cilantro.
2. Mix all of the sauce fixings.
3. Blend the barbecue sauce components and set aside.
4. Pull the pork apart and make the salad. Pour a glaze over the pork with a bit of the sauce.

Nutrition: 461 Calories | 33g Fat 28g Protein

Spaghetti Squash Meatball Casserole

Preparation Time: 35 minutes |Cooking Time: 30 minutes |Servings: 5

Ingredients:

- 1 medium spaghetti
- 1/2 teaspoon salt, divided
- 1/2 teaspoon fennel seed
- 1/4 teaspoon ground coriander
- 1/4 teaspoon dried basil
- 1/4 teaspoon dried oregano
- 1-pound lean ground beef (90% lean)
- 2 teaspoons olive oil
- 1 medium onion, chopped
- 1 garlic clove, minced
- 2 cups chopped collard greens
- 1 cup chopped fresh spinach
- 1 cup reduced-fat ricotta cheese
- 2 plum tomatoes, chopped
- 1 cup pasta sauce
- 1 cup shredded part-skim mozzarella cheese

Directions:

1. Cut the squash lengthwise in half, discard seeds. Place halves on a microwave-safe plate, cut side down. Microwave, uncovered, on high until tender, for 15-20 minutes. Cool slightly.
2. Preheat oven to 350°. Mix 1/4 teaspoon salt with remaining seasonings; add to beef, mixing lightly but thoroughly. Shape into 1-1/2-in. balls. In a large skillet, brown meatballs over medium heat; remove from pan.
3. In same pan, heat oil over medium heat; sauté onion until tender, 3-4 minutes. Add garlic; cook and stir 1 minute. Stir in collard greens, spinach, ricotta and remaining salt; remove from heat.
4. Using a fork, separate strands of spaghetti squash; stir into greens mixture. Transfer to a greased 13x9-in. or 3-qt. baking dish. Top with the plum tomatoes, meatballs, sauce and cheese. Bake, uncovered, until meatballs are cooked through, 30-35 minutes.

Nutrition: 358 Calories | 14g Fat| 28g Carb

Vegetarian Club Salad

Preparation Time: 10 minutes |Cooking Time: 22 minutes |Servings: 3

Ingredients:

- 2 tbsp. of each:
- -Mayonnaise
- -Sour cream
- ½ t. of each:
- -Onion powder
- -Garlic powder
- 1 tbsp. milk
- 1 t. dried parsley
- 3 large, hard-boiled eggs
- 4 oz. cheddar cheese
- ½ c. cherry tomatoes
- 1 c diced cucumber
- 3 c. torn romaine lettuce
- 1 tbsp. Dijon mustard

Direction

1. Slice the hard-boiled eggs and cube the cheese. Cut the tomatoes into halves and dice the cucumber.
2. Prepare the dressing (dried herbs, mayo, and sour cream) mixing well.
3. Add one tablespoon of milk to the mixture - and another if it's too thick.
4. Layer the salad with the vegetables, cheese, and egg slices. Scoop a spoonful of mustard in the center along with a drizzle of dressing.
5. Toss and enjoy it!

Nutrition. 329 Calories | 25g Fat | 15g Protein

Cauliflower 'Mac N Cheese'

Preparation Time: 10 minutes |Cooking Time: 30 minutes |Servings: 2

Ingredients:

- 3 tbsp. butter
- 1 head cauliflower
- 1 c. cheddar cheese

- Black pepper & sea salt to taste
- ¼ c. of each:
- -Unsweetened almond milk
- -Heavy cream

Direction

1. Cut the cauliflower into small florets and shred the cheese.
2. Prepare the oven to 450ºF. Cover a baking sheet with aluminum foil or parchment paper.
3. Melt 2 tbsp. of butter. Toss the florets and butter. Give it a shake of pepper and salt. Place the cauliflower on the baking pan and roast 10-15 minutes.
4. Warm up the rest of the butter, milk, heavy cream, and cheese in the microwave or double boiler. Pour in the cheese and serve.

Nutrition:2 94 Calories | 23g Fat | 11g Protein

Fettuccine Chicken Alfredo

Preparation Time: 13 minutes |Cooking Time: 30 minutes |Servings: 2

Ingredients:

- 2 tbsp. butter
- 2 minced garlic cloves
- ½ t. dried basil
- ½ c. heavy cream
- 4 tbsp. grated parmesan

for the Chicken and Noodles:

- 2 chicken thighs - no bones or skin
- 1 tbsp. olive oil
- 1 bag Miracle Noodle - Fettuccini
- Salt and pepper

Direction

1. For the Sauce: Add the cloves to a pan with the butter for two minutes. Empty the cream into the skillet and let it simmer two additional minutes. Toss in one tablespoon of the parmesan at a time. Add the pepper, salt, and dried basil. Simmer three to five minutes on the low heat setting.
2. For the Chicken: Pound the chicken with a meat tenderizer hammer until it is approximately ½-inch thick. Warm up the oil in a skillet using the medium heat setting and put the chicken in to cook for about seven minutes per side. Shred and set aside. For the Noodles: Prepare the package of noodles. Rinse, and boil them for two minutes in a pot of water.
3. Fold in the noodles along with the sauce and shredded chicken. Cook slowly for two minutes and enjoy it.

Nutrition: 585 Calories | 51g Fat | 25g Protein

Lemon Garlic Shrimp Pasta

Preparation Time: 16 minutes |Cooking Time: 32 minutes |Servings: 4

Ingredients:

- 2 bags of angel hair pasta
- 4 garlic cloves
- 2 tbsp. each:
- Olive oil
- Butter
- ½ lemon
- 1 lb. large raw shrimp
- ½ t. paprika
- Fresh basil
- Pepper and salt

Direction

1. Drain the water from the package of noodles and rinse them in cold water. Add them to a pot of boiling water for two minutes.
2. Transfer them to a hot skillet over medium heat to remove the excess liquid (dry roast). Set them to the side.
3. Use the same pan to warm the oil, butter, and smashed garlic. Sauté a few minutes but don't brown.
4. Slice the lemon into rounds and add them to the garlic along with the shrimp. Sauté for approximately three minutes per side.
5. Add the noodles and spices and stir to blend the flavors.

Nutrition: 360 Calories |21g Fat | 36 g Protein

BBQ Meat-Lover's Pizza *

Preparation Time: 9 minutes |Cooking Time: 30 minutes |Servings: 1

Ingredients:

- 2 c. (8 oz.) mozzarella
- 1 tbsp. psyllium husk powder
- ¾ c. almond flour
- 3 tbsp. (1 ½ oz.) cream cheese
- 1 large egg
- ½ t. of each:
- Black pepper
- Salt
- 1 tbsp. Italian seasoning

for the Topping:

- 1 c. (4 oz.) mozzarella cheese
- To Taste: BBQ sauce
- Sliced Kabana/hard salami
- Bacon slices
- Sprinkled oregano - optional

Direction

1. Set the temperature of the oven to 400ºF.
2. Melt the cheese in the microwave until it melts – about 45 seconds. Toss in the cream cheese and egg, mixing well.
3. Blend in the psyllium husk, flour, salt, pepper, and Italian seasoning. Make the dough as circular as possible.
4. Bake for ten minutes. Flip it onto a piece of parchment paper.
5. Cover the crust with the toppings and some more cheese. Bake until the cheese is golden, slice, and serve.

Nutrition 205 Calories | 27g Fat | 18g Protein

Beef Pizza

Preparation Time: 14 minutes |Cooking Time: 30 minutes |Servings: 4

Ingredients:

- 2 large eggs
- 1 pkg. (20 oz.) ground beef
- 28 pepperoni slices
- ½ c. of each:
- Shredded cheddar cheese
- Pizza sauce
- 4 oz. mozzarella cheese
- Also Needed: 1 Cast iron skillet

Direction

1. Combine the eggs, beef, and seasonings. Place in the skillet to form the crust. Bake until the meat is done or about 15 minutes.
2. Take it out and add the sauce, cheese, and toppings. Place the pizza in the oven for a few minutes until the cheese has melted. Remove and enjoy!

Nutrition: 610 Calories | 45g Fat | 44g Protein

Bell Pepper Basil Pizza *

Preparation Time: 13 minutes |Cooking Time: 30 minutes |Servings: 1

Ingredients

for the Pizza Base:

- 6 oz. mozzarella cheese
- 2 tbsp. of each:
- -Fresh parmesan cheese
- -Cream cheese
- -Psyllium Husk
- 1 t. Italian seasoning
- 1 large egg
- ½ t. of each:
- -Black pepper
- -Salt

for the Toppings:

- 4 oz. shredded cheddar cheese
- ¼ c. marinara sauce
- 1 med. vine-ripened tomato
- 2-3 med. bell peppers
- 2-3 tbsp. fresh basil – chopped

Direction

1. Set the temperature in the oven to 400ºF.
2. Melt the cheese in the microwave until melted and pliable or for 40-50 seconds.
3. Add the remainder of the pizza base

fixings to the cheese – mixing well with your hands.
4. Flatten the dough to form the two circular pizzas. Bake ten minutes. Remove and add the toppings. Take for about 8-10 additional minutes.
5. Let it cool and serve.

Nutrition: 410 Calories | 31g Fat | 21g Protein

Pita Pizza

Preparation Time: 12 minutes |Cooking Time: 30 minutes |Servings: 2

Ingredients:
- ½ c. marinara sauce
- 1 low-carb pita
- 2 oz. cheddar cheese
- 14 slices pepperoni
- 1 oz. roasted red peppers

Direction
1. Set the oven to 450ºF.
2. Slice the pita in half and put on a foil-lined baking tray. Rub with a bit of oil and toast for one to two minutes.
3. Pour the sauce over the bread, sprinkle with the cheese, and other toppings. Bake for another five minutes or until the cheese melts.

Nutrition: 250 Calories | 19g Fat | 13g Protein

Chipotle Fish Tacos

Preparation Time: 10 minutes |Cooking Time: 31 minutes |Servings: 4

Ingredients:
- ½ small diced yellow onion
- 2 pressed cloves of garlic
- 1 chopped fresh jalapeno
- 2 tbsp. olive oil
- 4 oz. chipotle peppers in adobo sauce
- 2 tbsp. each:
- -Mayonnaise
- -Butter
- 4 low-carb tortillas
- 1 lb. haddock fillets

Direction
1. In a skillet, fry the onion on med-high for five minutes.
2. Lower the temperature to the medium heat setting. Toss in the garlic, and jalapeno. Stir another two minutes.
3. Chop and add the chipotles, along with the adobo sauce into the pan.
4. Drop the butter, mayonnaise, and fish into the pan and cook about eight minutes.
5. Make the Tacos: Fry the tortilla for approximately two minutes for each side. Chill and shape them with the prepared fixings.

Nutrition 300 Calories | 20g Fat | 24g Protein

Cumin Spiced Beef Wraps *

Preparation Time: 10 minutes |Cooking Time: 35 minutes |Servings: 1

Ingredients:
- 1-2 tbsp. coconut oil
- ¼ onion – diced
- 2/3 lb. ground beef
- 2 tbsp. chopped cilantro
- 1 diced red bell pepper
- 1 t. minced ginger
- 2 t. cumin
- 4 minced garlic cloves
- Pepper and salt to your liking
- 8 large cabbage leaves

Direction:
1. Warm-up a frying pan and pour in the oil. Sauté the peppers, onions, and ground beef using medium heat.
2. When done, add the pepper, salt, cumin, ginger, cilantro, and garlic.
3. Fill a large pot with water (3/4 full) and wait for it to boil. Cook each leaf for 20 seconds, plunge it in cold water and drain before placing it on your serving dish.

4. Scoop the mixture onto each leaf, fold, and enjoy.

Nutrition: Calories: 375 | Fat: 26g |Protein: 30g

Balsamic Beef Pot Roast*

Preparation Time: 1 minutes |Cooking Time: 33 minutes |Servings: 1

Ingredients:

- 1 boneless (approx. 3 lb.) chuck roast
- 1 t. of each:
- Garlic powder
- Black ground pepper
- 1 tbsp. kosher salt
- ¼ c. balsamic vinegar
- ½ c. chopped onion
- 2 c. water
- ¼ t. xanthan gum

Direction

1. Combine the salt, garlic powder, and pepper and rub the chuck roast with the combined fixings.
2. Use a heavy skillet to sear the roast. Add the vinegar and deglaze the pan as you continue cooking for one more minute.
3. Toss the onion into a pot with the (two cups) boiling water along with the roast. Cover with a top and simmer for three to four hours on a low setting.
4. Take the meat from the pot and add to a cutting surface. Shred into chunks and remove any fat or bones.
5. Add the xanthan gum to the broth and whisk. Place the roast meat back in the pan to warm up. Serve with a favorite side dish.

Nutrition: Calories: 393|Fat: 28g|Protein: 30g

Cheeseburger Calzone

Preparation Time: 10 minutes |Cooking Time: 33 minutes |Servings: 2

Ingredients:

- ½ yellow diced onion
- 1 ½ lb. ground beef – lean
- 4 thick-cut bacon strips
- 4 dill pickle spears
- 8 oz. cream cheese – divided
- 1 egg
- ½ c. mayonnaise
- 1 c. of each:
- -Shredded cheddar cheese
- -Almond flour
- -Shredded mozzarella cheese

Direction

1. Program the oven to 425ºF. Prepare a cookie tin with parchment paper.
2. Chop the pickles into spears. Set aside for now.
3. Prepare the Crust: Combine ½ of the cream cheese and the mozzarella cheese. Microwave 35 seconds. When it melts, add the egg and almond flour to make the dough. Set aside.
4. Cook the beef on the stove using medium heat.
5. Cook the bacon (microwave for five minutes or stovetop). When cool, break into bits.
6. Dice the onion and add to the beef and cook until softened. Toss in the bacon, cheddar cheese, pickle bits, the rest of the cream cheese, and mayonnaise. Stir well.
7. Roll the dough onto the prepared baking tin. Scoop the mixture into the center. Fold the ends and side to make the calzone.
8. Bake until browned or about 15 minutes. Let it rest for 10 minutes before slicing.

Nutrition: Calories: 580 |Fat: 47g|Protein: 34g

Nacho Steak in the Skillet

Preparation Time: 11 minutes |Cooking Time: 36 minutes |Servings: 2

Ingredients:

- 1 tbsp. butter
- 8 oz. beef round tip steak

- 1/3 c. melted refined coconut oil
- ½ t. turmeric
- 1 t. chili powder
- 1 ½ pounds cauliflower
- 1 oz. each shredded:
- -Cheddar cheese
- -Monterey Jack cheese

Garnish:

- 1 oz. canned jalapeno slices
- 1/3 c. sour cream
- Avocado – Approx. 5 oz.

Direction:

1. Set the oven temperature to 400ºF.
2. Prepare the cauliflower into chip-like shapes.
3. Combine the turmeric, chili powder, and coconut oil in a mixing dish.
4. Toss in the cauliflower and add it to a tin. Set the baking timer for 20 to 25 minutes.
5. Over med-high heat in a cast-iron skillet, add the butter. Cook until both sides are done, flipping just once. Let it rest for five to ten minutes. Thinly slice, and sprinkle with some pepper and salt to the steak.
6. When done, transfer the florets to the skillet and add the steak strips. Top it off with the cheese and bake five to ten more minutes.
7. Serve with your favorite garnish but count those carbs.

Nutrition:
Calories: 385.4| Fat: 30.67g |Protein: 18.87g

Portobello Bun Cheeseburgers

Preparation Time: 9 minutes |Cooking Time: 32 minutes |Servings: 6

Ingredients:

- 1 lb. ground beef - lean 80/20
- 1 t. of each:
- 1 tbsp. Worcestershire sauce
- Pink Himalayan salt
- Ground black pepper
- 1 tbsp. avocado oil
- 6 slices sharp cheddar cheese
- 6 Portobello mushroom caps

Direction:

1. Remove the stem, rinse, and dab dry the mushrooms.
2. Combine the salt, pepper, beef, and Worcestershire sauce in a mixing container. Form into patties.
3. Warm up the oil (medium heat). Let the caps simmer about three to four minutes per side.
4. Transfer the mushrooms to a bowl - using the same pan - cook the patties four minutes, flip, and cook another five minutes until done.
5. Add the cheese to the burgers and cover for one minute to melt the cheese.
6. Add one of the mushroom caps to the burgers along with the desired garnishes and serve.

Nutrition: Calories: 336|Fat: 22g|Protein: 29g

Steak-Lovers Slow-Cooked Chili in the Slow Cooker

Preparation Time: 10 minutes |Cooking Time: 31 minutes |Servings: 3

Ingredients
for the Chili:

- 1 c. beef or chicken stock
- ½ c. sliced leeks
- 2 ½ lbs. (1-inch cubes) steak
- 2 c. whole tomatoes (canned with juices)
- 1/8 t. black pepper
- ½ t. salt
- ½ t. cumin
- ¼ t. ground cayenne pepper
- 1 tbsp. chili powder

Optional Toppings:

- 1 t. fresh chopped cilantro
- 2 tbsp. sour cream
- ¼ c/ shredded cheddar cheese
- ½ avocado – sliced or cubed

Direction

1. Toss all of the fixings into the cooker - except the toppings.

2. Use the cooker's high setting for about six hours.
3. Serve, add the toppings, and enjoy.

Nutrition:
Calories: 540|Fat: 41.32g|Protein: 32.4g

Vegetarian Keto Burger on a Bun*

Preparation Time: 10 minutes |Cooking Time: 35 minutes |Servings: 1

Ingredients:

- 1-2 tbsp. freshly chopped basil – 1 t. dried
- Mushroom
- 2 medium-large flat mushrooms – ex. Portobello
- 1 tbsp. of each:
- Coconut oil/ghee
- Freshly chopped oregano – ½ t. dried
- 1 crushed garlic clove
- ¼ t. salt
- Black pepper

Garnish:

- 2 large organic eggs
- 2 slices cheddar/gouda cheese
- 2 tbsp. mayonnaise
- 2 keto buns

Direction:

1. Prepare the mushrooms for marinating by seasoning with crushed garlic, pepper, salt, ghee (melted), and fresh herbs. Save a small amount for frying the eggs. Marinate for about one hour at room temperature.
2. Arrange the mushrooms in the pan with the top side facing upwards.
3. Cook for about five minutes on the med-high setting. Flip and continue cooking for another five minutes.
4. Remove the pan from the burner and flip the mushrooms over and add the cheese. When it is time to serve, put them under the broiler for a minute or so to melt the cheese.
5. With the remainder of the ghee, fry the eggs leaving the yolk runny. Remove from the heat.
6. Slice the buns and add them to the grill, cooking until crisp for about two to three minutes.
7. To assemble, add one tablespoon of mayonnaise to each bun and top them off with the mushroom, egg, tomato, and lettuce.
8. Put the tops on the buns and serve.

Nutrition: Calories: 637|Fat: 55g|Protein: 23g

Spaghetti Squash and Chickpea Bolognese

Preparation Time: 5 minutes |Cooking Time: 25 minutes |Servings: 4

Ingredient

- 1 (3- to 4-pound / 1.4- to 1.8-kg) spaghetti squash
- ½ teaspoon ground cumin
- 1 cup no-sugar-added spaghetti sauce
- 1 (15-ounce / 425-g) can low-sodium chickpeas, drained and rinsed
- 6 ounces (170 g) extra-firm tofu

Direction

1. Preheat the oven to 400°F (205°C).
2. Cut the squash in half lengthwise. Scoop out the seeds and discard.
3. Season both halves of the squash with the cumin and place them on a baking sheet cut side down. Roast for 25 minutes.
4. Meanwhile, heat a medium saucepan over low heat, and pour in the spaghetti sauce and chickpeas.
5. Press the tofu between two layers of paper towels, and gently squeeze out any excess water.
6. Crumble the tofu into the sauce and cook for 15 minutes.
7. Remove the squash from the oven, and comb through the flesh of each half with a fork to make thin strands.
8. Divide the “spaghetti” into four portions and top each portion with one-quarter of the sauce.

Nutrition: Calories: 276|fat: 7.1g|protein: 14.1g

Zucchini and Pinto Bean Casserole

Preparation Time: 15 minutes |Cooking Time: 15 minutes |Servings: 4

Ingredient

- 1 (6 to 7-inch) zucchini, trimmed
- 1 (15-ounce / 425-g) can pinto beans
- 1 1/3 cups salsa
- 1 1/3 cups shredded Mexican cheese blend
- Nonstick cooking spray

Direction

1. Slice the zucchini into rounds. You'll need at least 16 slices.
2. Spray a 6-inch cake pan with nonstick spray.
3. Put the beans into a medium bowl and mash some of them with a fork.
4. Cover the bottom of the pan with about 4 zucchini slices. Add about 1/3 of the beans, 1/3 cup of salsa, and 1/3 cup of cheese. Press down. Repeat for 2 more layers. Add the remaining zucchini, salsa, and cheese. (There are no beans in the top layer.)
5. Cover the pan loosely with foil.
6. Pour 1 cup of water into the electric pressure cooker.
7. Place the pan on the wire rack and carefully lower it into the pot.
8. Close and lock the lid of the pressure cooker. Set the valve to sealing.
9. Cook on high pressure for 15 minutes.
10. When the cooking is complete, hit Cancel and allow the pressure to release naturally.
11. Once the pin drops, unlock and remove the lid.
12. Carefully remove the pan from the pot, lifting by the handles of the wire rack. Let the casserole sit for 5 minutes before slicing into quarters and serving.

Nutrition: Calories: 251|fat: 12. protein: 16.1g

Eggplant-Zucchini Parmesan

Preparation Time: 10 minutes |Cooking Time: 2 hours |Servings: 3

Ingredient

- 1 medium eggplant, peeled and cut into 1-inch cubes
- 1 medium zucchini, cut into 1-inch pieces
- 1 medium onion, cut into thin wedges
- 1½ cups purchased light spaghetti sauce
- 2/3 cup reduced fat Parmesan cheese, grated

Direction

1. Place the vegetables, spaghetti sauce and 1/3 cup Parmesan in the crock pot. Stir to combine. Cover and cook on high for 2 to 2 ½ hours, or on low 4 to 5 hours.
2. Sprinkle remaining Parmesan on top before serving.

Nutrition: Calories: 82|Fat: 2.0g|Protein: 5.1g

Grilled Portobello and Zucchini Burger

Preparation Time: 5 minutes |Cooking Time: 10 minutes |Servings: 2

Ingredient

- 2 large portabella mushroom caps
- ½ small zucchini, sliced
- 2 slices low fat cheese
- 2 whole wheat sandwich thins
- 2 teaspoons roasted red bell peppers
- 2 teaspoons olive oil

Direction

1. Heat grill, or charcoal, to medium-high heat.
2. Lightly brush mushroom caps with olive oil. Grill mushroom caps and zucchini slices until tender, about 3 to 4 minutes per side.
3. Place on sandwich thin. Top with sliced cheese and roasted red bell pepper. Serve.

Nutrition: Calories: 178|Fat: 3. protein: 15.1g

Lemon Wax Beans

Preparation Time: 5 minutes |Cooking Time: 15 minutes |Servings: 2

Ingredient

- 2 pounds (907 g) wax beans
- Juice of ½ lemon
- From the Cupboard:
- 2 tablespoons extra-virgin olive oil
- Sea salt and freshly ground black pepper, to taste

Direction

1. Preheat the oven to 400ºF (205ºC).
2. Line a baking sheet with aluminum foil.
3. In a large bowl, toss the beans and olive oil. Season lightly with salt and pepper.
4. Transfer the beans to the baking sheet and spread them out.
5. Roast the beans until caramelized and tender, about 10 to 12 minutes.
6. Transfer the beans to a serving platter and sprinkle with the lemon juice.

Nutrition: Calories: 99|Fat: 7.1g|Protein: 2.1g

Wilted Dandelion Greens with Sweet Onion

Preparation Time: 15 minutes |Cooking Time: 12 minutes |Servings: 4

Ingredient

- 1 Vidalia onion, thinly sliced
- 2 garlic cloves, minced
- 2 bunches dandelion greens, roughly chopped
- ½ cup low-sodium vegetable broth
- 1 tablespoon extra-virgin olive oil
- Freshly ground black pepper, to taste

Direction

1. Heat the olive oil in a large skillet over low heat.
2. Cook the onion and garlic for 2 to 3 minutes until tender, stirring occasionally.
3. Add the dandelion greens and broth and cook for 5 to 7 minutes, stirring frequently, or until the greens are wilted.
4. Transfer to a plate and season with black pepper. Serve warm.

Nutrition: Calories: 81|Fat: 3.8g|Protein: 3.1g

Asparagus with Scallops

Preparation Time: 10 minutes |Cooking Time: 15 minutes |Servings: 4

Ingredient

- 1-pound (454 g) asparagus, trimmed and cut into 2-inch segments
- 1-pound (454 g) sea scallops
- ¼ cup dry white wine
- Juice of 1 lemon
- 2 garlic cloves, minced
- 3 teaspoons extra-virgin olive oil, divided
- 1 tablespoon butter
- ¼ teaspoon freshly ground black pepper

Direction

1. In a large skillet, heat 1½ teaspoons of oil over medium heat.
2. Add the asparagus and sauté for 5 to 6 minutes until just tender, stirring regularly. Remove from the skillet and cover with aluminum foil to keep warm.
3. Add the remaining 1½ teaspoons of oil and the butter to the skillet. When the butter is melted and sizzling, place the scallops in a single layer in the skillet. Cook for about 3 minutes on one side until nicely browned.
4. Use tongs to gently loosen and flip the scallops and cook on the other side for another 3 minutes until browned and cooked through. Remove and cover with foil to keep warm.
5. In the same skillet, combine the wine, lemon juice, garlic, and pepper. Bring to a simmer for 1 to 2 minutes, stirring to mix in any browned pieces left in the pan.
6. Return the asparagus and the cooked scallops to the skillet to coat with the sauce. Serve warm.

Nutrition: Calories: 253|Fat: 7g|Protein: 26.1g

Butter Cod with Asparagus

Preparation Time: 5 minutes |Cooking Time: 10 minutes |Servings: 4

Ingredient

- 4 (4-ounce / 113-g) cod fillets
- ¼ teaspoon garlic powder
- 24 asparagus spears, woody ends trimmed
- ½ cup brown rice, cooked
- 1 tablespoon freshly squeezed lemon juice
- ¼ teaspoon salt
- ¼ teaspoon freshly ground black pepper
- 2 tablespoons unsalted butter

Direction

1. In a large bowl, season the cod fillets with the garlic powder, salt, and pepper. Set aside.
2. Melt the butter in a skillet over medium-low heat.
3. Place the cod fillets and asparagus in the skillet in a single layer. Cook covered for 8 minutes, or until the cod is cooked through.
4. Divide the cooked brown rice, cod fillets, and asparagus among four plates. Serve drizzled with the lemon juice.

Nutrition: Calories: 233|Fat: 8. protein: 22.1g

Creamy Cod Fillet with Quinoa and Asparagus

Preparation Time: 5 minutes |Cooking Time: 15 minutes |Servings: 4

Ingredient

- ½ cup uncooked quinoa
- 4 (4-ounce / 113-g) cod fillets
- ½ teaspoon garlic powder, divided
- 24 asparagus spears, cut the bottom 1½ inches off
- 1 cup half-and-half
- ¼ teaspoon salt
- ¼ teaspoon freshly ground black pepper
- 1 tablespoon avocado oil

Direction

1. Put the quinoa in a pot of salted water. Bring to a boil. Reduce the heat to low and simmer for 15 minutes or until the quinoa is soft and has a white "tail". Cover and turn off the heat. Let sit for 5 minutes.
2. On a clean work surface, rub the cod fillets with ¼ teaspoon of garlic powder, salt, and pepper.
3. Heat the avocado oil in a nonstick skillet over medium-low heat.
4. Add the cod fillets and asparagus in the skillet and cook for 8 minutes or until they are tender. Flip the cod and shake the skillet halfway through the cooking time.
5. Pour the half-and-half in the skillet, and sprinkle with remaining garlic powder. Turn up the heat to high and simmer for 2 minutes until creamy.
6. Divide the quinoa, cod fillets, and asparagus in four bowls and serve warm.

Nutrition: Calories: 258|fat: 7.9g|Protein: 25.2g

Asparagus and Scallop Skillet with Lemony

Preparation Time: 10 minutes |Cooking Time: 15 minutes |Servings: 4

Ingredient

- 1-pound (454 g) asparagus, trimmed and cut into 2-inch segments
- 1-pound (454 g) sea scallops
- ¼ cup dry white wine
- 2 garlic cloves, minced
- Juice of 1 lemon
- 3 teaspoons extra-virgin olive oil, divided
- 1 tablespoon butter
- ¼ teaspoon freshly ground black pepper

Direction

1. Heat half of olive oil in a nonstick skillet over medium heat until shimmering.
2. Add the asparagus to the skillet and sauté for 6 minutes until soft. Transfer the cooked asparagus to a large plate and cover with aluminum foil.

3. Heat the remaining half of olive oil and butter in the skillet until the butter is melted.
4. Add the scallops to the skillet and cook for 6 minutes or until opaque and browned. Flip the scallops with tongs halfway through the cooking time. Transfer the scallops to the plate and cover with aluminum foil.
5. Combine the wine, garlic, lemon juice, and black pepper in the skillet. Simmer over medium-low heat for 2 minutes. Keep stirring during the simmering.
6. Pour the sauce over the asparagus and scallops to coat well, then serve warm.

Nutrition Calories: 256 |Fat: 7g |Protein: 26.1g

Snack

Almond Butter Cinnamon Bars *

Preparation Time: 35 minutes |Cooking Time: 0 minutes |Servings: 1

Ingredients:

- ½ Cup of creamed coconut, chopped into chunks
- 1/8 Teaspoon of ground cinnamon

For the first Icing:

- 1 Tablespoon of non-melted extra virgin coconut oil
- 1 Tablespoon of almond butter

For the Second Icing:

- 1 Tablespoon of extra virgin almond butter
- ½ Teaspoon of ground cinnamon

Directions:

1. Start by lining a muffin pan with muffin liners.
2. In a large mixing bowl and using both your hands, combine the coconut cream with cinnamon and mix very well.
3. Pat the mixture into the dish; make sure to fill 2 mini loaf sections.
4. Then prepare the first icing by whisking the coconut oil with the almond butter and spread the mixture over the creamed coconut.
5. Put the bars into the freezer for about 6 minutes. In the meantime, prepare the second Icing by whisking the icing almond butter with the cinnamon and drizzle it on top of the bars.
6. Place the bars in the refrigerator for about 30 minutes or for about 8 minutes in the freezer.
7. Cut the frozen batter into bars with a knife. Serve and enjoy your delicious bars!

Nutrition: Calories: 160 |Fat: 7g|Protein: 3.2g

Pistachio and Cocoa Squares

Preparation Time: 25 minutes |Cooking Time: 5 minutes |Servings: 5

Ingredients:

- ½ Cup of finely chopped and cacao butter
- 1 Cup of roasted almond butter
- 1 Cup of creamy coconut butter
- 1 Cup of firm coconut oil
- ½ Cup of full fat coconut milk, chilled for an overnight
- ¼ Cup of ghee
- 1 Tablespoon of pure vanilla extract
- 2 Teaspoons of chai spice
- ¼ Teaspoon of pure almond extract
- ¼ Teaspoon of Himalayan salt
- ¼ Cup of chopped raw pistachios, shelled

Directions:

1. Grease a square baking pan of about 9" sand line it with a parchment paper; make sure to leave a little bit hanging on both sides to help you unmold easily; then set aside.

2. Melt the cacao butter in the oven for about 30 seconds and reserve it.
3. Add the roasted almonds, the coconut butter, the coconut oil, the coconut milk, the ghee, the vanilla extract, the spice, the almond extract, the salt and the chopped pistachios to a large mixing bowl and mix very well starting with a low speed; then increase the speed and mix until the mixture become airy.
4. Pour the mixed and melted cacao butter into that of the almond and keep mixing on a high speed until you get an incorporated batter.
5. Transfer the prepared pan; then evenly spread the batter and sprinkle with the chopped pistachios.
6. Refrigerate your batter for about 4 hours or for an overnight.
7. Cut into about 36 squares; then serve and enjoy!

Nutrition: Calories: 170|Fat: 17g|Protein: 2g

Peppermint and Chocolate Keto Squares *

Preparation Time: 10 minutes |Cooking Time: 0 minutes |Servings: 1

Ingredients:

For the peppermint filling:

- ½ Cup of coconut butter
- 1 Tablespoon of melted coconut oil
- 1 Teaspoon of peppermint extract
- 2 Tablespoons of Stevia

For the chocolate layer:

- 2 Tablespoons of melted coconut oil
- 4 Oz of 100% dark chocolate

Directions:

1. In a large mixing bowl, combine all together the coconut butter with the melted coconut oil, the peppermint extract and the stevia and mix very well.
2. Pour a small quantity of peppermint mixture into silicone muffin trays to form a layer of about 1/3 inch of thickness.
3. Freeze for about 1 hour; then melt the dark chocolate with the coconut oil and mix again.
4. Remove the firm peppermint filling from the cups.
5. Pour a small quantity of the chocolate mixture into each of the cups in a way that it covers the base; then cover with more chocolate.
6. Repeat the same process with the remaining cups.
7. Let the patties cool for about 2 hours until it becomes solid; then let thaw for about 10 minutes.
8. Serve and enjoy your patties!

Nutrition: Calories: 153|Fat: 13g|Protein: 4g

Ginger Patties

Preparation Time: 10 minutes |Cooking Time: 0 minutes |Servings: 3

Ingredients:

- 1 Cup of coconut butter, softened
- 1 Cup of coconut oil, softened
- ½ Cup of shredded coconut; unsweetened
- 1 Teaspoon of stevia
- 1 Teaspoon of ginger powder

Directions:

1. Mix the softened coconut butter with the coconut oil, the stevia, the shredded coconut and the ginger powder and mix very well until your ingredients are very well dissolved.
2. Pour the batter into the silicon molds and refrigerate for about 10 minutes.
3. Serve and enjoy your ginger patties.

Nutrition: Calories: 123|Fat: 12g|Protein: 1g

Blueberry Fat Bombs *

Preparation Time: 5 minutes |Cooking Time: 0 minutes |Servings: 1

Ingredients:

- 4 Oz of soft goat's cheese
- ½ Cup of fresh blueberries
- 1 Cup of almond flour
- 1 Teaspoon of vanilla extract
- ½ Cup of pecans
- ½ Teaspoon of stevia
- ¼ Cup of unsweetened shredded coconut

Directions:

1. Process the goat cheese with the fresh blueberries, the almond flour, the vanilla extract, the pecans, the stevia and the unsweetened shredded coconut in a food processor and process very well
2. Roll the mixture into about 30 small fat bombs
3. Pour the coconut flakes in a bowl and lightly roll each of the fat bombs into the shredded coconut
4. Serve and enjoy your delicious fat bombs!

Nutrition: Calories: 49|Fat: 5g|Protein: 2.3g

Almond Oreo Cookies

Preparation Time: 15 minutes |Cooking Time: 12 minutes |Servings: 2

Ingredients:

- 2 and ¼ cups of hazelnut or almond flour
- 3 Tablespoons of coconut flour
- 4 Tablespoons of cocoa powder
- 1 Teaspoons of baking powder
- ½ Teaspoon of xanthan gum
- ¼ Teaspoon of salt
- ½ Cup of softened butter
- ½ Cup of stevia
- 1 Large egg
- 1 Teaspoon of vanilla extract

For the Cream Filling:

- 4 Oz of softened cream cheese
- 2 Tablespoons of almond butter
- ½ Teaspoons of pure vanilla extract
- ½ Cup of powdered of Swerve, you can just grind it in a spice grinder

Directions:

1. Preheat your oven to a temperature of about 350 degrees Fahrenheit.
2. Combine the hazelnut or the almond flour with the cocoa powder, the baking powder, the xanthan gum, the salt, the stevia, the egg and the vanilla extract in a large bowl and mix very well.
3. Add the almond butter and mix again.
4. In a separate medium bowl, cream all together the Swerve and the butter until it become light and extremely fluffy for 2 to 3 minutes.
5. Add the egg and the vanilla and mix until your ingredients are fully combined.
6. Add your already mixed dry ingredients and mix it until it is very well combined.
7. Roll out the obtained dough between two rectangular waxed paper sheets; make sure the thickness is about 1/8.
8. Place the dough over a cookie sheet lined with a parchment paper.
9. Roll the cookie dough again until the end.
10. Bake the cookies for about 12 minutes; then let cool completely before starting to fill.

To make the filling:

11. Cream the cream cheese with the butter; then cream all together and add the vanilla extract.
12. Gradually add in the powdered swerve.
13. Fill the Oreo cookies with the cream.
14. Serve and enjoy your delicious cookies!

Nutrition: Calories: 136|Fat: 12g|Protein: 4g

Almond Cheesecake Bites

Preparation Time: 15 minutes |Cooking Time: 0 minutes |Servings: 2

Ingredients:

- ½ cup reduced-fat cream cheese, soft
- ½ cup almonds, ground fine
- ¼ cup almond butter
- 2 drops liquid stevia

Direction:

1. In a large bowl, beat cream cheese, almond butter and stevia on high speed until mixture is smooth and creamy. Cover and chill 30 minutes.
2. Use your hands to shape the mixture into 12 balls.
3. Place the ground almonds in a shallow plate. Roll the balls in the nuts completely covering all sides. Store in an airtight container in the refrigerator.

Nutrition: Calories 68 |Protein 5g |Fat 5g

Almond Coconut Biscotti

Preparation Time: 5 minutes |Cooking Time: 51 minutes |Servings: 4

Ingredients:

- 1 egg, room temperature
- 1 egg white, room temperature
- ½ cup margarine, melted
- 2 ½ cup flour
- 1 1/3 cup unsweetened coconut, grated
- ¾ cup almonds, sliced
- 2/3 cup Splenda
- 2 tsp baking powder
- 1 tsp vanilla
- ½ tsp salt

Direction:

1. Heat oven to 350 degrees. Line a baking sheet with parchment paper.
2. In a large bowl, combine dry Ingredients.
3. In a separate mixing bowl, beat other Ingredients together. Add to dry Ingredients and mix until thoroughly combined.
4. Divide dough in half. Shape each half into a loaf measuring 8x2 ¾-inches. Place loaves on pan 3 inches apart.
5. Bake 25-30 minutes or until set and golden brown. Cool on wire rack 10 minutes.
6. With a serrated knife, cut loaf diagonally into ½-inch slices. Place the cookies, cut side down, back on the pan and bake another 20 minutes, or until firm and nicely browned. Store in airtight container. Serving size is 2 cookies.

Nutrition: Calories 234 |Protein 5g |Fat 18g

Almond Flour Crackers

Preparation Time: 5 minutes |Cooking Time: 15 minutes |Servings: 3

Ingredients:

- ½ cup coconut oil, melted
- 1 ½ cups almond flour
- ¼ cup Stevia

Direction:

1. Heat oven to 350 degrees. Line a cookie sheet with parchment paper.
2. In a mixing bowl, combine all Ingredients and mix well.
3. Spread dough onto prepared cookie sheet, ¼-inch thick. Use a paring knife to score into 24 crackers.
4. Bake 10 – 15 minutes or until golden brown.
5. Separate and store in air-tight container.

Nutrition: Calories 281 |Protein 4g |Fat 23g

Asian Chicken Wings

Preparation Time: 5 minutes |Cooking Time: 30 minutes |Servings: 3

Ingredients:

- 24 chicken wings
- 6 tbsp. soy sauce
- 6 tbsp. Chinese 5 spice
- Salt & pepper
- Nonstick cooking spray

Direction:
1. Heat oven to 350 degrees. Spray a baking sheet with cooking spray.
2. Combine the soy sauce, 5 spice, salt, and pepper in a large bowl. Add the wings and toss to coat.
3. Pour the wings onto the prepared pan. Bake 15 minutes. Turn chicken over and cook another 15 minutes until chicken is cooked through.
4. Serve with your favorite low carb dipping sauce.

Nutrition: Calories 178 |Protein 12g |Fat 11g

Banana Nut Cookies

Preparation Time: 10 minutes |Cooking Time: 15 minutes |Servings: 6

Ingredients:
- 1 ½ cup banana, mashed
- 2 cup oats
- 1 cup raisins
- 1 cup walnuts
- 1/3 cup sunflower oil
- 1 tsp vanilla
- ½ tsp salt

Direction:
1. Heat oven to 350 degrees.
2. In a large bowl, combine oats, raisins, walnuts, and salt.
3. In a medium bowl, mix banana, oil, and vanilla. Stir into oat mixture until combined. Let rest 15 minutes.
4. Drop by rounded tablespoonful onto 2 ungreased cookie sheets. Bake 15 minutes, or until a light golden brown. Cool and store in an airtight container. Serving size is 2 cookies.

Nutrition: Calories 148 |Protein 3g |Fat 9g

BLT Stuffed Cucumbers

Preparation Time: 15 minutes |Cooking Time: 15 minutes |Servings: 4

Ingredients:
- 3 slices bacon, cooked crisp and crumbled
- 1 large cucumber
- ½ cup lettuce, diced fine
- ½ cup baby spinach, diced fine
- ¼ cup tomato, diced fine
- What you'll need from store cupboard:
- 1 tbsp. + ½ tsp fat-free mayonnaise
- ¼ tsp black pepper
- 1/8 tsp salt

Direction:
1. Peel the cucumber and slice in half lengthwise. Use a spoon to remove the seeds.
2. In a medium bowl, combine remaining Ingredients and stir well.
3. Spoon the bacon mixture into the cucumber halves. Cut into 2-inch pieces and serve.

Nutrition: Calories 95 |Protein 6g |Fat 6g

Buffalo Bites

Preparation Time: 6 minutes |Cooking Time: 11 minutes |Servings: 4

Ingredients:
- 1 egg
- ½ head of cauliflower, separated into florets
- 1 cup panko breadcrumbs
- 1 cup low-fat ranch dressing
- ½ cup hot sauce
- ½ tsp salt
- ½ tsp garlic powder
- Black pepper
- Nonstick cooking spray

Direction:
1. Heat oven to 400 degrees. Spray a baking sheet with cooking spray.
2. Place the egg in a medium bowl and mix

in the salt, pepper and garlic. Place the panko crumbs into a small bowl.
3. Dip the florets first in the egg then into the panko crumbs. Place in a single layer on prepared pan.
4. Bake 8-10 minutes, stirring halfway through, until cauliflower is golden brown and crisp on the outside.
5. In a small bowl stir the dressing and hot sauce together. Use for dipping.

Nutrition: Calories 132 |Protein 6g |Fat 5g

Cinnamon Apple Popcorn

Preparation Time: 31 minutes |Cooking Time: 50 minutes |Servings: 10

Ingredients:

- 4 tbsp. margarine, melted
- 10 cup plain popcorn
- 2 cup dried apple rings, unsweetened and chopped
- ½ cup walnuts, chopped
- 2 tbsp. Splenda brown sugar
- 1 tsp cinnamon
- ½ tsp vanilla

Direction:

1. Heat oven to 250 degrees.
2. Place chopped apples in a 9x13-inch baking dish and bake 20 minutes. Remove from oven and stir in popcorn and nuts.
3. In a small bowl, whisk together margarine, vanilla, Splenda, and cinnamon. Drizzle evenly over popcorn and toss to coat.
4. Bake 30 minutes, stirring quickly every 10 minutes. If apples start to turn a dark brown, remove immediately.
5. Pout onto waxed paper to cool at least 30 minutes. Store in an airtight container.

Nutrition: Calories 133 |Protein 3g |Fat 8g

Crab & Spinach Dip

Preparation Time: 9 minutes |Cooking Time: 2 hours |Servings: 4

Ingredients:

- 1 pkg. frozen chopped spinach, thawed and squeezed nearly dry
- 8 oz. reduced-fat cream cheese
- 6 ½ oz. can crabmeat, drained and shredded
- 6 oz.jar marinated artichoke hearts, drained and diced fine
- ¼ tsp hot pepper sauce
- Melba toast or whole grain crackers (optional)

Direction:

1. Remove any shells or cartilage from crab.
2. Place all Ingredients in a small crock pot.
3. Cover and cook on high 1 ½ - 2 hours, or until heated through and cream cheese is melted. Stir after 1 hour.
4. Serve with Melba toast or whole grain crackers. Serving size is ¼ cup.

Nutrition: Calories 106 |Protein 5g |Fat 8g

Cranberry & Almond Granola Bars

Preparation Time: 14 minutes |Cooking Time: 21 minutes |Servings: 2

Ingredients:

- 1 egg
- 1 egg white
- 2 cup low-fat granola
- ¼ cup dried cranberries, sweetened
- ¼ cup almonds, chopped
- 2 tbsp. Splenda
- 1 teaspoon almond extract
- ½ tsp cinnamon

Direction:

1. Heat oven to 350 degrees. Line the bottom and sides of an 8-inch baking dish with parchment paper.
2. In a large bowl, combine dry Ingredients including the cranberries.
3. In a small bowl, whisk together egg, egg white and extract. Pour over dry Ingredients and mix until combined.

4. Press mixture into the prepared pan. Bake 20 minutes or until light brown.
5. Cool in the pan for 5 minutes. Then carefully lift the bars from the pan onto a cutting board. Use a sharp knife to cut into 12 bars. Cool completely and store in an airtight container.

Nutrition: Calories 85 |Protein 3g |Fat 3g

Keto Chocolate Bombs

Preparation Time: 30 minutes |Cooking Time: 0 minutes |Servings: 3

Ingredients:

- 2 Cups of smooth peanut butter
- ¾ Cup coconut of flour
- ½ Cup of sticky sweetener
- 2 Cups of sugar-free chocolate chips

Directions:

1. Start by lining a large tray with a parchment paper and set it aside.
2. In a large mixing bowl, combine all your ingredients together except for the chocolate chips, and combine your ingredients very well until it is completely combined
3. If your batter is too thick or is crumbly, you may add a small quantity of milk or water
4. With both your hands, try forming small balls from the batter and arrange it over a the already prepared lined tray and freeze for about 10 minutes
5. While your peanut butter balls are in the freezer, melt the sugar-free chocolate chips in the microwave for about 30 seconds to about 1 minute
6. Remove the peanut butter from the freezer; then carefully and gently dip each of the balls into the melted chocolate
7. Repeat the same process until all the chocolate balls are covered in chocolate and arrange over a platter
8. Once you finish covering all the balls, place the balls in the refrigerator for about 20 minutes or just until the chocolate firms up
9. Serve and enjoy your delicious chocolate balls!

Nutrition: Calories: 95|Fat: 9.7 g |Protein: 3 g

Coconut Keto Bombs

Preparation Time: 15 minutes |Cooking Time: 0 minutes |Servings: 3

Ingredients:

- 1 and ½ cups of walnuts or any type of nuts of your choice
- ½ Cup of shredded coconut
- ¼ Cup of coconut butter + 1 additional tablespoon of extra coconut butter
- 2 Tablespoons of almond butter
- 2 Tablespoons of chia seeds
- 2 Tablespoons of flax meal
- 2 Tablespoons of hemp seeds
- 1 Teaspoon of cinnamon
- ½ Teaspoon of vanilla bean powder
- ¼ Teaspoon of kosher salt
- 2 Tablespoons of cacao nibs

For the chocolate drizzle

- 1 Oz of unsweetened chocolate, chopped
- ½ Teaspoon of coconut oil

Directions:

1. In the mixing bowl of your food processor, combine the walnuts with the coconut butter; the almond butter, the chia seeds, the flax meal, the hemp seeds, the cinnamon, the vanilla bean powder, the shredded coconut and the chopped; then drizzle with the coconut oil.
2. Pulse your ingredients for about 1 to 2 minutes or until the mixture starts breaking down.
3. Keep processing your mixture until it starts to stick together; but just be careful not to over mix.
4. Add in the cacao nibs and pulse until your ingredients.

5. With a small cookie scoop or simply with a tablespoon, divide the mixture into pieces of equal size.
6. Use both your hands to toll the mixture into balls; then arrange it over a platter.
7. Store the balls in an airtight container or place it in the freezer for about 15 minutes.
8. Serve and enjoy your delicious balls!

Nutrition: Calories: 164|Fat: 14 g |Protein: 4g

Raspberry and Cashew Balls

Preparation Time: 15 minutes |Cooking Time: 0 minutes |Servings: 4

Ingredients:

- 1 1/3 Cup of raw cashews or almonds
- ¼ Cup of cashew or almond butter
- 2 Tablespoons of coconut oil
- 2 Pitted Medjool dates, pre-soaked into hot water for about 10 minutes
- ½ Teaspoon of vanilla extract
- ¼ Teaspoon of kosher salt
- ½ Cup of freeze-dried and lightly crashed raspberries
- 1/3 Cup of chopped dark chocolate

Directions:

1. In a high-powered blender or a Vitamix, combine the cashews or almonds with the butter, the coconut oil, the Medjool dates, the vanilla extract and the salt and pulse on a high speed for about 1 to 2 minutes or until the batter starts sticking together.
2. Pulse in the dried raspberries and the dark chocolate until your get a thick mixture.
3. With a tablespoon or a small cookie scoop, divide the mixture into balls of equal size.
4. Arrange the balls in a container or a zip-top bag in a refrigerator for about 2 weeks or just serve and enjoy your delicious cashew balls!

Nutrition: Calories: 108| Fat: 7.4g| Protein: 3g

Cocoa Balls

Preparation Time: 90 minutes |Cooking Time: 0 minutes |Servings: 4

Ingredients:

- 1 Cup of almond butter
- 1 Cup of coconut oil, at room temperature
- ½ Cup of unsweetened cocoa powder
- 1/3 Cup of coconut flour
- ¼ Teaspoon of powdered stevia
- 1/16 tsp of pink Himalayan salt

Directions:

1. In a small pot and over a medium high heat, melt the almond butter and combine it with the coconut oil.
2. Add the coconut flour, the cocoa powder and the Himalayan salt and stir.
3. Add the stevia and mix again; then let your mixture cool.
4. Pour the mixture in a large bowl and transfer it to the freezer to solidify for about 60 to 90 minutes.
5. Once solidified, remove the bowl from the freezer and form it into balls.
6. Form balls from the batter and arrange the balls over a tray lined with a parchment paper.
7. Refrigerate the balls for about 15 minutes.
8. Serve and enjoy your delicious Ketogenic bombs!

Nutrition: Calories: 157|Fat: 12g|Protein: 3.7g

Salted Macadamia Keto Bombs *

Preparation Time: 35 minutes |Cooking Time: 0 minutes |Servings: 1

Ingredients:

- 10 Tablespoons of Coconut Oil
- 5 Tablespoons of Unsweetened Cocoa Powder
- 1 Tablespoon of Granulated Stevia

- 3 Tablespoon of coarsely chopped Macadamia Nuts
- 1 Pinch of Coarse Sea Salt to taste

Directions:

1. Melt the coconut oil over the stove.
2. Add the cocoa powder and the granulated Stevia.
3. Mix your ingredients and remove it from the heat.
4. Spoon the mixture into silicone candy molds until the mound is about ¾ full.
5. Refrigerate the molds for about 5 minutes.
6. Sprinkle the macadamia nut in each of the silicone molds and press down; then return the molds to the refrigerator and let cool for about 30 minutes.
7. Sprinkle macadamia nuts into each well. Press down to distribute the nuts.
8. Once the chocolates are cool and set, remove it from the refrigerator; then let sit at room temperature and sprinkle with coarse salt.
9. Serve and enjoy your delicious macadamia salted balls!

Nutrition: Calories: 120|Fat: 13g|Protein: 2.5g

Brownie Cookies *

Preparation Time: 20 minutes |Cooking Time: 10 minutes |Servings: 1

Ingredients:

- 2 Tablespoons of softened almond butter
- 1 Large egg
- 1 Tablespoon of Trivia
- ¼ Cup of Splenda
- 1/8 Teaspoon of blackstrap molasses
- 1 Tablespoon of vita fiber syrup
- 1 Teaspoon of vanilla extract
- 6 Tablespoon of sugar-free chocolate-chips
- 1 Teaspoon of almond butter
- 6 Tablespoons of almond flour
- 1 Tablespoon of cocoa powder
- 1/8 Teaspoon of baking powder
- 1/8 Teaspoon of salt
- ¼ Teaspoon of xanthan gum
- ¼ Cup of chopped pecans
- 1 Tablespoon of sugar-free chocolate-chips

Directions:

1. In a medium bowl, and with a hand mixer, mix all together two tablespoons of almond butter with the egg, the sweeteners, the vita fiber and the vanilla and combine for about 2 minutes.
2. In a separate medium bowl, microwave the chocolate chips and about 1 tablespoon of the almond butter for about 30 seconds.
3. Beat the chocolate into the mixture of eggs and butter and mix until you get a smooth batter.
4. Stir in the remaining almond flour, the cocoa powder, the baking powder, the salt, the xanthan gum, the chopped pecans and the chocolate chips.
5. Place the batter in the freezer for about 7 to 8 minutes to firm up; then preheat your oven to about 350 F.
6. Spray a large baking sheet with oil and make the shape of cookies with your hands.
7. Arrange the cookies over the baking sheet and lightly flatten each of the cookies with your hand or with the back of an oiled spoon.
8. Bake your cookies for about 8 to 10min.
9. Let the cookies rest for about 10 minutes to cool.
10. Serve and enjoy your delicious cookies!

Nutrition: Calories: 61 |Fat: 4 g |Protein: 1.2g

Macadamia Cookies

Preparation Time: 20 minutes |Cooking Time: 10 minutes |Servings: 2

Ingredients:

- 1/2 cup coconut oil, melted
- 2 tablespoons almond butter

- 1 egg
- 1 1/2 cup almond flour
- 2 tablespoons unsweetened cocoa powder
- 1/2 cup granulated erythritol sweetener
- 1 teaspoon vanilla extract
- 1/2 teaspoon baking soda
- 1/4 cup chopped macadamia nuts
- 1 Pinch of salt

Directions:

1. Start by preheating your oven to a temperature of about 350 F.
2. Combine the almond butter with the coconut oil, the almond flour, the cocoa powder, the swerve, the vanilla extract, the baking soda, the chopped macadamia nut and the salt in a large mixing bowl.
3. Mix your ingredients very well with a fork or a spoon; then set it aside.
4. Line a cookie sheet with a parchment paper or just grease it very well.
5. Drop small balls of about 1 ½ inches wide; then gently flatten the cookies with your hands.
6. Bake your cookies for about 15 minutes; then remove them from the oven and set them aside to cool for about 10 minutes.
7. Serve and enjoy your cookies!

Nutrition: Calories: 179|Fat: 17g|Protein: 5g

Pistachio Muffins

Preparation Time: 10 minutes |Cooking Time: 30 minutes |Servings: 2

Ingredients:

- 4 Large Eggs, it is better to use brown Eggs
- ½ Cup of almond butter, unsalted
- ¼ Cup of confectioners Swerve
- ¼ Cup of Organic Stevia Blend by Pure
- 1 Teaspoon of Pistachio Extract
- ½ Cup of Almond Milk, unsweetened
- 1 Teaspoon of Vanilla Extract
- 1 Cup of blanched Almond Flour
- ½ Cup of Organic Coconut Flour
- 2 Teaspoons of Baking Powder
- ½ Teaspoon of Xanthan Gum
- 1 Teaspoon of Himalayan Pink Salt
- ½ Cup of crushed Pistachio Nuts

Directions:

1. Preheat your oven to about 325 F.
2. Whisk the eggs in a large mixing bowl until they become fluffy.
3. In a separate bowl, melt the almond butter until it becomes soft.
4. Add the butter to a bowl with the sweeteners, the extracts, and the almond milk.
5. Blend your ingredients until it is very well incorporated.
6. Add the Pistachio Extract, the vanilla Extract, the almond Flour, the coconut flour, the baking powder, the Xanthan gum and the salt.
7. Whisk your ingredients until they become very well mixed.
8. Add your dry ingredients into a large bowl and mix very we well.
9. Add the crushed pistachios; then fold until it is blended.
10. Grease a muffin tin of about 12 cups or liners.
11. Evenly pour the batter into each of the muffin cups.
12. Bake the muffins for about 25 to 30 minutes.
13. Let your muffins cool for about 5 minutes.
14. Serve and enjoy your muffins!

Nutrition: Calories: 198|Fat: 12g |Protein: 6g

Taco Cheese Bites

Preparation Time: 5 minutes |Cooking Time: 10 minutes |Servings: 3

Ingredients

- 2 Cups of Packaged Shredded Cheddar Cheese
- 2 Tablespoon of Chili Powder
- 2 Tablespoons of Cumin
- 1 Teaspoon of Salt

- 8 Teaspoons of coconut cream for garnishing
- Use Pico de Gallo for garnishing as well

Directions:

1. Preheat your oven to a temperature of about 350 F.
2. Over a baking sheet lined with a parchment paper, place 1 tablespoon piles of cheese and make sure to a space of 2 inches between each.
3. Place the baking sheet in your oven and bake for about 5 minutes.
4. Remove from the oven and let the cheese cool down for about 1 minute; then carefully lift up and press each into the cups of a mini muffin tin.
5. Make sure to press the edges of the cheese to form the shape of muffins mini.
6. Let the cheese cool completely; then remove it.
7. While you continue to bake the cheese and create your cups.
8. Fill the cheese cups with the coconut cream, then top with the Pico de Gallo.
9. Serve and enjoy your delicious snack!

Nutrition: Calories: 73|Fat: 5g |Protein: 4g

Garlic Kale Chips *

Preparation Time: 5 minutes |Cooking Time: 15 minutes |Servings: 1

Ingredients:

- 1 (16 oz.) bunch kale, trimmed and cut into 2-inch pieces
- 2 tablespoons extra-virgin olive oil
- 1 teaspoon sea salt
- ½ teaspoon garlic powder
- Pinch cayenne (optional, to taste)

Directions:

1. Preheat the oven to 350°F. Line two baking sheets with parchment paper.
2. Wash the kale and pat it completely dry.
3. In a large bowl, toss the kale with the olive oil, sea salt, garlic powder, and cayenne, if using.
4. Spread the kale in a single layer on the prepared baking sheets.
5. Bake until crisp, 12 to 15 minutes, rotating the sheets once.

Nutrition: Calories: 231 |Fat: 15g |Protein: 7g

Caprese Skewers

Preparation Time: 5 minutes |Cooking Time: 0 minutes |Servings: 2

Ingredients:

- 12 cherry tomatoes
- 12 basil leaves
- 8 (1-inch) pieces mozzarella cheese
- ¼ cup Italian Vinaigrette (optional, for serving)

Directions:

1. On each of 4 wooden skewers, thread the following: 1 tomato, 1 basil leaf, 1 piece of cheese, 1 tomato, 1 basil leaf, 1 piece of cheese, 1 basil leaf, 1 tomato.
2. Serve with the vinaigrette, if desired, for dipping.

Nutrition: Calories: 338|Fat: 24g |Protein: 25g

Turkey Roll-Ups with Veggie Cream Cheese

Preparation Time: 10 minutes |Cooking Time: 0 minutes |Servings: 2

Ingredients:

- ¼ cup cream cheese, at room temperature
- 2 tablespoons finely chopped red onion
- 2 tablespoons finely chopped red bell pepper
- 1 tablespoon chopped fresh chives
- 1 teaspoon Dijon mustard
- 1 garlic clove, minced
- ¼ teaspoon sea salt
- 6 slices deli turkey

Directions:

1. The cream cheese, red onion, bell

pepper, chives, mustard, garlic, and salt are mixed in a small bowl.
2. Spread the mixture on the turkey slices and roll-up.

Nutrition: Calories: 146 |Fat: 10g |Protein: 8g

Baked Parmesan Crisps *

Preparation Time: 5 minutes |Cooking Time: 5 minutes |Servings: 1

Ingredients:

- 1/2 cup grated Parmesan cheese

Directions:

1. Preheat the oven to 400°F. A rimmed baking sheet is lined with parchment paper.
2. Spread the Parmesan on the prepared baking sheet into 4 mounds, spreading each mound out so it is flat but not touching the others.
3. Bake until brown and crisp, 3 to 5 minutes.
4. Cool for 5 minutes. Use a spatula to remove to a plate to continue cooling.

Nutrition: Calories: 216 |Fat: 14g|Protein: 19g

Garlicky Hummus

Preparation Time: 5 minutes |Cooking Time: 10 minutes |Servings: 2

Ingredients:

- 1½ cups canned chickpeas, rinsed and drained
- ¼ cup tahini
- 2 teaspoons minced garlic
- 1 teaspoon ground cumin
- ½ teaspoon ground coriander
- ¼ cup freshly squeezed lemon juice
- 2 tablespoons olive oil
- Sea salt

Directions:

1. Put the chickpeas, tahini, garlic, cumin, coriander, and lemon juice in a food processor, and blend until smooth, scraping down the sides of the processor at least once.
2. Incorporate the olive oil and process until blended. Season with sea salt.
3. Store the hummus in a sealed container in the refrigerator for up to 1 week.

Nutrition: Calories: 147 |Protein: 5g |Fat: 9g

Pesto Veggie Pizza

Preparation Time: 05 minutes |Cooking Time: 15 minutes |Servings: 2

Ingredients:

- Olive oil, for greasing the parchment paper
- ¼ head cauliflower, cut into florets
- 3 tablespoons almond flour
- ½ teaspoons olive oil
- 1 egg, beaten
- Minced garlic
- Pinch sea salt
- ¼ cup Simple Tomato Sauce (here)
- ¼ zucchini, thinly sliced
- ¼ cup baby spinach leaves
- 2 ½ asparagus spears, woody ends trimmed, cut into 3-inch pieces
- Basil pesto

Directions:

1. Preheat the oven to 450°F. Put a baking sheet without a rim in the oven.
2. Prepare a piece of parchment paper by lightly brushing with olive oil and set aside.
3. Put a large saucepan filled halfway with water over high heat and bring it to a boil.
4. Put the cauliflower in a food processor, and pulse until very finely chopped, almost flour consistency.
5. Transfer the ground cauliflower to a fine mesh sieve and put it over the boiling water for about 1 minute, until the cauliflower is cooked.
6. Wring out all the water from the cauliflower using a kitchen towel. Transfer the cauliflower to a large bowl.
7. Stir in the almond flour, oil, egg, garlic, and salt, and mix to create a thick dough.

Use your hands to press the ingredients together and transfer the cauliflower mixture to the parchment paper.

8. Press the mixture out into a flat circle, about ½ inch thick. Slide the parchment paper onto the baking sheet in the oven.
9. Bake the crust for about 10 minutes, until it is crisp and turns golden brown.
10. Remove the crust from the oven and spread the sauce evenly to the edges of the crust.
11. Arrange the zucchini, spinach, and asparagus on the pizza.
12. Drizzle the pizza with basil pesto and put it back in the oven for about 2 minutes, until the vegetables are tender. Serve.

Nutrition: Calories: 107 |Protein: 5g |Fat: 7g

Apple Leather

Preparation Time: 10 minutes |Cooking Time: 8-10 hours Servings: 4

Ingredients:

- 5 apples, peeled, cored, and sliced
- ¼ cup water
- 1 teaspoon pure vanilla extract
- ¼ teaspoon ground ginger
- ¼ teaspoon ground cloves

Directions:

1. Put the apples, water, vanilla, ginger, and cloves in a large saucepan over medium heat.
2. Bring the mixture to a boil, reduce to low heat, and simmer for about 20 minutes, until the apples are very tender.
3. Transfer the apple mixture to a food processor, and purée until very smooth.
4. Set the oven on the lowest possible setting.
5. Line a baking sheet with parchment paper.
6. Pour the puréed apple mixture onto the baking sheet and spread it out very thinly and evenly.
7. Place the baking sheet in the oven, and bake for 8 to 10 hours, until the leather is smooth and no longer sticky.
8. Cut the apple leather with a pizza cutter into 24 strips, and store this treat in a sealed container in a cool, dark place for up to 2 weeks.

Nutrition: Calories: 41|Protein: 0.1g|Fat: 0.3g

Simple Appetizer Meatballs

Preparation Time: 25 minutes |Cooking Time: 25 minutes |Servings: 8 pieces

Ingredients:

- ½ pound lean ground beef
- ½ pound lean ground pork
- ½ cup sodium-free chicken broth
- ¼ cup almond flour
- 1 tablespoon low-sodium tamari sauce
- ½ teaspoon ground cumin
- ¼ teaspoon freshly ground black pepper

Directions:

1. Preheat the oven to 375°F.
2. Combine all the ingredients together until completely incorporated in a large bowl.
3. Roll the mixture into ¾-inch balls and place them on a parchment-lined baking sheet.
4. Bake the meatballs for 25 to 30 minutes, until they are cooked through and golden brown.
5. Serve.

Nutrition: Calories: 125 |Protein: 20g |Fat: 4g

French Bread Pizza

Preparation Time: 5 minutes |Cooking Time: 2-3 hours Servings: 2

Ingredients:

- ½ cup asparagus(diced)
- ½ cup Roma tomatoes(diced)
- ½ cup red bell pepper(diced)
- ½ tablespoon minced garlic
- ½ loaf French bread
- ½ cup pizza sauce

- ½ cup low-fat shredded mozzarella cheese

Directions:

1. Heat the oven to 400°F. Coat the baking sheet lightly with a cooking spray.
2. Add the asparagus, tomatoes, and pepper in a little dish. Add the garlic and stir gently to coat uniformly.
3. Adjust the French bread to the baking sheet. Apply ¼ cup of the pizza sauce and ¼ of the vegetable paste to each portion of the mixture. Sprinkle with ¼ cup of mozzarella cheese.
4. Bake until the cheese is finely browned, and the vegetables are tender for 8 to 10 minutes. Serve straight away.

Nutrition: Calories: 265|Fat: 5g|Protein: 15g

Candied Pecans *

Preparation Time: 5 minutes |Cooking Time: 11 minutes |Servings: 1

Ingredients:

- 1 ½ tsp butter
- 1 ½ cup pecan halves
- 2 ½ tbsp. Splenda, divided
- 1 tsp cinnamon
- ¼ tsp ginger
- 1/8 tsp cardamom
- 1/8 tsp salt

Direction:

1. In a small bowl, stir together 1 1/2 teaspoons Splenda, cinnamon, ginger, cardamom and salt. Set aside.
2. Melt butter in a medium skillet over med-low heat. Add pecans, and two tablespoons Splenda. Reduce heat to low and cook, stirring occasionally, until sweetener melts, about 5 to 8 minutes.
3. Add spice mixture to the skillet and stir to coat pecans. Spread mixture to parchment paper and let cool for 10-15 minutes. Store in an airtight container. Serving size is ¼ cup.

Nutrition: Calories 173 |Protein 2g |Fat 16g

Cauliflower Hummus

Preparation Time: 6 minutes |Cooking Time: 15 minutes |Servings: 6

Ingredients:

- 3 cup cauliflower florets
- 3 tbsp. fresh lemon juice
- 5 cloves garlic, divided
- 5 tbsp. olive oil, divided
- 2 tbsp. water
- 1 ½ tbsp. Tahini paste
- 1 ¼ tsp salt, divided
- Smoked paprika and extra olive oil for serving

Direction:

1. In a microwave safe bowl, combine cauliflower, water, 2 tablespoons oil, ½ teaspoon salt, and 3 whole cloves garlic. Microwave on high 15 minutes, or until cauliflower is soft and darkened.
2. Transfer mixture to a food processor or blender and process until almost smooth. Add tahini paste, lemon juice, remaining garlic cloves, remaining oil, and salt. Blend until almost smooth.
3. Place the hummus in a bowl and drizzle lightly with olive oil and a sprinkle or two of paprika. Serve with your favorite raw vegetables.

Nutrition: Calories 107 |Protein 2g |Fat 10g

Cheese Crisp Crackers

Preparation Time: 6 minutes |Cooking Time: 11 minutes |Servings: 4

Ingredients:

- 4 slices pepper Jack cheese, quartered
- 4 slices Colby Jack cheese, quartered
- 4 slices cheddar cheese, quartered

Direction:

1. Heat oven to 400 degrees. Line a cooking sheet with parchment paper.
2. Place cheese in a single layer on prepared pan and bake 10 minutes, or until cheese gets firm.

3. Transfer to paper towel line surface to absorb excess oil. Let cool, cheese will crisp up more as it cools.
4. Store in airtight container, or Ziploc bag. Serve with your favorite dip or salsa.

Nutrition: Calories 253|Protein 15g |Fat 20g

Cheesy Onion Dip

Preparation Time: 6 minutes |Cooking Time: 5 minutes |Servings: 5

Ingredients:

- 8 oz. low fat cream cheese, soft
- 1 cup onions, grated
- 1 cup low fat Swiss cheese, grated
- 1 cup lite mayonnaise

Direction:

1. Heat oven to broil.
2. Combine all Ingredients in a small casserole dish. Microwave on high, stirring every 30 seconds, until cheese is melted, and Ingredients are combined.
3. Place under the broiler for 1-2 minutes until the top is nicely browned. Serve warm with vegetables for dipping.

Nutrition: Calories 158 |Protein 9g |Fat 11g

Cheesy Pita Crisps

Preparation Time: 6 minutes |Cooking Time: 15 minutes |Servings: 2

Ingredients:

- ½ cup mozzarella cheese
- ¼ cup margarine, melted
- 4 whole-wheat pita pocket halves
- 3 tbsp. reduced fat parmesan
- ½ tsp garlic powder
- ½ tsp onion powder
- ¼ tsp salt
- ¼ tsp pepper
- Nonstick cooking spray

Direction:

1. Heat oven to 400 degrees. Spray a baking sheet with cooking spray.
2. Cut each pita pocket in half. Cut each half into 2 triangles. Place, rough side up, on prepared pan.
3. In a small bowl, whisk together margarine, parmesan and seasonings.
4. Spread each triangle with margarine mixture. Sprinkle mozzarella over top.
5. Bake 12-15 minutes or until golden brown.

Nutrition: Calories 131 |Protein 4g |Fat 7g

Cheesy Taco Chips

Preparation Time: 16 minutes |Cooking Time: 41 minutes |Servings: 2

Ingredients:

- 1 cup Mexican blend cheese, grated
- 2 large egg whites
- 1 1/2 cup crushed pork rinds
- 1 tbsp. taco seasoning
- ¼ tsp salt

Direction:

1. Heat oven to 300 degrees. Line a large baking sheet with parchment paper.
2. In a large bowl, whisk egg whites and salt until frothy. Stir in pork rinds, cheese, and seasoning and stir until thoroughly combined.
3. Turn out onto prepared pan. Place another sheet of parchment paper on top and roll out very thin, about 12x12-inches. Remove top sheet of parchment paper, and using a pizza cutter, score dough in 2-inch squares, then score each square in half diagonally.
4. Bake 20 minutes until they start to brown. Turn off oven and let them sit inside the oven until they are firm to the touch, about 10-20 minutes.
5. Remove from oven and cool completely before breaking apart. Eat them as is or with your favorite dip.

Nutrition: |Calories 260 |Protein 25g |at 17g

Chewy Granola Bars

Preparation Time: 11 minutes |Cooking Time: 35 minutes |Servings: 8

Ingredients:

- 1 egg, beaten
- 2/3 cup margarine, melted
- 3 ½ cup quick oats
- 1 cup almonds, chopped
- ½ cup honey
- ½ cup sunflower kernels
- ½ cup coconut, unsweetened
- ½ cup dried apples
- ½ cup dried cranberries
- ½ cup Splenda brown sugar
- 1 tsp vanilla
- ½ tsp cinnamon
- Nonstick cooking spray

Direction:

1. Heat oven to 350 degrees. Spray a large baking sheet with cooking spray.
2. Spread oats and almonds on prepared pan. Bake 12-15 minutes until toasted, stirring every few minutes.
3. In a large bowl, combine egg, margarine, honey, and vanilla. Stir in remaining Ingredients.
4. Stir in oat mixture. Press into baking sheet and bake 13-18 minutes, or until edges are light brown.
5. Cool on a wire rack. Cut into bars and store in an airtight container.

Nutrition: Calories 119 |Protein 2g |Fat 6g

Chili Lime Tortilla Chips

Preparation Time: 6 minutes |Cooking Time: 15 minutes |Servings: 4

Ingredients:

- 12 6-inch corn tortillas, cut into 8 triangles
- 3 tbsp. lime juice
- 1 tsp cumin
- 1 tsp chili powder

Direction:

1. Heat oven to 350 degrees.
2. Place tortilla triangles in a single layer on a large baking sheet.
3. In a small bowl stir together spices.
4. Sprinkle half the lime juice over tortillas, followed by ½ the spice mixture. Bake 7 minutes.
5. Remove from oven and turn tortillas over. Sprinkle with remaining lime juice and spices. Bake another 8 minutes or until crisp, but not brown.
6. Serve with your favorite salsa, serving size is 10 chips.

Nutrition: Calories 65 |Protein 2g |Fat 1g

Chocolate Chip Blondies

Preparation Time: 6 minutes |Cooking Time: 21 minutes |Servings: 6

Ingredients:

- 1 egg
- ½ cup semi-sweet chocolate chips
- 1/3 cup flour
- 1/3 cup whole wheat flour
- ¼ cup Splenda brown sugar
- ¼ cup sunflower oil
- 2 tbsp. honey
- 1 tsp vanilla
- ½ tsp baking powder
- ¼ tsp salt
- Nonstick cooking spray

Direction:

1. Heat oven to 350 degrees. Spray an 8-inch square baking dish with cooking spray.
2. In a small bowl, combine dry Ingredients.
3. In a large bowl, whisk together egg, oil, honey, and vanilla. Stir in dry Ingredients just until combined. Stir in chocolate chips.
4. Spread batter in prepared dish. Bake 20-22 minutes or until they pass the toothpick test. Cool on a wire rack then cut into bars.

Nutrition: Calories 136 |Protein 2g |Fat 6g

Cinnamon Apple Chips

Preparation Time: 6 minutes |Cooking Time: 11 minutes |Servings: 2

Ingredients:

- 1 medium apple, sliced thin
- ¼ tsp cinnamon
- ¼ tsp nutmeg
- Nonstick cooking spray

Direction:

1. Heat oven to 375. Spray a baking sheet with cooking spray.
2. Place apples in a mixing bowl and add spices. Toss to coat.
3. Arrange apples, in a single layer, on prepared pan. Bake 4 minutes, turn apples over and bake 4 minutes more.
4. Serve immediately or store in airtight container.

Nutrition: Calories 58 |Protein 0.1g |Fat 0.3g

Spicy Bruschetta

Preparation Time: 5 minutes |Cooking Time: 10 minutes |Servings: 2

Ingredients:

- 1 baguette roll
- Salt and white pepper
- ½ tomato
- ½ tbsp. acetic balsamic vinegar
- 37.5 g roasted peppers from the jar
- 2 tbsps. oil
- ½ clove of garlic
- 1 red chili
- ½ onion

Directions:

1. Halve the rolls and drizzle with 1 tablespoon of oil.
2. Preheat the oven to 200°C and roast the rolls on both sides for 2-3 minutes.
3. Pour boiling water over the tomato and let it steep for a moment. Then peel and core the tomato and dice the pulp.
4. Drain the peppers and cut them into small pieces. Peel and dice the garlic. Peel and chop the onion. Core the chili pepper and cut it into slices.
5. Mix all ingredients with 3 tablespoons of oil and vinegar. Season the mixture with salt and pepper.
6. Spread the vegetables on the rolls and briefly heat them again in the oven.

Nutrition: Calories: 205|Fat: 10g|Protein: 3.8g

Easy Pizza for Two

Preparation Time: 5 minutes |Cooking Time: 10 minutes |Servings: 2

Ingredients:

- ½ cup chunky no-salt-added
- Tomato sauce
- 1 ready-made whole-wheat flatbread (about 10-inch diameter)
- 2 slices of onion, (¼-inch wide)
- 4 sliced red bell pepper (¼-inch wide)
- ½ cup shredded low-fat mozzarella
- 2 tablespoons chopped fresh basil

Directions:

1. Heat the oven to 350ºF.
2. Coat the baking pan lightly with the cooking oil.
3. Spread the tomato sauce on the flatbread. Cover with tomato, chili pepper, mozzarella, and basil.
4. Place the pizza in a baking pan and cook until the cheese melts and becomes lightly browned approximately five minutes.

Nutrition: Calories: 163|Protein: 8g |Fat: 5g

Bean Salad with Balsamic Vinaigrette

Preparation Time: 5 minutes |Cooking Time: 0 minutes |Servings: 3

Ingredients:

For the Vinaigrette:

- 2 tablespoons balsamic vinegar
- 1/3 cup fresh parsley, chopped
- 4 garlic cloves, finely chopped
- Ground black pepper, to taste

- ¼ cup Extra-virgin olive oil

For the Salad:

- 1/3 can (15 oz.) low-sodium garbanzo beans, rinsed and drained
- 1/3 can (15 oz.) low-sodium black beans, rinsed and drained
- 1 small red onion, diced
- 2 lettuce leaves
- Celery, finely chopped

Directions:

1. In a small pan, mix the balsamic vinegar, the parsley, the garlic, and the pepper to prepare the vinaigrette. Slowly add the olive oil when whisking.
2. In a large pan, combine the beans and the onion.
3. Pour the vinaigrette over the mixture and stir softly, blend thoroughly and coat equally. Cover and refrigerate until ready to serve.
4. Put one lettuce leaf on each plate to serve. Divide the salad between the individual plates and garnish with the minced celery. Serve straight away.

Nutrition: Calories: 206 |Fat: 10g |Protein: 7g

Easy Cauliflower Hush Puppies

Preparation Time: 15 minutes |Cooking Time: 10 minutes |Servings: 8

Ingredients:

- 1 whole cauliflower, including stalks and florets, roughly chopped
- ¾ cup buttermilk
- ¾ cup low-fat milk
- 1 medium onion, chopped
- 2 medium eggs
- 2 cups yellow cornmeal
- 1½ teaspoons baking powder
- ½ teaspoon salt

Directions:

1. In a blender, combine the cauliflower, buttermilk, milk, and onion and purée. Transfer to a large mixing bowl.
2. Crack the eggs into the purée, and gently fold until mixed.
3. In a medium bowl, whisk the cornmeal, baking powder, and salt together.
4. Gently add the dry ingredients to the wet ingredients and mix until just combined, taking care not to overmix.
5. Working in batches, place 1/3-cup portions of the batter into the basket of an air fryer.
6. Set the air fryer to 390°F (199°C), close, and cook for 10 minutes. Transfer the hush puppies to a plate. Repeat until no batter remains.
7. Serve warm with greens.

Nutrition: Calories: 180|Fat: 8g|Protein: 4.1g

Cauliflower Mash *

Preparation Time: 7 minutes |Cooking Time: 20 minutes |Servings: 1

Ingredients:

- ½ head cauliflower, cored and cut into large florets
- ¼ teaspoon kosher salt
- ¼ teaspoon garlic pepper
- 1 tablespoon plain Greek yogurt
- Freshly grated Parmesan cheese
- ½ tablespoon unsalted butter or ghee (optional)
- Chopped fresh chives

Directions:

1. Pour 1 cup of water into the electric pressure cooker and insert a steamer basket or wire rack.
2. Place the cauliflower in the basket.
3. Secure the pressure cooker lid. Set the valve to sealing.
4. Cook on high pressure for 5 minutes.
5. When it beeps, hit Cancel and quickly release the pressure.
6. Remove the cauliflower from the pot and pour out the water. Return the cauliflower to the pot and add the salt, garlic pepper, yogurt, and cheese. Use an immersion blender or potato masher to purée or mash the cauliflower in the pot.

7. Spoon into a serving bowl, and garnish with butter (if using) and chives.

Nutrition: Calories: 141|Fat: 6g|Protein: 12.1g

Red Pepper, Goat Cheese, and Arugula Open-Faced Grilled Sandwich

Preparation Time: 5 minutes |Cooking Time: 15 minutes |Servings: 2

Ingredients:

- 1 red bell pepper, seeded
- Nonstick cooking spray
- 2 slice whole-wheat thin-sliced bread
- 4 tablespoons crumbled goat cheese
- Pinch dried thyme
- 1 cup arugula

Directions:

1. Preheat the broiler to high heat. Line a baking sheet with parchment paper.
2. Cut the ½ bell pepper lengthwise into two pieces and arrange on the prepared baking sheet with the skin facing up.
3. Broil until the skin is blackened for about 5 to 10 minutes. Transfer to a covered container to steam for 5 minutes, then remove the skin from the pepper using your fingers. Cut the pepper into strips.
4. Heat a small skillet over medium-high heat. Spray it with nonstick cooking spray and place the bread in the skillet. Top with the goat cheese and sprinkle with the thyme. Pile the arugula on top, followed by the roasted red pepper strips. Press down with a spatula to hold in place.
5. Cook for 2 to 3 minutes until the bread is crisp and browned and the cheese is warmed through.

Nutrition: Calories: 109 |Fat: 2g |Protein: 4g

Salad

Tuna Salad

Preparation Time: 10 minutes |Cooking Time: 0 minutes |Servings: 3

Ingredients:

- 1 can tuna (6 oz.)
- 1/3 cup fresh cucumber, chopped
- 1/3 cup fresh tomato, chopped
- 1/3 cup avocado, chopped
- 1/3 cup celery, chopped
- 2 garlic cloves, minced
- 4 tsp. olive oil
- 2 tbsp. lime juice
- Pinch of black pepper

Directions:

1. Prepare the dressing by combining olive oil, lime juice, minced garlic and black pepper.
2. Mix the salad ingredients in a salad bowl and drizzle with the dressing.

Nutrition: Calories 212 | Protein 14.3g|Carb 14g

Spinach Shrimp Salad

Preparation Time: 10 minutes |Cooking Time: 10 minutes |Servings: 4

Ingredients:

- 1 lb. uncooked shrimp, peeled and deveined
- 2 tablespoons parsley, minced
- ¾ cup halved cherry tomatoes
- 1 medium lemon
- 4 cups baby spinach
- 2 tablespoons butter
- 3 minced garlic cloves
- ¼ teaspoon pepper
- ¼ teaspoon salt

Directions:

1. Melt the butter over medium temperature in a nonstick skillet.

2. Add the shrimp.
3. Now cook the shrimp for 3 minutes until your shrimp becomes pink.
4. Add the parsley and garlic.
5. Cook for another minute. Take out from the heat.
6. Keep the spinach in your salad bowl.
7. Top with the shrimp mix and tomatoes.
8. Drizzle lemon juice on the salad.
9. Sprinkle pepper and salt.

Nutrition: Calories 201|Fat 10g |Protein 21g

Sweet Potato and Roasted Beet Salad

Preparation Time: 10 minutes |Cooking Time: 10 minutes |Servings: 4

Ingredients:

- 2 beets
- 1 sweet potato, peeled and cubed
- 1 garlic clove, minced
- 2 tablespoons walnuts, chopped and toasted
- 1 cup fennel bulb, sliced
- 3 tablespoons balsamic vinegar
- 1 teaspoon Dijon mustard
- 1 tablespoon honey
- 3 tablespoons olive oil
- ¼ teaspoon pepper
- ¼ teaspoon salt
- 3 tablespoons water

Directions:

1. Scrub the beets. Trim the tops to 1 inch.
2. Wrap in foil and keep on a baking sheet.
3. Bake until tender. Take off the foil. Combine water and sweet potato in a bowl.
4. Cover. Microwave for 5 minutes. Drain off.
5. Now peel the beets. Cut into small wedges.
6. Arrange the fennel, sweet potato and beets on 4 salad plates.
7. Sprinkle nuts.
8. Whisk the honey, mustard, vinegar, water, garlic, pepper and salt.
9. Whisk in oil gradually.
10. Drizzle over the salad.

Nutrition: Calories 270|Fat 13g|Protein 5g

Harvest Salad

Preparation Time: 9 minutes |Cooking Time: 25 minutes |Servings: 5

Ingredients:

- 10 oz. kale, deboned and chopped
- 1 ½ cup blackberries
- ½ butternut squash, cubed
- ¼ cup goat cheese, crumbled
- What you'll need from store cupboard:
- Maple Mustard Salad Dressing (chapter 16)
- 1 cup raw pecans
- 1/3 cup raw pumpkin seeds
- ¼ cup dried cranberries
- 3 1/2 tbsp. olive oil
- 1 ½ tbsp. sugar free maple syrup
- 3/8 tsp salt, divided
- Pepper, to taste
- Nonstick cooking spray

Directions:

1. Heat oven to 400 degrees. Spray a baking sheet with cooking spray.
2. Spread squash on the prepared pan, add 1 ½ tablespoons oil, 1/8 teaspoon salt, and pepper to squash and stir to coat the squash evenly. Bake 20-25 minutes.
3. Place kale in a large bowl. Add 2 tablespoons oil and ½ teaspoon salt and massage it into the kale with your hands for 3-4 minutes.
4. Spray a clean baking sheet with cooking spray. In a medium bowl, stir together pecans, pumpkin seeds, and maple syrup until nuts are coated. Pour onto prepared pan and bake 8-10 minutes, these can be baked at the same time as the squash.
5. To assemble the salad: place all of the ingredients in a large bowl. Pour dressing over and toss to coat. Serve.

Nutrition: Calories 436 |Protein 9g |Fat 37g

Asian Noodle Salad

Preparation Time: 20 minutes |Cooking Time: 15 minutes |Servings: 4

Ingredients:

- 2 carrots, sliced thin
- 2 radishes, sliced thin
- 1 English cucumber, sliced thin
- 1 mango, julienned
- 1 bell pepper, julienned
- 1 small serrano pepper, seeded and sliced
- 1 bag tofu Shirataki Fettuccini noodles
- ¼ cup lime juice
- ¼ cup fresh basil, chopped
- ¼ cup fresh cilantro, chopped
- 2 tbsp. fresh mint, chopped
- 2 tbsp. rice vinegar
- 2 tbsp. sweet chili sauce
- 2 tbsp. roasted peanuts finely chopped
- 1 tbsp. Splenda
- ½ tsp sesame oil

Directions:

1. Pickle the vegetables: In a large bowl, place radish, cucumbers, and carrots. Add vinegar, coconut sugar, and lime juice and stir to coat the vegetables. Cover and chill 15 – 20 minutes.
2. Prep the noodles: remove the noodles from the package and rinse under cold water. Cut into smaller pieces. Pat dry with paper towels.
3. To assemble the salad. Remove the vegetables from the marinade, reserving marinade, and place in a large mixing bowl. Add noodles, mango, bell pepper, chili, and herbs.
4. In a small bowl, combine 2 tablespoons marinade with the chili sauce and sesame oil. Pour over salad and toss to coat. Top with peanuts and serve.

Nutrition: Calories 158 |Protein 4g|Fat 4g

Avocado & Citrus Shrimp Salad

Preparation Time: 11 minutes |Cooking Time: 15 minutes |Servings: 4

Ingredients:

- 1 lb. medium shrimp, peeled and deveined, remove tails
- 8 cup salad greens
- 1 lemon
- 1 avocado, diced
- 1 shallot, diced fine
- ½ cup almonds, sliced and toasted
- 1 tbsp. olive oil
- Salt and freshly ground black pepper

Directions:

1. Cut the lemon in half and squeeze the juice, from both halves, into a small bowl, set aside. Slice the lemon into thin wedges.
2. Heat the oil in a skillet over medium heat. Add lemon wedges and let cook, about 1 minute, to infuse the oil with the lemons.
3. Add the shrimp and cook, stirring frequently, until shrimp turn pink. Discard the lemon wedges and let cool.
4. Place the salad greens in a large bowl: Add the shrimp, with the juices from the pan, and toss to coat. Add remaining Ingredients and toss to combine. Serve.

Nutrition Calories 425 |Protein 35g|Fat 26g

Healthy Taco Salad

Preparation Time: 20 minutes |Cooking Time: 9 minutes |Servings: 4

Ingredients:

- 2 whole Romaine hearts, chopped
- 1 lb. lean ground beef
- 1 whole avocado, cubed
- 3 oz. grape tomatoes, halved
- ½ cup cheddar cheese, cubed
- 2 tbsp. sliced red onion
- 1/2 batch Tangy Mexican Salad Dressing
- 1 tsp ground cumin
- Salt and pepper to taste

Directions:

1. Cook ground beef in a skillet over medium heat. Break the beef up into little pieces as it cooks. Add seasonings and stir

to combine. Drain grease and let cool for about 5 minutes.
2. To assemble the salad, place all Ingredients into a large bowl. Toss to mix then add dressing and toss. Top with reduced-fat sour cream and/or salsa if desired.

Nutrition: |Calories 449 |Protein 40g |Fat 22g

Chicken Guacamole Salad

Preparation Time: 6 minutes |Cooking Time: 25 minutes |Servings: 4

Ingredients:

- 1 lb. chicken breast, boneless & skinless
- 2 avocados
- 1-2 jalapeno peppers, seeded & diced
- 1/3 cup onion, diced
- 3 tbsp. cilantro, diced
- 2 tbsp. fresh lime juice
- 2 cloves garlic, diced
- 1 tbsp. olive oil
- Salt & pepper, to taste

Directions:

1. Heat oven to 400 degrees. Line a baking sheet with foil.
2. Season chicken with salt and pepper and place on prepared pan. Bake 20 minutes, or until chicken is cooked through. Let cool completely.
3. Once chicken has cooled, shred or dice and add to a large bowl. Add remaining Ingredients and mix well, mashing the avocado as you mix it in. Taste and season with salt and pepper as desired. Serve immediately.

Nutrition: Calories 324 |Protein 23g |Fat 22g|

Roasted Portobello Salad

Preparation Time: 10 minutes |Cooking Time: 0 minutes |Servings: 4

Ingredients:

- 11/2lb. Portobello mushrooms, stems trimmed
- 3 heads Belgian endive, sliced
- 1 small red onion, sliced
- 4 oz. blue cheese
- 8 oz. mixed salad greens

Dressing:

- 3 tbsp. red wine vinegar
- 1 tbsp. Dijon mustard
- 2/3 cup olive oil
- Salt and pepper to taste

Directions:

1. Preheat the oven to 450F.
2. Prepare the dressing by whisking together vinegar, mustard, salt and pepper. Slowly add olive oil while whisking.
3. Cut the mushrooms and arrange them on a baking sheet, stem-side up. Coat the mushrooms with some dressing and bake for 15 minutes.
4. In a salad bowl toss the salad greens with onion, endive and cheese. Sprinkle with the dressing.
5. Add mushrooms to the salad bowl.

Nutrition: Calories 501|Protein 14.9g|Carb 22g

Shredded Chicken Salad

Preparation Time: 5 minutes |Cooking Time: 10 minutes |Servings: 6

Ingredients:

- 2 chicken breasts, boneless, skinless
- 1 head iceberg lettuce, cut into strips
- 2 bell peppers, cut into strips
- 1 fresh cucumber, quartered, sliced
- 3 scallions, sliced
- 2 tbsp. chopped peanuts
- 1 tbsp. peanut vinaigrette
- Salt to taste
- 1 cup water

Directions:

1. In a skillet simmer one cup of salted water.
2. Add the chicken breasts, cover and cook on low for 5 minutes. Remove the cover.

Then remove the chicken from the skillet and shred with a fork.
3. In a salad bowl mix the vegetables with the cooled chicken, season with salt and sprinkle with peanut vinaigrette and chopped peanuts.

Nutrition: Calories 117|Protein 11g|Carb 9g

Broccoli Salad *

Preparation Time: 10 minutes |Cooking Time: 0 minutes |Servings: 1

Ingredients:

- 1 medium head broccoli, raw, florets only
- 1/2 cup red onion, chopped
- 12 oz. turkey bacon, chopped, fried until crisp
- 1/2 cup cherry tomatoes, halved
- ¼ cup sunflower kernels
- ¾ cup raisins
- ¾ cup mayonnaise
- 2 tbsp. white vinegar

Directions:

1. In a salad bowl combine the broccoli, tomatoes and onion.
2. Mix mayo with vinegar and sprinkle over the broccoli. Add the sunflower kernels, raisins and bacon and toss well.

Nutrition: Calories 220|Protein 11g|Carb 17g

Cherry Tomato Salad

Preparation Time: 10 minutes |Cooking Time: 10 minutes |Servings: 6

Ingredients:

- 40 cherry tomatoes, halved
- 1 cup mozzarella balls, halved
- 1 cup green olives, sliced
- 1 can (6 oz.) black olives, sliced
- 2 green onions, chopped
- 3 oz. roasted pine nuts

Dressing:

- 1/2 cup olive oil
- 2 tbsp. red wine vinegar
- 1 tsp. dried oregano
- Salt and pepper to taste

Directions:

1. In a salad bowl, combine the tomatoes, olives and onions.
2. Prepare the dressing by combining olive oil with red wine vinegar, dried oregano, salt and pepper.
3. Sprinkle with the dressing and add the nuts.
4. Let marinate in the fridge for 1 hour.

Nutrition: Protein 2.4g|Carb 10g|Sugar 3.6g

Ground Turkey Salad

Preparation Time: 10 minutes |Cooking Time: 35 minutes |Servings: 4

Ingredients:

- 1 lb. lean ground turkey
- 1/2-inch ginger, minced
- 2 garlic cloves, minced
- 1 onion, chopped
- 1 tbsp. olive oil
- 1 bag lettuce leaves (for serving)
- ¼ cup fresh cilantro, chopped
- 2 tsp. coriander powder
- 1 tsp. red chili powder
- 1 tsp. turmeric powder
- Salt to taste
- 4 cups water

Dressing:

- 2 tbsp. fat free yogurt
- 1 tbsp. sour cream, non-fat
- 1 tbsp. low fat mayonnaise
- 1 lemon, juiced
- 1 tsp. red chili flakes
- Salt and pepper to taste

Directions:

1. In a skillet sauté the garlic and ginger in olive oil for 1 minute. Add onion and season with salt. Cook for 10 minutes over medium heat.
2. Add the ground turkey and sauté for 3 more minutes. Add the spices (turmeric, red chili powder and coriander powder).

3. Add 4 cups water and cook for 30 minutes, covered.
4. Prepare the dressing by combining yogurt, sour cream, mayo, lemon juice, chili flakes, salt and pepper.
5. To serve arrange the salad leaves on serving plates and place the cooked ground turkey on them. Top with dressing.

Nutrition: Calories 176|Protein 17.8g|Ccarb 9g

Asian Cucumber Salad

Preparation Time: 10 minutes
Cooking time: 0 minute
Servings: 6
Ingredients:

- 1 lb. cucumbers, sliced
- 2 scallions, sliced
- 2 tbsp. sliced pickled ginger, chopped
- ¼ cup cilantro
- 1/2 red jalapeño, chopped
- 3 tbsp. rice wine vinegar
- 1 tbsp. sesame oil
- 1 tbsp. sesame seeds

Directions:

1. In a salad bowl combine all ingredients and toss together.

Nutrition: Calories 52|Protein 1g|Carb 5.7g

Cauliflower Tofu Salad

Preparation Time: 10 minutes |Cooking Time: 15 minutes |Servings: 4
Ingredients:

- 2 cups cauliflower florets, blended
- 1 fresh cucumber, diced
- 1/2 cup green olives, diced
- 1/3 cup red onion, diced
- 2 tbsp. toasted pine nuts
- 2 tbsp. raisins
- 1/3 cup feta, crumbled
- 1/2 cup pomegranate seeds
- 2 lemons (juiced, zest grated)
- 8 oz. tofu
- 2 tsp. oregano
- 2 garlic cloves, minced
- 1/2tsp. red chili flakes
- 3 tbsp. olive oil
- Salt and pepper to taste

Directions:

1. Season the processed cauliflower with salt and transfer to a strainer to drain.
2. Prepare the marinade for tofu by combining 2 tbsp. lemon juice, 1.5 tbsp. olive oil, minced garlic, chili flakes, oregano, salt and pepper. Coat tofu in the marinade and set aside.
3. Preheat the oven to 450F.
4. Bake tofu on a baking sheet for 12 minutes.
5. In a salad bowl mix the remaining marinade with onions, cucumber, cauliflower, olives and raisins. Add in the remaining olive oil and grated lemon zest.
6. Top with tofu, pine nuts, and feta and pomegranate seeds.

Nutrition: Calories 328|Protein 11g|Carb 28

Scallop Caesar Salad

Preparation Time: 5 minutes
Cooking Time: 2 minutes   Servings: 2
Ingredients:

- 8 sea scallops
- 4 cups romaine lettuce
- 2 tsp. olive oil
- 3 tbsp. Caesar Salad Dressing
- 1 tsp. lemon juice
- Salt and pepper to taste

Directions:

1. In a frying pan heat olive oil and cook the scallops in one layer no longer than 2 minutes per both sides. Season with salt and pepper to taste.
2. Arrange lettuce on plates and place scallops on top. Pour over the Caesar dressing and lemon juice.

Nutrition: Calories 340|Protein 30g|Carb 14g

Chicken Avocado Salad

Preparation Time: 30 minutes |Cooking Time: 15 minutes |Servings: 4

Ingredients:

- 1 lb. chicken breast, cooked, shredded
- 1 avocado, pitted, peeled, sliced
- 2 tomatoes, diced
- 1 cucumber, peeled, sliced
- 1 head lettuce, chopped
- 3 tbsp. olive oil
- 2 tbsp. lime juice
- 1 tbsp. cilantro, chopped
- Salt and pepper to taste

Directions:

1. In a bowl whisk together oil, lime juice, cilantro, salt, and a pinch of pepper.
2. Combine lettuce, tomatoes, cucumber in a salad bowl and toss with half of the dressing. Toss chicken with the remaining dressing and combine with vegetable mixture.
3. Top with avocado.

Nutrition: Calories 380|Protein38g|Carb 10g

California Wraps

Preparation Time: 5 minutes |Cooking Time: 15 minutes |Servings: 2

Ingredients:

- 4 slices turkey breast, cooked
- 4 slices ham, cooked
- 4 lettuce leaves
- 4 slices tomato
- 4 slices avocado
- 1 tsp. lime juice
- A handful watercress leaves
- 4 tbsp. Ranch dressing, sugar free

Directions:

1. Top a lettuce leaf with turkey slice, ham slice and tomato.
2. In a bowl combine avocado and lime juice and place on top of tomatoes. Top with water cress and dressing.
3. Repeat with the remaining ingredients for 4. Topping each lettuce leaf with a turkey slice, ham slice, tomato and dressing.

Nutrition: Calories 140|Protein 9g|Carb 4g

Chicken Salad in Cucumber Cups

Preparation Time: 5 minutes |Cooking Time: 15 minutes |Servings: 4

Ingredients:

- 1/2 chicken breast, skinless, boiled and shredded
- 2 long cucumbers, cut into 8 thick rounds each, scooped out (won't use in a).
- 1 tsp. ginger, minced
- 1 tsp. lime zest, grated
- 4 tsp. olive oil
- 1 tsp. sesame oil
- 1 tsp. lime juice
- Salt and pepper to taste

Directions:

1. In a bowl combine lime zest, juice, olive and sesame oils, ginger, and season with salt.
2. Toss the chicken with the dressing and fill the cucumber cups with the salad.

Nutrition: Calories 116|Protein 12g|Carb 4g

Sunflower Seeds and Arugula Garden Salad

Preparation Time: 5 minutes |Cooking Time: 10 minutes |Servings: 2

Ingredients:

- ¼ tsp. black pepper
- ¼ tsp. salt
- 1 tsp. fresh thyme, chopped
- 2 tbsp. sunflower seeds, toasted
- 2 cups red grapes, halved
- 7 cups baby arugula, loosely packed
- 1 tbsp. coconut oil
- 2 tsp. honey
- 3 tbsp. red wine vinegar
- 1/2tsp. stone-ground mustard

Directions:

1. In a small bowl, whisk together mustard, honey and vinegar. Slowly pour oil as you whisk.
2. In a large salad bowl, mix thyme, seeds, grapes and arugula.
3. Drizzle with dressing and serve.

Nutrition: Calories 86.7|Protein 1.6g|Fat 3g.

Supreme Caesar Salad

Preparation Time: 5 minutes |Cooking Time: 10 minutes |Servings: 4

Ingredients:

- ¼ cup olive oil
- ¾ cup mayonnaise
- 1 head romaine lettuce, torn into bite sized pieces
- 1 tbsp. lemon juice
- 1 tsp. Dijon mustard
- 1 tsp. Worcestershire sauce
- 3 cloves garlic, peeled and minced
- 3 cloves garlic, peeled and quartered
- 4 cups day old bread, cubed
- 5 anchovy filets, minced
- 6 tbsp. grated parmesan cheese, divided
- Ground black pepper to taste
- Salt to taste

Directions:

1. In a small bowl, whisk well lemon juice, mustard, Worcestershire sauce, 2 tbsp. parmesan cheese, anchovies, mayonnaise, and minced garlic. Season with pepper and salt to taste. Set aside in the ref.
2. On medium fire, place a large nonstick saucepan and heat oil.
3. Sauté quartered garlic until browned around a minute or two. Remove and discard.
4. Add bread cubes in same pan, sauté until lightly browned. Season with pepper and salt. Transfer to a plate.
5. In large bowl, place lettuce and pour in dressing. Toss well to coat. Top with remaining parmesan cheese.
6. Garnish with bread cubes, serve, and enjoy.

Nutrition: Calories: 443|Fat 32g|Protein 11.6g

Tabbouleh- Arabian Salad *

Preparation Time: 5 minutes |Cooking Time: 10 minutes |Servings: 1

Ingredients:

- ¼ cup chopped fresh mint
- 1 2/3 cups boiling water
- 1 cucumber, peeled, seeded and chopped
- 1 cup bulgur
- 1 cup chopped fresh parsley
- 1 cup chopped green onions
- 1 tsp. salt
- 1/3 cup lemon juice
- 1/3 cup olive oil
- 3 tomatoes, chopped
- Ground black pepper to taste

Directions:

1. In a large bowl, mix together boiling water and bulgur. Let soak and set aside for an hour while covered.
2. After one hour, toss in cucumber, tomatoes, mint, parsley, onions, lemon juice and oil. Then season with black pepper and salt to taste. Toss well and refrigerate for another hour while covered before serving.

Nutrition: Calories 185|Fat 13.1g|Protein 4.1g

Bacon-Broccoli Salad

Preparation Time: 10 minutes |Cooking Time: 10 minutes |Servings: 10

Ingredients:

- 8 cups broccoli florets
- 3 strips of bacon, cooked and crumbled
- ¼ cup sunflower kernels
- 1 bunch of green onion, sliced
- 3 tablespoons seasoned rice vinegar
- 3 tablespoons canola oil
- 1/2 cup dried cranberries

Directions:

1. Combine the green onion, cranberries, and broccoli in a bowl.

2. Whisk the vinegar, and oil in another bowl. Blend well.
3. Now drizzle over the broccoli mix.
4. Coat well by tossing.
5. Sprinkle bacon and sunflower kernels before serving.

Nutrition: Calories 121|Fat 7g |Protein 3g

Tenderloin Grilled Salad

Preparation Time: 10 minutes |Cooking Time: 20 minutes |Servings: 5

Ingredients:

- 1 lb. pork tenderloin
- 10 cups mixed salad greens
- 2 oranges, seedless, cut into bite-sized pieces
- 1 tablespoon orange zest, grated
- 2 tablespoons of cider vinegar
- 2 tablespoons olive oil
- 2 teaspoons Dijon mustard
- 1/2 cup juice of an orange
- 2 teaspoons honey
- 1/2 teaspoon ground pepper

Directions:

1. Bring together all the dressing ingredients in a bowl.
2. Grill each side of the pork covered over medium heat for 9 minutes.
3. Slice after 5 minutes.
4. Slice the tenderloin thinly.
5. Keep the greens on your serving plate.
6. Top with the pork and oranges.
7. Sprinkle nuts (optional).

Nutrition: Calories 211|Fat 9g|Protein 20g

Barley Veggie Salad *

Preparation Time: 10 minutes |Cooking Time: 20 minutes |Servings: 1

Ingredients:

- 1 tomato, seeded and chopped
- 2 tablespoons parsley, minced
- 1 yellow pepper, chopped
- 1 tablespoon basil, minced
- ¼ cup almonds, toasted
- 1-1/4 cups vegetable broth
- 1 cup barley
- 1 tablespoon lemon juice
- 2 tablespoons of white wine vinegar
- 3 tablespoons olive oil
- ¼ teaspoon pepper
- 1/2 teaspoon salt
- 1 cup of water

Directions:

1. Boil the broth, barley, and water in a saucepan.
2. Reduce heat. Cover and let it simmer for 10 minutes.
3. Take out from the heat.
4. In the meantime, bring together the parsley, yellow pepper, and tomato in a bowl.
5. Stir the barley in.
6. Whisk the vinegar, oil, basil, lemon juice, water, pepper and salt in a bowl.
7. Pour this over your barley mix. Toss to coat well.
8. Stir the almonds in before serving.

Nutrition: Calories 211|Fat 10g|Protein 6g

Warm Portobello Salad

Preparation Time: 20 minutes |Cooking Time: 9 minutes |Servings: 4

Ingredients:

- 6 cup mixed salad greens
- 1 cup Portobello mushrooms, sliced
- 1 green onion, sliced
- Walnut or Warm Bacon Vinaigrette (chapter 16)
- 1 tbsp. olive oil
- 1/8 tsp ground black pepper

Directions:

1. Heat oil in a nonstick skillet over med-high heat. Add mushrooms and cook, stirring occasionally, 10 minutes, or until they are tender. Stir in onions and reduce heat to low.
2. Place salad greens on serving plates, top with mushrooms and sprinkle with

pepper. Drizzle lightly with your choice of vinaigrette.

Nutrition: Calories 81|Protein 4g |Fat 4g

Layered Salad

Preparation Time: 9 minutes |Cooking Time: 15 minutes |Servings: 2

Ingredients:

- 6 slices bacon, chopped and cooked crisp
- 2 tomatoes, diced
- 2 stalks celery, sliced
- 1 head romaine lettuce, diced
- 1 red bell pepper, diced
- 1 cup frozen peas, thawed
- 1 cup sharp cheddar cheese, grated
- 1/4 cup red onion, diced fine
- What you'll need from the store cupboard
- 1 cup fat-free ranch dressing

Directions:

1. Use a 9x13- inch glass baking dish and layer half the lettuce, pepper, celery, tomatoes, peas, onion, cheese, bacon, and dressing.
2. Repeat. Serve or cover and chill until ready to serve.

Nutrition: Calories 130 |Protein 6g |Fat 6g

Baked "Potato" Salad

Preparation Time: 6 minutes |Cooking Time: 15 minutes |Servings: 6

Ingredients:

- 2 lb. cauliflower, separated into small florets
- 6-8 slices bacon, chopped and fried crisp
- 6 boiled eggs, cooled, peeled, and chopped
- 1 cup sharp cheddar cheese, grated
- ½ cup green onion, sliced
- 1 cup reduced-fat mayonnaise
- 2 tsp yellow mustard
- 1 ½ tsp onion powder, divided
- Salt and fresh-ground black pepper to taste

Directions:

1. Place cauliflower in a vegetable steamer, or a pot with a steamer insert, and steam 5-6 minutes.
2. Drain the cauliflower and set aside.
3. In a small bowl, whisk together mayonnaise, mustard, 1 teaspoon onion powder, salt, and pepper.
4. Pat cauliflower dry with paper towels and place in a large mixing bowl. Add eggs, salt, pepper, remaining ½ teaspoon onion powder, then dressing. Mix gently to combine Ingredients together.
5. Fold in the bacon, cheese, and green onion. Serve warm or cover and chill before serving.

Nutrition: Calories 247|Protein 17g |Fat 17g

Caprese Salad *

Preparation Time: 6 minutes |Cooking Time: 15 minutes |Servings: 1

Ingredients:

- 3 medium tomatoes, cut into 8 slices
- 2 (1-oz.) slices mozzarella cheese, cut into strips
- ¼ cup fresh basil, sliced thin
- 2 tsp extra-virgin olive oil
- 1/8 tsp salt
- Pinch black pepper

Directions:

1. Place tomatoes and cheese on serving plates. Sprinkle with salt and pepper. Drizzle oil over and top with basil. Serve.

Nutrition: Calories 77 |Protein 5g|Fat 5g

Chopped Veggie Salad

Preparation Time: 4 minutes |Cooking Time: 15 minutes |Servings: 4

Ingredients:

- 1 cucumber, chopped
- 1-pint cherry tomatoes, cut in half
- 3 radishes, chopped
- 1 yellow bell pepper chopped
- ½ cup fresh parsley, chopped

- What you'll need from store cupboard:
- 3 tbsp. lemon juice
- 1 tbsp. olive oil
- Salt to taste

Directions:

1. Place all Ingredients in a large bowl and toss to combine. Serve immediately or cover and chill until ready to serve.

Nutrition: Calories 70 |Protein 2g |Fat 4g

Tofu Salad Sandwiches

Preparation Time: 9 minutes
Cooking Time: 16 minutes
Serving: 4
Ingredients:

- 1 pkg. silken firm tofu, pressed
- 4 lettuce leaves
- 2 green onions, diced
- ¼ cup celery, diced
- 8 slices bread, (chapter 14)
- ¼ cup lite mayonnaise
- 2 tbsp. sweet pickle relish
- 1 tbsp. Dijon mustard
- ¼ tsp turmeric
- ¼ tsp salt
- 1/8 tsp cayenne pepper

Directions:

1. Press tofu between layers of paper towels for 15 minutes to remove excess moisture. Cut into small cubes.
2. In a medium bowl, stir together remaining Ingredients. Fold in tofu. Spread over 4 slices of bread. Top with a lettuce leaf and another slice of bread. Serve.

Nutrition: Calories 378 |Protein 24g |Fat 20g

Grilled Chicken salad with Avocado *

Preparation Time: 20 minutes |Cooking Time: 15 minutes |Servings: 6
Ingredients:

- 1 Chicken breasts (145g)
- 1/2 Greek yogurt
- 2tbsp lemon juice
- 1tbsp fresh thyme
- 12 cm cucumber, deseeded and sliced
- 1tbsp natural yogurt
- 90 g mooli or radish, thinly sliced
- 80 g beans sprouts
- 1 punnet of cress
- ½ avocado
- 2 onions
- 1tbsp rice wine vinegar
- 1bsp chopped coriander
- 1tbsp sesame oil
- 1 punnet of cress
- 1tbsp chopped coriander
- 1tbsp toasted sesame seeds

Direction:

1. Put the chicken breasts between two sheets of cling film and beat with a rolling pin until 1cm thick. Stir together the yogurt, lemon and thyme and season with pepper.
2. Put the chicken and marinade in a bowl and leave for 15 mins.
3. Meanwhile, put the mooli, cucumber, onions, bean sprouts and cress in a large salad bowl and toss.
4. Add the avocado, vinegar, oil, coriander and yogurt to a blender and blitz until smooth. Cook the chicken on a BBQ, in a chargrill pan or under the grill for approx. 8 mins, turning once.
5. Drizzle the dressing over the salad, scatter over the sesame seeds, add the sliced chicken on top and serve.

Nutrition:349 Calories | 38g Protein | 8g Carb

Lobster Roll Salad with Bacon Vinaigrette

Preparation Time: 20 minutes |Cooking Time: 15 minutes |Servings: 6
Ingredients:

- 6 slices bacon
- 2 whole grain ciabatta rolls, halved horizontally
- 3 medium tomatoes, cut into wedges
- 2 (8 oz.) spiny lobster tails, fresh or frozen (thawed)
- 2 cups fresh baby spinach
- 2 cups romaine lettuce, torn
- 1 cup seeded cucumber, diced

- 1 cup red sweet peppers, diced
- 2 tablespoons shallot, diced fine
- 2 tablespoons fresh chives, diced fine
- What you'll need from the store cupboard
- 2 cloves garlic, diced fine
- 3 tbsp. white wine vinegar
- 3 tbsp. olive oil, divided

Directions:

1. Heat a grill to medium heat, or medium heat charcoals.
2. Rinse lobster and pat dry. Butterfly lobster tails. Place on the grill, cover and cook 25 – 30 minutes, or until meat is opaque.
3. Remove lobster and let cool.
4. In a small bowl, whisk together 2 tablespoons olive oil and garlic. Brush the cut sides of the rolls with oil mixture. Place on grill, cut side down, and cook until crisp, about 2 minutes. Transfer to cutting board.
5. While lobster is cooking, chop bacon and cook in a medium skillet until crisp. Transfer to paper towels. Reserve 1 tablespoon bacon grease.
6. To make the vinaigrette: combine reserved bacon grease, vinegar, shallot, remaining 1 tablespoons oil and chives in a glass jar with an air-tight lid. Screw on the lid and shake to combine.
7. Remove the lobster from the shells and cut into 1 ½-inch pieces. Cut rolls into 1-inch cubes.
8. To assemble salad: in a large bowl, combine spinach, romaine, tomatoes, cucumber, peppers, lobster, and bread cubes. Toss to combine. Transfer to serving platter and drizzle with vinaigrette. Sprinkle bacon over top and serve.

Nutrition: |Calories 255 |Protein 20g|Fat 11g

Pomegranate & Brussels Sprouts Salad

Preparation Time: 8 minutes |Cooking Time: 12 minutes |Servings: 6

Ingredients:

- 3 slices bacon, cooked crisp & crumbled
- 3 cup Brussels sprouts, shredded
- 3 cup kale, shredded
- 1 ½ cup pomegranate seeds
- ½ cup almonds, toasted & chopped
- ¼ cup reduced fat parmesan cheese, grated
- Citrus Vinaigrette, (chapter 16)

Directions:

1. Combine all Ingredients in a large bowl.
2. Drizzle vinaigrette over salad and toss to coat well. Serve garnished with more cheese if desired.

Nutrition: Calories 256 |Protein 9g |Fat 18g

Strawberry & Avocado Salad

Preparation Time: 6 minutes |Cooking Time: 9 minutes |Servings: 4

Ingredients:

- 6 oz. baby spinach
- 2 avocados, chopped
- 1 cup strawberries, sliced
- ¼ cup feta cheese, crumbled
- Creamy Poppy Seed Dressing (chapter 16)
- ¼ cup almonds, sliced

Directions:

1. Add spinach, berries, avocado, nuts and cheese to a large bowl and toss to combine.
2. Pour ½ recipe of Creamy Poppy Seed Dressing over salad and toss to coat. Add more dressing if desired. Serve.

Nutrition: Calories 253 |Protein 4g |Fat 19g

Shrimp & Avocado Salad

Preparation Time: 11 minutes |Cooking Time: 5 minutes |Servings: 4

Ingredients:

- ½ lb. raw shrimp, peeled and deveined
- 3 cups romaine lettuce, chopped
- 1 cup Napa cabbage, chopped
- 1 avocado, pit removed and sliced

- ¼ cup red cabbage, chopped
- 1/4 cucumber, julienned
- 2 tbsp. green onions, diced fine
- 2 tbsp. fresh cilantro, diced
- 1 tsp fresh ginger, diced fine
- 2 tbsp. coconut oil
- 1 tbsp. sesame seeds
- 1 tsp Chinese five spice
- Fat-free Ranch dressing

Directions:

1. Toast sesame seeds in a medium skillet over medium heat. Shake the skillet to prevent them from burning. Cook until they start to brown, about 2 minutes. Set aside.
2. Add the coconut oil to the skillet. Pat the shrimp dry and sprinkle with the five spice. Add to hot oil. Cook 2 minutes per side, or until they turn pink. Set aside.
3. Arrange lettuce and cabbage on a serving platter. Top with green onions, cucumber, and cilantro. Add shrimp and avocado.
4. Drizzle with desired amount of dressing and sprinkle sesame seeds over top. Serve.

Nutrition: Calories 306 |Protein 15g |Fat 19g

Kale Salad with Avocado Dressing

Preparation Time: 10 minutes |Cooking Time: 0 minutes |Servings: 6

Ingredient

- 6 cups chopped kale
- 1 cup finely chopped red bell pepper
- 1 bunch scallions, white and green parts, finely chopped
- 1 avocado, pitted and peeled
- ½ cup raw cashews
- 3 garlic cloves, peeled
- Juice of ½ lemon
- ¼ cup extra-virgin olive oil
- Salt
- Freshly ground black pepper

Direction

1. In a large bowl, toss together the kale, red bell pepper, and scallions.
2. In a high-speed blender or food processor, combine the avocado, cashews, garlic, lemon juice, and olive oil, and process until smooth. Add up to ½ cup of water as needed to create a pourable dressing. Season with salt and pepper. Pour the dressing over the kale, mix well, and serve.

Nutrition: Calories: 232 |Fat: 18g|Protein: 5g

Cucumber Salad *

Preparation Time: 10 minutes |Cooking Time: 0 minutes |Servings: 1

Ingredient

- 2 medium cucumbers, peeled and chopped
- 1 cup cherry tomatoes, halved
- ½ red onion, thinly sliced
- 2 tablespoons red wine vinegar
- 2 tablespoons extra-virgin olive oil
- ¼ teaspoon dried oregano
- ¼ teaspoon salt, plus more as needed
- Freshly ground black pepper

Direction

1. In a medium bowl, combine the cucumbers, tomatoes, and red onion.
2. In a small bowl, whisk the vinegar, olive oil, oregano, salt, and some pepper. Pour the vinaigrette over the vegetables and toss to coat.
3. Taste and season with more salt and pepper, if desired. Serve immediately or refrigerate in an airtight container for 2 to 3 days.

Nutrition: Calories: 98 |Fat: 7g|Protein: 2g

Roasted Beet Salad

Preparation Time: 20 minutes |Cooking Time: 70 minutes |Servings: 4

Ingredient

- 6 medium beets, scrubbed, tops removed
- ¼ cup balsamic vinegar
- ¼ cup extra-virgin olive oil
- 1 teaspoon Dijon mustard
- Salt

- Freshly ground black pepper
- ¼ cup walnuts
- 6 ounces baby arugula
- 2 ounces feta cheese, crumbled

Direction

1. Preheat the oven to 400°F.
2. Wrap each beet tightly in aluminum foil and arrange on a baking sheet. Roast for 45 to 60 minutes, depending on their size, until tender when pierced with a knife. Remove from the oven, carefully unwrap each beet, and let cool for 10 minutes.
3. Reduce the oven temperature to 350°F.
4. Meanwhile, in a medium bowl, whisk the vinegar, olive oil, and mustard. Season with salt and pepper.
5. On the same baking sheet, spread the walnuts in a single layer. Toast for 5 to 7 minutes, until lightly browned.
6. Using a small knife, peel and slice the beets, and place them in another medium bowl. Add half the vinaigrette and toss to coat.
7. Add the arugula to the remaining vinaigrette and toss to coat.
8. On a serving platter, arrange the arugula and top with the beets. Sprinkle the toasted walnuts and feta cheese over the top and serve.

Nutrition: Calories: 267|Fat: 20g|Protein: 7g

Black Bean and Corn Salad

Preparation Time: 20 minutes |Cooking Time: 0 minutes |Servings: 5

Ingredient

- 2 (15-ounce) cans reduced-sodium black beans, rinsed and drained
- 1 red bell pepper, chopped
- 1 cucumber, chopped
- 1 avocado, peeled, seeded, and chopped
- 1 cup fresh, frozen and thawed, or canned and drained corn
- ½ cup minced red onion
- 1 jalapeño pepper, seeded and minced
- ¼ cup chopped fresh cilantro
- ¼ cup extra-virgin olive oil
- 3 tablespoons freshly squeezed lime juice
- 1 teaspoon honey
- 1 teaspoon ground cumin
- Salt
- Freshly ground black pepper

Direction

1. In a large bowl, stir together the black beans, red bell pepper, cucumber, avocado, corn, red onion, jalapeño, and cilantro.
2. In a small bowl, whisk the olive oil, lime juice, honey, and cumin. Season with salt and pepper. Pour the dressing over the salad, mix well to coat, and serve.

Nutrition: Calories: 313|Fat: 19g|Protein: 9g

Perfect Quinoa Salad

Preparation Time: 16 minutes |Cooking Time: 14 minutes |Servings: 2

Ingredient

- 1 cup quinoa, rinsed
- 1½ cups water
- 1 cucumber, finely chopped
- 1 red bell pepper, finely chopped
- ½ red onion, chopped
- ½ cup fresh flat-leaf parsley
- ¼ cup extra-virgin olive oil
- Juice of 2 lemons
- 3 garlic cloves, minced
- ½ teaspoon salt
- ¼ teaspoon freshly ground black pepper

Direction

1. In a small saucepan over high heat, combine the quinoa and water. Bring to a boil, reduce the heat to low, cover the pot, and cook for 10 to 15 minutes, until the water is absorbed. Turn off the heat, fluff with a fork, re-cover, and let rest for about 5 minutes.
2. Meanwhile, in a large bowl, toss the cucumber, red bell pepper, red onion, and parsley.

3. In a small bowl, whisk the olive oil, lemon juice, garlic, salt, and pepper. Pour the dressing over the vegetables and toss well to coat. Fold in the quinoa and serve.

Nutrition: Calories: 200 |Fat: 10g |Protein: 5g

Tropical Fruit Salad with Coconut Milk *

Preparation Time: 10 minutes |Cooking Time: 0 minutes |Servings: 1

Ingredient

- 2 cups pineapple chunks
- 2 kiwi fruits, peeled and sliced
- 1 mango, peeled and chopped
- ¼ cup canned light coconut milk
- 1 tablespoon freshly squeezed lime juice
- 1 tablespoon honey

Direction

1. In a medium bowl, toss together the pineapple, kiwi, and mango.
2. In a small bowl, combine the coconut milk, lime juice, and honey, stirring until the honey dissolves. Pour the mixture over the fruits and toss to coat. Serve immediately or refrigerate in an airtight container for up to 3 days.

Nutrition: Calories: 70 Total fat: 1g Protein: 1g

Cucumber, Tomato, and Avocado Salad

Preparation Time: 10 minutes |Cooking Time: 0 minutes |Servings: 2

Ingredient

- 1 cup cherry tomatoes, halved
- 1 large cucumber, chopped
- 1 small red onion, thinly sliced
- 1 avocado, diced
- 2 tablespoons chopped fresh dill
- 2 tablespoons extra-virgin olive oil
- Juice of 1 lemon
- ¼ teaspoon salt
- ¼ teaspoon freshly ground black pepper

Direction

1. In a large mixing bowl, combine the tomatoes, cucumber, onion, avocado, and dill.
2. In a small bowl, combine the oil, lemon juice, salt, and pepper, and mix well.
3. Drizzle the dressing over the vegetables and toss to combine. Serve.

Nutrition: Calories: 151|Fat: 12g|Protein: 2g

Cabbage Slaw Salad

Preparation Time: 20 minutes |Cooking Time: 0 minutes |Servings: 6

Ingredient

- 2 cups finely chopped green cabbage
- 2 cups finely chopped red cabbage
- 2 cups grated carrots
- 3 scallions, both white and green parts, sliced
- 2 tablespoons extra-virgin olive oil
- 2 tablespoons rice vinegar
- 1 teaspoon honey
- 1 garlic clove, minced
- ¼ teaspoon salt

Direction

1. In a large bowl, toss together the green and red cabbage, carrots, and scallions.
2. In a small bowl, whisk together the oil, vinegar, honey, garlic, and salt.
3. Pour the dressing over the veggies and mix to thoroughly combine.
4. Serve immediately or cover and chill for several hours before serving.

Nutrition: Calories: 80| Fat: 5g|Protein: 1g

Green Salad with Blackberries, Goat Cheese, and Sweet Potatoes

Preparation Time: 20 minutes |Cooking Time: 15 minutes |Servings: 4

Ingredient

For the vinaigrette

- 1-pint blackberries
- 2 tablespoons red wine vinegar
- 1 tablespoon honey
- 3 tablespoons extra-virgin olive oil
- ¼ teaspoon salt
- Freshly ground black pepper

For the salad

- 1 sweet potato, cubed
- 1 teaspoon extra-virgin olive oil
- 8 cups salad greens (baby spinach, spicy greens, romaine)
- ½ red onion, sliced
- ¼ cup crumbled goat cheese

Direction

1. To make the vinaigrette
2. In a blender jar, combine the blackberries, vinegar, honey, oil, salt, and pepper, and process until smooth. Set aside.
3. To make the salad
4. Preheat the oven to 425°F. Line a baking sheet with parchment paper.
5. In a medium mixing bowl, toss the sweet potato with the olive oil.
6. Transfer to the prepared baking sheet and roast for 20 minutes, stirring once halfway through, until tender. Remove and cool for a few minutes.
7. In a large bowl, toss the greens with the red onion and cooled sweet potato, and drizzle with the vinaigrette. Serve topped with 1 tablespoon of goat cheese per serving.

Nutrition: Calories: 196| Fat: 12g|Protein: 3g

Three Bean and Basil Salad

Preparation Time: 20 minutes |Cooking Time: 0 minutes |Servings: 4

Ingredient

- 1 (15-ounce) can low-sodium chickpeas, drained and rinsed
- 1 (15-ounce) can low-sodium kidney beans, drained and rinsed
- 1 (15-ounce) can low-sodium white beans, drained and rinsed
- 1 red bell pepper, seeded and finely chopped
- ¼ cup chopped scallions, both white and green parts
- ¼ cup finely chopped fresh basil
- 3 garlic cloves, minced
- 2 tablespoons extra-virgin olive oil
- 1 tablespoon red wine vinegar
- 1 teaspoon Dijon mustard
- ¼ teaspoon freshly ground black pepper

Direction

1. In a large mixing bowl, combine the chickpeas, kidney beans, white beans, bell pepper, scallions, basil, and garlic. Toss gently to combine.
2. In a small bowl, combine the olive oil, vinegar, mustard, and pepper. Toss with the salad.
3. Cover and refrigerate for an hour before serving, to allow the flavors to mix.
4. Substitution tip: Feel free to substitute home-cooked beans in place of canned, using about 1½ cups per variety.

Nutrition: Calories: 193|Fat: 5g |Protein: 10g

Rainbow Black Bean Salad

Preparation Time: 16 minutes |Cooking Time: 16 minutes |Servings: 5

Ingredient

- 1 (15-ounce) can low-sodium black beans, drained and rinsed
- 1 avocado, diced
- 1 cup cherry tomatoes, halved
- 1 cup chopped baby spinach
- ½ cup finely chopped red bell pepper
- ¼ cup finely chopped jicama
- ½ cup chopped scallions, both white and green parts
- ¼ cup chopped fresh cilantro
- 2 tablespoons freshly squeezed lime juice
- 1 tablespoon extra-virgin olive oil
- 2 garlic cloves, minced
- 1 teaspoon honey
- ¼ teaspoon salt
- ¼ teaspoon freshly ground black pepper

Direction

1. In a large bowl, combine the black beans, avocado, tomatoes, spinach, bell pepper, jicama, scallions, and cilantro.
2. In a small bowl, mix the lime juice, oil, garlic, honey, salt, and pepper. Add to the salad and toss.
3. Chill for 1 hour before serving.

Nutrition: Calories: 169 | Fat: 7g |Protein: 6g

Warm Barley and Squash Salad with Balsamic Vinaigrette

Preparation Time: 20 minutes |Cooking Time: 41 minutes |Servings: 4

Ingredient

- 1 small butternut squash
- 3 teaspoons plus 2 tablespoons extra-virgin olive oil, divided
- 2 cups broccoli florets
- 1 cup pearl barley
- 1 cup toasted chopped walnuts
- 2 cups baby kale
- ½ red onion, sliced
- 2 tablespoons balsamic vinegar
- 2 garlic cloves, minced
- ½ teaspoon salt
- ¼ teaspoon freshly ground black pepper

Direction

1. Preheat the oven to 400°F. Line a baking sheet with parchment paper.
2. Peel and seed the squash and cut it into dice. In a large bowl, toss the squash with 2 teaspoons of olive oil. Transfer to the prepared baking sheet and roast for 20 minutes.
3. While the squash is roasting, toss the broccoli in the same bowl with 1 teaspoon of olive oil. After 20 minutes, flip the squash and push it to one side of the baking sheet.
4. Add the broccoli to the other side and continue to roast for 20 more minutes until tender.
5. While the veggies are roasting, in a medium pot, cover the barley with several inches of water. Bring to a boil, then reduce the heat, cover, and simmer for 30 minutes until tender. Drain and rinse.
6. Transfer the barley to a large bowl, and toss with the cooked squash and broccoli, walnuts, kale, and onion.
7. In a small bowl, mix the remaining 2 tablespoons of olive oil, balsamic vinegar, garlic, salt, and pepper. Toss the salad with the dressing and serve.

Nutrition: Calories: 274 Fat: 15g|Protein: 6g

Winter Chicken and Citrus Salad

Preparation Time: 20 minutes |Cooking Time: 0 minutes |Servings: 4

Ingredient

- 4 cups baby spinach
- 2 tablespoons extra-virgin olive oil
- 1 tablespoon freshly squeezed lemon juice
- 1/8 teaspoon salt
- Freshly ground black pepper
- 2 cups chopped cooked chicken
- 2 mandarin oranges, peeled and sectioned
- ½ peeled grapefruit, sectioned
- ¼ cup sliced almonds

Direction

1. In a large mixing bowl, toss the spinach with the olive oil, lemon juice, salt, and pepper.
2. Add the chicken, oranges, grapefruit, and almonds to the bowl. Toss gently.
3. Arrange on 4 plates and serve.

Nutrition: Calories: 249| Fat: 12g|Protein: 24g

Blueberry and Chicken Salad on a Bed of Greens

Preparation Time: 20 minutes |Cooking Time: 0 minutes |Servings: 4

Ingredient

- 2 cups chopped cooked chicken
- 1 cup fresh blueberries
- ¼ cup finely chopped almonds
- 1 celery stalk, finely chopped
- ¼ cup finely chopped red onion
- 1 tablespoon chopped fresh basil
- 1 tablespoon chopped fresh cilantro
- ½ cup plain, nonfat Greek yogurt or vegan mayonnaise
- ¼ teaspoon salt
- ¼ teaspoon freshly ground black pepper

- 8 cups salad greens (baby spinach, spicy greens, romaine)

Direction

1. In a large mixing bowl, combine the chicken, blueberries, almonds, celery, onion, basil, and cilantro. Toss gently to mix.
2. In a small bowl, combine the yogurt, salt, and pepper. Add to the chicken salad and stir to combine.
3. Arrange 2 cups of salad greens on each of 4 plates and divide the chicken salad among the plates to serve.

Nutrition: Calories: 207 | Fat: 6g|Protein: 28g

Salmon, Quinoa, and Avocado Salad *

Preparation Time: 20 minutes |Cooking Time: 15 minutes |Servings: 1

Ingredient

- ½ cup quinoa
- 1 cup water
- 4 (4-ounce) salmon fillets
- 1-pound asparagus, trimmed
- 1 teaspoon extra-virgin olive oil, plus 2 tablespoons
- ½ teaspoon salt, divided
- ½ teaspoon freshly ground black pepper, divided
- ¼ teaspoon red pepper flakes
- 1 avocado, chopped
- ¼ cup chopped scallions, both white and green parts
- ¼ cup chopped fresh cilantro
- 1 tablespoon minced fresh oregano
- Juice of 1 lime

Direction

1. In a small pot, combine the quinoa and water, and bring to a boil over medium-high heat. Cover, reduce the heat, and simmer for 15 minutes.
2. Preheat the oven to 425°F. Line a large baking sheet with parchment paper.
3. Arrange the salmon on one side of the prepared baking sheet. Toss the asparagus with 1 teaspoon of olive oil and arrange on the other side of the baking sheet. Season the salmon and asparagus with ¼ teaspoon of salt, ¼ teaspoon of pepper, and the red pepper flakes. Roast for 12 minutes until browned and cooked through.
4. While the fish and asparagus are cooking, in a large mixing bowl, gently toss the cooked quinoa, avocado, scallions, cilantro, and oregano.
5. Add the remaining 2 tablespoons of olive oil and the lime juice, and season with the remaining ¼ teaspoon of salt and ¼ teaspoon of pepper.
6. Break the salmon into pieces, removing the skin and any bones, and chop the asparagus into bite-sized pieces. Fold into the quinoa and serve warm or at room temperature.

Nutrition: Calories: 397| Fat: 22g|Protein: 29g

Sides

Onion Rings

Preparation Time: 10 minutes |Cooking Time: 32 minutes |Servings: 4

Ingredients:

- 1 large white onion, peeled
- 2/3 cup pork rinds

- 3 tablespoons almond flour
- 1/2 teaspoon garlic powder
- 1/2 teaspoon paprika
- 1/4 teaspoon sea salt
- 3 tablespoons coconut flour
- 2 eggs, pastured

Direction:

1. Switch on the air fryer, insert fryer basket, grease it with olive oil, then shut with its lid, set the fryer at 400 degrees F and preheat for 10 minutes.
2. Meanwhile, slice the peeled onion into ½ inch thick rings.
3. Take a shallow dish, add almond flour and stir in garlic powder, paprika, and pork rinds; take another shallow dish, add coconut flour and salt and stir until mixed.
4. Crack eggs in a bowl and then whisk until combined.
5. Working on one onion ring at a time, first coat onion ring in coconut flour mixture, then it in egg, and coat with pork rind mixture by scooping over the onion until evenly coated.
6. Open the fryer, place coated onion rings in it in a single layer, spray oil over onion rings, close with its lid and cook for 16 minutes until nicely golden and thoroughly cooked, flipping the onion rings halfway through the frying.
7. When air fryer beeps, open its lid, transfer onion rings onto a serving plate and cook the remaining onion rings in the same manner.
8. Serve straight away.

Nutrition: Calories: 135 |Fat: 7g |Protein: 8g

Cauliflower Fritters

Preparation Time: 10 minutes |Cooking Time: 14 minutes |Servings: 2

Ingredients:

- 5 cups chopped cauliflower florets
- 1/2 cup almond flour
- 1/2 teaspoon baking powder
- ½ teaspoon ground black pepper
- ½ teaspoon salt
- 2 eggs, pastured

Direction:

1. Add chopped cauliflower in a blender or food processor, pulse until minced and then tip the mixture in a bowl.
2. Add remaining ingredients, stir well and then shape the mixture into 1/3-inch patties, an ice cream scoop of mixture per patty.
3. Switch on the air fryer, insert fryer basket, grease it with olive oil, then shut with its lid, set the fryer at 390 degrees F and preheat for 5 minutes.
4. Then open the fryer, add cauliflower patties in it in a single layer, spray oil over patties, close with its lid and cook for 14 minutes at the 375 degrees F until nicely golden and cooked, flipping the patties halfway through the frying.
5. Serve straight away with the dip.

Nutrition: Calories: 272|Fat: 0.3g|Protein: 11g

Zucchini Fritters *

Preparation Time: 20 minutes |Cooking Time: 12 minutes |Servings: 1

Ingredients:

- 2 medium zucchinis, ends trimmed
- 3 tablespoons almond flour
- 1 tablespoon salt
- 1 teaspoon garlic powder
- ¼ teaspoon paprika
- ¼ teaspoon ground black pepper
- ¼ teaspoon onion powder
- 1 egg, pastured

Direction:

1. Wash and pat dry the zucchini, then cut its ends and grate the zucchini.
2. Place grated zucchini in a colander, sprinkle with salt and let it rest for 10 minutes.
3. Then wrap zucchini in a kitchen cloth and squeeze moisture from it as much as possible and place dried zucchini in another bowl.

4. Add remaining ingredients into the zucchini and then stir until mixed.
5. Take fryer basket, line it with parchment paper, grease it with oil and drop zucchini mixture on it by a spoonful, about 1-inch apart and then spray well with oil.
6. Switch on the air fryer, insert fryer basket, then shut with its lid, set the fryer at 360 degrees F and cook the fritter for 12 minutes until nicely golden and cooked, flipping the fritters halfway through the frying.
7. Serve straight away.

Nutrition Calories: 57 |Fat: 1g |Protein: 3g

Air-Fried Kale Chips *

Preparation Time: 5 minutes |Cooking Time: 7 minutes |Servings: 1

Ingredients:

- 1 large bunch of kale
- ¾ teaspoon red chili powder
- 1 teaspoon salt
- ¾ teaspoon ground black pepper

Direction:

1. Remove the hard spines form the kale leaves, then cut kale into small pieces and place them in a fryer basket.
2. Spray oil over kale, then sprinkle with salt, chili powder and black pepper and toss until well mixed.
3. Switch on the air fryer, insert fryer basket, then shut with its lid, set the fryer at 375 degrees F and cook for 7 minutes until kale is crispy, shaking halfway through the frying.
4. When air fryer beeps, open its lid, transfer kale chips onto a serving plate and serve.

Nutrition: Calories: 66|Fat: 4g |Protein: 2.5g

Radish Chips *

Preparation Time: 5 minutes |Cooking Time: 20 minutes |Servings: 1

Ingredients:

- 8 ounces radish slices
- ½ teaspoon garlic powder
- 1 teaspoon salt
- ½ teaspoon onion powder
- ½ teaspoon ground black pepper

Direction:

1. Wash the radish slices, pat them dry, place them in a fryer basket, and then spray oil on them until well coated.
2. Sprinkle salt, garlic powder, onion powder, and black pepper over radish slices and then toss until well coated.
3. Switch on the air fryer, insert fryer basket, then shut with its lid, set the fryer at 370 degrees F and cook for 10 minutes, stirring the slices halfway through.
4. Then spray oil on radish slices, shake the basket and continue frying for 10 minutes, stirring the chips halfway through.
5. Serve straight away.

Nutrition: Calories: 21 |Fat: 1.8g |Protein: 0.2 g

Zucchini Fries

Preparation Time: 10 minutes |Cooking Time: 20 minutes |Servings: 4

Ingredients:

- 2 medium zucchinis
- ½ cup almond flour
- 1/8 teaspoon ground black pepper
- ½ teaspoon garlic powder
- 1/8 teaspoon salt
- 1 teaspoon Italian seasoning
- ½ cup grated parmesan cheese, reduced fat
- 1 egg, pastured, beaten

Direction:

1. Switch on the air fryer, insert fryer basket, grease it with olive oil, then shut with its lid, set the fryer at 400 degrees F and preheat for 10 minutes.
2. Meanwhile, cut each zucchini in half and then cut each zucchini half into 4-inch-long pieces, each about ½-inch thick. Place flour in a shallow dish, add remaining ingredients except for the egg and stir until mixed.

3. Crack the egg in a bowl and then whisk until blended.
4. Working on one zucchini piece at a time, first dip it in the egg, then coat it in the almond flour mixture and place it on a wire rack.
5. Open the fryer, add zucchini pieces in it in a single layer, spray oil over zucchini, close with its lid and cook for 10 minutes until nicely golden and crispy, shaking halfway through the frying.
6. Cook remaining zucchini pieces in the same manner and serve.

Nutrition: Calories: 147 |Fat: 10 g |Protein: 9 g

Avocado Fries *

Preparation Time: 10 minutes |Cooking Time: 20 minutes |Servings: 1

Ingredients:

- 1 medium avocado, pitted
- 1 egg
- 1/2 cup almond flour
- ¼ teaspoon salt
- ¼ teaspoon ground black pepper
- 1/2 teaspoon salt

Direction:

1. Switch on the air fryer, insert fryer basket, grease it with olive oil, then shut with its lid, set the fryer at 400 degrees F and preheat for 10 minutes.
2. Meanwhile, cut the avocado in half and then cut each half into wedges, each about ½-inch thick.
3. Place flour in a shallow dish, add salt and black pepper and stir until mixed.
4. Crack the egg in a bowl and then whisk until blended.
5. Working on one avocado piece at a time, first dip it in the egg, then coat it in the almond flour mixture and place it on a wire rack.
6. Open the fryer, add avocado pieces in it in a single layer, spray oil over avocado, close with its lid and cook for 10 minutes until nicely golden and crispy, shaking halfway through the frying.
7. When air fryer beeps, open its lid, transfer avocado fries onto a serving plate and serve.

Nutrition: Calories: 251|Fat: 17 g |Protein: 6 g

Roasted Peanut Butter Squash *

Preparation Time: 5 minutes |Cooking Time: 22 minutes |Servings: 1

Ingredients:

- 1 butternut squash, peeled
- 1 teaspoon cinnamon
- 1 tablespoon olive oil

Direction:

1. Switch on the air fryer, insert fryer basket, grease it with olive oil, then shut with its lid, set the fryer at 220 degrees F and preheat for 5 minutes.
2. Meanwhile, peel the squash400 cut it into 1-inch pieces, and then place them in a bowl.
3. Drizzle oil over squash pieces, sprinkle with cinnamon and then toss until well coated.
4. Open the fryer, add squash pieces in it, close with its lid and cook for 17 minutes until nicely golden and crispy, shaking every 5 minutes.
5. When air fryer beeps, open its lid, transfer squash onto a serving plate and serve.

Nutrition: Calories: 116 |Fat: 3 g |Protein: 1 g

Roasted Chickpeas *

Preparation Time: 35 minutes |Cooking Time: 25 minutes |Servings: 1

Ingredients:

- 15-ounce cooked chickpeas
- 1 teaspoon garlic powder
- 1 tablespoon nutritional yeast
- 1/8 teaspoon cumin
- 1 teaspoon smoked paprika
- 1/2 teaspoon salt
- 1 tablespoon olive oil

Direction:

1. Take a large baking sheet, line it with paper towels, then spread chickpeas on it, cover the peas with paper towels, and let rest for 30 minutes or until chickpeas are dried.
2. Then switch on the air fryer, insert fryer basket, grease it with olive oil, then shut with its lid, set the fryer at 355 degrees F and preheat for 5 minutes.
3. Place dried chickpeas in a bowl, add remaining ingredients and toss until well coated.
4. Open the fryer, add chickpeas in it, close with its lid and cook for 20 minutes until nicely golden and crispy, shaking the chickpeas every 5 minutes.
5. When air fryer beeps, open its lid, transfer chickpeas onto a serving bowl and serve.

Nutrition: Calories: 124|Fat: 4.4g |Protein: 4g

Aromatic Toasted Pumpkin Seeds

Preparation Time: 5 minutes |Cooking Time: 45 minutes |Servings: 4

Ingredients:

- 1 cup pumpkin seeds
- 1 teaspoon cinnamon
- 2 packets stevia
- 1 tablespoon canola oil
- ¼ teaspoon sea salt

Direction

1. Prep the oven to 300°F (150°C).
2. Combine the pumpkin seeds with cinnamon, stevia, canola oil, and salt in a bowl. Stir to mix well.
3. Pour the seeds in the single layer on a baking sheet, then arrange the sheet in the preheated oven.
4. Bake for 45 minutes or until well toasted and fragrant. Shake the sheet twice to bake the seeds evenly.
5. Serve immediately.

Nutrition: 202 calories|5.1g Carb|2.3g fiber

Bacon-Wrapped Shrimps

Preparation Time: 10 minutes |Cooking Time: 6 minutes |Servings: 10

Ingredient:

- 20 shrimps, peeled and deveined
- 7 slices bacon
- 4 leaves romaine lettuce

Direction

1. Set the oven to 205ºC.
2. Wrap each shrimp with each bacon strip, then arrange the wrapped shrimps in a single layer on a baking sheet, seam side down.
3. Broil for 6 minutes. Flip the shrimps halfway through the cooking time.
4. Take out from the oven and serve on lettuce leaves.

Nutrition: 70 calories |4.5g fat|7g protein

Cheesy Broccoli Bites *

Preparation Time: 10 minutes |Cooking Time: 25 minutes |Servings: 1

Ingredient:

- 2 tablespoons olive oil
- 2 heads broccoli, trimmed
- 1 egg
- 1/3 cup reduced-fat shredded Cheddar cheese
- 1 egg white
- ½ cup onion, chopped
- 1/3 cup breadcrumbs
- ¼ teaspoon salt
- ¼ teaspoon black pepper

Direction:

1. Ready the oven at 400ºF (205ºC). Coat a large baking sheet with olive oil.
2. Arrange a colander in a saucepan, then place the broccoli in the colander. Pour the water into the saucepan to cover the bottom. Boil, then reduce the heat to low. Close and simmer for 6 minutes. Allow cooling for 10 minutes.
3. Blend broccoli and remaining ingredients in a food processor. Let sit for 10 minutes.
4. Make the bites: Drop 1 tablespoon of the mixture on the baking sheet. Repeat with the remaining mixture.
5. Bake in the preheated oven for 25

minutes. Flip the bites halfway through the cooking time.

6. Serve immediately.

Nutrition: 100 Calories|Carb 13g | Fiber 3g

Easy Caprese Skewers

Preparation Time: 5 minutes |Cooking Time: 0 minutes |Servings: 2

Ingredient:

- 12 cherry tomatoes
- 8 (1-inch) pieces Mozzarella cheese
- 12 basil leaves
- ¼ cup Italian Vinaigrette, for serving

Direction

1. Thread the tomatoes, cheese, and bay leave alternatively through the skewers.
2. Place the skewers on a huge plate and baste with the Italian Vinaigrette. Serve immediately.

Nutrition: Calories 230|Carb 8.5g|Fiber 2g

Turkey stuffed bell peppers

Preparation Time: 30 minutes |Cooking Time: 20 minutes |Servings: 5

Ingredients:

- 5 medium green, red or yellow peppers
- 2 teaspoons olive oil
- 1-1/4 pounds extra-lean ground turkey
- 1 large onion, chopped
- 1 garlic clove, minced
- 2 teaspoons ground cumin
- 1 teaspoon Italian seasoning
- 1/2 teaspoon salt
- 1/2 teaspoon pepper
- 2 medium tomatoes, finely chopped
- 1-3/4 cups shredded cheddar
- 1-1/2 cups soft breadcrumbs
- 1/4 teaspoon paprika

Directions:

1. Preheat oven to 325°. Cut peppers lengthwise in half; remove seeds. Place in a 15x10x1-in. pan coated with cooking spray.
2. In a large skillet, heat oil over medium-high heat. Cook and crumble turkey with onion, garlic and seasonings over medium-high heat until meat is no longer pink, 6-8 minutes. Cool slightly. Stir in tomatoes, cheese and breadcrumbs.
3. Fill with turkey mixture. Sprinkle with paprika. Bake, uncovered, until filling is heated through, and peppers are tender, 20-25 minutes.

Nutrition: 321 Calories|9g Fat|18g Carb

Grilled Tofu with Sesame Seeds *

Preparation Time: 45 minutes |Cooking Time: 20 minutes |Servings: 1

Ingredient:

- 1½ tablespoons brown rice vinegar
- 1 scallion
- 1 tablespoon ginger root
- 1 tablespoon no-sugar-added applesauce
- 2 tablespoons naturally brewed soy sauce
- ¼ teaspoon dried red pepper flakes
- 2 teaspoons sesame oil, toasted
- 1 (14-ounce / 397-g) package extra-firm tofu
- 2 tablespoons fresh cilantro
- 1 teaspoon sesame seeds

Direction

1. Combine the vinegar, scallion, ginger, applesauce, soy sauce, red pepper flakes, and sesame oil in a large bowl. Stir to mix well.
2. Dunk the tofu pieces in the bowl, then refrigerate to marinate for 30 minutes.
3. Preheat a grill pan over medium-high heat.
4. Place the tofu on the grill pan with tongs, reserve the marinade, then grill for 8 minutes or until the tofu is golden brown and have deep grilled marks on both sides. Flip the tofu halfway through the cooking time. You may need to work in batches to avoid overcrowding.
5. Transfer the tofu to a large plate and sprinkle with cilantro leaves and sesame seeds. Serve with the marinade alongside.

Nutrition: 90 Calories|3g Carb|1g fiber

Kale Chips *

Preparation Time: 5 minutes |Cooking Time: 15 minutes |Servings: 15

Ingredients:

- ¼ teaspoon garlic powder
- Pinch cayenne to taste
- 1 tablespoon extra-virgin olive oil
- ½ teaspoon sea salt, or to taste
- 1 (8-ounce) bunch kale

Direction

1. Prepare oven at 180ºC. Line two baking sheets with parchment paper.
2. Toss the garlic powder, cayenne pepper, olive oil, and salt in a large bowl, then dunk the kale in the bowl.
3. Situate kale in a single layer on one of the baking sheets.
4. Arrange the sheet in the preheated oven and bake for 7 minutes. Remove the sheet from the oven and pour the kale into the single layer of the other baking sheet.
5. Move the sheet of kale back to the oven and bake for another 7 minutes.
6. Serve immediately.

Nutrition: 136 Calories|3g Carb|1.1g fiber

Simple Deviled Eggs

Preparation Time: 5 minutes |Cooking Time: 8 minutes |Servings: 6

Ingredients:

- 6 large eggs
- 1/8 teaspoon mustard powder
- 2 tablespoons light mayonnaise

Direction:

1. Sit the eggs in a saucepan, then pour in enough water to cover the egg. Bring to a boil, then boil the eggs for another 8 minutes. Turn off the heat and cover, then let sit for 15 minutes.
2. Transfer the boiled eggs to a pot of cold water and peel under the water.
3. Transfer the eggs to a large plate, then cut in half. Remove the egg yolks and place them in a bowl, then mash with a fork.
4. Add the mustard powder, mayo, salt, and pepper to the bowl of yolks, then stir to mix well.
5. Spoon the yolk mixture in the egg white on the plate. Serve immediately.

Nutrition:45 Calories|1g Carb|0.9g fiber

Sautéed Collard Greens and Cabbage

Preparation Time: 10 minutes |Cooking Time: 10 minutes |Servings: 2

Ingredients:

- 2 tablespoons extra-virgin olive oil
- 1 collard greens bunch
- ½ small green cabbage
- 6 garlic cloves
- 1 tablespoon low-sodium soy sauce

Direction:

1. Cook olive oil in a large skillet over medium-high heat.
2. Sauté the collard greens in the oil for about 2 minutes, or until the greens start to wilt.
3. Toss in the cabbage and mix well. Set to medium-low, cover, and cook for 5 to 7 minutes, stirring occasionally, or until the greens are softened.
4. Fold in the garlic and soy sauce and stir to combine. Cook for about 30 seconds more until fragrant.
5. Remove from the heat to a plate and serve.

Nutrition: 73 Calories|5.9g Carb|2.9g fiber

Roasted Delicate Squash with Thyme *

Preparation Time: 10 minutes |Cooking Time: 20 minutes |Servings: 1

Ingredients:

- 1 (1½-pound) Delicate squash
- 1 tablespoon extra-virgin olive oil
- ½ teaspoon dried thyme
- ¼ teaspoon salt
- ¼ teaspoon freshly ground black pepper

Direction:

1. Prep the oven to 400ºF (205ºC). Ready baking sheet with parchment paper and set aside.

2. Add the squash strips, olive oil, thyme, salt, and pepper in a large bowl, and toss until the squash strips are fully coated.
3. Place the squash strips on the prepared baking sheet in a single layer. Roast for about 20 minutes, flipping the strips halfway through.
4. Remove from the oven and serve on plates.

Nutrition: 78 Calories|11.8g Carb|2.1g fiber

Roasted Asparagus and Red Peppers

Preparation Time: 5 minutes |Cooking Time: 15 minutes |Servings: 4

Ingredients:

- 1-pound (454 g) asparagus
- 2 red bell peppers, seeded
- 1 small onion
- 2 tablespoons Italian dressing

Direction:

1. Ready oven to (205°C). Wrap baking sheet with parchment paper and set aside.
2. Combine the asparagus with the peppers, onion, dressing in a large bowl, and toss well.
3. Arrange the vegetables on the baking sheet and roast for about 15 minutes. Flip the vegetables with a spatula once during cooking.
4. Transfer to a large platter and serve.

Nutrition: 92 Calories|10.7g Carb|4g fiber

Tarragon Spring Peas

Preparation Time: 10 minutes |Cooking Time: 12 minutes |Servings: 5

Ingredients:

- 1 tablespoon unsalted butter
- ½ Vidalia onion
- 1 cup low-sodium vegetable broth
- 3 cups fresh shelled peas
- 1 tablespoon minced fresh tarragon

Directions:

1. Cook butter in a pan at medium heat.
2. Sauté the onion in the melted butter for about 3 minutes, stirring occasionally.
3. Pour in the vegetable broth and whisk well. Add the peas and tarragon to the skillet and stir to combine.
4. Reduce the heat to low, cover, cook for about 8 minutes more, or until the peas are tender.
5. Let the peas cool for 5 minutes and serve warm.

Nutrition: 82 Calories|12g Carb|3.8g fiber

Butter-Orange Yams *

Preparation Time: 7 minutes |Cooking Time: 45 minutes |Servings: 1

Ingredients:

- 2 medium jewel yams
- 2 tablespoons unsalted butter
- Juice of 1 large orange
- 1½ teaspoons ground cinnamon
- ¼ teaspoon ground ginger
- ¾ teaspoon ground nutmeg
- 1/8 teaspoon ground cloves

Direction:

1. Set oven at 180°C.
2. Arrange the yam dices on a rimmed baking sheet in a single layer. Set aside.
3. Add the butter, orange juice, cinnamon, ginger, nutmeg, and garlic cloves to a medium saucepan over medium-low heat. Cook for 3 to 5 minutes, stirring continuously. Spoon the sauce over the yams and toss to coat well.
4. Bake in the prepared oven for 40 minutes. Let the yams cool for 8 minutes on the baking sheet before removing and serving.

Nutrition: 129 Calories |24.7g Carb|5g fiber

Roasted Tomato Brussels Sprouts

Preparation Time: 15 minutes |Cooking Time: 20 minutes |Servings: 4

Ingredients:

- 1-pound (454 g) Brussels sprouts
- 1 tablespoon extra-virgin olive oil
- ½ cup sun-dried tomatoes
- 2 tablespoons lemon juice
- 1 teaspoon lemon zest

Directions:

1. Set oven 205ºC. Prep large baking sheet with aluminum foil.
2. Toss the Brussels sprouts in the olive oil in a large bowl until well coated. Sprinkle with salt and pepper.
3. Spread out the seasoned Brussels sprouts on the prepared baking sheet in a single layer.
4. Roast for 20 minutes, shake halfway through.
5. Remove from the oven then situate in a bowl. Whisk tomatoes, lemon juice, and lemon zest, to incorporate. Serve immediately.

Nutrition: 111 Calories|13.7g Carb|4.9g fiber

Simple Sautéed Greens

Preparation Time: 10 minutes |Cooking Time: 10 minutes |Servings: 4

Ingredients:

- 2 tablespoons extra-virgin olive oil
- 1 pound (454 g) Swiss chard
- 1-pound (454 g) kale
- ½ teaspoon ground cardamom
- 1 tablespoon lemon juice

Direction:

1. Heat up olive oil in a big skillet over medium-high heat.
2. Stir in Swiss chard, kale, cardamom, lemon juice to the skillet, and stir to combine. Cook for about 10 minutes, stirring continuously, or until the greens are wilted.
3. Sprinkle with the salt and pepper and stir well.
4. Serve the greens on a plate while warm.

Nutrition:|139 Calories |15.8g Carb|3.9g fiber

Garlicky Mushrooms

Preparation Time: 10 minutes |Cooking Time: 12 minutes |Servings: 4

Ingredients:

- 1 tablespoon butter
- 2 teaspoons extra-virgin olive oil
- 2 pounds button mushrooms
- 2 teaspoons minced fresh garlic
- 1 teaspoon chopped fresh thyme

Direction:

1. Warm up butter and olive oil in a huge skillet over medium-high heat.
2. Add the mushrooms and sauté for 10 minutes, stirring occasionally.
3. Stir in the garlic and thyme and cook for an additional 2 minutes.
4. Season and serve on a plate.

Nutrition: 96 Calories |8.2g Carb|1.7g fiber

Green Beans in Oven

Preparation Time: 5 minutes |Cooking Time: 17 minutes |Servings: 3

Ingredients

- 12 oz. green bean pods
- 1 tbsp. olive oil
- 1/2 tsp. onion powder
- 1/8 tsp. pepper
- 1/8 tsp. salt

Directions

1. Preheat oven to 350°F. Mix green beans with onion powder, pepper, and oil.
2. Spread the seeds on the baking sheet.
3. Bake 17 minutes or until you have a delicious aroma in the kitchen.

Nutrition: 37 Calories|1.4g Protein|5.5g Carb

Parmesan Broiled Flounder *

Preparation Time: 10 minutes |Cooking Time: 7 minutes |Servings: 1

Ingredients

- 2 (4-oz) flounder
- 1,5 tbsp Parmesan cheese
- 1,5 tbsp mayonnaise
- 1/8 tsp soy sauce
- 1/4 tsp chili sauce
- 1/8 tsp salt-free lemon-pepper seasoning

Directions

1. Preheat flounder.
2. Mix cheese, reduced-fat mayonnaise, soy sauce, chili sauce, seasoning.
3. Put fish on a baking sheet coated with

cooking spray, sprinkle with salt and pepper.
4. Spread Parmesan mixture over flounder. Broil 6 to 8 minutes or until a crust appears on the fish.

Nutrition: 200 Calories |17g Fat |7g Carb

Fish with Fresh Tomato - Basil Sauce

Preparation Time: 10 minutes |Cooking Time: 15 minutes |Servings: 2

Ingredients:

- 2 (4-oz) tilapia fillets
- 1 tbsp fresh basil, chopped
- 1/8 tsp salt
- 1 pinch of crushed red pepper
- 1 cup cherry tomatoes, chopped
- 2 tsp extra virgin olive oil

Directions

1. Preheat oven to 400°F.
2. Arrange rinsed and patted dry fish fillets on foil (coat a foil baking sheet with cooking spray).
3. Sprinkle tilapia fillets with salt and red pepper.
4. Bake 12 - 15 minutes.
5. Meanwhile, mix leftover ingredients in a saucepan.
6. Cook over medium-high heat until tomatoes are tender.
7. Top fish fillets properly with tomato mixture.

Nutrition: 130 Calories |30g Protein |1g Carb

Baked Chicken

Preparation Time: 15 minutes |Cooking Time: 25 minutes |Servings: 4

Ingredients

- 2 (6-oz) bone-in chicken breasts
- 1/8 tsp salt
- 1/8 tsp pepper
- 3 tsp extra virgin olive oil
- 1/2 tsp dried oregano
- 7 pitted kalamata olives
- 1 cup cherry tomatoes
- 1/2 cup onion
- 1 (9-oz) pkg frozen artichoke hearts
- 1 lemon

Directions

1. Preheat oven to 400°F.
2. Sprinkle chicken with pepper, salt, and oregano.
3. Heat oil, add chicken and cook until it browned.
4. Place chicken in a baking dish. Arrange tomatoes, coarsely chopped olives, and onion, artichokes and lemon cut into wedges around the chicken.
5. Bake 20 minutes or until chicken is done and vegetables are tender.

Nutrition: 160 Calories 3g Fat |1g Carb

Seared Chicken with Roasted Vegetables *

Preparation Time: 20 minutes |Cooking Time: 30 minutes |Servings: 1

Ingredients

- 1 (8-oz) boneless, skinless chicken breasts
- 3/4 lb. small Brussels sprouts
- 2 large carrots
- 1 large red bell pepper
- 1 small red onion
- 2 cloves garlic halved
- 2 tbsp extra virgin olive oil
- 1/2 tsp dried dill
- 1/4 tsp pepper
- 1/4 tsp salt

Directions

1. 1.Preheat oven to 425°F.
2. Match Brussels sprouts cut in half, red onion cut into wedges, sliced carrots, bell pepper cut into pieces and halved garlic on a baking sheet.
3. Sprinkle with 1 tbsp oil and with 1/8 tsp salt and 1/8 tsp pepper. Bake until well-roasted, cool slightly.
4. In the Meantime, sprinkle chicken with dill, remaining 1/8 tsp salt and 1/8 tsp pepper.
5. Cook until chicken is done. Put roasted vegetables with drippings over chicken.

Nutrition: 170 Calories |7g Fat |12g Protein

Fish Simmered in Tomato-Pepper Sauce

Preparation Time: 5 minutes |Cooking Time: 10 minutes |Servings: 2

Ingredients

- 2 (4-oz) cod fillets
- 1 big tomato
- 1/3 cup red peppers (roasted)
- 3 tbsp almonds
- 2 cloves garlic
- 2 tbsp fresh basil leaves
- 2 tbsp extra virgin olive oil
- 1/4 tsp salt
- 1/8 tsp pepper

Directions

1. Toast sliced almonds in a pan until fragrant.
2. Grind almonds, basil, minced garlic, 1-2 tsp oil in a food processor until finely ground.
3. Add coarsely chopped tomato and red peppers, grind until smooth.
4. Season fish with salt and pepper.
5. Cook in hot oil in a large pan over medium-high heat until fish is browned. Pour sauce around fish. Cook 6 minutes more.

Nutrition: 90 Calories |5g Fat |7g Carb

Cheese Potato and Pea Casserole *

Preparation Time: 10 minutes |Cooking Time: 35 minutes |Servings: 1

Ingredients

- 1 tbsp olive oil
- ¾ lb. red potatoes
- ¾ cup green peas
- ½ cup red onion
- ¼ tsp dried rosemary
- ¼ tsp salt
- 1/8 tsp pepper

Direction

1. Prepare oven to 350°F.
2. Cook 1 tsp oil in a skillet. Stir in thinly sliced onions and cook. Remove from pan.
3. Situate half of the thinly sliced potatoes and onions in bottom of skillet; top with peas, crushed dried rosemary, and 1/8 tsp each salt and pepper.
4. Place remaining potatoes and onions on top. Season with remaining 1/8 tsp salt.
5. Bake 35 minutes, pour remaining 2 tsp oil and sprinkle with cheese.

Nutrition: 80 Calories|2g Protein|18g Carb

Oven-Fried Tilapia

Preparation Time: 7 minutes |Cooking Time: 15 minutes |Servings: 2

Ingredients

- 2 (4-oz) tilapia fillets
- 1/4 cup yellow cornmeal
- 2 tbsp light ranch dressing
- 1 tbsp canola oil
- 1 tsp dill (dried) - 1/8 tsp salt

Directions

1. Preheat oven to 425°F. Brush both sides of rinsed and patted dry tilapia fish fillets with dressing.
2. Combine cornmeal, oil, dill, and salt.
3. Sprinkle fish fillets with cornmeal mixture.
4. Put fish on a prepared baking sheet.
5. Bake 15 minutes.

Nutrition: 96 Calories |21g Protein |2g Fat

Chicken with Coconut Sauce

Preparation Time: 15 minutes |Cooking Time: 20 minutes |Servings: 2

Ingredients

- 1/2 lb. chicken breasts
- 1/3 cup red onion
- 1 tbsp paprika (smoked)
- 2 tsp cornstarch
- 1/2 cup light coconut milk
- 1 tsp extra virgin olive oil
- 2 tbsp fresh cilantro
- 1 (10-oz) can tomatoes and green chilis
- 1/4 cup water

Directions

1. Cut chicken into little cubes; sprinkle with 1,5 tsp paprika.

2. Heat oil, add chicken and cook 3 to 5 minutes.
3. Remove from skillet, and fry finely chopped onion 5 minutes.
4. Return chicken to pan. Add tomatoes,1,5 tsp paprika, and water. Bring to a boil, and then simmer 4 minutes.
5. Mix cornstarch and coconut milk; stir into chicken mixture and cook until it has done. Sprinkle with chopped cilantro.

Nutrition: 200 Calories |13g Protein |10g Fat

Fish with Fresh Herb Sauce *

Preparation Time: 10 minutes |Cooking Time: 10 minutes |Servings: 1

Ingredients

- 2 (4-oz) cod fillets
- 1/3 cup fresh cilantro
- 1/4 tsp cumin
- 1 tbsp red onion
- 2 tsp extra virgin olive oil
- 1 tsp red wine vinegar
- 1 small clove garlic
- 1/8 tsp salt
- 1/8 black pepper

Directions

1. Combine chopped cilantro, finely chopped onion, oil, red wine vinegar, minced garlic, and salt.
2. Sprinkle both sides of fish fillets with cumin and pepper.
3. Cook fillets 4 minutes per side. Top each fillet with cilantro mixture.

Nutrition: 90 Calories |4g Fat |3g Carb

Skillet Turkey Patties

Preparation Time: 7 minutes |Cooking Time: 8 minutes |Servings: 2

Ingredients

- 1/2 lb. lean ground turkey
- 1/2 cup low-sodium chicken broth
- 1/4 cup red onion
- 1/2 tsp Worcestershire sauce
- 1 tsp extra virgin olive oil
- 1/4 tsp oregano (dried)
- 1/8 tsp pepper

Directions

1. Combine turkey, chopped onion, Worcestershire sauce, dried oregano, and pepper; make 2 patties.
2. Warm up oil and cook patties 4 minutes per side; set aside.
3. Add broth to skillet, bring to a boil. Boil 2 minutes, spoon sauce over patties.

Nutrition: 180 Calories |11g Fat |9g Carb

Turkey Loaf

Preparation Time: 10 minutes |Cooking Time: 50 minutes |Servings: 2

Ingredients

- 1/2 lb. 93% lean ground turkey
- 1/3 cup panko breadcrumbs
- 1/2 cup green onion
- 1 egg
- 1/2 cup green bell pepper
- 1 tbsp ketchup
- 1/4 cup sauce (Picante)
- 1/2 tsp cumin (ground)

Directions

1. Preheat oven to 350°F. Mix lean ground turkey, 3 tbsp Picante sauce, panko breadcrumbs, egg, chopped green onion, chopped green bell pepper and cumin in a bowl (mix well).
2. Put the mixture into a baking sheet; shape into an oval (about 1,5 inches thick). Bake 45 minutes.
3. Mix remaining Picante sauce and the ketchup; apply over loaf. Bake 5 minutes longer. Let stand 5 minutes.

Nutrition: 161 Calories |20g Protein |8g Fat

Mushroom Pasta

Preparation Time: 7 minutes |Cooking Time: 10 minutes |Servings: 2

Ingredients

- 4 oz whole-grain linguine
- 1 tsp extra virgin olive oil
- 1/2 cup light sauce
- 2 tbsp green onion
- 1 (8-oz) pkg mushrooms

- 1 clove garlic
- 1/8 tsp salt
- 1/8 tsp pepper

Directions

1. Cook pasta according to package directions, drain.
2. Fry sliced mushrooms 4 minutes.
3. Stir in fettuccine minced garlic, salt and pepper. Cook 2 minutes.
4. Heat light sauce until heated; top pasta mixture properly with sauce and with finely chopped green onion.

Nutrition 300 Calories |1g Fat |15g Carb

Chicken Tikka Masala

Preparation Time: 5 minutes |Cooking Time: 15 minutes |Servings: 2

Ingredients

- 1/2 lb. chicken breasts
- 1/4 cup onion
- 1.5 tsp extra virgin olive oil
- 1 (14.5-oz) can tomatoes
- 1 tsp ginger
- 1 tsp fresh lemon juice
- 1/3 cup plain Greek yogurt (fat-free)
- 1 tbsp garam masala
- 1/4 tsp salt
- 1/4 tsp pepper

Directions

1. Flavor chicken cut into 1-inch cubes with 1,5 tsp garam masala,1/8 tsp salt and pepper. Cook chicken and diced onion 4 to 5 minutes.
2. Add diced tomatoes, grated ginger, 1.5 tsp garam masala, 1/8 tsp salt. Cook 8 to 10 minutes. Add lemon juice and yogurt until blended.

Nutrition: 200 Calories |26g Protein |10g Fat

Tomato and Roasted Cod

Preparation Time: 10 minutes |Cooking Time: 35 minutes |Servings: 2

Ingredients

- 2 (4-oz) cod fillets
- 1 cup cherry tomatoes
- 2/3 cup onion
- 2 tsp orange rind
- 1 tbsp extra virgin olive oil
- 1 tsp thyme (dried)
- 1/4 tsp salt, divided
- 1/4 tsp pepper, divided

Directions

1. Preheat oven to 400°F. Mix in half tomatoes, sliced onion, grated orange rind, extra virgin olive oil, dried thyme, and 1/8 salt and pepper. Fry 25 minutes. Remove from oven.
2. Arrange fish on pan, and flavor with remaining 1/8 tsp each salt and pepper. Put reserved tomato mixture over fish. Bake 10 minutes.

Nutrition: 120 Calories |9g Protein |2g Fat

Ravioli

Preparation Time: 5 minutes |Cooking Time: 16 minutes |Servings: 4

Ingredients:

- 8 ounces frozen vegan ravioli, thawed
- 1 teaspoon dried basil
- 1 teaspoon garlic powder
- 1/8 teaspoon ground black pepper
- ¼ teaspoon salt
- 1 teaspoon dried oregano
- 2 teaspoons nutritional yeast flakes
- 1/2 cup marinara sauce, unsweetened
- 1/2 cup panko breadcrumbs
- 1/4 cup liquid from chickpeas can

Direction:

1. Place breadcrumbs in a bowl, sprinkle with salt, basil, oregano, and black pepper, add garlic powder and yeast and stir until mixed.
2. Take a bowl and then pour in chickpeas liquid in it.
3. Working on one ravioli at a time, first dip a ravioli in chickpeas liquid and then coat with breadcrumbs mixture.
4. Prepare remaining ravioli in the same manner, then take a fryer basket, grease it well with oil and place ravioli in it in a single layer.

5. Switch on the air fryer, insert fryer basket, sprinkle oil on ravioli, shut with its lid, set the fryer at 390 degrees F, then cook for 6 minutes, turn the ravioli and continue cooking 2 minutes until nicely golden and heated thoroughly.
6. Cook the remaining ravioli in the same manner and serve with marinara sauce.

Nutrition: Calories: 150 |Fat: 3 g |Protein: 5 g

Cabbage Wedges

Preparation Time: 10 minutes |Cooking Time: 29 minutes |Servings: 6

Ingredients:

- 1 small head of green cabbage
- 6 strips of bacon, thick cut, pastured
- 1 teaspoon onion powder
- ½ teaspoon ground black pepper
- 1 teaspoon garlic powder
- ¾ teaspoon salt
- 1/4 teaspoon red chili flakes
- 1/2 teaspoon fennel seeds
- 3 tablespoons olive oil

Direction:

1. Switch on the air fryer, insert fryer basket, grease it with olive oil, then shut with its lid, set the fryer at 350 degrees F and preheat for 5 minutes.
2. Open the fryer, add bacon strips in it, close with its lid and cook for 10 minutes until nicely golden and crispy, turning the bacon halfway through the frying.
3. Meanwhile, prepare the cabbage and for this, remove the outer leaves of the cabbage and then cut it into eight wedges, keeping the core intact.
4. Prepare the spice mix and for this, place onion powder in a bowl, add black pepper, garlic powder, salt, red chili, and fennel and stir until mixed.
5. Drizzle cabbage wedges with oil and then sprinkle with spice mix until well coated.
6. When air fryer beeps, open its lid, transfer bacon strips to a cutting board and let it rest.
7. Add seasoned cabbage wedges into the fryer basket, close with its lid, then cook for 8 minutes at 400 degrees F, flip the cabbage, spray with oil and continue air frying for 6 minutes until nicely golden and cooked.
8. When done, transfer cabbage wedges to a plate.
9. Chop the bacon, sprinkle it over cabbage and serve.

Nutrition: Calories 123 |Fat: 11g| Protein: 4 g

Buffalo Cauliflower Wings

Preparation Time: 5 minutes |Cooking Time: 30 minutes |Servings: 4

Ingredients:

- 1 tablespoon almond flour
- 1 medium head of cauliflower
- 1 ½ teaspoon salt
- 4 tablespoons hot sauce
- 1 tablespoon olive oil

Direction:

1. Switch on the air fryer, insert fryer basket, grease it with olive oil, then shut with its lid, set the fryer at 400 degrees F and preheat for 5 minutes.
2. Meanwhile, cut cauliflower into bite-size florets and set aside.
3. Place flour in a large bowl, whisk in salt, oil and hot sauce until combined, add cauliflower florets and toss until combined.
4. Open the fryer, add cauliflower florets in it in a single layer, close with its lid and cook for 15 minutes until nicely golden and crispy, shaking halfway through the frying.
5. When air fryer beeps, open its lid, transfer cauliflower florets onto a serving plate and keep warm.
6. Cook the remaining cauliflower florets in the same manner and serve.

Nutrition: Calories: 48 |Fat: 4 g |Protein: 1 g

Sweet Potato Cauliflower Patties

Preparation Time: 20 minutes |Cooking Time: 40 minutes |Servings: 7

Ingredients:

- 1 green onion, chopped
- 1 large, sweet potato, peeled
- 1 teaspoon minced garlic
- 1 cup cilantro leaves
- 2 cup cauliflower florets
- ¼ teaspoon ground black pepper
- 1/4 teaspoon salt
- 1/4 cup sunflower seeds
- 1/4 teaspoon cumin
- 1/4 cup ground flaxseed
- 1/2 teaspoon red chili powder
- 2 tablespoons ranch seasoning mix
- 2 tablespoons arrowroot starch

Direction:

1. Cut peeled sweet potato into small pieces, then place them in a food processor and pulse until pieces are broken up.
2. Then add onion, cauliflower florets, and garlic, pulse until combined, add remaining ingredients and pulse more until incorporated.
3. Tip the mixture in a bowl, shape the mixture into seven 1 ½ inch thick patties, each about ¼ cup, then place them on a baking sheet and freeze for 10 minutes.
4. Switch on the air fryer, insert fryer basket, grease it with olive oil, then shut with its lid, set the fryer at 400 degrees F and preheat for 10 minutes.
5. Open the fryer, add patties in it in a single layer, close with its lid and cook for 20 minutes until nicely golden and cooked, flipping the patties halfway through the frying.
6. When air fryer beeps, open its lid, transfer patties onto a serving plate and keep them warm.
7. Cook the remaining patties in the same manner and serve.

Nutrition: Calories: |85 Fat: 3g| Protein: 2.7g

Okra

Preparation Time: 10 minutes |Cooking Time: 10 minutes |Servings: 4

Ingredients:

- 1 cup almond flour
- 8 ounces fresh okra
- 1/2 teaspoon sea salt
- 1 cup milk, reduced fat
- 1 egg, pastured

Direction:

1. Crack the egg in a bowl, pour in the milk and whisk until blended.
2. Cut the stem from each okra, then cut it into ½-inch pieces, add them into egg and stir until well coated.
3. Mix flour and salt and add it into a large plastic bag.
4. Working on one okra piece at a time, drain the okra well by letting excess egg drip off, add it to the flour mixture, then seal the bag and shake well until okra is well coated.
5. Place the coated okra on a grease air fryer basket, coat remaining okra pieces in the same manner and place them into the basket.
6. Switch on the air fryer, insert fryer basket, spray okra with oil, then shut with its lid, set the fryer at 390 degrees F and cook for 10 minutes until nicely golden and cooked, stirring okra halfway through the frying.
7. Serve straight away.

Nutrition: Calories: 250 |Fat: 9 g |Protein: 3 g

Creamed Spinach

Preparation Time: 10 minutes |Cooking Time: 20 minutes |Servings: 2

Ingredients:

- 1/2 cup chopped white onion
- 10 ounces frozen spinach, thawed
- 1 teaspoon salt
- 1 teaspoon ground black pepper
- 2 teaspoons minced garlic
- 1/2 teaspoon ground nutmeg
- 4 ounces cream cheese, reduced fat, diced

- 1/4 cup shredded parmesan cheese, reduced fat

Direction:

1. Switch on the air fryer, insert fryer basket, grease it with olive oil, then shut with its lid, set the fryer at 350 degrees F and preheat for 5 minutes.
2. Meanwhile, take a 6-inches baking pan, grease it with oil and set aside.
3. Place spinach in a bowl, add remaining ingredients except for parmesan cheese, stir until well mixed and then add the mixture into prepared baking pan.
4. Open the fryer, add pan in it, close with its lid and cook for 10 minutes until cooked and cheese has melted, stirring halfway through.
5. Then sprinkle parmesan cheese on top of spinach and continue air fryer for 5 minutes at 400 degrees F until top is nicely golden and cheese has melted.
6. Serve straight away.

Nutrition: Calories: 273 |Fat: 23 g |Protein: 8 g

Eggplant Parmesan

Preparation Time: 20 minutes |Cooking Time: 15 minutes |Servings: 4

Ingredients:

- 1/2 cup and 3 tablespoons almond flour, divided
- 1.25-pound eggplant, ½-inch sliced
- 1 tablespoon chopped parsley
- 1 teaspoon Italian seasoning
- 2 teaspoons salt
- 1 cup marinara sauce
- 1 egg, pastured
- 1 tablespoon water
- 3 tablespoons grated parmesan cheese, reduced fat
- 1/4 cup grated mozzarella cheese, reduced fat

Direction:

1. Slice the eggplant into ½-inch pieces, place them in a colander, sprinkle with 1 ½ teaspoon salt on both sides and let it rest for 15 minutes.
2. Meanwhile, place ½ cup flour in a bowl, add egg and water and whisk until blended.
3. Place remaining flour in a shallow dish, add remaining salt, Italian seasoning, and parmesan cheese and stir until mixed.
4. Switch on the air fryer, insert fryer basket, grease it with olive oil, then shut with its lid, set the fryer at 360 degrees F and preheat for 5 minutes.
5. Meanwhile, drain the eggplant pieces, pat them dry, and then dip each slice into the egg mixture and coat with flour mixture.
6. Open the fryer, add coated eggplant slices in it in a single layer, close with its lid and cook for 8 minutes until nicely golden and cooked, flipping the eggplant slices halfway through the frying.
7. Then top each eggplant slice with a tablespoon of marinara sauce and some of the mozzarella cheese and continue air frying for 1 to 2 minutes or until cheese has melted.
8. When air fryer beeps, open its lid, transfer eggplants onto a serving plate and keep them warm.
9. Cook remaining eggplant slices in the same manner and serve.

Nutrition: Calories: 193 |Fat: 5g |Protein: 10g

Cauliflower Rice

Preparation Time: 10 minutes |Cooking Time: 27 minutes |Servings: 4

Ingredients:

For the Tofu:

- 1 cup diced carrot
- 6 ounces tofu, extra-firm, drained
- 1/2 cup diced white onion
- 2 tablespoons soy sauce
- 1 teaspoon turmeric

For the Cauliflower:

- 1/2 cup chopped broccoli
- 3 cups cauliflower rice

- 1 tablespoon minced garlic
- 1/2 cup frozen peas
- 1 tablespoon minced ginger
- 2 tablespoons soy sauce
- 1 tablespoon apple cider vinegar
- 1 1/2 teaspoons toasted sesame oil

Direction:

1. Switch on the air fryer, insert fryer pan, grease it with olive oil, then shut with its lid, set the fryer at 370 degrees F and preheat for 5 minutes.
2. Meanwhile, place tofu in a bowl, crumble it, then add remaining ingredients and stir until mixed.
3. Open the fryer, add tofu mixture in it, spray with oil, close with its lid and cook for 10 minutes until nicely golden and crispy, stirring halfway through the frying.
4. Meanwhile, place all the ingredients for cauliflower in a bowl and toss until mixed.
5. When air fryer beeps, open its lid, add cauliflower mixture, shake the pan gently to mix and continue cooking for 12 minutes, shaking halfway through the frying.
6. Serve straight away.

Nutrition: Calories: 258| Fat: 13g| Protein: 18g

Air-Fried Brussels Sprouts *

Preparation Time: 5 minutes |Cooking Time: 10 minutes |Servings: 1

Ingredients:

- 1 cups Brussels sprouts
- 1/4 teaspoon sea salt
- 1 tablespoon olive oil
- 1 tablespoon apple cider vinegar

Direction:

1. Switch on the air fryer, insert fryer basket, grease it with olive oil, then shut with its lid, set the fryer at 400 degrees F and preheat for 5 minutes.
2. Meanwhile, cut the sprouts lengthwise into ¼-inch thick pieces, add them in a bowl, add remaining ingredients and toss until well coated.
3. Open the fryer, add sprouts in it, close with its lid and cook for 10 minutes until crispy and cooked, shaking halfway through the frying.
4. When air fryer beeps, open its lid, transfer sprouts onto a serving plate and serve.

Nutrition: Calories: 88 |Fat: 4. g |Protein: 3.9g

Green Beans

Preparation Time: 5 minutes |Cooking Time: 13 minutes |Servings: 4

Ingredients:

- 1-pound green beans
- ¾ teaspoon garlic powder
- ¾ teaspoon ground black pepper
- 1 ¼ teaspoon salt
- ½ teaspoon paprika

Direction:

1. Switch on the air fryer, insert fryer basket, grease it with olive oil, then shut with its lid, set the fryer at 400 degrees F and preheat for 5 minutes.
2. Meanwhile, place beans in a bowl, spray generously with olive oil, sprinkle with garlic powder, black pepper, salt, and paprika and toss until well coated.
3. Open the fryer, add green beans in it, close with its lid and cook for 8 minutes until nicely golden and crispy, shaking halfway through the frying.
4. When air fryer beeps, open its lid, transfer green beans onto a serving plate and serve.

Nutrition: Calories: 45 |Fat: 1 g |Protein: 2 g

Asparagus Avocado Soup

Preparation Time: 10 minutes |Cooking Time: 20 minutes |Servings: 4

Ingredients:

- 1 avocado, peeled, pitted, cubed
- 12 ounces asparagus

- ½ teaspoon ground black pepper
- 1 teaspoon garlic powder
- 1 teaspoon sea salt
- 2 tablespoons olive oil, divided
- 1/2 of a lemon, juiced
- 2 cups vegetable stock

Direction:

1. Switch on the air fryer, insert fryer basket, grease it with olive oil, then shut with its lid, set the fryer at 425 degrees F and preheat for 5 minutes.
2. Meanwhile, place asparagus in a shallow dish, drizzle with 1 tablespoon oil, sprinkle with garlic powder, salt, and black pepper and toss until well mixed.
3. Open the fryer, add asparagus in it, close with its lid and cook for 10 minutes until nicely golden and roasted, shaking halfway through the frying.
4. When air fryer beeps, open its lid and transfer asparagus to a food processor.
5. Add remaining ingredients into a food processor and pulse until well combined and smooth.
6. Tip the soup in a saucepan, pour in water if the soup is too thick and heat it over medium-low heat for 5 minutes until thoroughly heated.
7. Ladle soup into bowls and serve.

Nutrition: Calories: 208 |Fat: 16 g |Protein: 6 g

Coffee-Steamed Carrots

Preparation Time: 10 minutes |Cooking Time: 3 minutes |Servings: 4

Ingredients:

- 1 cup brewed coffee
- 1 teaspoon light brown sugar
- ½ teaspoon kosher salt
- Freshly ground black pepper
- 1-pound baby carrots
- Chopped fresh parsley
- 1 teaspoon grated lemon zest

Directions:

1. Pour the coffee into the electric pressure cooker. Stir in the brown sugar, salt, and pepper. Add the carrots.
2. Close the pressure cooker. Set to sealing.
3. Cook on high pressure for minutes.
4. Once complete, click Cancel and quick release the pressure.
5. Once the pin drops, open and remove the lid.
6. Using a slotted spoon, portion carrots to a serving bowl. Topped with the parsley and lemon zest and serve.

Nutrition: 51 Calories |12g Carb | 4g Fiber

Rosemary Potatoes

Preparation Time: 10 minutes |Cooking Time: 25 minutes |Servings: 2

Ingredients:

- 1lb red potatoes
- 1 cup vegetable stock
- 2tbsp olive oil
- 2tbsp rosemary sprigs

Directions:

1. Situate potatoes in the steamer basket and add the stock into the Instant Pot.
2. Steam the potatoes in your Instant Pot for 15 minutes.
3. Depressurize and pour away the remaining stock.
4. Set to sauté and add the oil, rosemary, and potatoes.
5. Cook until brown.

Nutrition: 195 Calories|31g Carb|1g Fat

Corn on the Cob

Preparation Time: 10 minutes |Cooking Time: 5 minutes |Servings: 6

Ingredients:

- 6 ears corn

Directions:

1. Take off husks and silk from the corn. Cut or break each ear in half.
2. Pour 1 cup of water into the bottom of the electric pressure cooker. Insert a wire rack or trivet.

3. Place the corn upright on the rack, cut side down. Seal lid of the pressure cooker.
4. Cook on high pressure for 5 minutes.
5. When its complete, select Cancel and quick release the pressure.
6. When pin drops, unlock and take off lid.
7. Pull out the corn from the pot. Season as desired and serve immediately.

Nutrition: 62 Calories|14g Carb|1g Fiber

Chili Lime Salmon *

Preparation Time: 6 minutes |Cooking Time: 10 minutes |Servings: 1

Ingredients:

For Sauce:

- 1 jalapeno pepper
- 1 tablespoon chopped parsley
- 1 teaspoon minced garlic
- 1/2 teaspoon cumin
- 1/2 teaspoon paprika
- 1/2 teaspoon lime zest
- 1 tablespoon honey
- 1 tablespoon lime juice
- 1 tablespoon olive oil
- 1 tablespoon water

For Fish:

- 2 salmon fillets, each about 5 ounces
- 1 cup water
- 1/2 teaspoon salt
- 1/8 teaspoon ground black pepper

Directions:

1. Prepare salmon and for this, season salmon with salt and black pepper until evenly coated.
2. Plugin instant pot, insert the inner pot, pour in water, then place steamer basket and place seasoned salmon on it.
3. Seal instant pot with its lid, press the 'steam' button, then press the 'timer' to set the cooking time to 5 minutes and cook on high pressure, for 5 minutes.
4. Transfer all the ingredients for the sauce in a bowl, whisk until combined and set aside until required.
5. When the timer beeps, press 'cancel' button and do quick pressure release until pressure nob drops down.
6. Open the instant pot, then transfer salmon to a serving plate and drizzle generously with prepared sauce.
7. Serve straight away.

Nutrition: 305 Calories|29g Carbo|6g Fiber

Collard Greens

Preparation Time: 5 minutes |Cooking Time: 6 hours Servings: 10

Ingredients:

- 2 pounds chopped collard greens
- ¾ cup chopped white onion
- 1 teaspoon onion powder
- 1 teaspoon garlic powder
- 1 teaspoon salt
- 2 teaspoons brown sugar
- ½ teaspoon ground black pepper
- ½ teaspoon red chili powder
- ¼ teaspoon crushed red pepper flakes
- 3 tablespoons apple cider vinegar
- 2 tablespoons olive oil
- 14.5-ounce vegetable broth
- 1/2 cup water

Directions:

1. Plugin instant pot, insert the inner pot, add onion and collard and then pour in vegetable broth and water.
2. Close instant pot with its lid, seal, press the 'slow cook' button, then press the 'timer' to set the cooking time to 6 hours at high heat setting.
3. When the timer beeps, press 'cancel' button and do natural pressure release until pressure nob drops down.
4. Open the instant pot, add remaining ingredients and stir until mixed.
5. Then press the 'sauté/simmer' button and cook for 3 to minutes or more until collards reach to desired texture.
6. Serve straight away.

Nutrition: 49 Calories|2.3g Carb|0.5g Fiber

Mashed Pumpkin

Preparation Time: 9 minutes |Cooking Time: 15 minutes |Servings: 2

Ingredients:

- 2 cups chopped pumpkin
- 0.5 cup water
- 2tbsp powdered sugar-free sweetener of choice
- 1tbsp cinnamon

Directions:

1. Place the pumpkin and water in your Instant Pot.
2. Seal and cook on Stew 15 minutes.
3. Remove and mash with the sweetener and cinnamon.

Nutrition: 12 Calories|3g Carb|1g Sugar

Parmesan-Topped Acorn Squash *

Preparation Time: 8 minutes |Cooking Time: 20 minutes |Servings: 4

Ingredients:

- 1 acorn squash (about 1 pound)
- 1 tablespoon extra-virgin olive oil
- 1 teaspoon dried sage leaves, crumbled
- ¼ teaspoon freshly grated nutmeg
- 1/8 teaspoon kosher salt
- 1/8 teaspoon freshly ground black pepper
- 2 tablespoons freshly grated Parmesan cheese

Directions:

1. Chop acorn squash in half lengthwise and remove the seeds. Cut each half in half for a total of 4 wedges. Snap off the stem if it's easy to do.
2. In a small bowl, combine the olive oil, sage, nutmeg, salt, and pepper.
3. Brush the cut sides of the squash with the olive oil mixture.
4. Fill 1 cup of water into the electric pressure cooker and insert a wire rack or trivet.
5. Place the squash on the trivet in a single layer, skin-side down.
6. Set the lid of the pressure cooker on sealing.
7. Cook on high pressure for 20 minutes.
8. Once done, press Cancel and quick release the pressure.
9. Once the pin drops, open it.
10. Carefully remove the squash from the pot, sprinkle with the Parmesan, and serve.

Nutrition: 85 Calories|12g Carb|2g Fiber

Quinoa Tabbouleh

Preparation Time: 8 minutes |Cooking Time: 16 minutes |Servings: 6

Ingredients:

- 1 cup quinoa, rinsed
- 1 large English cucumber
- 2 scallions, sliced
- 2 cups cherry tomatoes, halved
- 2/3 cup chopped parsley
- 1/2 cup chopped mint
- ½ teaspoon minced garlic
- 1/2 teaspoon salt
- ½ teaspoon ground black pepper
- 2 tablespoon lemon juice
- 1/2 cup olive oil

Directions:

1. Plugin instant pot, insert the inner pot, add quinoa, then pour in water and stir until mixed.
2. Close instant pot with its lid and turn the pressure knob to seal the pot.
3. Select 'manual' button, then set the 'timer' to 1 minute and cook in high pressure, it May take7 minutes.
4. Once the timer stops, select 'cancel' button and do natural pressure release for 10 minutes and then do quick pressure release until pressure nob drops down.
5. Open the instant pot, fluff quinoa with a fork, then spoon it on a rimmed baking sheet, spread quinoa evenly and let cool.
6. Meanwhile, place lime juice in a small bowl, add garlic and stir until just mixed.
7. Then add salt, black pepper, and olive oil and whisk until combined.
8. Transfer cooled quinoa to a large bowl, add remaining ingredients, then drizzle generously with the prepared lime juice mixture and toss until evenly coated.

9. Taste quinoa to adjust seasoning and then serve.

Nutrition: 283 Calories|30.6g Carb |3.4g Fiber

Wild Rice Salad with Cranberries and Almonds

Preparation Time: 6 minutes |Cooking Time: 25 minutes |Servings: 4

Ingredients:

For the rice

- 2 cups wild rice blend, rinsed
- 1 teaspoon kosher salt
- 2½ cups Vegetable Broth

For the dressing

- ¼ cup extra-virgin olive oil
- ¼ cup white wine vinegar
- 1½ teaspoons grated orange zest
- Juice of 1 medium orange (about ¼ cup)
- 1 teaspoon honey or pure maple syrup

For the salad

- ¾ cup unsweetened dried cranberries
- ½ cup sliced almonds, toasted
- Freshly ground black pepper

Directions:

1. To make the rice
2. In the electric pressure cooker, combine the rice, salt, and broth.
3. Close and lock the lid. Set the valve to sealing.
4. Cook on high pressure for 25 minutes.
5. When the cooking is complete, hit Cancel and allow the pressure to release naturally for 1minutes, then quick release any remaining pressure.
6. Once the pin drops, unlock and remove the lid.
7. Let the rice cool briefly, then fluff it with a fork.
8. To make the dressing
9. While the rice cooks, make the dressing: In a small jar with a screw-top lid, combine the olive oil, vinegar, zest, juice, and honey. (If you don't have a jar, whisk the ingredients together in a small bowl.) Shake to combine.
10. To make the salad
11. Mix rice, cranberries, and almonds.
12. Add the dressing and season with pepper.
13. Serve warm or refrigerate.

Nutrition: 126 Calories|18g Carb|2g Fiber

Low Fat Roasties

Preparation Time: 8 minutes |Cooking Time: 25 minutes |Servings: 2

Ingredients:

- 1lb roasting potatoes
- 1 garlic clove
- 1 cup vegetable stock
- 2tbsp olive oil

Directions:

1. Position potatoes in the steamer basket and add the stock into the Instant Pot.
2. Steam the potatoes in your Instant Pot for 15 minutes.
3. Depressurize and pour away the remaining stock.
4. Set to sauté and add the oil, garlic, and potatoes. Cook until brown.

Nutrition: 201 Calories|3g Carb|6g Fat

Roasted Parsnips

Preparation Time: 9 minutes |Cooking Time: 25 minutes |Servings: 2

Ingredients:

- 1lb parsnips
- 1 cup vegetable stock
- 2tbsp herbs
- 2tbsp olive oil

Directions:

1. Put the parsnips in the steamer basket and add the stock into the Instant Pot.
2. Steam the parsnips in your Instant Pot for 15 minutes.
3. Depressurize and pour away the remaining stock.
4. Set to sauté and add the oil, herbs and parsnips.
5. Cook until golden and crisp.

Nutrition: 130 Calories|14g Carb |4g Protein

Lower Carb Hummus

Preparation Time: 9 minutes |Cooking Time: 60 minutes |Servings: 2

Ingredients:

- 0.5 cup dry chickpeas
- 1 cup vegetable stock
- 1 cup pumpkin puree
- 2tbsp smoked paprika
- salt and pepper to taste

Directions:

1. Soak the chickpeas overnight.
2. Place the chickpeas and stock in the Instant Pot.
3. Cook on Beans 60 minutes.
4. Depressurize naturally.
5. Blend the chickpeas with the remaining ingredients.

Nutrition: 135 Calories|18g Carb | 3g Fat

Sweet and Sour Red Cabbage

Preparation Time: 7 minutes |Cooking Time: 10 minutes |Servings: 4

Ingredients:

- 2 cups Spiced Pear Applesauce
- 1 small onion, chopped
- ½ cup apple cider vinegar
- ½ teaspoon kosher salt
- 1 head red cabbage

Directions:

1. In the electric pressure cooker, combine the applesauce, onion, vinegar, salt, and cup of water. Stir in the cabbage.
2. Seal lid of the pressure cooker.
3. Cook on high pressure for 10 minutes.
4. When the cooking is complete, hit Cancel and quick release the pressure.
5. Once the pin drops, unlock and remove the lid. Spoon into a bowl or platter and serve.

Nutrition: 91 Calories |18g Carb 4g Fiber

Pinto Beans

Preparation Time: 6 minutes |Cooking Time: 55 minutes |Servings: 8

Ingredients:

- 2 cups pinto beans, dried
- 1 medium white onion
- 1 ½ teaspoon minced garlic
- ¾ teaspoon salt
- 1/4 teaspoon ground black pepper
- 1 teaspoon red chili powder
- 1/4 teaspoon cumin
- 1 tablespoon olive oil
- 1 teaspoon chopped cilantro
- 5 ½ cup vegetable stock

Directions:

1. Plugin instant pot, insert the inner pot, press sauté/simmer button, add oil and when hot, add onion and garlic and cook for 3 minutes or until onions begin to soften.
2. Add remaining ingredients, stir well, then press the cancel button, shut the instant pot with its lid and seal the pot.
3. Click 'manual' button, then press the 'timer' to set the cooking time to 45 minutes and cook at high pressure.
4. Once done, click 'cancel' button and do natural pressure release for 10 minutes until pressure nob drops down.
5. Open the instant pot, spoon beans into plates and serve.

Nutrition:107 Calories|11.7g Carb|4g Fiber

Parmesan Cauliflower Mash

Preparation Time: 19 minutes |Cooking Time: 5 minutes |Servings: 4

Ingredients:

- 1 head cauliflower
- ½ teaspoon kosher salt
- ½ teaspoon garlic pepper
- 2 tablespoons plain Greek yogurt
- ¾ cup freshly grated Parmesan cheese
- 1 tablespoon unsalted butter or ghee (optional)
- Chopped fresh chives

Directions:

1. Pour cup of water into the electric pressure cooker and insert a steamer basket or wire rack.
2. Place the cauliflower in the basket.

3. Cover lid of the pressure cooker to seal.
4. Cook on high pressure for 5 minutes.
5. Once complete, hit Cancel and quick release the pressure.
6. When the pin drops, remove the lid.
7. Remove the cauliflower from the pot and pour out the water. Return the cauliflower to the pot and add the salt, garlic pepper, yogurt, and cheese. Use an immersion blender to purée or mash the cauliflower in the pot.
8. Spoon into a serving bowl, and garnish with butter (if using) and chives.

Nutrition: 141 Calories|12g Carb|4g Fiber

Steamed Asparagus

Preparation Time: 3 minutes |Cooking Time: 2 minutes |Servings: 4

Ingredients:

- 1 lb. fresh asparagus, rinsed and tough ends trimmed
- 1 cup water

Direction:

1. Place the asparagus into a wire steamer rack and set it inside your Instant Pot.
2. Add water to the pot. Close and seal the lid, turning the steam release valve to the "Sealing" position.
3. Select the "Steam" function to cook on high pressure for 2 minutes.
4. Once done, do a quick pressure release of the steam.
5. Lift the wire steamer basket out of the pot and place the asparagus onto a serving plate.
6. Season as desired and serve.

Nutrition: 22 Calories |4g Carb|2g Protein

Squash Medley

Preparation Time: 10 minutes |Cooking Time: 20 minutes |Servings: 2

Ingredients:

- 2 lbs. mixed squash
- ½ cup mixed veg
- 1 cup vegetable stock
- 2 tbsps. olive oil
- 2 tbsps. mixed herbs

Direction:

1. Put the squash in the steamer basket and add the stock into the Instant Pot.
2. Steam the squash in your Instant Pot for 10 minutes.
3. Depressurize and pour away the remaining stock.
4. Set to sauté and add the oil and remaining ingredients.
5. Cook until a light crust form.

Nutrition: 100 Calories |10g Carb|6g Fat

Eggplant Curry

Preparation Time: 15 minutes |Cooking Time: 20 minutes |Servings: 2

Ingredients:

- 3 cups chopped eggplant
- 1 thinly sliced onion
- 1 cup coconut milk
- 3 tbsps. curry paste
- 1 tbsp. oil or ghee

Direction:

1. Select Instant Pot to sauté and put the onion, oil, and curry paste.
2. Once the onion is soft, stir in remaining ingredients and seal.
3. Cook on Stew for 20 minutes. Release the pressure naturally.

Nutrition: 350 Calories |15g Carb|25g Fat

Lentil and Eggplant Stew

Preparation Time: 15 minutes |Cooking Time: 35 minutes |Servings: 2

Ingredients:

- 1 lb. eggplant
- 1 lb. dry lentils
- 1 cup chopped vegetables
- 1 cup low sodium vegetable broth

Direction:

1. Incorporate all the ingredients in your Instant Pot, cook on Stew for 35 minutes.
2. Release the pressure naturally and serve.

Nutrition: 310 Calories |22g Carb|10g Fat

Tofu Curry

Preparation Time: 15 minutes |Cooking Time: 20 minutes |Servings: 2

Ingredients:

- 2 cups cubed extra firm tofu
- 2 cups mixed stir fry vegetables
- ½ cup soy yogurt
- 3 tbsps. curry paste
- 1 tbsp. oil or ghee

Direction:

1. Set the Instant Pot to sauté and add the oil and curry paste.
2. Once soft, place the remaining ingredients except for the yogurt and seal.
3. Cook on Stew for 20 minutes.
4. Release the pressure naturally and serve with a scoop of soy yogurt.

Nutrition: 300 Calories |9g Carb|14g Fat

Lentil and Chickpea Curry

Preparation Time: 15 minutes |Cooking Time: 20 minutes |Servings: 2

Ingredients:

- 2 cups dry lentils and chickpeas
- 1 thinly sliced onion
- 1 cup chopped tomato
- 3 tbsps. curry paste
- 1 tbsp. oil or ghee

Direction:

1. Press Instant Pot to sauté and mix onion, oil, and curry paste.
2. Once the onion is cooked, stir the remaining ingredients and seal.
3. Cook on Stew for 20 minutes.
4. Release the pressure naturally and serve.

Nutrition: 360 Calories |26g Carb|19g Fat

Split Pea Stew

Preparation Time: 5 minutes |Cooking Time: 35 minutes |Servings: 2

Ingredients:

- 1 cup dry split peas
- 1 lb. chopped vegetables
- 1 cup mushroom soup
- 2 tbsps. old bay seasoning

Direction:

1. Incorporate all the ingredients in Instant Pot, cook for 33 minutes.
2. Release the pressure naturally.

Nutrition: 300 Calories |7g Carb| 2g Fat

Kidney Bean Stew

Preparation Time: 15 minutes |Cooking Time: 15 minutes |Servings: 2

Ingredients:

- 1 lb. cooked kidney beans
- 1 cup tomato passata
- 1 cup low sodium beef broth
- 3 tbsps. Italian herbs

Direction:

1. Incorporate all the ingredients in your Instant Pot, cook on Stew for 15 minutes.
2. Release the pressure naturally and serve.

Nutrition: 270 Calories |16g Carb|10g Fat

Fried Tofu Hotpot

Preparation Time: 15 minutes |Cooking Time: 15 minutes |Servings: 2

Ingredients:

- ½ lb. fried tofu
- 1 lb. chopped Chinese vegetable mix
- 1 cup low sodium vegetable broth
- 2 tbsps. 5 spice seasoning
- 1 tbsp. smoked paprika

Direction:

1. Combine all the ingredients in your Instant Pot, set on Stew for 15 minutes. Release the pressure naturally and serve.

Nutrition: 320 Calories |11g Carb| 23g Fat

Chili Sin Carne

Preparation Time: 15 minutes |Cooking Time: 35 minutes |Servings: 2

Ingredients:

- 3 cups mixed cooked beans
- 2 cups chopped tomatoes
- 1 tbsp. yeast extract
- 2 squares very dark chocolate
- 1 tbsp. red chili flakes

Direction:

1. Combine all the ingredients in your Instant Pot, cook for 35 minutes.
2. Release the pressure naturally and serve.

Nutrition: 240 Calories |20g Carb| 3g Fat

Brussels Sprouts *

Preparation Time: 5 minutes |Cooking Time: 3 minutes |Servings: 1

Ingredients:

- 1 tsp. extra-virgin olive oil
- 1 lb. halved Brussels sprouts
- 3 tbsps. apple cider vinegar
- 3 tbsps. gluten-free tamari soy sauce
- 3 tbsps. chopped sun-dried tomatoes

Direction:

1. Select the "Sauté" function on your Instant Pot, add oil and allow the pot to get hot.
2. Cancel the "Sauté" function and add the Brussels sprouts.
3. Stir well and allow the sprouts to cook in the residual heat for 2-3 minutes.
4. Add the tamari soy sauce and vinegar, and then stir.
5. Cover the Instant Pot, sealing the pressure valve by pointing it to "Sealing."
6. Select the "Manual, High Pressure" setting and cook for 3 minutes.
7. Once the cook cycle is done, do a quick pressure release, and then stir in the chopped sun-dried tomatoes.
8. Serve immediately.

Nutrition: 62 Calories |10g Carb|1g Fat

Garlic and Herb Carrots

Preparation Time: 2 minutes |Cooking Time: 18 minutes |Servings: 3

Ingredients:

- 2 tbsps. butter
- 1 lb. baby carrots
- 1 cup water
- 1 tsp. fresh thyme or oregano
- 1 tsp. minced garlic
- Black pepper
- Coarse sea salt

Direction:

1. Fill water to the inner pot of the Instant Pot, and then put in a steamer basket.
2. Layer the carrots into the steamer basket.
3. Close and seal the lid, with the pressure vent in the "Sealing" position.
4. Select the "Steam" setting and cook for 2 minutes on high pressure.
5. Quick release the pressure and then carefully remove the steamer basket with the steamed carrots, discarding the water.
6. Add butter to the inner pot of the Instant Pot and allow it to melt on the "Sauté" function.
7. Add garlic and sauté for 30 seconds, and then add the carrots. Mix well.
8. Stir in the fresh herbs and cook for 2-3 minutes.
9. Season with salt and black pepper, and the transfer to a serving bowl.
10. Serve warm and enjoy!

Nutrition: 122 Calories |12g Carb |7g Fat

Cilantro Lime Drumsticks

Preparation Time: 5 minutes |Cooking Time: 15 minutes |Servings: 6

Ingredients:

- 1 tbsp. olive oil
- 6 chicken drumsticks
- 4 minced garlic cloves
- ½ cup low-sodium chicken broth
- 1 tsp. cayenne pepper
- 1 tsp. crushed red peppers
- 1 tsp. fine sea salt
- Juice of 1 lime

To Serve:

- 2 tbsp. chopped cilantro
- Extra lime zest

Direction:

1. Pour olive oil to the Instant Pot and set it on the "Sauté" function.
2. Once the oil is hot adding the chicken drumsticks, and season them well.
3. Using tongs, stir the drumsticks and brown the drumsticks for 2 minutes per side.
4. Add the lime juice, fresh cilantro, and chicken broth to the pot.
5. Lock and seal the lid, turning the pressure valve to "Sealing."
6. Cook the drumsticks on the "Manual, High Pressure" setting for 9 minutes.
7. Once done let the pressure release naturally.

8. Carefully transfer the drumsticks to an aluminum-foiled baking sheet and broil them in the oven for 3-5 minutes until golden brown.
9. Serve warm, garnished with more cilantro and lime zest.

Nutrition: 480 Calories |3.3g Carb|29g Fat

Eggplant Spread

Preparation Time: 5 minutes |Cooking Time: 18 minutes |Servings: 5

Ingredients:

- 4 tbsps. extra-virgin olive oil
- 2 lbs. eggplant
- 4 skin-on garlic cloves
- ½ cup water
- ¼ cup pitted black olives
- 3 sprigs fresh thyme
- Juice of 1 lemon
- 1 tbsp. tahini
- 1 tsp. sea salt
- Fresh extra-virgin olive oil

Direction:

1. Peel the eggplant in alternating stripes, leaving some areas with skin and some with no skin.
2. Slice into big chunks and layer at the bottom of your Instant Pot.
3. Add olive oil to the pot, and on the "Sauté" function, fry and caramelize the eggplant on one side, about 5 minutes.
4. Add in the garlic cloves with the skin on.
5. Flip over the eggplant and then add in the remaining uncooked eggplant chunks, salt, and water.
6. Close the lid, ensure the pressure release valve is set to "Sealing."
7. Cook for 5 minutes on the "Manual, High Pressure" setting.
8. Once done, carefully open the pot by quick releasing the pressure through the steam valve.
9. Discard most of the brown cooking liquid.
10. Remove the garlic cloves and peel them.
11. Add the lemon juice, tahini, cooked and fresh garlic cloves and pitted black olives to the pot.
12. Using a hand-held immersion blender, process all the ingredients until smooth.
13. Pour out the spread into a serving dish and season with fresh thyme, whole black olives and some extra-virgin olive oil, prior to serving.

Nutrition: |155 Calories |16.8g Carb|11.7g Fat

Carrot Hummus *

Preparation Time: 15 minutes |Cooking Time: 10 minutes |Servings: 1

Ingredients:

- 1 chopped carrot
- 2 oz. cooked chickpeas
- 1 tsp. lemon juice
- 1 tsp. tahini
- 1 tsp. fresh parsley

Direction:

1. Place the carrot and chickpeas in your Instant Pot.
2. Add a cup of water, seal, cook for 10 minutes on Stew.
3. Depressurize naturally. Blend with the remaining ingredients.

Nutrition: 58 Calories |8g Carb|2g Fat

Vegetable

Eggplant Pasta

Preparation Time: 05 min
Cooking Time: 20 min Servings: 4
Gluten-free, Vegetarian
Ingredients

- 3 tablespoons olive oil, divided
- 1 lemon, 1/2 zested and juiced, 1/2 cut into wedges
- 1/8 teaspoon salt plus 1/4 tsp., divided
- 1 large eggplant (about 1 lb.), sliced into 1/2-inch-thick rounds
- 1/4 cup grated Parmesan cheese
- 2 ounces' rotini or penne
- 1 large garlic clove, minced
- 11/3 cups roasted red peppers
- 3 cups packed baby kale
- 2 tablespoons thinly sliced fresh basil
- 2 tablespoons walnuts, toasted

Directions:

1. Preheat the oven to 450 degrees. Line a large baking sheet with parchment paper.
2. Mix 2 tbsp. Oil, 1 1/2 tsp. Lemon juice and 1/8 tsp. Salt in a small bowl. Place the eggplant slices on the prepared baking sheet. Brush both sides of the eggplant with the lemon juice mixture. Sprinkle the top with Parmesan. Grill, about 20 to 25 minutes, until the eggplant is golden and tender.
3. In the meantime, bring a large pot of water to a boil. Add the pasta and cook according to package directions for about 8 minutes. Drain.
4. Return the pasta to the pot. Add the lemon zest, garlic, roasted red pepper, spinach and the remaining tablespoon. Oil and 1/4 tsp. Salt.
5. Cook over medium heat, about 3 minutes, stirring gently, until the spinach is tender. 66
6. Serve the eggplant with the pasta and vegetables. Sprinkle with basil and walnuts. Serve with lemon wedges.

Nutrition: Calories 223 |Fat 13.8g |Carb 21g

Garlic-Parmesan Asparagus

Preparation Time: 05 min
Cooking Time: 10 min Servings: 4
Ingredients:

- 3 tablespoons extra-virgin olive oil
- 2 cloves garlic, minced
- 1/2 teaspoon ground pepper
- 1/4 teaspoon salt
- 11/2 pounds fresh asparagus, trimmed
- 1/2 cup finely grated Parmesan cheese
- 3 tablespoons whole-wheat panko breadcrumbs
- 3 tablespoons chopped walnuts

Directions:

1. Preheat the oven to 425 degrees. Line a large baking sheet with aluminum foil or parchment paper. Combine oil, garlic, pepper, and salt in a large bowl; Add asparagus and massage to coat evenly. Spread the asparagus evenly on the prepared baking sheet.
2. Combine parmesan, panko, and walnuts in a small bowl, Sprinkle over the asparagus. Grill for 12 to 15 minutes until the panko is golden brown and the asparagus is tender. Serve immediately.

Nutrition: Calories 166 | Fat 14.8g

Green Beans with Sizzled Garlic

Preparation Time: 10 min
Cooking Time: 15 min Servings: 4
Ingredients

- 3 tablespoons coconut oil, divided
- 4 cloves garlic, thinly sliced
- 1-pound green beans, trimmed and cut into 1 1/2-inch pieces
- 1/4 teaspoon salt
- 1/3Cup water
- 1 cup grape tomatoes, halved
- 1/4 cup chopped fresh basil

Directions:

1. Heat 2 tbsp. Oil in a large skillet over medium heat. Add the garlic; cook, stirring occasionally, until golden brown, 2 to 3 minutes. Using a slotted spoon on a small plate, remove the garlic and leave the oil.
2. Add the beans and salt to the pan. Stir to coat. Add water; Cover and cook, stirring occasionally, until the beans are tender and most of the water has evaporated (about 8 minutes). Add the remaining tablespoon. Of oil, tomatoes to the pan. Cook, stirring occasionally, about 2 minutes, until the tomatoes begin to break. Remove the stove.
3. Add the basil and sizzled garlic. Stir to combine.

Nutrition: Calories 136 | Fat 10.5g| Carb 9g

Grilled broccoli Steaks

Preparation Time: 10 min
Cooking Time: 20 min Servings: 4
Ingredients

- 1 large head broccoli
- 2 cloves garlic, minced
- 31/2 tablespoons olive oil, divided
- 1 teaspoon ancho Chile powder
- 1 teaspoon ground cumin, divided
- 1/2 teaspoon salt, divided
- 1/2 teaspoon ground pepper, divided
- 1/2 teaspoon lime zest
- 2 tablespoons lime juice
- 1 tablespoon chopped fresh cilantro

1 teaspoon maple syrup
Directions:

1. Preheat the grill to medium to high heat. Place a grill basket on the grill while preheating.
2. Remove the tough outer leaves from the broccoli. Cut the stem to get a flat base, leaving the core intact. Place the broccoli upright on a cutting board. Holding the broccoli in place, use a large chef's knife to cut four 1 1/2-inch-thick leaves from the center, creating 2 large and 2 small fillets. Reserve the florets in bulk.
3. Combine the garlic, 1 1/2 tsp. Oil, chili powder, 1/2 tsp. Cumin, 1/4 teaspoon of salt and 1/4 teaspoon. Place the pepper in a small bowl. Evenly rub the broccoli fillets and florets.
4. Stir in the lime zest, lime juice, cilantro, honey and the remaining 2 tbsp. Oil, 1/2 teaspoon of cumin, 1/4 teaspoon of salt and 1/4 teaspoon. Place the pepper in a small bowl. Spoon 2 tbsp. Mix cilantro in separate small bowl for brushing; reserve the rest to serve.
5. Place the broccoli steaks on the grill and the florets in the grill basket; baste the broccoli with 1 Tbsp. of the cilantro mixture. Grill until well-marked and charred in some spots, 7 to 8 minutes. Flip the steaks and florets and baste with 1 Tbsp. cilantro mixture. Grill until the other side is tender and well-marked and charred in some spots, 7 to 8 minutes more. Transfer to a serving dish. Pour the remaining sauce over the roasted broccoli.

Nutrition: Calories 114 | Fat 10.7g|Carb 6g

Roasted Brussels Sprouts with Goat Cheese

Preparation Time: 05 min
Cooking Time: 20 min Servings: 4
Ingredients

- 1 pound Brussels sprouts, trimmed and halved
- 1 large shallot, sliced
- 1 tablespoon extra-virgin olive oil
- 1/4 teaspoon salt
- 1/4 teaspoon ground pepper
- 21/2 teaspoons 2-3 teaspoons white balsamic vinegar
- 1/3 cup crumbled goat cheese
- 1/4 cup pomegranate seeds

Directions:

1. Preheat oven to 400 degrees F. Combine Brussels sprouts with shallot, oil, salt and

pepper in a medium bowl. Spread out on a large, rimmed baking sheet.

2. Roast Brussels sprouts until tender, 20 to 22 minutes. Return to the bowl and toss with vinegar to taste. Sprinkle with goat cheese and pomegranate seeds.

Nutrition: Calories 103 |Fat 5g | Carb 13g

Mushroom & Tofu Stir-Fry

Preparation Time: 05 min
Cooking Time: 10 min
Servings: 4
Ingredients

- 4 tablespoons coconut oil, divided
- 1-pound mixed mushrooms, sliced
- 1 medium red bell pepper, diced
- 1 bunch scallions, trimmed and cut into 2-inch pieces
- 1 tablespoon grated fresh ginger
- 1 large clove garlic, grated
- 1 (8 ounce) container baked tofu or smoked tofu, diced

Directions:

1. Heat 2 tablespoons of oil in a large flat-bottomed wok or cast-iron skillet over high heat. Add mushrooms and bell peppers; cook, stirring occasionally, until smooth, about 4 minutes. Add the scallions, ginger and garlic; Cook for 30 seconds. Transfer the vegetables to a bowl.
2. Add the remaining 2 tablespoons of oil and tofu to the pan. Flip once, cook 3 to 4 minutes, until browned.
3. Add the vegetables and the oyster sauce. Cook for 1 minute, stirring constantly.

Nutrition: Calories 739|Fat 36g| Carb 53g

Roasted Carrots

Preparation Time: 05 min
Cooking Time: 20 min
Servings: 4
Ingredients

- 2 tablespoons balsamic vinegar
- 1 tablespoon pure maple syrup
- 2 tablespoons olive oil, divided
- 1-pound carrots, preferably multicolored, cut into 2-inch pieces
- 1/4 teaspoon salt
- 2 tablespoons chopped toasted pine nuts

Directions:

1. Preheat the oven to 400 degrees. Whisk the vinegar, maple syrup and 1 tablespoon of oil in a small bowl; put aside.
2. Combine carrots, salt and remaining 1 tablespoon of oil in large bowl; toss to coat. Spread in a layer on a baking sheet. Cook the carrots for 16 to 18 minutes, until they begin to brown and are almost tender but not completely cooked. Pour the balsamic mixture over the carrots and cover completely with a spatula.
3. Continue roasting until carrots are tender and glazed, another 5 minutes. If desired, sprinkle with toasted pine nuts. Serve immediately.

Nutrition: Calories 150| Fat 10g |Carb 13.1g

Baked Zucchini Chips

Preparation Time: 05 min
Cooking Time: 20 min Servings: 2
Ingredients

- 2 medium zucchini, trimmed (about 7 oz. each)
- 1 serving cooking spray
- 2 teaspoons lime juice
- 1/4 teaspoon chili powder
- 1/4 teaspoon salt

Directions:

1. Place the racks in the upper and lower thirds of the oven. Preheat to 225 degrees. Line 2 large baking sheets with parchment paper.
2. Cut the zucchini into 1/8-inch-thick slices (a mandolin slicer will help you with this). Lay the slices in a layer on the prepared forms and dry them with paper towels. (The slices should not overlap, but it's okay if they are close together.) Brush

lightly with cooking spray. Sprinkle with lemon juice, chili powder and salt.

3. Bake for 1 hour, halving the positions of the shapes. Flip the zucchini slices over and cook for another 45 to 55 minutes, until golden brown and not moist. (Check every 5-10 minutes after the first hour and season the darker slices as soon as they are cooked.) Transfer the zucchini chips to a wire rack to cool.

Nutrition: Calories 104|Fat 7g|Carb 10g

Black Bean Tortilla Wraps

Preparation Time: 5 min
Cooking Time: 20 min Servings: 4
Ingredients

- 1/2 cup reduced-fat sour cream
- 1/2 teaspoon ground cumin
- 1 (15-ounce) can black beans, rinsed and drained
- 1 cup ripe diced peeled avocado
- 1/2 poblano Chile, finely chopped
- 1/4 cup finely chopped red onion
- 1/4 cup chopped fresh cilantro leaves
- 3 tablespoons fresh lime juice
- 1/4 teaspoon salt
- 4 (8-inch) flour tortillas

Directions:

1. Combine sour cream and cumin seeds in a small bowl; Stir with a whisk.
2. Combine the beans and the next 6 ingredients in a bowl. Place equal amounts of the black bean mixture in the center of each tortilla. Roll it up, cut it in half and secure it with wooden pickaxes if necessary. Serve with the sour cream mixture.

Nutrition: Calories 568 | Fat 15g|Carb 86g

Asparagus-Tofu Stir-Fry

Preparation Time: 10 min
Cooking Time: 10 min Servings: 6
Ingredients

- 3/4-pound asparagus spears
- 3/4 cup vegetable broth
- 1/4 cup low-sodium soy sauce
- 2 teaspoons corn-starch
- 2 tablespoons sesame oil, divided
- 1 (8-ounce) package tofu thinly sliced
- 4 garlic cloves, minced
- 1/2 teaspoon crushed red pepper
- 1 (6-ounce) package sliced shiitake mushrooms

Directions:

1. Remove the tough ends from the asparagus. Cut the spears diagonally into 2-inch pieces. Put aside.
2. Combine vegetable broth, soy sauce and cornstarch in a small bowl; Beat with whisk until smooth. Put aside.
3. Heat 1 tablespoon of sesame oil in a large nonstick skillet over medium-high heat. Add tofu and sauté 4 to 5 minutes or until golden brown. Take the tofu out of the pan; put aside.
4. Heat the remaining tablespoon of sesame oil in the same pan. Add the garlic, red peppers, asparagus and mushrooms to the pan and sauté for 3 minutes or until the asparagus is crisp and tender. Add the broth; Bring to a boil and cook for 2 to 3 minutes or until thickened. Add tofu and cook 1 minute or until heated through. Serve with brown rice.

Nutrition: Calories 215 | Fat 12g|Carb 17g

Black Bean-Orange Chili

Preparation Time: 10 min
Cooking Time: 10 min Servings: 4
Ingredients

- 2 tablespoons olive oil
- 1 large onion, chopped
- 1 medium green pepper, chopped
- 3 garlic cloves, minced
- 1 teaspoon ground cinnamon
- 1 teaspoon ground cumin
- 1 teaspoon chili powder
- 1/4 teaspoon pepper

- 3 cans (14-1/2 ounces each) diced tomatoes, undrained
- 2 cans (15 ounces each) black beans, rinsed and drained - 1 cup orange juice

Directions:

1. In a Dutch oven, heat the oil over medium-high heat.
2. Add onion and green pepper; cook and stir 8 to 10 minutes or until tender. Add garlic and spices; Cook for 1 more minute.

3. Add remaining ingredients; bring to a boil. Reduce the heat; Simmer, covered, 20-25 minutes to allow flavors to combine, stirring occasionally.

Nutrition: Calories 473| Fat 9g| Carb 73G

Cumin Quinoa Patties

Preparation Time: 10 min
Cooking Time: 10 min Servings: 4
Ingredients

- 1 cup water - 1/2 cup quinoa, rinsed
- 1 medium carrot, cut into 1-inch pieces
- 1 cup canned cannellini beans, rinsed and drained
- 1/4 cup panko breadcrumbs
- 3 green onions, chopped
- 3 teaspoons ground cumin
- 1/4 teaspoon salt
- 1/8 teaspoon pepper
- 2 tablespoons olive oil

Directions:

1. Bring the water to a boil in a small saucepan. Add the quinoa. Reduce the heat; Cook, covered, over low heat for 12 to 15 minutes until the liquid is absorbed. Remove from heat.
2. In the meantime, put the carrot in the food processor. Mix until coarsely chopped. Add the beans; mix until chopped. Transfer the mixture to a large bowl. Stir in the cooked quinoa, breadcrumbs, onion, and spices. Shape into 8 patties with the mixture.
3. In a large skillet, heat the oil over medium heat. Add the patties. Cook until thermometer reads 160 °, 3-4 minutes per side, turning carefully.
4. Serve with optional garnishes if desired.

Nutrition: Calories 351 | Fat 10g |Carb 44g

Kale Quesadillas

Preparation Time: 05 min
Cooking Time: 10 min Servings: 4
Ingredients

- 3 ounces' fresh baby kale (about 4 cups)
- 4 green onions, chopped
- 1 small tomato, chopped
- 2 tablespoons lemon juice
- 1 teaspoon ground cumin
- 1/4 teaspoon garlic powder
- 1 cup shredded reduced-fat Monterey Jack cheese
- 1/4 cup reduced-fat ricotta cheese
- 6 flour tortillas (6 inches)

Directions:

1. In a large non-stick skillet, cook the first 6 ingredients and stir until the kale is tender. Remove from heat; Add cheese.
2. Top half of each tortilla with the kale mixture; Fold the other half over the filling. Place on a pan covered with cooking spray. Cook over medium heat for 1 to 2 minutes per side until golden brown. Cut the quesadillas in half; Serve with sour cream if desired.

Nutrition: Calories 236|Fat 11g |Carb 19g

Quinoa-Stuffed Zucchini

Preparation Time: 10 min
Cooking Time: 20 min Servings: 8
Ingredients

- 4 Zucchini
- 3 teaspoons olive oil, divided
- 1/8 teaspoon pepper
- 1 teaspoon salt, divided
- 1-1/2 cups vegetable broth

- 1 cup quinoa, rinsed
- 1 can (15 ounces) chickpeas or garbanzo beans, rinsed and drained
- 1/4 cup dried cranberries
- 1 green onion, thinly sliced
- 1 teaspoon minced fresh sage
- 1/2 teaspoon grated lemon zest
- 1 teaspoon lemon juice
- 1/2 cup crumbled goat cheese

Directions:

1. Preheat the oven to 450 °.
2. Cut each zucchini in half lengthwise; Remove and discard the seeds. Lightly brush cut sides with 1 teaspoon of oil. Sprinkle with pepper and 1/2 teaspoon of salt. Place them face down on a baking sheet. Bake for 15-20 minutes until tender.

3. Combine broth and quinoa in a large saucepan. Bring to a boil. Reduce the heat; Cook, covered, over low heat for 12 to 15 minutes until the liquid is absorbed.
4. Add the chickpeas, cranberries, green onions, sage, lemon zest, lemon juice and remaining oil and salt; pour into the pumpkin. Sprinkle with cheese.

Nutrition: Calories216 | Fat 5g | Carb 31g

Quinoa with vegetable stir fry

Preparation Time: 10 min
Cooking Time: 20 min Servings: 4
Ingredients

- 1 tablespoon olive oil
- 1 cup quinoa, rinsed and well drained
- 2 garlic cloves, minced
- 1 medium zucchini, chopped
- 2 cups water
- 3/4 cup canned chickpeas, rinsed and drained
- 1 medium tomato, finely chopped
- 1/2 cup crumbled feta cheese
- 2 tablespoons minced fresh basil
- 1/4 teaspoon pepper

Directions:

1. In a large saucepan, heat oil over medium-high heat.
2. Add the quinoa and garlic; cook and stir for 2-3 minutes or until quinoa is lightly browned.
3. Add zucchini and water; bring to a boil. Reduce the heat; Cook, covered, over low heat for 12 to 15 minutes until the liquid is absorbed.
4. Add remaining ingredients; Serve hot.

Nutrition: Calories 389 | Fat 12g |Carb 53g

Kale with Garlic, Raisins and Peanuts

Preparation Time: 10 min
Cooking Time: 20 min Servings: 4
Ingredients

- 1 tablespoon peanut oil
- 2 garlic cloves, thinly sliced
- A pinch dried hot red pepper flakes
- 1 small red bell pepper, cored, seeded and cut into thin strips
- 2 pounds' fresh baby kale, rinsed and spun
- 1/4 cup golden raisins
- 1/4 cup unsalted dry-roasted peanuts, chopped
- Salt and freshly ground black pepper

Directions:

1. In a large non-stick skillet, heat oil over medium-high heat. Add the garlic and chili flakes and cook
2. Add the red pepper and cook for another minute, stirring or stirring. Add kale, raisins and peanuts; with the help of tongs, turn the kale upside down to distribute the mixture and cook evenly.
3. Fry only until wilted and most of the released water have evaporated, about 2 minutes. Season with salt and pepper.

Nutrition: Calories 104 | Fat 4.7g | Carb 14

Asian Fried Eggplant

Preparation Time: 10 minutes
Cooking Time: 40 minutes Servings: 4

Ingredients:

- 1 large eggplant, sliced into fourths
- 3 green onions, diced, green tips only
- 1 teaspoon fresh ginger, peeled diced fine
- 1/4 cup + 1 teaspoon cornstarch
- 1 1/2 tablespoon. Soy sauce
- 1 1/2 tablespoon. Sesame oil
- 1 tablespoon. Vegetable oil
- 1 tablespoon. Fish sauce
- 2 teaspoon Splenda
- 1/4 teaspoon salt

Directions:

1. Place eggplant on paper towels and sprinkle both sides with salt. Let for 1 hour to remove excess moisture. Pat dry with more paper towels.
2. In a small bowl, whisk together soy sauce, sesame oil, fish sauce, Splenda, and 1 teaspoon cornstarch.
3. Coat both sides of the eggplant with the 1/4 cup cornstarch, use more if needed.
4. Heat oil in a large skillet, over med-high heat. Add 1/2 the ginger and 1 green onion, then lay 2 slices of eggplant on top. Use 1/2 the sauce mixture to lightly coat both sides of the eggplant. Cook 8-10 minutes per side. Repeat.
5. Serve garnished with remaining green onions.

Nutrition: Calories 155| Carb 18g |Protein 2g

Cucumber Dill Salad *

Preparation Time: 5 minutes
Cooking Time: 0 minutes Serving: 1
Ingredients:

- 1 Persian cucumber, peeled and sliced into very thin rounds
- 6 tablespoons nonfat Greek yogurt
- 1 teaspoon seasoned rice vinegar
- 1/2 teaspoon dill, fresh or dried
- 1/4 teaspoon garlic powder

Directions:

1. Combine all of the ingredients in a small bowl.

Nutrition: Calories 20| Carb 3g | Protein 2g

Beet and Walnut Salad

Preparation Time: 5 minutes
Cooking Time: 0 minutes Servings: 4
Ingredients:

- 4 cups salad greens
- 1 cup chopped beets (canned and rinsed, or fresh cooked and cooled)
- 2 tablespoons chopped walnuts
- 2 tablespoons goat cheese
- Maple Mustard Vinaigrette

Directions:

1. Combine all of the ingredients in a large bowl and toss with the dressing.

Nutrition: Calories 65| Fat 5g |Carb 5g

Broccoli Salad

Preparation Time: 10 minutes
Cooking Time: 0 minutes
Servings: 5
Ingredients:

- 1/2 cup nonfat Greek yogurt
- 1/2 cup light mayonnaise
- 2 tablespoons seasoned rice vinegar
- 1 tablespoon sugar
- 5 cups chopped raw broccoli
- 1/4 cup raisins, dried currants, or dried cranberries
- 1/4 cup chopped nuts, such as cashews, pecans, or almonds

Directions:

1. In a medium bowl, combine the yogurt, mayonnaise, vinegar, and sugar. Stir in the broccoli, dried fruit, and nuts.
2. Mix well until evenly coated with the dressing.

Nutrition: Nutrition 80|Fat 4.5g|Carb 2g

Dried Fruit Squash

Preparation time: 15 minutes
Cooking time: 40 minutes Servings: 4

Ingredients:

- 1/4 cup water
- 1 medium butternut squash, halved and seeded
- 1/2 tablespoon olive oil
- 1/2 tablespoon balsamic vinegar
- Salt and ground black pepper, to taste
- 4 large dates, pitted and chopped
- 4 fresh figs, chopped
- 3 tablespoons pistachios, chopped
- 2 tablespoons pumpkin seeds

Directions:

1. Preheat the oven to 375°F.
2. Place the water in the bottom of a baking dish. Arrange the squash halves in a large baking dish, hollow side up, and drizzle with oil and vinegar. Sprinkle with salt and black pepper. Spread the dates, figs, and pistachios on top. Bake for about 40 minutes, or until squash becomes tender.
3. Serve hot with the garnishing of pumpkin seeds.

Nutrition: Calories 227| Fat 5g |Carb 42g

Banana Curry

Preparation time: 15 minutes
Cooking time: 15 minutes Servings: 3
Ingredients:

- 2 tablespoons olive
- 2 yellow onions, chopped
- 8 garlic cloves, minced
- 2 tablespoons curry powder
- 1 tablespoon ground ginger
- 1 tablespoon ground cumin
- 1 teaspoon ground turmeric
- 1 teaspoon ground cinnamon
- 1 teaspoon red chili powder
- Salt and ground black pepper, to taste
- 2/3 cup soy yogurt
- 1 cup tomato puree
- 2 bananas, peeled and sliced
- 3 tomatoes, chopped finely
- 1/4 cup unsweetened coconut flakes

Directions:

1. In a large pan, heat the oil over medium heat and sauté onion for about 4–5 minutes. Add the garlic, curry powder, and spices, and sauté for about 1 minute.
2. Add the soy yogurt and tomato sauce and bring to a gentle boil. Stir in the bananas and simmer for about 3 minutes.
3. Stir in the tomatoes and simmer for about 1–2 minutes. Stir in the coconut flakes and immediately remove from the heat.
4. Serve hot.

Nutrition: Calories 382 | Fat 18g|Carb 52g

Mushroom Curry

Preparation time: 15 minutes
Cooking time: 20 minutes
Servings: 3
Ingredients:

- 2 cups tomatoes, chopped
- 1 green chili, chopped
- 1 teaspoon fresh ginger, chopped
- 1/4 cup cashews
- 2 tablespoons canola oil
- 1/2 teaspoon cumin seeds
- 1/4 teaspoon ground coriander
- 1/4 teaspoon ground turmeric
- 1/4 teaspoon red chili powder
- 11/2 cups fresh shiitake mushrooms, sliced
- 11/2 cups fresh button mushrooms, sliced
- 1 cup frozen corn kernels
- 11/4 cups water
- 1/4 cup unsweetened coconut milk
- Salt and ground black pepper, to taste

Directions:

1. In a food processor, add the tomatoes, green chili, ginger, and cashews, and pulse until a smooth paste forms.
2. In a pan, heat the oil over medium heat and sauté the cumin seeds for about 1 minute. Add the spices and sauté for about 1 minute. Add the tomato paste and cook for about 5 minutes.

3. Stir in the mushrooms, corn, water, and coconut milk, and bring to a boil.
4. Cook for about 10–12 minutes, stirring occasionally. Season with salt and black pepper and remove from the heat.
5. Serve hot.

Nutrition: Calories 311| Fat 20g | Carb 28g

Veggie Combo

Preparation time: 15 minutes
Cooking time: 25 minutes
Servings: 4
Ingredients:

- 1 tablespoon olive oil
- 1 small yellow onion, chopped
- 1 teaspoon fresh thyme, chopped
- 1 garlic clove, minced
- 8 ounces' fresh button mushroom, sliced
- 1 pound Brussels sprouts
- 3 cups fresh spinach
- 4 tablespoons walnuts
- Salt and ground black pepper, to taste

Directions:

1. In a large skillet, heat the oil over medium heat and sauté the onion for about 3–4 minutes. Add the thyme and garlic and sauté for about 1 minute.
2. Add the mushrooms and cook for about 15 minutes, or until caramelized.
3. Add the Brussels sprouts and cook for about 2–3 minutes.
4. Stir in the spinach and cook for about 3–4 minutes. Stir in the walnuts, salt, and black pepper, and remove from the heat.
5. Serve hot.

Nutrition: Calories 153|Fat 8g|Carb 15g

Beet Soup

Preparation time: 10 minutes
Cooking time: 5 minutes
Servings: 2
Ingredients:

- 2 cups coconut yogurt
- 4 teaspoons fresh lemon juice
- 2 cups beets, trimmed, peeled, and chopped
- 2 tablespoons fresh dill
- Salt, to taste
- 1 tablespoon pumpkin seeds
- 2 tablespoons coconut cream
- 1 tablespoon fresh chives, minced

Directions:

1. In a high-speed blender, add all ingredients and pulse until smooth.
2. Transfer the soup into a pan over medium heat and cook for about 3–5 minutes or until heated through. Serve immediately with the garnishing of chives and coconut cream.

Nutrition: Calories 230 | Fat 8g |Carb 28g

Veggie Stew

Preparation time: 15 minutes
Cooking time: 30 minutes Servings: 3
Ingredients:

- 2 tablespoons olive oil
- 1 large onion, chopped
- 2 garlic cloves, minced
- 1/4 teaspoon fresh ginger, grated finely
- 1 teaspoon ground cumin
- 1 teaspoon cayenne pepper
- Salt and ground black pepper, to taste
- 2 cups homemade vegetable broth
- 11/2 cups small broccoli florets
- 11/2 cups small cauliflower florets
- 1 tablespoon fresh lemon juice
- 1 cup cashews
- 1 teaspoon fresh lemon zest, grated finely

Directions:

1. In a large soup pan, heat oil over medium heat and sauté the onion for about 3–4 minutes.

1. Add the garlic, ginger, and spices and sauté for about 1 minute.
2. Add 1 cup of the broth and bring to a boil.
3. Add the vegetables and again bring to a boil.
4. Cover the soup pan and cook for about 15–20 minutes, stirring occasionally.
5. Stir in the lemon juice and remove from the heat.
6. Serve hot with the topping of cashews and lemon zest.

Nutrition: Calories 425|Fat 32g|Carb 26g

Tofu with Brussels sprouts

Preparation time: 15 minutes
Cooking time: 15 minutes
Servings: 3
Ingredients:

- 11/2 tablespoons olive oil, divided
- 8 ounces' extra-firm tofu, drained, pressed, and cut into slices
- 2 garlic cloves, chopped
- 1/3 cup pecans, toasted, and chopped
- 1 tablespoon unsweetened applesauce
- 1/4 cup fresh cilantro, chopped
- 1/2-pound Brussels sprouts, trimmed and cut into wide ribbons
- 3/4-pound mixed bell peppers, seeded and sliced

Directions:

1. In a skillet, heat 1/2 tablespoon of the oil over medium heat and sauté the tofu and for about 6–7 minutes, or until golden-brown.
2. Add the garlic and pecans and sauté for about 1 minute.
3. Add the applesauce and cook for about 2 minutes.
4. Stir in the cilantro and remove from heat.
5. Transfer tofu into a plate and set aside
6. In the same skillet, heat the remaining oil over medium-high heat and cook the Brussels sprouts and bell peppers for about 5 minutes.
7. Stir in the tofu and remove from the heat. Serve immediately.

Nutrition: Calories 238|Fat 18g|Carb 13g

Tofu with Peas

Preparation time: 15 minutes
Cooking time: 20 minutes
Servings: 5
Ingredients:

- 1 tablespoon chili-garlic sauce
- 3 tablespoons low-sodium soy sauce
- 2 tablespoons canola oil, divided
- 1 (16-ounce) package extra-firm tofu, drained, pressed, and cubed
- 1 cup yellow onion, chopped
- 1 tablespoon fresh ginger, minced
- 2 garlic cloves, minced
- 2 large tomatoes, chopped finely
- 5 cups frozen peas, thawed
- 1 teaspoon white sesame seeds

Directions:

1. For sauce: in a bowl, add the chili-garlic sauce and soy sauce and mix until well combined.
2. In a large skillet, heat 1 tablespoon of oil over medium-high heat and cook the tofu for about 4–5 minutes or until browned completely, stirring occasionally.
3. Transfer the tofu into a bowl.
4. In the same skillet, heat the remaining oil over medium heat and sauté the onion for about 3–4 minutes.
5. Add the ginger and garlic and sauté for about 1 minute.
6. Add the tomatoes and cook for about 4–5 minutes, crushing with the back of spoon.
7. Stir in all three peas and cook for about 2–3 minutes.
8. Stir in the sauce mixture and tofu and cook for about 1–2 minutes.
9. Serve hot with the garnishing of sesame seeds.

Nutrition: Calories 291| Fat 12g |Carb 30g

Carrot Soup with Tempeh

Preparation time: 15 minutes
Cooking time: 45 minutes
Servings: 6
Ingredients:

- 1/4 cup olive oil, divided
- 1 large yellow onion, chopped
- Salt, to taste
- 2 pounds' carrots, peeled, and cut into 1/2-inch rounds
- 2 tablespoons fresh dill, chopped
- 41/2 cups homemade vegetable broth
- 12 ounces' tempeh, cut into 1/2-inch cubes
- 1/4 cup tomato paste
- 1 teaspoon fresh lemon juice

Directions:

1. In a large soup pan, heat 2 tablespoons of the oil over medium heat and cook the onion with salt for about 6–8 minutes, stirring frequently.
2. Add the carrots and stir to combine.
3. Lower the heat to low and cook, covered for about 5 minutes, stirring frequently.
4. Add in the broth and bring to a boil over high heat.
5. Lower the heat to a low and simmer, covered for about 30 minutes.
6. Meanwhile, in a skillet, heat the remaining oil over medium-high heat and cook the tempeh for about 3–5 minutes.
7. Stir in the dill and cook for about 1 minute.
8. Remove from the heat.
9. Remove the pan of soup from heat and stir in tomato paste and lemon juice.
10. With an immersion blender, blend the soup until smooth and creamy.
11. Serve the soup hot with the topping of tempeh.

Nutrition: Calories 294|Fat 16g|Carb 26g

Tempeh with Bell Peppers

Preparation time: 15 minutes
Cooking time: 15 minutes
Servings: 3
Ingredients:

- 2 tablespoons balsamic vinegar
- 2 tablespoons low-sodium soy sauce
- 2 tablespoons tomato sauce
- 1 teaspoon maple syrup
- 1/2 teaspoon garlic powder
- 1/8 teaspoon red pepper flakes, crushed
- 1 tablespoon vegetable oil
- 8 ounces' tempeh, cut into cubes
- 1 medium onion, chopped
- 2 large green bell peppers, seeded and chopped

Directions:

1. In a small bowl, add the vinegar, soy sauce, tomato sauce, maple syrup, garlic powder, and red pepper flakes and beat until well combined. Set aside.
2. Heat 1 tablespoon of oil in a large skillet over medium heat and cook the tempeh about 2–3 minutes per side.
3. Add the onion and bell peppers and heat for about 2–3 minutes.
4. Stir in the sauce mixture and cook for about 3–5 minutes, stirring frequently.
5. Serve hot.

Nutrition: Calories 241|Fat 13g|Carb 18g

Squash Medley

Preparation time: 10 minutes.
Cooking time: 20 minutes. Servings: 2
Ingredients:

- 2lbs mixed squash
- 0.5 cup mixed veg
- 1 cup vegetable stock
- 2tbsp olive oil
- 2tbsp mixed herbs

Directions:

1. Put the squash in the steamer basket and add the stock into the Instant Pot.

2. Steam the squash in your Instant Pot for 10 minutes.
3. Depressurize and pour away the remaining stock. Set to sauté and add the oil and remaining ingredients.
4. Cook until a light crust forms.

Nutrition: Calories 100|Fato 6g|Carb 90

Eggplant Curry

Preparation time: 15 minutes
Cooking time: 20 minutes
Servings:2
Ingredients:

- 2-3 cups chopped eggplant
- 1 thinly sliced onion
- 1 cup coconut milk
- 3tbsp curry paste
- 1tbsp oil or ghee

Directions:

1. Set the Instant Pot to sauté and add the onion, oil, and curry paste.
2. When the onion is soft, add the remaining ingredients and seal. Cook on Stew for 20 minutes. Release the pressure naturally.

Nutrition: Calories 350|Fat 25g| Carb 15g

Chickpea Soup

Preparation time: 15 minutes
Cooking time: 35 minutes Servings:2
Ingredients:

- 1lb cooked chickpeas
- 1lb chopped vegetables
- 1 cup low sodium vegetable broth
- 2tbsp mixed herbs

Directions:

1. Mix all the ingredients in your Instant Pot.
2. Cook on Stew for 35 minutes.
3. Release the pressure naturally.

Nutrition: Calories 310|Fat 5g|Carb 20g

Fried Tofu Hotpot

Preparation time: 15 minutes
Cooking time: 15 minutes Servings: 2
Ingredients:

- 0.5lb fried tofu
- 1lb chopped Chinese vegetable mix
- 1 cup low sodium vegetable broth
- 2tbsp 5 spice seasoning
- 1tbsp smoked paprika

Directions:

1. Mix all the ingredients in your Instant Pot.
2. Cook on Stew for 15 minutes.
3. Release the pressure naturally.

Nutrition: Calories 320|Fat 23g|Carb 11g

Pea and Mint Soup

Preparation time: 15 minutes
Cooking time: 35 minutes Servings:2
Ingredients:

- 1lb green peas
- 2 cups low sodium vegetable broth
- 3tbsp mint sauce

Directions:

1. Mix all the ingredients in your Instant Pot.
2. Cook on Stew for 35 minutes.
3. Release the pressure naturally.
4. Blend into a rough soup.

Nutrition: Calories 130| Fat 4g| Carb 17g

Lentil and Eggplant Stew

Preparation time: 15 minutes
Cooking time: 35 minutes Servings: 2
Ingredients:

- 1lb eggplant
- 1lb dry lentils
- 1 cup chopped vegetables
- 1 cup low sodium vegetable broth

Directions:

1. Mix all the ingredients in your Instant Pot.
2. Cook on Stew for 35 minutes.
3. Release the pressure naturally.

Nutrition: Calories 310|Fat 10g|Carb 22g

Tofu Curry *

Preparation time: 15 minutes
Cooking time: 20 minutes
Servings: 1
Ingredients:

- 2 cups cubed extra firm tofu
- 2 cups mixed stir fry vegetables
- 0.5 cup soy yogurt
- 3tbsp curry paste
- 1tbsp oil or ghee

Directions:

1. Set the Instant Pot to sauté and add the oil and curry paste.
2. When the onion is soft, add the remaining ingredients except the yogurt and seal.
3. Cook on Stew for 20 minutes.
4. Release the pressure naturally and serve with a scoop of soy yogurt.

Nutrition: Calories 300| Fat 14g|Carb 9g

Fake On-Stew

Preparation time: 15 minutes
Cooking time: 25 minutes Servings: 2
Ingredients:

- 0.5lb soy bacon
- 1lb chopped vegetables
- 1 cup low sodium vegetable broth
- 1tbsp nutritional yeast

Directions:

1. Mix all the ingredients in your Instant Pot.
2. Cook on Stew for 25 minutes.
3. Release the pressure naturally.

Nutrition: Calories 200 |Fat7g|Carb 8g

Lentil and Chickpea Curry

Preparation time: 15 minutes
Cooking time: 20 minutes Servings: 2
Ingredients:

- 2 cups dry lentils and chickpeas
- 1 thinly sliced onion
- 1 cup chopped tomato
- 3tbsp curry paste
- 1tbsp oil or ghee

Directions:

1. Set the Instant Pot to sauté and add the onion, oil, and curry paste.
2. When the onion is soft, add the remaining ingredients and seal.
3. Cook on Stew for 20 minutes.
4. Release the pressure naturally.

Nutrition: Calories:360 |Fat 19g|Carb 26g

Seitan Roast

Preparation time: 15 minutes
Cooking time: 35 minutes Servings: 2
Ingredients:

- 1lb seitan roulade
- 1lb chopped winter vegetables
- 1 cup low sodium vegetable broth
- 4tbsp roast rub

Directions:

1. Rub the roast rub into your roulade.
2. Place the roulade and vegetables in your Instant Pot.
3. Add the broth. Seal.
4. Cook on Stew for 35 minutes.
5. Release the pressure naturally.

Nutrition:
Calories: 260 Carbs: 9 Sugar: 2 Fat: 2 Protein: 49
GL: 4

Zucchini with Tomatoes

Preparation Time: 15 minutes
Cooking Time: 11 minutes Servings: 8
Ingredients:

- 6 medium zucchinis, chopped roughly
- 1-pound cherry tomatoes
- 2 small onions, chopped roughly
- 2 tablespoons fresh basil, chopped
- 1 cup water
- 1 tablespoon olive oil
- 2 garlic cloves, minced
- Salt and ground black pepper, as required

Directions:

1. In the Instant Pot, place oil and press "Sauté". Now add the onion, garlic, ginger, and spices and cook for about 3-4 minutes.
2. Add the zucchinis and tomatoes and cook for about 1-2 minutes.

3. Press "Cancel" and stir in the remaining ingredients except basil.
4. Close the lid and place the pressure valve to "Seal" position.
5. Press "Manual" and cook under "High Pressure" for about 5 minutes.
6. Press "Cancel" and allow a "Natural" release.
7. Open the lid and transfer the vegetable mixture onto a serving platter.
8. Garnish with basil and serve.

Nutrition:
Calories: 57 Fats: 2.1g Carbohydrates: 9g
Sugar: 4.8gProteins: 2.5g Sodium: 39mg

Chickpea on Mixed Greens

Preparation Time: 10 minutes
Cooking Time: 0 minutes Servings: 2
Ingredients

- 123/4 ounces canned chickpeas, drained, rinsed, coarsely mashed
- 11/3 ounces celery, chopped
- 11/3 ounces red pepper, chopped
- 4 tablespoons red onion, chopped
- 1/8 teaspoon ground black pepper
- 2 tablespoons low fat mayonnaise
- 1/2 (5-ounce) package mixed baby salad greens

Directions:

1. Combine chickpeas, celery, red pepper, onion, pepper, and mayonnaise. Toss to mix.
2. Divide mix green among plates. Top with chickpeas mixture and serve.

Nutrition
Calories: 206 Carbohydrates (g): 26
Protein (g): 10 Fats (g): 3 Sodium (mg): 55

Tomato and Basil Salad

Preparation Time: 10 minutes
Cooking Time: 0 minutes Servings: 2
Ingredients

- 4 medium tomatoes, finely diced
- 1 garlic clove, crushed
- 6 basil leaves, rolled tightly and thinly sliced crosswise to form strips (chiffonade)
- 2 tablespoons organic extra virgin olive oil
- 1 tablespoon balsamic vinegar
- 1/2 teaspoon black pepper

Directions:

1. In a bowl, combine all the ingredients. Toss to mix. Season with pepper.

2. Divide among plates and serve.

Nutrition
Calories: 99
Carbohydrates (g): 3
Protein (g): 1
Fats (g): 7
Sodium (mg): 8

Annie's Everyday Salad

Preparation Time: 20 minutes
Cooking Time: 0 minutes Servings: 6
Ingredients

- 4 blood oranges, skinned, pitted, sliced
- 3 ripe avocados, pitted, halved, cubed to 1/2-inch thickness
- 1 teaspoon ground black pepper
- 2 fennel bulbs, outer layer removed, thinly sliced
- Juice of 1 lemon
- 2 tablespoons organic extra virgin olive oil

Directions:

1. On a large platter, arrange sliced orange in a single layer.
2. Season cubed avocado with black pepper. Arrange on top of sliced oranges.
3. Place fennel in a bowl. Add lemon juice and olive oil. Toss to mix. Transfer fennel onto sliced orange.
4. Drizzle juice and oil mixtures onto salad.
5. Serve salad on platter.

Nutrition
Calories: 251 Carbohydrates (g): 13
Protein (g): 4 Fats (g): 17 Sodium (mg): 17

The Potato Head Salad, 20

Preparation Time: 20
Cooking Time: 0 minutes
Servings: 10
Ingredients

- 11/2 pounds russet potatoes, peeled, cooked, cubed, warm
- 1 cup celery, sliced
- 1/2 cup green onions, sliced
- 1/4 cup green and red bell pepper, chopped
- 1/4 cup sweet pickle relish
- 2 hard cooked eggs, chopped
- 4 slices bacon, fried, well drained, crumbled
- 1 cup fat free mayonnaise
- 1/2 fat free sour cream
- 2 tablespoons cider vinegar
- 1 tablespoon yellow mustard
- 1/2 teaspoon celery seeds
- 1/8 teaspoon sea salt
- 1/8 teaspoon pepper

Directions:

1. In a bowl, combine potatoes, celery, green onions, green and red pepper, pickle relish, eggs and bacon. Toss and mix well. Add mayonnaise, sour cream, cider vinegar, yellow mustard and celery seeds. Toss and mix well. Season with sea salt and pepper.
2. Divide among plates and serve.

Nutrition
Calories: 132
Carbohydrates (g): 25
Protein (g): 4
Fats (g): 3
Sodium (mg): 495

Italian Crunchy Salad

Preparation Time: 20 minutes
cooking Time: 0 minutes Servings: 8
Ingredients:

- Fat Free Italian Dressing
- 1 (3/4-ounce) package Good Seasons Italian dressing mix
- 2 tablespoons plus 2 teaspoons lemon juice, freshly squeezed
- 1 cup water
- 1 teaspoon fructose
- 11/2 teaspoons instant thickener
- 11/2 cups fresh tomato, chunked to 1-inch
- 11/2 cups cucumber peeled, chunked to 1-inch
- 1/4 cup onion, chopped
- 1/2 cup black olives, sliced
- 1/2 cup avocado chunked to 1-inch
- 1/4 cup fat free Italian Dressing

Directions:

1. Prepare the Italian dressing. In a blender, combine all ingredients. Blend till well mixed. Transfer to bowl and let stand for 10 minutes. Set aside 1/4 cup and refrigerate the rest for later use.
2. In a bowl, combine all the ingredients. Toss to mix well.
3. Divide among plates and serve.

Nutrition
Calories: 39 Carbohydrates (g): 4 Protein (g): 1
Fats (g): 3 Sodium (mg): 145

Grilled Vegetables Salad with Herb Vinaigrette

Preparation Time: 25 minutes
Cooking Time: 0 minutes Servings: 6
Ingredients:

- Herb Vinaigrette
- 1 tablespoon organic extra virgin olive oil
- 2 teaspoons cider vinegar
- 1 teaspoon fresh parsley, snipped
- 1/4 teaspoon fresh thyme, snipped
- 1/4 teaspoon fresh rosemary, snipped
- 1/8 teaspoon sea salt
- 1/8 teaspoon ground black pepper
- 1 medium eggplant, cut crosswise into 1/2-inch slices
- 1 medium onion, cut into 1/2-inch wedges

- 2 green or red sweet peppers, halved, stemmed, seeded, membranes removed
- 3 roma tomatoes, halved lengthwise
- 6 large cremini mushrooms, stemmed
- 3 tablespoons organic extra virgin olive oil
- 1 tablespoon cider vinegar
- Herb Vinaigrette

Directions:

1. Prepare the herb vinaigrette. In a small bowl, combine all ingredients. Mix well and set aside.
2. In a very large bowl, combine eggplant, onion, sweet peppers, tomatoes and mushrooms. Drizzle oil and vinegar over vegetables. Toss to coat.
3. Preheat grill over medium heat. Uncover and grill vegetables till tender turning once midway through the grilling (about 6 minutes). Remove and cool for 5 minutes.
4. Cut halved sweet pepper to strips. Divide grilled vegetables among plates. Drizzle with herb vinaigrette and serve warm.

Nutrition
Calories: 126
Carbohydrates (g): 11 Protein (g): 2
Fats (g): 9 Sodium (mg): 55

Fruits and Beans Salad

Preparation Time: 25 minutes
Cooking Time: 0 minutes Servings: 8
Ingredients

- Honey Lime Dressing
- 2 tablespoons organic extra virgin olive oil
- 2 tablespoons water
- 1 tablespoon raw honey
- 1 tablespoon tarragon wine vinegar
- 1 tablespoon lime zest, grated
- 3 teaspoons lime juice
- 1/2 teaspoon dried mint leaves
- 1/8 teaspoon of sea salt
- 4 large ripe mangoes, peeled, pitted, cubed
- 1 cup pineapple, cubed
- 1/2 medium cucumber, seeded, sliced
- 1/4 cup red bell pepper, finely chopped
- 1/4 cup green onions, sliced
- 1 (15-ounce) can black beans, rinsed, drained
- 1/3Cup honey lime dressing
- 1 teaspoon mint sprigs

Directions:

1. Prepare the honey lime dressing. In a bowl, combine all the ingredients. Stir to mix and set aside 1/3 cup. In a salad bowl, combine all the ingredients (excluding mint). Toss to mix. To serve, transfer to plates and top with mint sprigs.

Nutrition
Calories: 164 Carbohydrates (g): 33 Protein (g): 5
Fats (g): 4
Sodium (mg): 169

Tomato Cucumber Mint Salad

Preparation Time: 25 minutes
Cooking Time: 0 minutes
Servings: 6
Ingredients

- 2 cucumbers, cut to 1/2-inch-wide pieces
- 1/3 cup red wine vinegar
- 1 teaspoon sugar
- 1/2 teaspoon sea salt
- 2 cups tomatoes, chopped
- 2/3Cup red onion, chopped
- 1/4 cup fresh mint, chopped
- 2 tablespoons organic extra virgin olive oil

Directions:

1. In a medium blow, combine cucumbers, vinegar, sugar and sea salt. Mix well and let stand in room temperature for 15 minutes.
2. Add tomatoes, red onion, mint and olive oil. Toss to mix.
3. Divide and transfer salad to plates and serve.

Nutrition

Calories: 68 Carbohydrates (g): 7 Protein (g): 1 Fats (g): 5 Sodium (mg): 202

Asparagus Mashed Eggs Salad

Preparation Time: 30 minutes
Cooking Time: 10 minutes Servings: 4
Ingredients

- 5 hard cooked eggs, shell removed
- 1/4 cup red onion, minced
- 2 tablespoons full fat mayonnaise
- 1 rib celery, finely diced
- 1 tablespoon lemon juice, freshly squeezed
- 1 tablespoon fresh parsley, chopped
- 2 teaspoons Dijon mustard
- 1 teaspoon of water
- 20 large asparagus spears (about 1 pound), peeled, ends trimmed

Directions:

1. Prepare the salad dressing. Halved eggs and separate the whites and yolks.
2. In 2 separate bowls, mash all the egg whites and 2 egg yolks. Set aside. (Save the remaining 3 egg yolks for other uses.)
3. In a bowl, combine the onion, mayonnaise, celery, lemon juice, parsley, mustard and water. Mix till blended. Add egg white mixture and stir to mix.
4. Bring a medium saucepan half fill with water to a boil over high heat. In a large bowl, half fill with ice water.
5. Cook asparagus till al dente (about 8 minutes). Remove and soak in ice water to retain color. Pat dry cooled asparagus with paper towels. Divide the asparagus spears among 4 plates. Spoon salad dressing over asparagus spears and top with minced egg yolks.

Nutrition
Calories: 105 Carbohydrates (g): 8 Protein (g): 8
Fats (g): 5 Sodium (mg): 199

Green Bean, Tomato and Onion Salad

Preparation Time: 30 minutes
Cooking Time: 5 minutes
Servings: 6
Ingredients

- 1/2 teaspoon sea salt
- 1-pound young green beans, trimmed
- 8 small plum tomatoes (about 1 pound), halved lengthwise
- 2 green onions, sliced
- Ingredients - Dressing
- 1/4 cup organic extra virgin olive oil
- 4 teaspoon red wine vinegar
- 1 tablespoon grainy mustard
- 1 clove garlic, minced
- 1/2 teaspoon granulated sugar
- 1/4 teaspoon sea salt
- 1/4 teaspoon ground black pepper
- 1/4 cup fresh parsley, chopped

Directions:

1. Half fill a medium saucepan with water. Add sea salt and bring to a boil. Add beans and cook till crispy and tender (about 3 minutes).
2. Remove from heat. Drain and cool bean in chill water. Drain and pat dry with paper towels.
3. With a small metal spoon scoop out center of plum tomatoes and discard. Halve each plum tomato again. Combine beans, tomatoes and green onions in a large bowl. Set aside.
4. Next, prepare the dressing. In a small bowl combine oil, vinegar, mustard, garlic, sugar, sea salt and pepper. Mix well. Add parsley and stir briefly. Pour dressing over salad and toss well.
5. Divide salad among plates and serve.

Nutrition
Calories: 128 Carbohydrates (g): 10 Protein (g): 2 Fats (g): 10 Sodium (mg): 150

Nutritional Berries-Pecan with Spinach Salad

Preparation Time: 45 minutes
Cooking Time: 20 minutes Servings: 6
Ingredients

- Oil Free Raspberry Dressing:

- 3 (3/4-ounce) packages Good Seasons Italian dressing mix
- 1/2 cup plus 1 tablespoon lemon juice, fresh squeezed
- 2 cups water
- 6 tablespoons raspberry-white grape juice frozen concentrate
- 1/3Cup instant food thickener
- 15 cloves garlic, peeled
- 1/4 cup pecans, chopped
- 1/3Cup oil free raspberry dressing
- 121/2 cups packed baby leaf spinach
- 1/2 cup red onion, thinly sliced
- 11/2 cups mixed berries, sliced
- Nonstick cooking spray

Directions:

1. Preheat oven to 275°F.
2. Prepare raspberry dressing. Combine all ingredients in a blender. Blend till smooth (about 30 seconds). Set aside 1/3 cup and refrigerate the rest for a maximum of 10 days.
3. Spread out pecans on baking sheet. Bake till slightly browned (about 10 minutes). Remove from oven and let cool for 15 minutes.
4. Meanwhile, increase oven to 300°F. Keep garlic in foil pouch. Lightly coat with a layer of nonstick cooking spray. Seal pouch and bake for 10 minutes. Remove from oven.
5. Combine all ingredients in a large bowl. Toss and mix well.
6. Divide among plates and serve.

Nutrition

Calories: 76 Carbohydrates (g): 10
Protein (g): 3 Fats (g): 4 Sodium (mg): 181

Vegetable Kabob Salad

Preparation Time: 50 minutes
Cooking Time: 15 minutes
Servings: 4
Ingredients - Dressing

- 2 tablespoons organic extra virgin olive oil
- 1 tablespoon red wine vinegar
- 1 tablespoon balsamic vinegar
- 1 teaspoon Dijon mustard
- 1 large clove garlic, minced
- 1 tablespoon fresh parsley, finely chopped
- 2 teaspoons fresh rosemary, finely chopped
- 1/2 teaspoon sea salt
- 1/2 teaspoon ground black pepper

Ingredients

- 1 Vidalia onion, sliced to 4 rounds
- 1 red bell pepper, quartered, ribbed, seeded
- 1 yellow bell pepper, quartered, ribbed, seeded
- 3 small zucchini, halved crosswise then lengthwise
- Nonstick cooking spray

Directions:

1. Prepare the dressing. Combine oil, vinegars, mustard, garlic, parsley, rosemary, sea salt and pepper in a bowl. Mix well. Brush vegetables with dressing.
2. Set vegetables aside to marinate for at least 30 minutes.
3. Preheat grill at medium-high heat after lightly coated with nonstick cooking spray.
4. Insert bamboo skewers through sliced onions. Arrange all vegetables on baking sheet.
5. Place baking sheet over grill and cook till vegetables are crispy and tender (about 12 minutes). Turn occasionally.
6. Divide vegetables among plates and serve warm.

Nutrition

Calories: 72 Carbohydrates (g): 10 Protein (g): 1
Fats (g): 1 Sodium (mg): 165

Fennel Garlic Salad

Preparation Time: 70 minutes
Cooking Time: 0 minutes
Servings: 4
Ingredients

- 11/2 fennel bulbs (about 18 ounces total), very thinly sliced with a mandoline
- 5 large cloves garlic, very thinly sliced
- 1/4 cup organic extra virgin olive oil
- Juice of 1/2 large lemon
- 1/8 teaspoon of coarse sea salt
- 1/8 teaspoon of ground black pepper
- 1 teaspoon fresh chives, minced
- 1 teaspoon fresh parsley leaves, minced

Directions:

1. In a stainless-steel bowl, combine fennel and garlic. Chill for 1 hour.
2. In another steel bowl, combine oil, lemon juice, sea salt and pepper. Mix well.
3. Remove fennel and garlic from fridge. Pour dressing over fennel and garlic. Toss well. Add chives and parsley. Toss to mix.
4. Divide and transfer salad to 4 plates and serve.

Nutrition
Calories: 173
Carbohydrates (g): 11
Protein (g): 2
Fats (g): 14
Sodium (mg): 97

Grandma Wendy's Multi-Layer Salad

Preparation Time: 70 minutes
Cooking Time: 0 minutes
Servings: 8
Ingredients:
Dressing:

- 1/4 cup organic extra virgin olive oil
- 2 tablespoon lime juice, freshly squeezed
- 1 tablespoon raw honey
- 2 teaspoon Dijon mustard
- 3/4 teaspoon ground cumin
- 1 clove garlic, minced
- 1/2 teaspoon sea salt
- 1/2 teaspoon pepper

Ingredients

- 1 (10-ounce) package fresh baby spinach, stemmed, coarsely chopped
- 11/2 cups mushrooms, sliced
- 2 cups carrots, peeled, shredded
- 11/2 cups seedless cucumber, halved lengthwise, sliced
- 1 small red onion, thinly sliced
- 1/3Cupdark raisins

Directions:

1. Prepare the dressing. In a bowl, combine oil, lime juice, honey, mustard, cumin, garlic, sea salt and pepper. Cover and chill.
2. Divide spinach into 3 portions. In a large bowl, layer 1 portion of spinach with mushrooms, another portion of spinach with carrots, then the final portion with spinach only. Top with cucumbers, onion and raisins. Cover and refrigerate 1 hour.
3. Remove salad and dressing from refrigerator. Divide salad among plates. Drizzle dressing over salad and serve.

Nutrition
Calories: 122
Carbohydrates (g): 14
Protein (g): 2
Fats (g): 7
Sodium (mg): 220

Bean and Chickpea Salad with Mustard-Herb Dressing

Preparation Time: 80 minutes
Cooking Time: 3 minutes
Servings: 6
Ingredients

- 1/2 teaspoon sea salt
- 1-pound green beans, end trimmed, cut to 1-inch length
- 1 (19-ounce) can chickpeas, drained, rinsed
- 1/3Cup red onions, chopped

Ingredients - Dressing

- 2 tablespoons organic extra virgin olive oil
- 2 tablespoons red wine vinegar
- 1 tablespoon granulated sugar
- 1 tablespoon Dijon mustard
- 1/4 teaspoon freshly ground black pepper
- 1/4 teaspoon sea salt
- 2 tablespoons fresh dill, finely chopped

Directions:

1. Half fill a medium saucepan with water. Add sea salt and bring to a boil. Add beans and cook till crispy and tender (about 3 minutes). Remove from heat. Drain and cool bean in chill water. Drain and pat dry with paper towels
2. In a bowl, combine green beans, chickpeas and onions. Set aside.
3. Next, prepare the dressing. In a small bowl, combine oil, vinegar, sugar, mustard, pepper and sea salt. Mix till smooth. Stir in dill. Drizzle over salad and toss well. Let chill for 1 hour.
4. Divide salad among plates and serve.

Nutrition

Calories: 161 Carbohydrates (g): 23

Protein (g): 6 Fats (g): 6 Sodium (mg): 325

Most Irresistible Potato Salad

Preparation Time: 105 minutes

Cooking Time: 20 minutes

Servings: 8

Ingredients:

- 6 medium potatoes, rinsed
- 3/4 teaspoon sea salt, divided
- 3/4 cup frozen peas, thawed
- 2 tablespoon red wine vinegar
- 1 tablespoon Dijon mustard
- 1 clove garlic, minced
- 4 green onions, sliced
- 2 stalks celery, diced
- 1/4 cup fresh parsley, chopped
- 3 hard cooked eggs, chopped
- 1/2 cup light mayonnaise
- 1/4 cup plain low-fat yogurt
- 1/4 teaspoon ground black pepper

Directions:

1. Half fill a medium saucepan with water. Add sea salt and bring water to a boil. Cook potatoes till tender (about 20 minutes). Remove from heat. Drain and let cool for 10 minutes. Peel skin and cut to 1/2-inch cubes. Place in large bowl and set aside.
2. Rinse peas with boiling water. Drain well.
3. Combine vinegar, mustard and garlic in small bowl. Mix well. Add potatoes. Toss gently to mix. Add onions, celery, parsley, eggs and peas. Mix well.
4. In a separate large bowl, combine mayonnaise, yogurt, 1/4 teaspoon sea salt and pepper. Mix well. Fold in potato mixture till evenly coated. Chill for at least 1 hour.
5. To serve, divide salad among plates.

Nutrition

Calories: 162 Carbohydrates (g): 20

Protein (g): 5 Fats (g): 7 Sodium (mg): 395

Salad on the Rock

Preparation Time: 130 minutes

Cooking Time: 0 minutes

Servings: 8

Ingredients

- 2 cups cauliflower, finely chopped
- 1 cup broccoli florets, finely chopped
- 1/2 cup red apple, diced
- 2 tablespoons raw sunflower seeds
- 2 tablespoons dried cranberries
- 1/4 cup Mayonnaise spread
- 11/2 teaspoons lemon juice, freshly squeezed
- 1/8 teaspoon sea salt
- 2 tablespoons frozen apple juice concentrate, thawed
- 1/8 teaspoon cayenne pepper

Directions:

1. In a medium bowl, combine all ingredients. Toss well. Cover and chill for at least 2 hours.
2. Remove from refrigerator. Transfer to plates and serve.

Nutrition

Calories: 58

Carbohydrates (g): 7

Protein (g): 2

Fats (g): 3

Sodium (mg): 87

Fresh Tomato with Minty Lentil Salad

Preparation Time: 160 minutes

Cooking Time: 15 minutes
Servings: 6
Ingredients

- 1 cup dry lentils
- 2 cups water
- 1/2 cup onion, chopped
- 2 teaspoons garlic, minced
- 1/4 cup celery, chopped
- 1/2 cup green pepper, chopped
- 1/2 cup parsley, finely chopped
- 2 tablespoons fresh mint, finely chopped
- 1/4 cup lemon juice
- 1/4 cup extra virgin olive oil
- 1/2 teaspoon sea salt
- 1 cup fresh tomato, diced

Directions:

1. In a medium saucepan, combine lentils and water and bring to a boil. Reduce heat till simmering, cover and let simmer till lentils are tender (about 15 minutes). Remove from heat, drain and transfer to medium bowl.
2. Add onion, garlic, celery, green pepper, parsley and mint. Mix well.
3. In a small bowl, combine lemon juice, olive oil, and sea salt. Mix well. Drizzle over lentils mixture and toss to mix. Cover and refrigerate for 2 hours or more.
4. To serve, remove salad from refrigerator, mix in tomatoes and divide salad among plates.

Nutrition
Calories: 136
Carbohydrates (g): 11
Protein (g): 4
Fats (g): 9
Sodium (mg): 211

Delicious Caribbean Potato Salad

Preparation Time: 3 hours 10 minutes
Cooking Time: 0 minutes
Servings: 8
Ingredients

- 11/2 pounds sweet potatoes, peeled, cooked, 3/4-inch cubed
- 11/2 pounds russet potatoes, peeled, cooked, 3/4 -inch cubed
- 1/4 cup small pimiento stuffed olives
- 3/4 cup fat free mayonnaise
- 1/2 cup fat free milk
- 2 teaspoons lime juice
- 2 green onions, sliced
- 1 teaspoon ground cumin
- 1/8 teaspoon red cayenne pepper
- 1/8 teaspoon sea salt

Directions:

1. In a bowl, combine potatoes and olives. Add mayonnaise, milk, lime juice, green onions, cumin and pepper. Toss and mix well. Season with sea salt.
2. Chill for 3 hours.
3. Remove from fridge. Divide among plates and serve.

Nutrition
Calories: 167 Carbohydrates (g): 37
Protein (g): 3 Fats (g): 1
Sodium (mg): 416

Ten Vegetables Salad

Preparation Time: 10 minutes +8 hours refrigerate
Cooking Time: 0 minutes
Servings: 8
Ingredients

- Herbed Sour Cream Dressing:
- 3/4 cup fat free mayonnaise
- 3/4 cup sour cream
- 2 cloves garlic, minced
- 1/2 teaspoon dried basil
- 1/2 teaspoon tarragon leaves
- 1/4 teaspoon sea salt
- 1/4 teaspoon pepper

Ingredients

- 2 cups romaine lettuce, thinly sliced
- 1 cup red cabbage, sliced
- 1 cup mushrooms, sliced
- 1 cup carrots, sliced
- 1 cup green bell pepper, sliced
- 1 cup cherry tomatoes, halved
- 1 cup small broccoli

- 1/2 cup cucumber, sliced
- 1/2 cup red onion, sliced
- 11/2 cup sour cream dressing
- 4 teaspoons parsley, finely chopped

Directions:

1. Prepare the herbed sour cream dressing. Combine all ingredients in a bowl. Mix well.
2. In a (11/2-quart) bowl, arrange lettuce at the bottom. Arrange and layer remaining vegetables on top of lecture. Top with sour cream dressing and garnish with parsley.
3. Cover and refrigerate for 8 hours.
4. Remove from fridge. Toss to mix. Transfer to plates and serve.

Nutrition
Calories: 68
Carbohydrates (g): 15
Protein (g): 3
Fats (g): 0
Sodium (mg): 380

Butter Beans

Preparation Time: 5 minutes
Cooking Time: 12 minutes Serving: 4
Ingredients

- 2 garlic cloves, minced
- Red pepper flakes to taste
- Salt to taste
- 2 tablespoons clarified butter
- 4 cups green beans, trimmed

Directions

1. Bring a pot of salted water to boil
2. Once the water starts to boil, add beans and cook for 3 minutes
3. Take a bowl of ice water and drain beans, plunge them in the ice water
4. Once cooled, keep them on the side
5. Take a medium skillet and place it over medium heat, add ghee and melt
6. Add red pepper, salt, garlic
7. Cook for 1 minute
8. Add beans and toss until coated well, cook for 3 minutes
9. Serve and enjoy!

Nutrition:
Calories: 93 Fat: 8g
Carbohydrates: 4g Protein: 2g

Walnuts and Asparagus

Preparation Time: 5 minutes
Cooking Time: 5 minutes
Serving: 4
Ingredients

- 1 and1/2 tablespoons olive oil
- 3/4-pound asparagus, trimmed
- 1/4 cup walnuts, chopped
- Salt and pepper to taste

Directions

1. Place a skillet over medium heat add olive oil and let it heat up
2. Add asparagus, Sauté for 5 minutes until browned Season with salt and pepper
3. Remove heat
4. Add walnuts and toss Serve warm!

Nutrition:
Calories: 124 Fat: 12g Carbohydrates: 2g
Protein: 3g

Roasted Cauliflower

Preparation Time: 5 minutes
Cooking Time: 30 minutes
Serving: 8
Ingredients

- 1 large cauliflower head
- 2 tablespoons melted coconut oil
- 2 tablespoons fresh thyme
- 1 teaspoon Celtic Sea salt
- 1 teaspoon fresh ground pepper
- 1 head roasted garlic
- 8 ounces burrata cheese, for garnish
- 2 tablespoons fresh thyme for garnish

Directions

1. Preheat your oven to 425 degrees F
2. Rinse cauliflower and trim, core and sliced
3. Lay cauliflower evenly on a rimmed baking tray
4. Drizzle coconut oil evenly over cauliflower, sprinkle thyme leaves
5. Season with a pinch of salt and pepper

6. Squeeze roasted garlic
7. Roast cauliflower until slightly caramelize for about 30 minutes, making sure to turn once
8. Garnish with fresh thyme leaves and burrata
9. Enjoy!

Nutrition:
Calories: 129
Fat: 11g
Carbohydrates: 6g
Protein: 7g

Cool Brussels Platter

Preparation Time: 5 minutes
Cooking Time: 10-15 minutes
Serving: 2
Ingredients

- 1/4 cup parmesan cheese, grated
- 1/4 cup hazelnuts, whole and skinless
- 1 tablespoon olive oil
- 1 pound Brussels sprouts
- Salt to taste

Directions

1. Pre-heat your oven 350 degrees F
2. Line a baking sheet with parchment paper and trim bottom of Brussels
3. Put leaves in a medium-sized bowl, making sure that they are broken
4. Toss leaves with olive oil and season with salt
5. Spread leaves on baking sheet
6. Roast for 10-15 minutes until crispy
7. Divide between bowls and toss with remaining ingredients
8. Serve and enjoy!

Nutrition:
Calories: 287 Fat: 19g Carbohydrates: 13g Protein: 14g

Tangy Pineapple Coleslaw

Preparation Time: 10 minutes
Cooking Time: 0 minutes
Servings: 6
Ingredients:

- 1/4 cup nonfat Greek yogurt
- 1/4 cup light mayonnaise
- 1/4 cup finely chopped canned pineapple (packed in its own juice)
- 2 tablespoons pineapple juice (from the canned pineapple)
- 21/2 cups shredded cabbage
- 1/2 cup shredded carrots

Directions:

1. In a medium bowl, combine the yogurt, mayonnaise, pineapple, and pineapple juice. Put in the cabbage and carrots and mix well until evenly covered with the dressing.

Nutrition:
Calories: 60 Protein: 1g Carbohydrates: 6g Fat: 3.5g Saturated Fat: 0.5g Cholesterol: 0mg Sodium: 85mg Fiber: 1g

Vegetarian Antipasto Salad

Preparation Time: 10 minutes
Cooking Time: 0 minutes
Servings: 8

- Ingredients:
- 1 cup halved marinated mushrooms
- 1 cup chopped canned artichokes
- 1 cup chopped roasted red peppers
- 1/2 cup sliced black olives
- 1 cup cubed light mozzarella cheese
- 1/2 cup chopped fresh basil
- 4 cups chopped romaine lettuce

Directions:

1. Dressing of your choice
2. Toss all of the ingredients in a large bowl and serve.
3. Calorie-Cutting Tips
4. To keep calories low, try to find the veggies packed/marinated in water or vinegar. If you select the ones packed in oil, simply rinse them before using.

Nutrition:
Calories: 80 Protein: 5g Carbohydrates: 9g Fat: 3.5g Saturated Fat: 1g Cholesterol: 5mg Sodium: 480mg Fiber: 3g

Watermelon and Feta Salad

Preparation Time: 10 minutes
Cooking Time: 0 minutes Servings: 4
Ingredients:

- 4 cups 1/2"-cubed watermelon
- 2 tablespoons fresh chopped basil
- 4 tablespoons white balsamic vinegar
- 2 tablespoons water
- 2 teaspoons honey
- Squeeze of fresh lemon juice
- 1/4 cup reduced-fat feta cheese

Directions:

1. Put the watermelon into a medium bowl.
2. In a smaller bowl, whisk together the basil, vinegar, water, honey, and lemon. Pour over the watermelon. Mix well to evenly coat. Sprinkle with cheese and lightly stir.

Nutrition:
Calories: 80 Protein: 2g Carbohydrates: 19g Fat: 1g Saturated Fat: 1g Cholesterol: 5mg Sodium: 125mg Fiber: 1g

Generous Fiery Tomato Salad

Preparation Time: 10 minutes
Cooking Time: 25 minutes Serving: 4
Ingredients

- 1/2 cup scallions, chopped
- 1-pound cherry tomatoes
- 3teaspoons olive oil
- Sea salt and freshly ground black pepper, to taste
- 1 tablespoon red wine vinegar

Directions:

1. Season tomatoes with spices and oil
2. Heat your oven to 450 degrees Fahrenheit
3. Take a baking sheet and spread the tomatoes
4. Bake for 15 minutes
5. Stir and turn the tomatoes
6. Then again, bake for 10 minutes
7. Take a bowl and mix the roasted tomatoes with all the remaining ingredients
8. Serve and enjoy!

Nutrition:
Calories: 115
Fat: 10.4g
Carbohydrates: 5.4g
Protein: 12g

Juicy Ground Beef Casserole

Preparation Time: 10 minutes
Cooking Time: 35 minutes
Serving: 6
Ingredients

- 2 teaspoons onion flakes
- 1 tablespoon gluten-free Worcestershire sauce
- 2 pounds ground beef
- 2 garlic clove, peeled and minced
- Salt and pepper to taste
- 1 cup mozzarella cheese, shredded
- 2 cups cheddar cheese, shredded
- 1 cup Russian dressing
- 2 tablespoons sesame seeds, toasted
- 20 dill pickle slices
- 1 romaine lettuce head, torn

Directions:

1. Take a pan and place it over medium heat
2. Add beef, onion flakes, Worcestershire sauce, salt, pepper, and garlic
3. Stir for 5 minutes
4. Transfer to a baking dish and add a 1 cup of cheddar, mozzarella cheese, half of the dressing
5. Stir and spread evenly
6. Arrange pickle slices on top
7. Sprinkle remaining cheddar and sesame seeds
8. Transfer to oven and bake for 20 minutes at 350 degrees F
9. Turn oven to broil and broil for 5 minutes
10. Divide lettuce between serving platters and top with remaining dressing
11. Enjoy!

Nutrition:
Calories: 554
Fat: 51g
Carbohydrates: 5g
Protein: 45g

Seafood

Salmon Cakes in Air Fryer

Preparation Time: 10 minutes
Cooking Time: 10 minutes
Serving: 2
Ingredients

- Fresh salmon fillet 8 oz.
- Egg 1
- Salt 1/8 tsp
- Garlic powder ¼ tsp
- Sliced lemon 1

Direction

1. In the bowl, chop the salmon, add the egg & spices.
2. Form tiny cakes.
3. Let the Air fryer preheat to 390. On the bottom of the air fryer bowl lay sliced lemons—place cakes on top.
4. Cook them for seven minutes. Based on your diet preferences, eat with your chosen dip.

Nutrition
Calories: 194
Fat: 9g
Protein: 25g

Coconut Shrimp

Preparation Time: 10 minutes
Cooking Time: 30 minutes
Serving: 4
Ingredients

- Pork Rinds: ½ cup (Crushed)
- Jumbo Shrimp:4 cups. (deveined)
- Coconut Flakes preferably: ½ cup
- Eggs: two
- Flour of coconut: ½ cup
- Any oil of your choice for frying at least half-inch in pan
- Freshly ground black pepper & kosher salt to taste

Dipping sauce (Pina colada flavor)

- Powdered Sugar as Substitute: 2-3 tablespoon
- Mayonnaise: 3 tablespoons
- Sour Cream: ½ cup
- Coconut Extract or to taste: ¼ tsp
- Coconut Cream: 3 tablespoons
- Pineapple Flavoring as much to taste: ¼ tsp
- Coconut Flakes preferably unsweetened this is optional: 3 tablespoons

Direction
Pina Colada (Sauce)

1. Mix all the ingredients into a tiny bowl for the Dipping sauce (Pina colada flavor). Combine well and put in the fridge until ready to serve.

Shrimps

1. Whip all eggs in a deep bowl, and a small, shallow bowl, add the crushed pork rinds, coconut flour, sea salt, coconut flakes, and freshly ground black pepper.
2. Put the shrimp one by one in the mixed eggs for dipping, then in the coconut flour blend. Put them on a clean plate or put them on your air fryer's basket.
3. Place the shrimp battered in a single layer on your air fryer basket. Spritz the shrimp with oil and cook for 8-10 minutes at 360 ° F, flipping them through halfway.
4. Enjoy hot with dipping sauce.

Nutrition
Calories 340
Protein 25g
Fat 16g

Crispy Fish Sticks in Air Fryer

Preparation Time: 10 minutes
Cooking Time: 15 minutes

Serving: 4

Ingredients

- Whitefish such as cod 1 lb.
- Mayonnaise ¼ c
- Dijon mustard 2 tbsp.
- Water 2 tbsp.
- Pork rind 1&1/2 c
- Cajun seasoning ¾ tsp
- Kosher salt& pepper to taste

Direction

1. Spray non-stick cooking spray to the air fryer rack.
2. Pat the fish dry & cut into sticks about 1 inch by 2 inches' broad
3. Stir together the mayo, mustard, and water in a tiny, small dish. Mix the pork rinds & Cajun seasoning into another small container.
4. Adding kosher salt& pepper to taste (both pork rinds & seasoning can have a decent amount of kosher salt, so you can dip a finger to see how salty it is).
5. Working for one slice of fish at a time, dip to cover in the mayo mix & then tap off the excess. Dip into the mixture of pork rind, then flip to cover. Place on the rack of an air fryer.
6. Set at 400F to Air Fry & bake for 5 minutes, then turn the fish with tongs and bake for another 5 minutes. Serve.

Nutrition

Calories: 263

Fat: 16g

Protein: 26.4g

Honey-Glazed Salmon

Preparation Time: 10 minutes

Cooking Time: 15 minutes

Serving: 2

Ingredients

- Gluten-free Soy Sauce: 6 tsp
- Salmon Fillets: 2 pcs
- Sweet rice wine: 3 tsp
- Water: 1 tsp
- Honey: 6 tbsp.

Direction

1. In a bowl, mix sweet rice wine, soy sauce, honey, and water.
2. Set half of it aside.
3. In the half of it, marinate the fish and let it rest for two hours.
4. Let the air fryer preheat to 180 C
5. Cook the fish for 8 minutes, flip halfway through and cook for another five minutes.
6. Baste the salmon with marinade mixture after 3 or 4 minutes.
7. The half of marinade, pour in a saucepan reduce to half, serve with a sauce.

Nutrition

Calories 254

Fat 12g

Protein 20g

Basil-Parmesan Crusted Salmon

Preparation Time: 5 minutes

Cooking Time: 15 minutes

Serving: 4

Ingredients

- Grated Parmesan: 3 tablespoons
- Skinless four salmon fillets
- Salt: 1/4 teaspoon
- Freshly ground black pepper
- Low-fat mayonnaise: 3 tablespoons
- Basil leaves, chopped
- Half lemon

Direction

1. Let the air fryer preheat to 400F. Spray the basket with olive oil.
2. With salt, pepper, and lemon juice, season the salmon.
3. In a bowl, mix two tablespoons of Parmesan cheese with mayonnaise and basil leaves.
4. Add this mix and more parmesan on top of salmon and cook for seven minutes or until fully cooked. Serve hot.

Nutrition: Calories 289|Protein 30g|Fat 18.5g

Cajun Shrimp in Air Fryer

Preparation Time: 10 minutes

Cooking Time: 21 minutes

Serving: 4
Ingredients

- Peeled, 24 extra-jumbo shrimp
- Olive oil: 2 tablespoons
- Cajun seasoning: 1 tablespoon
- one zucchini, thick slices (half-moons)
- Cooked Turkey: ¼ cup
- Yellow squash, sliced half-moons
- Kosher salt: 1/4 teaspoon

Direction

1. In a bowl, mix the shrimp with Cajun seasoning.
2. In another bowl, add zucchini, turkey, salt, squash, and coat with oil.
3. Let the air fryer preheat to 400F
4. Move the shrimp and vegetable mix to the fryer basket and cook for three minutes.
5. Serve hot.

Nutrition
Calories: 284
Protein: 31g
Fat: 14g

Crispy Air Fryer Fish

Preparation Time: 10 minutes
Cooking Time: 17 minutes
Serving: 4
Ingredients

- Old bay: 2 tsp
- 4-6, cut in half, Whiting Fish fillets
- Fine cornmeal: ¾ cup
- Flour: ¼ cup
- Paprika: 1 tsp
- Garlic powder: half tsp
- Salt: 1 and ½ tsp
- Freshly ground black pepper: half tsp

Direction

1. In a Ziploc bag, add all ingredients and coat the fish fillets with it.
2. Spray oil on the basket of air fryer and put the fish in it.
3. Cook for ten minutes at 400 F. flip fish if necessary and coat with oil spray and cook for another seven-minute.
4. Serve with salad green.

Nutrition
Calories 254 fat 12.7g
protein 17.5g

Air Fryer Lemon Cod

Preparation Time: 5 minutes
Cooking Time: 10 minutes
Serving: 1
Ingredients

- One cod fillet
- Dried parsley
- Kosher salt and pepper to taste
- Garlic powder
- One lemon

Direction

1. In a bowl, mix all ingredients and coat the fish fillet with spices.
2. Slice the lemon and lay at the bottom of the air fryer basket.
3. Put spiced fish on top. Cover the fish with lemon slices.
4. Cook for ten minutes at 375F, the internal temperature of fish should be 145F.
5. Serve with microgreen salad.

Nutrition
Calories: 101 Protein: 16g
Fat: 1g

Sweet salmon with green beans

Preparation Time: 20 minutes |Cooking Time: 15 minutes |Servings: 4
Ingredients:

- 4 salmon fillets
- 1 tablespoon butter
- 2 tablespoons brown sugar
- 2 tablespoons reduced-sodium soy sauce
- 2 tablespoons Dijon mustard
- 1 tablespoon olive oil
- 1/2 teaspoon pepper
- 1/8 teaspoon salt
- 1-pound fresh green beans, trimmed

Directions:

1. Preheat oven to 425°. Place fillets in a 15x10x1-in. baking pan coated with cooking spray. In a small skillet, melt butter; stir in brown sugar, soy sauce, mustard, oil, pepper and salt. Brush half of the mixture over salmon.
2. Place green beans in a large bowl; drizzle with remaining brown sugar mixture and toss to coat. Arrange green beans around fillets. Roast until fish just begins to flake easily with a fork and green beans are crisp-tender, 14-16 minutes.

Nutrition: 388 Calories|19g Fat|14g Carb

Air Fryer Salmon Fillets

Preparation Time: 5 minutes
Cooking Time: 15 minutes
Serving: 2
Ingredients

- Low-fat Greek yogurt: 1/4 cup
- Two salmon fillets
- Fresh dill: 1 tbsp. (chopped)
- One lemon and lemon juice
- Garlic powder: half tsp.
- Kosher salt and pepper

Direction

1. Cut the lemon in slices and lay at the bottom of the air fryer basket.
2. Season the salmon with kosher salt and pepper. Put salmon on top of lemons.
3. Let it cook at 330 degrees for 15 minutes.
4. In the meantime, mix garlic powder, lemon juice, salt, pepper with yogurt and dill.
5. Serve the fish with sauce.

Nutrition
Calories: 194 Protein: 25g Fat: 7g

Air Fryer Fish & Chips

Preparation Time: 10 minutes
Cooking Time: 35 minutes
Serving: 4
Ingredients

- 4 cups of any fish fillet
- flour: 1/4 cup
- Whole wheat breadcrumbs: one cup
- One egg
- Oil: 2 tbsp.
- Potatoes
- Salt: 1 tsp.

Direction

1. Cut the potatoes in fries. Then coat with oil and salt.
2. Cook in the air fryer for 20 minutes at 400 F, toss the fries halfway through.
3. In the meantime, coat fish in flour, then in the whisked egg, and finally in breadcrumbs mix.
4. Place the fish in the air fryer and let it cook at 330F for 15 minutes.
5. Flip it halfway through, if needed.
6. Serve with tartar sauce and salad green.

Nutrition
Calories: 409 Protein: 30g
Fat: 11g

Grilled Salmon with Lemon

Preparation Time: 10 minutes
Cooking Time: 21 minutes
Serving: 4
Ingredients

- Olive oil: 2 tablespoons
- Two Salmon fillets
- Lemon juice
- Water: 1/3 cup
- Gluten-free light soy sauce: 1/3 cup
- Honey: 1/3 cup
- Scallion slices
- Cherry tomato
- Freshly ground black pepper, garlic powder, kosher salt to taste

Direction

1. Season salmon with pepper and salt
2. In a bowl, mix honey, soy sauce, lemon juice, water, oil. Add salmon in this marinade and let it rest for least two hours.

3. Let the air fryer preheat at 180°C
4. Place fish in the air fryer and cook for 8 minutes.
5. Move to a dish and top with scallion slices.

Nutrition
Calories 211
Fat 9g
Protein 15g

Air-Fried Fish Nuggets

Preparation Time: 15 minutes
Cooking Time: 10 minutes
Serving: 4
Ingredients

- Fish fillets in cubes: 2 cups(skinless)
- 1 egg, beaten
- Flour: 5 tablespoons
- Water: 5 tablespoons
- Kosher salt and pepper to taste
- Breadcrumbs mix
- Smoked paprika: 1 tablespoon
- Whole wheat breadcrumbs: ¼ cup
- Garlic powder: 1 tablespoon

Direction

1. Season the fish cubes with kosher salt and pepper.
2. In a bowl, add flour and gradually add water, mixing as you add.
3. Then mix in the egg. And keep mixing but do not over mix.
4. Coat the cubes in batter, then in the breadcrumb mix. Coat well
5. Place the cubes in a baking tray and spray with oil.
6. Let the air fryer preheat to 200 C.
7. Place cubes in the air fryer and cook for 12 minutes or until well cooked and golden brown.
8. Serve with salad greens.

Nutrition
184 Calories
19g Protein
3.3g Fat

Garlic Rosemary Grilled Prawns

Preparation Time: 6 minutes
Cooking Time: 11 minutes
Serving: 2
Ingredients

- Melted butter: 1/2 tbsp.
- Green capsicum: slices
- Eight prawns
- Rosemary leaves
- Kosher salt& freshly ground black pepper
- 3-4 cloves of minced garlic

Direction

1. In a bowl, mix all the ingredients and marinate the prawns in it for at least 60 minutes or more
2. Add two prawns and two slices of capsicum on each skewer.
3. Let the air fryer preheat to 180 C.
4. Cook for 5-6 minutes. Then change the temperature to 200 C and cook for another minute. Serve with lemon wedges.

Nutrition
Calories 194 Fat: 10g Carbohydrates: 12g

Air-Fried Crumbed Fish

Preparation Time: 10 minutes
Cooking Time: 13 minutes
Serving: 2
Ingredients

- Four fish fillets
- Olive oil: 4 tablespoons
- One egg beaten
- Whole wheat breadcrumbs: ¼ cup

Direction

1. Let the air fryer preheat to 180 C.
2. In a bowl, mix breadcrumbs with oil. Mix well
3. First, coat the fish in the egg mix (egg mix with water) then in the breadcrumb mix. Coat well
4. Place in the air fryer, let it cook for 10-12 minutes.
5. Serve hot with salad green and lemon.

Nutrition

Calories 254
Fat 12.7g
Protein 15.5g

Parmesan Garlic Crusted Salmon

Preparation Time: 5 minutes
Cooking Time: 15 minutes
Serving: 2
Ingredients

- Whole wheat breadcrumbs: 1/4 cup
- 4 cups of salmon
- Butter melted: 2 tablespoons
- ¼ tsp of freshly ground black pepper
- Parmesan cheese: 1/4 cup(grated)
- Minced garlic: 2 teaspoons
- Half teaspoon of Italian seasoning

Direction

1. Let the air fryer preheat to 400 F, spray the oil over the air fryer basket.
2. Pat dries the salmon. In a bowl, mix Parmesan cheese, Italian seasoning, and breadcrumbs. In another pan, mix melted butter with garlic and add to the breadcrumbs mix. Mix well
3. Add kosher salt and freshly ground black pepper to salmon. On top of every salmon piece, add the crust mix and press gently.
4. Let the air fryer preheat to 400 F and add salmon to it. Cook until done to your liking. Serve hot with vegetable side dishes.

Nutrition
Calories 330 Fat 19g Protein 31g

Air Fryer Salmon with Maple Soy Glaze

Preparation Time: 6 minutes
Cooking Time: 8 minutes
Serving: 4
Ingredients

- Pure maple syrup: 3 tbsp.
- Gluten-free soy sauce: 3 tbsp.
- Sriracha hot sauce: 1 tbsp.
- One clove of minced garlic
- Salmon: 4 fillets, skinless

Direction

1. In a Ziploc bag, mix sriracha, maple syrup, garlic, and soy sauce with salmon.
2. Mix well and let it marinate for at least half an hour.
3. Let the air fryer preheat to 400F with oil spray the basket
4. Take fish out from the marinade, pat dry.
5. Put the salmon in the air fryer, cook for 7 to 8 minutes, or longer.
6. In the meantime, in a saucepan, add the marinade, let it simmer until reduced to half.
7. Add glaze over salmon and serve.

Nutrition
Calories 292 Protein: 35g Fat: 11g

Air Fried Cajun Salmon *

Preparation Time: 10 minutes
Cooking Time: 21 minutes
Serving: 1
Ingredients

- Fresh salmon: 1 piece
- Cajun seasoning: 2 tbsp.
- Lemon juice.

Direction

1. Let the air fryer preheat to 180 C.
2. Pat dries the salmon fillet. Rub lemon juice and Cajun seasoning over the fish fillet.
3. Place in the air fryer, cook for 7 minutes. Serve with salad greens and lime wedges.

Nutrition
Calories 216 Fat 19g Protein 19.2g

Air Fryer Shrimp Scampi

Preparation Time: 5 minutes
Cooking Time: 11 minutes
Serving: 2
Ingredients

- Raw Shrimp: 4 cups
- Lemon Juice: 1 tablespoon
- Chopped fresh basil
- Red Pepper Flakes: 2 teaspoons
- Butter: 2.5 tablespoons

- Chopped chives
- Chicken Stock: 2 tablespoons
- Minced Garlic: 1 tablespoon

Direction

1. Let the air fryer preheat with a metal pan to 330F
2. In the hot pan, add garlic, red pepper flakes, and half of the butter. Let it cook for two minutes.
3. Add the butter, shrimp, chicken stock, minced garlic, chives, lemon juice, basil to the pan. Let it cook for five minutes. Bathe the shrimp in melted butter.
4. Take out from the air fryer and let it rest for one minute.
5. Add fresh basil leaves and chives and serve.

Nutrition

Calories 287

Fat 5.5g

Protein 18g

Sesame Seeds Fish Fillet *

Preparation Time: 10 minutes

Cooking Time: 22 minutes

Serving: 1

Ingredients

- Plain flour: 3 tablespoons
- One egg, beaten
- Five frozen fish fillets

For Coating

- Oil: 2 tablespoons
- Sesame seeds: 1/2 cup
- Rosemary herbs
- 5-6 biscuit's crumbs
- Kosher salt& pepper, to taste

Direction

1. For two-minute sauté the sesame seeds in a pan, without oil. Brown them and set it aside.
2. In a plate, mix all coating ingredients
3. Place the aluminum foil on the air fryer basket and let it preheat at 200 C.
4. First, coat the fish in flour. Then in egg, then in the coating mix.
5. Place in the Air fryer. If fillets are frozen, cook for ten minutes, then turn the fillet and cook for another four minutes.
6. If not frozen, then cook for eight minutes and two minutes.

Nutrition

Calories 250 Fat: 8g Protein: 20g

Lemon Pepper Shrimp in Air Fryer

Preparation Time: 6 minutes

Cooking Time: 11 minutes

Serving: 2

Ingredients

- Raw shrimp: 1 and 1/2 cup peeled, deveined
- Olive oil: 1/2 tablespoon
- Garlic powder: ¼ tsp
- Lemon pepper: 1 tsp
- Paprika: ¼ tsp
- Juice of one lemon

Direction

1. Let the air fryer preheat to 400 F
2. In a bowl, mix lemon pepper, olive oil, paprika, garlic powder, and lemon juice. Mix well. Add shrimps and coat well
3. Add shrimps in the air fryer, cook for 8 minutes and top with lemon slices and serve

Nutrition

Calories 237 Fat 6g

Protein 36g

Monk-Fish Curry

Preparation Time: 15 minutes

Cooking Time: 21 minutes

Serving: 2

Ingredients:

- 0.5lb monkfish
- 1 thinly sliced sweet yellow onion
- 0.5 cup chopped tomato
- 3tbsp strong curry paste
- 1tbsp oil or ghee

Direction

1. Set the Instant Pot to sauté and add the onion, oil, and curry paste.

2. When the onion is soft, add the remaining ingredients and seal.
3. Cook on Stew for 20 minutes.
4. Release the pressure naturally.

Nutrition:
Calories: 270 Fat: 11g Protein: 45g

Salmon Bake

Preparation Time: 15 minutes
Cooking Time: 15 minutes Serving: 2
Ingredients:

- 1lb salmon
- 1lb chopped Mediterranean vegetables
- 1 cup low sodium fish broth
- juice of half a lemon
- sea salt as desired

Direction:

1. Mix all the ingredients except the broth in a foil pouch.
2. Place the pouch in the steamer basket your Instant Pot.
3. Pour the broth into your Instant Pot.
4. Cook on Steam for 15 minutes.
5. Release the pressure naturally.

Nutrition:
Calories: 260
Fat: 12g
Protein: 36g

Mixed Chowder

Preparation Time: 16 minutes
Cooking Time: 35 minutes
Serving: 2
Ingredients:

- 1lb fish stew mix
- 2 cups white sauce
- 3tbsp old bay seasoning

Direction

1. Mix all the ingredients in your Instant Pot.
2. Cook on Stew for 35 minutes.
3. Release the pressure naturally.

Nutrition:
Calories: 320 Fat: 16g Protein: 41g

Trout Bake

Preparation Time: 10 minutes
Cooking Time: 38 minutes
Serving: 2
Ingredients:

- 1lb trout fillets, boneless
- 1lb chopped winter vegetables
- 1 cup low sodium fish broth
- 1tbsp mixed herbs
- sea salt as desired

Direction:

1. Mix all the ingredients except the broth in a foil pouch.
2. Place the pouch in the steamer basket your Instant Pot.
3. Pour the broth into the Instant Pot.
4. Cook on Steam for 35 minutes.
5. Release the pressure naturally.

Nutrition:
Calories: 310
Fat: 12g
Protein: 40g

Tuna Sweetcorn Casserole

Preparation Time: 16 minutes
Cooking Time: 35 minutes
Serving: 2
Ingredients:

- 3 small tins of tuna
- 0.5lb sweetcorn kernels
- 1lb chopped vegetables
- 1 cup low sodium vegetable broth
- 2tbsp spicy seasoning

Direction:

1. Mix all the ingredients in your Instant Pot.
2. Cook on Stew for 35 minutes.
3. Release the pressure naturally.

Nutrition:
Calories: 300
Fat: 9g
Protein: 43g

Swordfish Steak

Preparation Time: 16 minutes

Cooking Time: 35 minutes
Serving: 2
Ingredients:

- 1lb swordfish steak, whole
- 1lb chopped Mediterranean vegetables
- 1 cup low sodium fish broth
- 2tbsp soy sauce

Direction:

1. Mix all the ingredients except the broth in a foil pouch.
2. Place the pouch in the steamer basket for your Instant Pot.
3. Pour the broth into the Instant Pot. Lower the steamer basket into the Instant Pot.
4. Cook on Steam for 35 minutes.
5. Release the pressure naturally.

Nutrition:
Calories: 270
Fat: 10g
Protein: 48g

Shrimp Coconut Curry

Preparation Time: 14 minutes
Cooking Time: 25 minutes
Serving: 2
Ingredients:

- 0.5lb cooked shrimp
- 1 thinly sliced onion
- 1 cup coconut yogurt
- 3tbsp curry paste
- 1tbsp oil or ghee

Direction:

1. Set the Instant Pot to sauté and add the onion, oil, and curry paste.
2. When the onion is soft, add the remaining ingredients and seal.
3. Cook on Stew for 20 minutes.
4. Release the pressure naturally.

Nutrition:
Calories: 380
Fat: 22g
Protein: 40g

Tuna and Cheddar

Preparation Time: 20 minutes
Cooking Time: 31 minutes
Serving: 2
Ingredients:

- 3 small cans tuna
- 1lb finely chopped vegetables
- 1 cup low sodium vegetable broth
- 0.5 cup shredded cheddar

Direction:

1. Mix all the ingredients in your Instant Pot.
2. Cook on Stew for 35 minutes.
3. Release the pressure naturally.

Nutrition:
Calories: 320 Fat: 11g
Protein: 37g

Chili Shrimp

Preparation Time: 16 minutes
Cooking Time: 35 minutes Serving: 2
Ingredients:

- 1.5lb cooked shrimp
- 1lb stir fry vegetables
- 1 cup ready-mixed fish sauce
- 2tbsp chili flakes

Direction:

1. Mix all the ingredients in your Instant Pot.
2. Cook on Stew for 35 minutes.
3. Release the pressure naturally.

Nutrition:
Calories: 270 Fat: 8g
Protein: 51g

Sardine Curry

Preparation Time: 15 minutes
Cooking Time: 35 minutes
Serving: 2
Ingredients:

- 5 tins of sardines in tomato
- 1lb chopped vegetables
- 1 cup low sodium fish broth
- 3tbsp curry paste

Direction:

1. Mix all the ingredients in your Instant Pot.

2. Cook on Stew for 35 minutes.
3. Release the pressure naturally.

Nutrition:
Calories: 320
Fat: 16g
Protein: 42g

Mussels and Spaghetti Squash

Preparation Time: 14 minutes
Cooking Time: 35 minutes
Serving: 2
Ingredients:

- 1lb cooked, shelled mussels
- 1/2 a spaghetti squash, to fit the Instant Pot
- 1 cup low sodium fish broth
- 3tbsp crushed garlic
- sea salt to taste

Direction:

1. Mix the mussels with the garlic and salt.
2. Place the mussels inside the squash.
3. Lower the squash into your Instant Pot.
4. Pour the broth around it.
5. Cook on Stew for 35 minutes.
6. Release the pressure naturally.
7. Shred the squash, mixing the "spaghetti" with the mussels.

Nutrition:
Calories: 265
Fat: 9g
Protein: 48g

Cod in White Sauce

Preparation Time: 16 minutes
Cooking Time: 5 minutes
Serving: 2
Ingredients:

- 1lb cod fillets
- 1lb chopped swede and carrots
- 2 cups white sauce
- 1 cup peas
- 3tbsp black pepper

Direction:

1. Mix all the ingredients in your Instant Pot.
2. Cook on Stew for 5 minutes.
3. Release the pressure naturally.

Nutrition:
Calories: 390 Fat: 26g Protein: 41g

Lemon Sole

Preparation Time: 16 minutes
Cooking Time: 5 minutes
Serving: 2
Ingredients:

- 1lb sole fillets, boned and skinned
- 1 cup low sodium fish broth
- 2 shredded sweet onions
- juice of half a lemon
- 2tbsp dried cilantro

Direction:

1. Mix all the ingredients in your Instant Pot.
2. Cook on Stew for 5 minutes.
3. Release the pressure naturally.

Nutrition:
Calories: 230 Fat: 6g
Protein: 46g

Cod in Parsley Sauce

Preparation Time: 17 minutes
Cooking Time: 5 minutes Serving: 2
Ingredients:

- 1lb boneless, skinless cod fillets
- 0.5lb green peas
- 1 cup white sauce
- juice of a lemon
- 2tbsp dry parsley

Direction:

1. Mix all the ingredients in your Instant Pot.
2. Cook on Stew for 35 minutes.
3. Release the pressure naturally.

Nutrition:
Calories: 330 Fat: 19g Protein: 40g

Crab Curry

Preparation Time: 13 minutes
Cooking Time: 25 minutes
Serving: 2
Ingredients:

- 0.5lb chopped crab
- 1 thinly sliced red onion
- 0.5 cup chopped tomato
- 3tbsp curry paste
- 1tbsp oil or ghee

Direction:

1. Set the Instant Pot to sauté and add the onion, oil, and curry paste.
2. When the onion is soft, add the remaining ingredients and seal.
3. Cook on Stew for 20 minutes.
4. Release the pressure naturally.

Nutrition:

Calories: 250 Fat: 10g Protein: 24g

Shrimp with Tomatoes and Feta

Preparation Time: 10 minutes
Cooking Time: 30 minutes
Serving: 4
Ingredient

- 3 tomatoes, coarsely chopped
- ½ cup chopped sun-dried tomatoes
- 2 teaspoons minced garlic
- 2 teaspoons extra-virgin olive oil
- 1 teaspoon chopped fresh oregano
- Freshly ground black pepper
- 1½ pounds (16–20 count) shrimp, peeled, deveined, tails removed
- 4 teaspoons freshly squeezed lemon juice
- ½ cup low-sodium feta cheese, crumbled

Direction

1. Heat the oven to 450°F.
2. In a medium bowl, toss the tomatoes, sun-dried tomatoes, garlic, oil, and oregano until well combined.
3. Season the mixture lightly with pepper.
4. Transfer the tomato mixture to a 9-by-13-inch glass baking dish.
5. Bake until softened, about 15 minutes.
6. Stir the shrimp and lemon juice into the hot tomato mixture and top evenly with the feta.
7. Bake until the shrimp are cooked through, about 15 minutes more.

Nutrition
Calories: 306
Fat: 11g
Protein: 39g

Orange-Infused Scallops

Preparation Time: 10 minutes
Cooking Time: 12 minutes
Serving: 4
Ingredient

- 2 pounds sea scallops
- Sea salt
- Freshly ground black pepper
- 2 tablespoons extra-virgin olive oil
- 1 tablespoon minced garlic
- ¼ cup freshly squeezed orange juice
- 1 teaspoon orange zest
- 2 teaspoons chopped fresh thyme, for garnish

Direction

1. Clean the scallops and pat them dry with paper towels, then season them lightly with salt and
2. pepper.
3. Place a large skillet over medium-high heat and add the olive oil.
4. Sauté the garlic until it is softened and translucent, about 3 minutes.
5. Add the scallops to the skillet and cook until they are lightly seared and just cooked through, turning once, about 4 minutes per side.
6. Transfer the scallops to a plate, cover to keep warm, and set them aside.
7. Add the orange juice and zest to the skillet and stir to scrape up any cooked bits.
8. Spoon the sauce over the scallops and serve, garnished with the thyme.

Nutrition
Calories: 267
Fat: 8g
Protein: 38g

Crab Cakes with Honeydew Melon Salsa

Preparation Time: 90 minutes

Cooking Time: 13 minutes
Serving: 4
Ingredient
For the salsa

- 1 cup finely chopped honeydew melon
- 1 scallion, white and green parts, finely chopped
- 1 red bell pepper, seeded, finely chopped
- 1 teaspoon chopped fresh thyme
- Pinch sea salt
- Pinch freshly ground black pepper

For the crab cakes

- 1-pound lump crabmeat, drained and picked over
- ¼ cup finely chopped red onion
- ¼ cup panko breadcrumbs
- 1 tablespoon chopped fresh parsley
- 1 teaspoon lemon zest
- 1 egg
- ¼ cup whole-wheat flour
- Nonstick cooking spray

Direction
For salsa

1. In a small bowl, stir together the melon, scallion, bell pepper, and thyme.
2. Season the salsa with salt and pepper and set aside.

For crab cakes

3. In a medium bowl, mix together the crab, onion, breadcrumbs, parsley, lemon zest, and egg until very well combined.
4. Divide the crab mixture into 8 equal portions and form them into patties about ¾-inch thick.
5. Chill the crab cakes in the refrigerator for at least 1 hour to firm them up.
6. Dredge the chilled crab cakes in the flour until lightly coated, shaking off any excess flour.
7. Place a large skillet over medium heat and lightly coat it with cooking spray.
8. Cook the crab cakes until they are golden brown, turning once, about 5 minutes per side.
9. Serve warm with the salsa.

Nutrition
Calories: 232
Fat: 3g
Protein: 32g

Seafood Stew

Preparation Time: 20 minutes
Cooking Time: 31 minutes
Serving: 6
Ingredient

- 1 tablespoon extra-virgin olive oil
- 1 sweet onion, chopped
- 2 teaspoons minced garlic
- 3 celery stalks, chopped
- 2 carrots, peeled and chopped
- 1 (28-ounce) can sodium-free diced tomatoes, undrained
- 3 cups low-sodium chicken broth
- ½ cup clam juice
- ¼ cup dry white wine
- 2 teaspoons chopped fresh basil
- 2 teaspoons chopped fresh oregano
- 2 (4-ounce) haddock fillets, cut into 1-inch chunks
- 1-pound mussels, scrubbed, debearded
- 8 ounces (16–20 count) shrimp, peeled, deveined, quartered
- Sea salt
- Freshly ground black pepper
- 2 tablespoons chopped fresh parsley

Direction

1. Place a large saucepan over medium-high heat and add the olive oil.
2. Sauté the onion and garlic until softened and translucent, about 3 minutes.
3. Stir in the celery and carrots and sauté for 4 minutes.
4. Stir in the tomatoes, chicken broth, clam juice, white wine, basil, and oregano.
5. Bring the sauce to a boil, then reduce the heat to low. Simmer for 15 minutes.
6. Add the fish and mussels, cover, and cook until the mussels open, about 5 minutes.

7. Discard any unopened mussels. Add the shrimp to the pan and cook until the shrimp are opaque, about 2 minutes.
8. Season with salt and pepper. Serve garnished with the chopped parsley.

Nutrition
Calories: 248
Fat: 7g
Protein: 28g

Sole Piccata

Preparation Time: 10 minutes
Cooking Time: 22 minutes
Serving: 4
Ingredient

- 1 teaspoon extra-virgin olive oil
- 4 (5-ounce) sole fillets, patted dry
- 3 tablespoons butter
- 2 teaspoons minced garlic
- 2 tablespoons all-purpose flour
- 2 cups low-sodium chicken broth
- Juice and zest of ½ lemon
- 2 tablespoons capers

Direction

1. Place a large skillet over medium-high heat and add the olive oil.
2. Pat the sole fillets dry with paper towels then pan-sear them until the fish flakes easily when tested with a fork, about 4 minutes on each side. Transfer the fish to a plate and set it aside.
3. Return the skillet to the stove and add the butter.
4. Sauté the garlic until translucent, about 3 minutes.
5. Whisk in the flour to make a thick paste and cook, stirring constantly, until the mixture is golden brown, about 2 minutes.
6. Whisk in the chicken broth, lemon juice, and lemon zest.
7. Cook until the sauce has thickened, about 4 minutes.
8. Stir in the capers and serve the sauce over the fish.

Nutrition
Calories: 271
Fat: 13g
Protein: 30g

Spicy Citrus Sole

Preparation Time: 10 minutes
Cooking Time: 12 minutes
Serving: 4
Ingredient

- 1 teaspoon chili powder
- 1 teaspoon garlic powder
- ½ teaspoon lime zest
- ½ teaspoon lemon zest
- ¼ teaspoon freshly ground black pepper
- ¼ teaspoon smoked paprika
- Pinch sea salt
- 4 (6-ounce) sole fillets, patted dry
- 1 tablespoon extra-virgin olive oil
- 2 teaspoons freshly squeezed lime juice

Direction

1. Preheat the oven to 450°F.
2. Line a baking sheet with aluminum foil and set it aside.
3. In a small bowl, stir together the chili powder, garlic powder, lime zest, lemon zest, pepper, paprika, and salt until well mixed.
4. Pat the fish fillets dry with paper towels, place them on the baking sheet, and rub them lightly all over with the spice mixture.
5. Drizzle the olive oil and lime juice on the top of the fish.
6. Bake until the fish flakes when pressed lightly with a fork, about 8 minutes. Serve immediately.

Nutrition
Calories: 184
Fat: 5g
Protein: 32g

Haddock with Creamy Cucumber Sauce

Preparation Time: 10 minutes
Cooking Time: 13 minutes
Serving: 4
Ingredient

- ¼ cup 2 percent plain Greek yogurt
- ½ English cucumber, grated, liquid squeezed out
- ½ scallion, white and green parts, finely chopped
- 2 teaspoons chopped fresh mint
- 1 teaspoon honey
- Sea salt
- 4 (5-ounce) haddock fillets
- Freshly ground black pepper
- Nonstick cooking spray

Direction

1. In a small bowl, stir together the yogurt, cucumber, scallion, mint, honey, and a pinch of salt. Set it aside.
2. Pat the fish fillets dry with paper towels and season them lightly with salt and pepper.
3. Place a large skillet over medium-high heat and spray lightly with cooking spray.
4. Cook the haddock, turning once, until it is just cooked through, about 5 minutes per side.
5. Remove the fish from the heat and transfer to plates.
6. Serve topped with the cucumber sauce.

Nutrition

Calories: 164 Fat: 2g Protein: 27g

Herb-Crusted Halibut

Preparation Time: 10 minutes
Cooking Time: 21 minutes
Serving: 4
Ingredient

- 4 (5-ounce) halibut fillets
- Extra-virgin olive oil, for brushing
- ½ cup coarsely ground unsalted pistachios
- 1 tablespoon chopped fresh parsley
- 1 teaspoon chopped fresh thyme
- 1 teaspoon chopped fresh basil
- Pinch sea salt
- Pinch freshly ground black pepper

Direction

1. Preheat the oven to 350°F.
2. Line a baking sheet with parchment paper.
3. Pat the halibut fillets dry with a paper towel and place them on the baking sheet.
4. Brush the halibut generously with olive oil.
5. In a small bowl, stir together the pistachios, parsley, thyme, basil, salt, and pepper.
6. Spoon the nut and herb mixture evenly on the fish, spreading it out so the tops of the fillets are covered.
7. Bake the halibut until it flakes when pressed with a fork, about 20 minutes.
8. Serve immediately.

Nutrition

Calories: 262 Fat: 11g Protein: 32g

Salmon Florentine

Preparation Time: 10 minutes
Cooking Time: 32 minutes
Serving: 4
Ingredient

- 1 teaspoon extra-virgin olive oil
- ½ sweet onion, finely chopped
- 1 teaspoon minced garlic
- 3 cups baby spinach
- 1 cup kale, tough stems removed, torn into 3-inch pieces
- Sea salt
- Freshly ground black pepper
- 4 (5-ounce) salmon fillets
- Lemon wedges, for serving

Direction

1. Preheat the oven to 350°F.
2. Place a large skillet over medium-high heat and add the oil.
3. Sauté the onion and garlic until softened and translucent, about 3 minutes.
4. Add the spinach and kale and sauté until the greens wilt, about 5 minutes.
5. Remove the skillet from the heat and season the greens with salt and pepper.

6. Place the salmon fillets so they are nestled in the greens and partially covered by them. Bake the salmon until it is opaque, about 20 minutes.
7. Serve immediately with a squeeze of fresh lemon.

Nutrition

Calories: 281 Fat: 16g Protein: 29g

Baked Salmon with Lemon Sauce

Preparation Time: 10 minutes
Cooking Time: 15 minutes
Serving: 4

Ingredient

- 4 (5-ounce) salmon fillets
- Sea salt
- Freshly ground black pepper
- 1 tablespoon extra-virgin olive oil
- ½ cup low-sodium vegetable broth
- Juice and zest of 1 lemon
- 1 teaspoon chopped fresh thyme
- ½ cup fat-free sour cream
- 1 teaspoon honey
- 1 tablespoon chopped fresh chives

Direction

1. Preheat the oven to 400°F.
2. Season the salmon lightly on both sides with salt and pepper.
3. Place a large ovenproof skillet over medium-high heat and add the olive oil.
4. Sear the salmon fillets on both sides until golden, about 3 minutes per side.
5. Transfer the salmon to a baking dish and bake until it is just cooked through, about 10 minutes.
6. While the salmon is baking, whisk together the vegetable broth, lemon juice, zest, and thyme in a small saucepan over medium-high heat until the liquid reduces by about one-quarter, about 5 minutes.
7. Whisk in the sour cream and honey.
8. Stir in the chives and serve the sauce over the salmon.

Nutrition

Calories: 310 Fat: 18g Protein: 29g

Tomato Tuna Melts

Preparation Time: 6 minutes
Cooking Time: 5 minutes
Serving: 2

Ingredient

- 1 (5-ounce) can chunk light tuna packed in water, drained
- 2 tablespoons plain nonfat Greek yogurt
- 2 teaspoons freshly squeezed lemon juice
- 2 tablespoons finely chopped celery
- 1 tablespoon finely chopped red onion
- Pinch cayenne pepper
- 1 large tomato, cut into ¾-inch-thick rounds
- ½ cup shredded cheddar cheese

Direction

1. Preheat the broiler to high.
2. In a medium bowl, combine the tuna, yogurt, lemon juice, celery, red onion, and cayenne pepper. Stir well.
3. Arrange the tomato slices on a baking sheet. Top each with some tuna salad and cheddar cheese.
4. Broil for 3 to 4 minutes until the cheese is melted and bubbly. Serve.

Nutrition:

Calories: 243
Fat: 10g
Protein: 30g

Peppercorn-Crusted Baked Salmon

Preparation Time: 6 minutes
Cooking Time: 22 minutes
Serving: 4

Ingredient

- Nonstick cooking spray
- ½ teaspoon freshly ground black pepper
- ¼ teaspoon salt
- Zest and juice of ½ lemon
- ¼ teaspoon dried thyme
- 1-pound salmon fillet

Direction

1. Preheat the oven to 425°F. Spray a baking sheet with nonstick cooking spray.
2. In a small bowl, combine the pepper, salt, lemon zest and juice, and thyme. Stir to combine.
3. Place the salmon on the prepared baking sheet, skin-side down. Spread the seasoning mixture evenly over the fillet.
4. Bake for 15 to 20 minutes, depending on the thickness of the fillet, until the flesh flakes easily.

Nutrition:
Calories: 163
Fat: 7g
Protein: 23g

Roasted Salmon with Honey-Mustard Sauce

Preparation Time: 6 minutes
Cooking Time: 21 minutes
Serving: 4
Ingredient

- Nonstick cooking spray
- 2 tablespoons whole-grain mustard
- 1 tablespoon honey
- 2 garlic cloves, minced
- ¼ teaspoon salt
- ¼ teaspoon freshly ground black pepper
- 1-pound salmon fillet

Direction

1. Preheat the oven to 425°F. Spray a baking sheet with nonstick cooking spray.
2. In a small bowl, whisk together the mustard, honey, garlic, salt, and pepper.
3. Place the salmon fillet on the prepared baking sheet, skin-side down. Spoon the sauce onto the salmon and spread evenly.
4. Roast for 15 to 20 minutes, depending on the thickness of the fillet, until the flesh flakes easily.

Nutrition: Calories: 186|Fat: 7g|Protein: 23g

Ginger-Glazed Salmon and Broccoli

Preparation Time: 10 minutes
Cooking Time: 15 minutes
Serving: 4
Ingredient

- Nonstick cooking spray
- 1 tablespoon low-sodium tamari or gluten-free soy sauce
- Juice of 1 lemon
- 1 tablespoon honey
- 1 (1-inch) piece fresh ginger, grated
- 1 garlic clove, minced
- 1-pound salmon fillet
- ¼ teaspoon salt, divided
- 1/8 teaspoon freshly ground black pepper
- 2 broccoli heads, cut into florets
- 1 tablespoon extra-virgin olive oil

Direction

1. Preheat the oven to 400°F. Spray a baking sheet with nonstick cooking spray.
2. In a small bowl, mix the tamari, lemon juice, honey, ginger, and garlic. Set aside.
3. Place the salmon skin-side down on the prepared baking sheet. Season with 1/8 teaspoon of salt and the pepper.
4. In a large mixing bowl, toss the broccoli and olive oil. Season with the remaining 1/8 teaspoon of salt. Arrange in a single layer on the baking sheet next to the salmon. Bake for 15 to 20 minutes until the salmon flakes easily with a fork and the broccoli is fork tender.
5. In a small pan over medium heat, bring the tamari-ginger mixture to a simmer and cook for 1 to 2 minutes until it just begins to thicken.
6. Drizzle the sauce over the salmon and serve.

Nutrition:
Calories: 238
Fat: 11g
Protein: 25g

Roasted Salmon with Salsa Verde

Preparation Time: 6 minutes
Cooking Time: 25 minutes
Serving: 4
Ingredient

- Nonstick cooking spray
- 8 ounces tomatillos, husks removed
- ½ onion, quartered
- 1 jalapeño or serrano pepper, seeded
- 1 garlic clove, unpeeled
- 1 teaspoon extra-virgin olive oil
- ½ teaspoon salt, divided
- 4 (4-ounce) wild-caught salmon fillets
- ¼ teaspoon freshly ground black pepper
- ¼ cup chopped fresh cilantro
- Juice of 1 lime

Direction

1. Preheat the oven to 425°F. Spray a baking sheet with nonstick cooking spray.
2. In a large bowl, toss the tomatillos, onion, jalapeño, garlic, olive oil, and ¼ teaspoon of salt to coat. Arrange in a single layer on the prepared baking sheet, and roast for about 10 minutes until just softened. Transfer to a dish or plate and set aside.
3. Arrange the salmon fillets skin-side down on the same baking sheet, and season with the remaining ¼ teaspoon of salt and the pepper. Bake for 12 to 15 minutes until the fish is firm and flakes easily.
4. Meanwhile, peel the roasted garlic and place it and the roasted vegetables in a blender or food processor. Add a scant ¼ cup of water to the jar, and process until smooth.
5. Add the cilantro and lime juice and process until smooth. Serve the salmon topped with the salsa Verde.

Nutrition:
199 Calories
9g Fat
23g Protein

Dinner

Pork Chop Diane

Preparation Time: 10 minutes
Cooking Time: 20 minutes Serving: 4
Ingredients:

- ¼ cup low-sodium chicken broth
- 1 tablespoon freshly squeezed lemon juice
- 2 teaspoons Worcestershire sauce
- 2 teaspoons Dijon mustard
- 4 (5-ounce) boneless pork top loin chops
- 1 teaspoon extra-virgin olive oil
- 1 teaspoon lemon zest
- 1 teaspoon butter
- 2 teaspoons chopped fresh chives

Direction:

1. Blend together the chicken broth, lemon juice, Worcestershire sauce, and Dijon mustard and set it aside.
2. Season the pork chops lightly.
3. Situate large skillet over medium-high heat and add the olive oil.
4. Cook the pork chops, turning once, until they are no longer pink, about 8 minutes per side. Put aside the chops.
5. Pour the broth mixture into the skillet and cook until warmed through and thickened, about 2 minutes.
6. Blend lemon zest, butter, and chives.
7. Garnish with a generous spoonful of sauce.

Nutrition:
200 Calories8g Fatb1g Carbohydrates

Autumn Pork Chops with Red Cabbage and Apples

Preparation Time: 15 minutes
Cooking Time: 30 minutes
Serving: 4

Ingredients:

- ¼ cup apple cider vinegar
- 2 tablespoons granulated sweetener
- 4 (4-ounce) pork chops, about 1 inch thick
- 1 tablespoon extra-virgin olive oil
- ½ red cabbage, finely shredded
- 1 sweet onion, thinly sliced
- 1 apple, peeled, cored, and sliced
- 1 teaspoon chopped fresh thyme

Direction:

1. Scourge together the vinegar and sweetener. Set it aside.
2. Season the pork with salt and pepper.
3. Position huge skillet over medium-high heat and add the olive oil.
4. Cook the pork chops until no longer pink, turning once, about 8 minutes per side.
5. Put chops aside.
6. Add the cabbage and onion to the skillet and sauté until the vegetables have softened, about 5 minutes.
7. Add the vinegar mixture and the apple slices to the skillet and bring the mixture to a boil.
8. Adjust heat to low and simmer, covered, for 5 additional minutes.
9. Return the pork chops to the skillet, along with any accumulated juices and thyme, cover, and cook for 5 more minutes.

Nutrition:
223 Calories
12g Carbohydrates
3g Fiber

Chipotle Chili Pork Chops

Preparation Time: 4 hours
Cooking Time: 20 minutes
Serving: 4
Ingredients:

- Juice and zest of 1 lime
- 1 tablespoon extra-virgin olive oil
- 1 tablespoon chipotle chili powder
- 2 teaspoons minced garlic
- 1 teaspoon ground cinnamon
- Pinch sea salt
- 4 (5-ounce) pork chops

Direction:

1. Combine the lime juice and zest, oil, chipotle chili powder, garlic, cinnamon, and salt in a resealable plastic bag. Add the pork chops. Remove as much air as possible and seal the bag.
2. Marinate the chops in the refrigerator for at least 4 hours, and up to 24 hours, turning them several times.
3. Ready the oven to 400°F and set a rack on a baking sheet. Let the chops rest at room temperature for 15 minutes, then arrange them on the rack and discard the remaining marinade.
4. Roast the chops until cooked through, turning once, about 10 minutes per side.
5. Serve with lime wedges.

Nutrition:
204 Calories
1g Carbohydrates
1g Sugar

Orange-Marinated Pork Tenderloin

Preparation Time: 2 hours
Cooking Time: 30 minutes
Serving: 4
Ingredients:

- ¼ cup freshly squeezed orange juice
- 2 teaspoons orange zest
- 2 teaspoons minced garlic
- 1 teaspoon low-sodium soy sauce
- 1 teaspoon grated fresh ginger
- 1 teaspoon honey
- 1½ pounds pork tenderloin roast
- 1 tablespoon extra-virgin olive oil

Direction:

1. Blend together the orange juice, zest, garlic, soy sauce, ginger, and honey.
2. Pour the marinade into a resealable plastic bag and add the pork tenderloin.
3. Remove as much air as possible and seal the bag. Marinate the pork in the refrigerator, turning the bag a few times, for 2 hours.

4. Preheat the oven to 400°F.
5. Pull out tenderloin from the marinade and discard the marinade.
6. Position big ovenproof skillet over medium-high heat and add the oil.
7. Sear the pork tenderloin on all sides, about 5 minutes in total.
8. Position skillet to the oven and roast for 25 minutes.
9. Put aside for 10 minutes before serving.

Nutrition:
228 Calories 4g Carbohydrates 3g Sugar

Homestyle Herb Meatballs

Preparation Time: 10 minutes
Cooking Time: 15 minutes
Serving: 4
Ingredients:

- ½ pound lean ground pork
- ½ pound lean ground beef
- 1 sweet onion, finely chopped
- ¼ cup breadcrumbs
- 2 tablespoons chopped fresh basil
- 2 teaspoons minced garlic
- 1 egg

Direction:

1. Preheat the oven to 350°F.
2. Ready baking tray with parchment paper and set it aside.
3. In a large bowl, mix together the pork, beef, onion, breadcrumbs, basil, garlic, egg, salt, and pepper until very well mixed.
4. Roll the meat mixture into 2-inch meatballs.
5. Transfer the meatballs to the baking sheet and bake until they are browned and cooked through, about 15 minutes.
6. Serve the meatballs with your favorite marinara sauce and some steamed green beans.

Nutrition:
332 Calories 13g Carbohydrates 3g Sugar

Lime-Parsley Lamb Cutlets

Preparation Time: 4 hours
Cooking Time: 10 minutes
Serving: 4
Ingredients:

- ¼ cup extra-virgin olive oil
- ¼ cup freshly squeezed lime juice
- 2 tablespoons lime zest
- 2 tablespoons chopped fresh parsley
- 12 lamb cutlets (about 1½ pounds total)

Direction:

1. Scourge the oil, lime juice, zest, parsley, salt, and pepper.
2. Pour marinade to a resealable plastic bag.
3. Add the cutlets to the bag and remove as much air as possible before sealing.
4. Marinate the lamb in the refrigerator for about 4 hours, turning the bag several times.
5. Preheat the oven to broil.
6. Remove the chops from the bag and arrange them on an aluminum foil–lined baking sheet. Discard the marinade.
7. Broil the chops for 4 minutes per side for medium doneness.
8. Let the chops rest for 5 minutes before serving.

Nutrition:
413 Calories 1g Carbohydrates 31g Protein

Mediterranean Steak Sandwiches

Preparation Time: 1 hour
Cooking Time: 10 minutes Serving: 4
Ingredients:

- 2 tablespoons extra-virgin olive oil
- 2 tablespoons balsamic vinegar
- 2 teaspoons garlic
- 2 teaspoons lemon juice
- 2 teaspoons fresh oregano
- 1 teaspoon fresh parsley
- 1-pound flank steak
- 4 whole-wheat pitas
- 2 cups shredded lettuce
- 1 red onion, thinly sliced
- 1 tomato, chopped
- 1 ounce low-sodium feta cheese

Direction:

1. Scourge olive oil, balsamic vinegar, garlic, lemon juice, oregano, and parsley.
2. Add the steak to the bowl, turning to coat it completely.
3. Marinate the steak for 1 hour in the refrigerator, turning it over several times.
4. Preheat the broiler. Line a baking sheet with aluminum foil.
5. Put steak out of the bowl and discard the marinade.
6. Situate steak on the baking sheet and broil for 5 minutes per side for medium.
7. Set aside for 10 minutes before slicing.
8. Stuff the pitas with the sliced steak, lettuce, onion, tomato, and feta.

Nutrition:
344 Calories 22g Carbohydrates
3g Fiber

Roasted Beef with Peppercorn Sauce

Preparation Time: 10 minutes
Cooking Time: 90 minutes
Serving: 4
Ingredients:

- 1½ pounds top rump beef roast
- 3 teaspoons extra-virgin olive oil
- 3 shallots, minced
- 2 teaspoons minced garlic
- 1 tablespoon green peppercorns
- 2 tablespoons dry sherry
- 2 tablespoons all-purpose flour
- 1 cup sodium-free beef broth

Direction:

1. Heat the oven to 300°F.
2. Season the roast with salt and pepper.
3. Position huge skillet over medium-high heat and add 2 teaspoons of olive oil.
4. Brown the beef on all sides, about 10 minutes in total, and transfer the roast to a baking dish.
5. Roast until desired doneness, about 1½ hours for medium. When the roast has been in the oven for 1 hour, start the sauce.
6. In a medium saucepan over medium-high heat, sauté the shallots in the remaining 1 teaspoon of olive oil until translucent, about 4 minutes.
7. Stir in the garlic and peppercorns and cook for another minute. Whisk in the sherry to deglaze the pan.
8. Whisk in the flour to form a thick paste, cooking for 1 minute and stirring constantly.
9. Fill in the beef broth and whisk for 4 minutes. Season the sauce.
10. Serve the beef with a generous spoonful of sauce.

Nutrition:
330 Calories
4g Carbohydrates
36g Protein

Coffee-and-Herb-Marinated Steak

Preparation Time:2 hours
Cooking Time: 10 minutes
Serving: 3
Ingredients:

- ¼ cup whole coffee beans
- 2 teaspoons garlic
- 2 teaspoons rosemary
- 2 teaspoons thyme
- 1 teaspoon black pepper
- 2 tablespoons apple cider vinegar
- 2 tablespoons extra-virgin olive oil
- 1-pound flank steak, trimmed of visible fat

Direction:

1. Place the coffee beans, garlic, rosemary, thyme, and black pepper in a coffee grinder or food processor and pulse until coarsely ground.
2. Transfer the coffee mixture to a resealable plastic bag and add the vinegar and oil. Shake to combine.
3. Add the flank steak and squeeze the excess air out of the bag. Seal it. Marinate the steak in the refrigerator for at least 2 hours, occasionally turning the bag over.
4. Preheat the broiler. Line a baking sheet with aluminum foil.

5. Pull the steak out and discard the marinade.
6. Position steak on the baking sheet and broil until it is done to your liking.
7. Put aside for 10 minutes before cutting it.
8. Serve with your favorite side dish.

Nutrition:
313 Calories
20g Fat
31g Protein

Traditional Beef Stroganoff

Preparation Time: 10 minutes
Cooking Time: 30 minutes
Serving: 4
Ingredients:

- 1 teaspoon extra-virgin olive oil
- 1-pound top sirloin, cut into thin strips
- 1 cup sliced button mushrooms
- ½ sweet onion, finely chopped
- 1 teaspoon minced garlic
- 1 tablespoon whole-wheat flour
- ½ cup low-sodium beef broth
- ¼ cup dry sherry
- ½ cup fat-free sour cream
- 1 tablespoon chopped fresh parsley

Direction:

1. Position the skillet over medium-high heat and add the oil.
2. Sauté the beef until browned, about 10
3. minutes, then remove the beef with a slotted spoon to a plate and set it aside.
4. Add the mushrooms, onion, and garlic to the skillet and sauté until lightly browned, about 5 minutes.
5. Whisk in the flour and then whisk in the beef broth and sherry.
6. Return the sirloin to the skillet and bring the mixture to a boil.
7. Reduce the heat to low and simmer until the beef is tender, about 10 minutes.
8. Stir in the sour cream and parsley. Season with salt and pepper.

Nutrition: 257 Calories 6g Carb 1g Fiber

Chicken and Roasted Vegetable Wraps

Preparation Time: 10 minutes
Cooking Time: 20 minutes
Serving: 4
Ingredients:

- ½ small eggplant
- 1 red bell pepper
- 1 medium zucchini
- ½ small red onion, sliced
- 1 tablespoon extra-virgin olive oil
- 2 (8-ounce) cooked chicken breasts, sliced
- 4 whole-wheat tortilla wraps

Direction:

1. Preheat the oven to 400°F.
2. Wrap baking sheet with foil and set it aside.
3. In a large bowl, toss the eggplant, bell pepper, zucchini, and red onion with the olive oil.
4. Transfer the vegetables to the baking sheet and lightly season with salt and pepper.
5. Roast the vegetables until soft and slightly charred, about 20 minutes.
6. Divide the vegetables and chicken into four portions.
7. Wrap 1 tortilla around each portion of chicken and grilled vegetables and serve.

Nutrition: 483 Calories 45g Carb 3g Fiber

Parmesan Chicken Artichoke Hearts

Preparation Time: 20 minutes |Cooking Time: 20 minutes |Servings: 4

Ingredients:

- 4 boneless skinless chicken breast halves
- 3 teaspoons olive oil, divided
- 1 teaspoon dried rosemary, crushed
- 1/2 teaspoon dried thyme
- 1/2 teaspoon pepper
- 2 cans (14 ounces each) water-packed artichoke hearts, drained and quartered

- 1 medium onion, coarsely chopped
- 1/2 cup white wine or reduced-sodium chicken broth
- 2 garlic cloves, chopped
- 1/4 cup shredded Parmesan cheese
- 1 lemon, cut into 8 slices
- 2 green onions, thinly sliced

Directions:
1. Preheat oven to 375°. Place chicken in a 15x10x1-in. baking pan coated with cooking spray; drizzle with 1-1/2 teaspoons oil. In a small bowl, mix rosemary, thyme and pepper, sprinkle half over chicken.
2. In a large bowl, combine artichoke hearts, onion, wine, garlic, remaining oil and remaining herb mixture; toss to coat. Arrange around chicken. Sprinkle chicken with cheese; top with lemon slices.
3. Roast until a thermometer inserted in chicken reads 165°, 20-25 minutes. Sprinkle with green onions.

Nutrition: 328 Calories |8g Fat|15g Carb

Spicy Chicken Cacciatore

Preparation Time: 20 minutes
Cooking Time: 1 hour
Serving: 6
Ingredients:
- 1 (2-pound) chicken
- ¼ cup all-purpose flour
- 2 tablespoons extra-virgin olive oil
- 3 slices bacon
- 1 sweet onion
- 2 teaspoons minced garlic
- 4 ounces button mushrooms, halved
- 1 (28-ounce) can low-sodium stewed tomatoes
- ½ cup red wine
- 2 teaspoons chopped fresh oregano

Direction:
1. Cut the chicken into pieces: 2 drumsticks, 2 thighs, 2 wings, and 4 breast pieces.
2. Dredge the chicken pieces in the flour and season each piece with salt and pepper.
3. Place a large skillet over medium-high heat and add the olive oil.
4. Brown the chicken pieces on all sides, about 20 minutes in total. Transfer the chicken to a plate.
5. Cook chopped bacon to the skillet for 5 minutes. With a slotted spoon, transfer the cooked bacon to the same plate as the chicken.
6. Pour off most of the oil from the skillet, leaving just a light coating. Sauté the onion, garlic, and mushrooms in the skillet until tender, about 4 minutes.
7. Stir in the tomatoes, wine, oregano, and red pepper flakes.
8. Bring the sauce to a boil. Return the chicken and bacon, plus any accumulated juices from the plate to the skillet.
9. Reduce the heat to low and simmer until the chicken is tender, about 30 minutes.

Nutrition: 230 Calories 14g Carb 2g Fiber

Ginger Citrus Chicken Thighs

Preparation Time: 15 minutes
Cooking Time: 30 minutes Serving: 4
Ingredients:
- 4 chicken thighs, bone-in, skinless
- 1 tablespoon grated fresh ginger
- 1 tablespoon extra-virgin olive oil
- Juice and zest of ½ lemon
- Juice and zest of ½ orange
- 2 tablespoons honey
- 1 tablespoon reduced-sodium soy sauce
- 1 tablespoon chopped fresh cilantro

Direction:
1. Rub the chicken thighs with the ginger and season lightly with salt.
2. Place a large skillet over medium-high heat and add the oil.
3. Brown the chicken thighs, turning once, for about 10 minutes.

4. While the chicken is browning, stir together the lemon juice and zest, orange juice and zest, honey, soy sauce, and red pepper flakes in a small bowl.
5. Add the citrus mixture to the skillet, cover, and reduce the heat to low.
6. Braise chicken for 20 minutes, adding a couple of tablespoons of water if the pan is too dry.
7. Serve garnished with the cilantro.

Nutrition: 114 Calories|9g Carb|ar9g Protein

Chicken with Creamy Thyme Sauce

Preparation Time: 15 minutes
Cooking Time: 30 minutes
Serving: 4
Ingredients:

- 4 (4-ounce) chicken breasts
- 1 tablespoon extra-virgin olive oil
- ½ sweet onion, chopped
- 1 cup low-sodium chicken broth
- 2 teaspoons chopped fresh thyme
- ¼ cup heavy (whipping) cream
- 1 tablespoon butter
- 1 scallion

Direction:

1. Preheat the oven to 375°F.
2. Season the chicken breasts slightly.
3. Position large ovenproof skillet over medium-high heat and add the olive oil.
4. Brown the chicken, turning once, about 10 minutes in total. Transfer the chicken to a plate.
5. In the same skillet, sauté the onion until softened and translucent, about 3 minutes.
6. Add the chicken broth and thyme, and simmer until the liquid has reduced by half, about 6 minutes.
7. Stir in the cream and butter and return the chicken and any accumulated juices from the plate to the skillet.
8. Transfer the skillet to the oven. Bake until cooked through, about 10 minutes.
9. Serve topped with the chopped scallion.

Nutrition: 287 Calories|4g Carb|1g Fiber

One-Pot Roast Chicken Dinner

Preparation Time: 10 minutes
Cooking Time: 40 minutes
Serving: 6
Ingredients:

- ½ head cabbage
- 1 sweet onion
- 1 sweet potato
- 4 garlic cloves
- 2 tablespoons extra-virgin olive oil
- 2 teaspoons minced fresh thyme
- 2½ pounds bone-in chicken thighs and drumsticks

Directions:

1. Preheat the oven to 450°F.
2. Lightly grease a large roasting pan and arrange the cabbage, onion, sweet potato, and garlic in the bottom. Drizzle with 1 tablespoon of oil, sprinkle with the thyme, and season the vegetables lightly with salt and pepper.
3. Season the chicken with salt and pepper.
4. Place a large skillet over medium-high heat and brown the chicken on both sides in the remaining 1 tablespoon of oil, about 10 minutes in total.
5. Situate browned chicken on top of the vegetables in the roasting pan. Roast for 30 minutes.

Nutrition: 540 Calories|14g Carb|4g Fiber

Mushrooms with Bell Peppers

Preparation Time: 15 minutes
Cooking Time: 10 minutes
Servings: 4

Ingredients:

- 1 tablespoon grapeseed oil
- 3 cups fresh button mushrooms, sliced
- ¾ cups red bell peppers
- ¾ cups green bell peppers strips
- 1½ cup white onions strips
- 2 teaspoons fresh sweet basil
- 2 teaspoons fresh oregano

- ½ teaspoon cayenne powder
- Sea salt, as required
- 2 teaspoons onion powder

Directions:

1. Cook the oil over medium-high heat and sauté the mushrooms, bell peppers and onion for about 5-6 minutes.
2. Add the herbs and spices and cook for about 2-3 minutes. Stir in the lime juice and serve hot.

Nutrition: 80 Calories|3.9g Fat|2.8g Protein

Bell Peppers & Tomato Casserole

Preparation Time: 15 minutes
Cooking Time: 35 minutes
Serves: 6
Ingredients:
For Herb Sauce

- 4 garlic cloves, chopped
- ½ cup fresh parsley, chopped
- ½ cup fresh cilantro, chopped
- 3 tablespoons avocado oil
- 2 tablespoons fresh key lime juice
- ½ teaspoon ground cumin
- ½ teaspoon cayenne powder
- Sea salt, as required

For Veggies

- 1 large green bell pepper
- 1 large yellow bell pepper
- 1 large orange bell pepper
- 1 large red bell pepper
- 1-pound plum tomatoes wedges
- 2 tablespoons avocado oil

Directions:

1. Lightly, grease the baking dish and preheat the oven to 350 degrees. For the sauce: transfer all ingredients in food processor and pulse till smooth. In a large bowl, add the bell peppers and sauce and herb sauce and gently, toss to coat.
2. Transfer the bell pepper mixture into prepared baking dish. Drizzle with oil. Enclose the baking dish with foil and bake for about 35 minutes.
3. Take off the cover of the baking dish and bake for another 20-30 minutes. Serve hot.

Nutrition: 61 Calories|2g Fat|2g Protein

Veggies Casserole

Preparation Time: 20 minutes
Cooking Time: 45 minutes
Servings: 5
Ingredients:

- 3 plum tomatoes
- 3 tablespoons spring water
- 3 tablespoons avocado oil, divided
- ½ onion, chopped
- 3 tablespoons garlic, minced
- Sea salt, as required
- Cayenne powder as required
- 1 zucchini
- 1 yellow squash
- 1 green bell pepper
- 1 red bell pepper
- 1 yellow bell pepper
- 1 tablespoon fresh thyme leaves
- 1 tablespoon fresh key lime juice

Directions:

1. Preheat oven to 375 degrees. Blend the tomatoes and water until pureed.
2. In a bowl, add the tomato puree, 1 tablespoon of oil, onion, garlic, salt and black pepper and blend nicely. In the bottom of a 10x10-inch baking dish, spread the tomato paste mixture evenly.
3. Arrange alternating vegetable slices, starting at the outer edge of the baking dish and working concentrically towards the center. Pour some remaining oil in the vegetables and sprinkle with salt and cayenne powder, followed by the thyme. Arrange a piece of parchment paper over the vegetables. Bake for about 45 minutes. Serve hot.

Nutrition: 77 Calories 1.6g Fat | 3.2g Protein

Sweet & Spicy Chickpeas

Preparation Time: 15 minutes
Cooking Time: 1 hour 10 minutes
Servings: 4
Ingredients:

- 6 plum tomatoes
- 3 tablespoons agave nectar
- ¼ cup date sugar
- 2 teaspoons onion powder
- ½ teaspoon ground ginger
- ¼ teaspoon cayenne powder
- Sea salt, as required
- 3 cups cooked chickpeas
- ¼ cup green bell peppers
- ¼ cup white onions, chopped

Directions:

1. In a blender, add the tomatoes, agave, date sugar and spices and pulse until smooth. In a pan, add the tomato mixture, chickpeas, bell peppers and onion over medium heat and bring to a boil.
2. Cook for about 5 minutes. Reduce the heat to low and simmer for about 1 hour. Serve hot.

Nutrition: 327 Calories |2g Fat |13.3g Protein

Chickpeas & Veggie Stew

Preparation Time: 20 minutes
Cooking Time: 1 hour 5 minutes
Servings: 6
Ingredients:

- 3 cups portabella mushrooms
- 4 cups spring water
- 1 cup cooked chickpeas
- 1 cup fresh kale
- 1 cup white onion
- ½ cup red onion
- 1 cup green bell peppers
- ½ cup butternut squash
- 2 plum tomatoes, chopped
- 2 tablespoons grapeseed oil
- 1 teaspoon dried oregano
- 1 teaspoon dried basil
- ½ teaspoon dried thyme
- 2 teaspoons onion powder
- 1 teaspoon cayenne powder
- ½ teaspoon ginger powder
- Sea salt, as required

Directions:

1. Transfer all the ingredients over high heat and bring to a boil.
2. Reduce the heat to low and simmer, covered for about 1 hour, stirring occasionally.
3. Serve hot.

Nutrition:138 Calories |5.4g Fat |5.1g Protein

Almond-Crusted Salmon

Preparation Time: 10 minutes
Cooking Time: 15 minutes
Servings: 4
Ingredients:

- ¼ cup almond meal
- ¼ cup whole-wheat breadcrumbs
- ¼ teaspoon ground coriander
- 1/8 teaspoon ground cumin
- 4 (6-ounce) boneless salmon fillets
- 1 tablespoon fresh lemon juice
- Salt and pepper

Direction:

1. Ready the oven at 500°F and line a small baking dish with foil.
2. Combine the almond meal, breadcrumbs, coriander, and cumin in a small bowl.
3. Rinse the fish in cool water then pat dry and brush with lemon juice.
4. Season the fish with salt and pepper then dredge in the almond mixture on both sides.
5. Situate fish in the baking dish and bake for 15 minutes.

Nutrition: 232 Calories |5.8g Carb 1.7g Sugar:

Chicken & Veggie Bowl with Brown Rice

Preparation Time: 10 minutes
Cooking Time: 20 minutes
Servings: 4

Ingredients:

- 1 cup instant brown rice
- ¼ cup tahini
- ¼ cup fresh lemon juice
- 2 cloves minced garlic
- ¼ teaspoon ground cumin
- Pinch salt
- 1 tablespoon olive oil
- 4 (4-ounce) chicken breast halves
- ½ medium yellow onion, sliced
- 1 cup green beans, trimmed
- 1 cup chopped broccoli
- 4 cups chopped kale

Direction:

1. Bring 1-cup water to boil in a small saucepan.
2. Stir in the brown rice and simmer for 5 minutes then cover and set aside.
3. Meanwhile, whisk together the tahini with ¼-cup water in a small bowl.
4. Stir in the lemon juice, garlic, and cumin with a pinch of salt and stir well.
5. Heat up oil in a big cast-iron skillet over medium heat.
6. Season the chicken with salt and pepper then add to the skillet.
7. Cook for 3 to 5 minutes on each side until cooked through then remove to a cutting board and cover loosely with foil.
8. Reheat the skillet and cook the onion for 2 minutes then stir in the broccoli and beans.
9. Sauté for 2 minutes then stir in the kale and sauté 2 minutes more.
10. Add 2 tablespoons of water then cover and steam for 2 minutes while you slice the chicken.
11. Build the bowls with brown rice, sliced chicken, and sautéed veggies.
12. Serve hot drizzled with the lemon tahini dressing.

Nutrition: 435 Calories |24g Carb|4.8g Fiber

Beef Steak Fajitas

Preparation Time: 10 minutes
Cooking Time: 15 minutes
Servings: 4
Ingredients:

- 1 lbs. lean beef sirloin, sliced thin
- 1 tablespoon olive oil
- 1 medium red onion, sliced
- 1 red pepper, sliced thin
- 1 green pepper, sliced thin
- ½ teaspoon ground cumin
- ½ teaspoon chili powder
- 8 (6-inch) whole-wheat tortillas
- Fat-free sour cream

Direction:

1. Preheat huge cast-iron skillet over medium heat then add the oil.
2. Add the sliced beef and cook in a single layer for 1 minute on each side.
3. Remove the beef to a bowl and cover to keep warm.
4. Reheat the skillet then add the onions and peppers – season with cumin and chili powder.
5. Stir-fry the veggies to your liking then add to the bowl with the beef.
6. Serve hot in small whole-wheat tortillas with sliced avocado and fat-free sour cream.

Nutrition: 430 Calories |30.5g Carb|17g Fiber

Italian Pork Chops

Preparation Time: 5 minutes
Cooking Time: 45 minutes Serving: 4
Ingredients:

- 4 pork chops, boneless
- 3 garlic cloves, minced
- 1 tsp. dried rosemary, crushed
- ¼ tsp. pepper
- ¼ tsp. sea salt

Direction:

1. Prepare the oven to 425 F/ 218 C.
2. Line baking tray with cooking spray and season pork chops with pepper and salt.
3. Combine garlic and rosemary and rub all over pork chops.
4. Place pork chops in a prepared baking tray.

5. Roast pork chops in preheated oven for 10 minutes.
6. Set temperature to 180 C and roast for 25 minutes.
7. Serve and enjoy

Nutrition

261 Calories 1g Carbohydrates 18g Protein

Chicken Mushroom Stroganoff

Preparation Time: 5 minutes
Cooking Time: 25 minutes
Servings: 6
Ingredients:

- 1 cup fat-free sour cream
- 2 tablespoons flour
- 1 tablespoon Worcestershire sauce
- ½ teaspoon dried thyme
- 1 chicken bouillon cube, crushed
- Salt and pepper
- ½ cup water
- 1 medium yellow onion
- 8 ounces sliced mushrooms
- 1 tablespoon olive oil
- 2 cloves minced garlic
- 12 ounces chicken breast
- 6 ounces whole-wheat noodles, cooked

Direction:

1. Whisk together 2/3 cup of the sour cream with the flour, Worcestershire sauce, thyme, and crushed bouillon in a medium bowl.
2. Season with salt and pepper then slowly stir in the water until well combined.
3. Cook oil in a large skillet over medium-high heat.
4. Sauté onions, mushrooms for 3 minutes.
5. Cook garlic for 2 minutes more then add the chicken.
6. Pour in the sour cream mixture and cook until thick and bubbling.
7. Reduce heat and simmer for 2 minutes.
8. Spoon the chicken and mushroom mixture over the cooked noodles and garnish with the remaining sour cream to serve.

Nutrition: 295 Calories |29.6g Carb|2.9g Fiber

Grilled Tuna Kebabs

Preparation Time: 20 minutes
Cooking Time: 10 minutes
Servings: 4
Ingredients:

- 2 ½ tablespoons rice vinegar
- 2 tablespoons fresh grated ginger
- 2 tablespoons sesame oil
- 2 tablespoons soy sauce
- 2 tablespoons fresh chopped cilantro
- 1 tablespoon minced green chili
- 1 ½ pounds fresh tuna
- 1 large red pepper
- 1 large red onion

Directions:

1. Whisk together the rice vinegar, ginger, sesame oil, soy sauce, cilantro, and chili in a medium bowl – add a few drops of liquid stevia extract to sweeten.
2. Toss in the tuna and chill for 20 minutes, covered.
3. Meanwhile, grease a grill pan with cooking spray and soak wooden skewers in water.
4. Slide the tuna cubes onto the skewers with red pepper and onion.
5. Grill for 4 minutes per side and serve hot.

Nutrition: 240 Calories |8.5g Carb| 1.7g Fiber

Cast-Iron Pork Loin

Preparation Time: 10 minutes
Cooking Time: 20 minutes
Servings: 6
Ingredients:

- 1 (1 ½ pounds) boneless pork loin
- Salt and pepper
- 2 tablespoons olive oil
- 2 tablespoons dried herb blend

Direction:

1. Heat the oven to 425°F.
2. Cut the excess fat from the pork and season.
3. Heat the oil in a large cast-iron skillet over medium heat.

4. Add the pork and cook for 2 minutes on each side.
5. Sprinkle the herbs over the pork and transfer to the oven.
6. Roast for 10 to 15 minutes.
7. Put aside for 10 minutes before cutting to serve.

Nutrition: 205 Calories |1g Carb|29g Protein

Crispy Baked Tofu

Preparation Time: 5 minutes
Cooking Time: 25 minutes
Servings: 4
Ingredients:

- 1 (14-ounce) block extra-firm tofu
- 1 tablespoon olive oil
- 1 tablespoon cornstarch
- ½ teaspoon garlic powder
- Salt and pepper

Direction:

1. Spread paper towels out on a flat surface.
2. Cut the tofu into slices up to about ½-inch thick and lay them out.
3. Cover the tofu with another paper towel and place a cutting board on top.
4. Let the tofu drain for 10 to 15 minutes.
5. Preheat the oven to 400°F and line a baking sheet with foil or parchment.
6. Slice tofu into cubes and situate in a large bowl.
7. Toss with the olive oil, cornstarch, and garlic powder, salt and pepper.
8. Spread on the baking sheet and bake for 10 minutes.
9. Flip the tofu and bake for another 10 to 15 minutes. Serve hot.

Nutrition: 140 Calories |2.1g Carb| 0.1g Fiber

Tilapia with Coconut Rice

Preparation Time: 10 minutes
Cooking Time: 15 minutes
Servings: 4
Ingredients:

- 4 (6-ounce) boneless tilapia fillets
- 1 tablespoon ground turmeric
- 1 tablespoon olive oil
- 2 packets precooked whole-grain rice
- 1 cup light coconut milk
- ½ cup fresh chopped cilantro
- 1 ½ tablespoons fresh lime juice

Direction:

1. Season the fish with turmeric, salt, and pepper.
2. Cook oil in a large skillet at medium heat and add the fish.
3. Cook for 2 to 3 minutes per side until golden brown.
4. Remove the fish to a plate and cover to keep warm.
5. Reheat the skillet and add the rice, coconut milk, and a pinch of salt.
6. Simmer on high heat until thickened, about 3 to 4 minutes.
7. Stir in the cilantro and lime juice.
8. Spoon the rice onto plates and serve with the cooked fish.

Nutrition: 460 Calories |27.1g Carb| 3.7g Fiber

Spicy Turkey Tacos

Preparation Time: 5 minutes
Cooking Time: 25 minutes
Servings: 8
Ingredients:

- 1 tablespoon olive oil
- 1 medium yellow onion, diced
- 2 cloves minced garlic
- 1 pound 93% lean ground turkey
- 1 cup tomato sauce, no sugar added
- 1 jalapeno, seeded and minced
- 8 low-carb multigrain tortillas

Direction:

1. Heat up oil in a big skillet over medium heat.
2. Add the onion and sauté for 4 minutes then stir in the garlic and cook 1 minute more.
3. Stir in the ground turkey and cook for 5 minutes until browned, breaking it up with a wooden spoon.

4. Sprinkle on the taco seasoning and cayenne then stir well.
5. Cook for 30 seconds and mix in the tomato sauce and jalapeno.
6. Simmer on low heat for 10 minutes while you warm the tortillas in the microwave.
7. Serve the meat in the tortillas with your favorite taco toppings.

Nutrition: 195 Calories |15.4g Carb| 8g Fiber

Quick and Easy Shrimp Stir-Fry

Preparation Time: 15 minutes
Cooking Time: 15 minutes
Servings: 5
Ingredients:

- 1 tablespoon olive oil
- 1-pound uncooked shrimp
- 1 tablespoon sesame oil
- 8 ounces snow peas
- 4 ounces broccoli, chopped
- 1 medium red pepper, sliced
- 3 cloves minced garlic
- 1 tablespoon fresh grated ginger
- ½ cup soy sauce
- 1 tablespoon cornstarch
- 2 tablespoons fresh lime juice
- ¼ teaspoon liquid stevia extract

Direction:

1. Cook olive oil in a huge skillet over medium heat.
2. Add the shrimp and season then sauté for 5 minutes.
3. Remove the shrimp to a bowl and keep warm.
4. Reheat the skillet with the sesame oil and add the veggies.
5. Sauté until the veggies are tender, about 6 to 8 minutes.
6. Cook garlic and ginger for 1 minute more.
7. Whisk together the remaining ingredients and pour into the skillet.
8. Toss to coat the veggies then add the shrimp and reheat. Serve hot.

Nutrition: 220 Calories |12.7g Carb|2.6g Fiber

Chicken Burrito Bowl with Quinoa

Preparation Time: 15 minutes
Cooking Time: 10 minutes
Servings: 6
Ingredients:

- 1 tablespoon chipotle chills in adobo
- 1 tablespoon olive oil
- ½ teaspoon garlic powder
- ½ teaspoon ground cumin
- 1-pound boneless skinless chicken breast
- 2 cups cooked quinoa
- 2 cups shredded romaine lettuce
- 1 cup black beans
- 1 cup diced avocado
- 3 tablespoons fat-free sour cream

Direction:

1. Stir together the chipotle chills, olive oil, garlic powder, and cumin in a small bowl.
2. Preheat a grill pan to medium-high and grease with cooking spray.
3. Season the chicken with salt and pepper and add to the grill pan.
4. Grill for 5 minutes then flip it and brush with the chipotle glaze.
5. Cook for another 3 to 5 minutes until cooked through.
6. Remove to a cutting board and chop the chicken.
7. Assemble the bowls with 1/6 of the quinoa, chicken, lettuce, beans, and avocado.
8. Top each with a half tablespoon of fat-free sour cream to serve.

Nutrition: |410 Calories |37.4g Carb|8.5g Fiber

Baked Salmon Cakes

Preparation Time: 10 minutes
Cooking Time: 20 minutes
Servings: 4
Ingredients:

- 15 ounces canned salmon, drained
- 1 large egg, whisked
- 2 teaspoons Dijon mustard

- 1 small yellow onion, minced
- 1 ½ cups whole-wheat breadcrumbs
- ¼ cup low-fat mayonnaise
- ¼ cup nonfat Greek yogurt, plain
- 1 tablespoon fresh chopped parsley
- 1 tablespoon fresh lemon juice
- 2 green onions, sliced thin

Direction:

1. Set the oven to 450°F and prep baking sheet with parchment.
2. Flake the salmon into a medium bowl then stir in the egg and mustard.
3. Mix in the onions and breadcrumbs by hand, blending well, then shape into 8 patties.
4. Grease a large skillet and heat it over medium heat.
5. Fry patties for 2 minutes per side.
6. Situate patties to the baking sheet and bake for 15 minutes.
7. Meanwhile, whisk together the remaining ingredients.
8. Serve the baked salmon cakes with the creamy herb sauce.

Nutrition: 240 Calories | 9.3g Carb| 1.5g Fiber

Rice and Meatball Stuffed Bell Peppers

Preparation Time 15 minutes
Cooking Time: 20 minutes
Serving 4

Ingredients

- 4 bell peppers
- 1-tablespoon olive oil
- 1 small onion, chopped
- 2 cloves garlic, minced
- 1 cup frozen cooked rice, thawed
- 16 to 20 small frozen precooked meatballs
- ½-cup tomato sauce
- 2 tablespoons Dijon mustard

Directions

1. To prepare the peppers, cut off about ½ inch of the tops. Carefully take-out membranes and seeds from inside the peppers. Set aside.
2. In a 6-by-6-by-2-inch pan, combine the olive oil, onion, and garlic. Bake in the air fryer for 2 to 4 minutes or until crisp and tender. Remove the vegetable mixture from the pan and set aside in a medium bowl.
3. Add the rice, meatballs, tomato sauce, and mustard to the vegetable mixture and stir to combine
4. Stuff the peppers with the meat-vegetable mixture.
5. Situate peppers in the air fryer basket and bake for 9 to 13 minutes or until the filling is hot and the peppers are tender.

Nutrition: 487 Calories |57g Carb|6g Fiber

Stir-Fried Steak and Cabbage

Preparation Time: 15 minutes
Cooking Time: 10 minutes
Serving 4
Ingredients

- ½-pound sirloin steak, cut into strips
- 2 teaspoons cornstarch
- 1-tablespoon peanut oil
- 2 cups chopped red or green cabbage
- 1 yellow bell pepper, chopped
- 2 green onions, chopped
- 2 cloves garlic, sliced
- ½-cup commercial stir-fry sauce

Directions

1. Toss the steak with the cornstarch and set aside
2. In a 6-inch metal bowl, combine the peanut oil with the cabbage. Place in the basket and cook for 3 to 4 minutes.
3. Remove the bowl from the basket and add the steak, pepper, onions, and garlic. Return to the air fryer and cook for 3 to 5 minutes. Add the stir-fry sauce and cook for 2 to 4 minutes. Serve over rice.

Nutrition:180 Calories |9g Carb|2g Fiber

Nori-Burritos

Preparation time: 15 minutes
Cooking Time: 20 minutes Servings: 2
Ingredients

- 1 avocado, ripe
- 450 gr. cucumber (seeded)
- 1/2 mango, ripe
- 4 sheets nori seaweed
- 1 zucchini, small
- Handful of amaranth or dandelion greens
- Handful of sprouted hemp seeds
- 1 tbs. tahini
- Sesame seeds, to taste

Directions:

1. Set the Nori sheet on a cutting board, gleaming side facing down. Arrange all the ingredients on the nori sheet, leaving to the right one-inch broad margin of exposed nori.
2. Fold nori's sheet from the side nearest to you, roll it up and over the fillings, use both hands. Put some sesame seeds on top and slice into thick pieces.

Nutrition: 201 Calories |26g protein| 14g fiber

Grilled Zucchini Hummus Wrap

Preparation Time: 15 minutes
Cooking Time: 25 minutes Servings: 4

Ingredients

- 1 zucchini, ends removed and sliced
- 1 plum tomato, sliced, or cherry tomatoes, halved
- 1/4 sliced red onion
- 1 cup romaine lettuce or wild arugula
- 4 tbsp. homemade hummus (mashed garbanzo beans)
- 2 spelt flour tortillas
- 1 tbsp. grapeseed oil
- Sea salt and cayenne pepper, to taste

Directions

1. Heat a skillet to medium heat or grill. In grapeseed oil, mix the sliced zucchini and sprinkle with sea salt and cayenne pepper.
2. Place tossed, sliced zucchini directly on grill and let cook for 3 minutes, flip over and cook for another 2 minutes. Set aside Zucchini.
3. Place the tortillas on the grill for around a minute, or until the grill marks are noticeable and the tortillas are fold able. Remove tortillas from grill and prepare wraps, 2 tablespoons of hummus, slices of zucchini, 1/2 cup greens, slices of onion and tomato. Wrap firmly, and instantly savor.

Nutrition:98 Calories|20g protein|12g fiber

Zucchini Bread Pancakes

Preparation Time: 5 minutes
Cooking Time: 20 minutes
Servings: 5
Ingredients

- 2 cups spelt or kamut flour
- 2 tbsp. date sugar
- 1/4 cup mashed burro banana
- 1 cup finely shredded zucchini
- 2 cups homemade walnut milk
- 1/2 cup chopped walnuts
- 1 tbsp. grapeseed oil

Directions

1. Whisk flour in a large bowl with date sugar. Mix in walnut milk and mashed banana burro. Stir until just blended, make sure the bowl's bottom is scraped so there are no dry mix pockets. Stir in shredded walnuts and Zucchini. Heat the grapeseed oil over medium high heat in a griddle or skillet.
2. To make your pancakes, add batter onto the griddle. Cook on each side for 4-5 minutes. Serve with a syrup of agave and enjoy!

Nutrition: 101 Calories|27g protein|14g fiber

Classic Homemade Hummus

Preparation Time: 5 minutes
Cooking Time: 10 minutes
Servings: 3
Ingredients

- 1 cup cooked chickpeas
- 1/3 cup homemade tahini butter
- 2 tbsp. olive oil
- 2 tbsp. key lime juice
- A dash of onion powder
- Sea salt, to taste

Directions

1. Blend everything in a food processor or high-powered blender and serve.

Nutrition: 87 calories|16g protein|8g fiber

Veggie Fajitas Tacos

Preparation Time: 10 minutes
Cooking Time: 15 minutes
Servings: 3
Ingredients

- 1 onion
- Juice of 1/2 key lime
- 2 bell peppers
- Your choice of approved seasonings (onion powder, cayenne pepper)
- 6 corn-free tortillas
- 1 Tbsp. grapeseed oil
- Avocado
- 2-3 large portobello mushrooms

Directions

1. Remove mushroom stems, spoon gills out if necessary, and clear tops clean. Slice into approximately 1/3 "thick slices. Slice the onion and bell peppers in thin slices.
2. Pour 1 Tbsp Grapeseed oil into a big size skillet on medium heat and onions and peppers. Cook for 2 minutes. Mix in seasonings and mushrooms. Stir frequently and cook for another seven-eight minutes or until tender.
3. Heat the spoon and tortillas the fajita material into the middle of the tortilla. Serve with key lime juice and avocado.

Nutrition: 108 calories 20g protein 14g fiber

Lemon Chicken with Peppers

Preparation Time: 5 minutes
Cooking Time: 20 minutes
Serving: 6
Ingredients

- 1 tsp cornstarch
- 1 tbsp. low sodium soy sauce
- 12 oz. chicken breast tenders, cut in thirds
- 1/4 cup fresh lemon juice
- 1/4 cup low sodium soy sauce
- 1/4 cup fat-free chicken broth
- 1 tsp. fresh ginger, minced
- 2 cloves garlic, minced
- 1 tablespoon Splenda
- 1 teaspoon cornstarch
- 1 tablespoon vegetable oil
- 1/4 cup red bell pepper
- 1/4 cup green bell pepper

Direction

1. Scourge 1 teaspoon cornstarch and 1 tablespoon soy sauce. Add sliced chicken tenders. Chill to marinate for 10 minutes.
2. Stir the lemon juice, 1/4 cup soy sauce, chicken broth, ginger, garlic, Splenda and 1 teaspoon cornstarch together.
3. Warm up oil in a medium frying pan. Cook chicken over medium-high heat for 4 minutes.
4. Add sauce and sliced peppers. Cook 1 to 2 minutes more.

Nutrition: 150 Calories |1g fiber| 6g Carb

Dijon Herb Chicken

Preparation Time: 7 minutes
Cooking Time: 25 minutes
Serving: 4
Ingredients

- 4 skinless, boneless chicken breast halves

- 1 tablespoon butter
- 1 tablespoon olive or vegetable oil
- 2 garlic cloves, finely minced
- 1/2 cup dry white wine
- 1/4 cup water
- 2 tablespoons Dijon-style mustard
- 1/2 teaspoon dried dill weed
- 1/4 teaspoon coarsely ground pepper
- 1/3 cups chopped fresh parsley

Direction

1. Situate chicken breasts between sheets of plastic wrap or waxed paper, and pound with a kitchen mallet until they are evenly about 1/4-inch thick.
2. Warm up butter and oil over medium-high heat; cook chicken pieces for 3 minutes per side. Transfer chicken to a platter; keep warm and set aside.
3. Sauté garlic for 15 seconds in skillet drippings; stir in wine, water, mustard, dill weed, salt and pepper. Boil and reduce volume by 1/2, stirring up the browned bits at the bottom of the skillet.
4. Drizzle sauce over chicken cutlets. Sprinkle with parsley and serve.

Nutrition: 223 calories|1g fiber|6g Carb

Sesame Chicken Stir Fry

Preparation Time: 10 minutes
Cooking Time: 30 minutes
Serving: 6

Ingredients

- 12 ounces skinless, boneless chicken breast
- 1 tablespoon vegetable oil
- 2 garlic cloves, finely minced
- 1 cup broccoli florets
- 1 cup cauliflowers
- 1/2-pound fresh mushrooms, sliced
- 4 green onions, cut into 1-inch pieces
- 2 tablespoons low-sodium soy sauce
- 3 tablespoon dry sherry
- 1 teaspoon finely minced fresh ginger
- 1 teaspoon cornstarch melted in 2 tablespoons water
- 1/4 teaspoon sesame oil
- 1/4 cup dry-roasted peanuts

Directions

1. Cut off fat from chicken and thinly slice diagonally into 1-inch strips.
2. In a huge non-stick skillet, heat oil and stir-fry chicken 4 minutes Remove; put aside and keep warm.
3. Stir-fry garlic for 15 seconds; then broccoli and cauliflower, stir-fry 2 minutes. Then fry mushrooms, green onions, soy sauce, sherry and ginger for 2 minutes.
4. Pour dissolved arrowroot, sesame oil, peanuts and the chicken. Cook until heated through and sauce has thickened.

Nutrition: 256 Calories|9g Carb|30g protein

Rosemary Chicken

Preparation Time: 9 minutes
Cooking Time: 30 minutes
Serving: 4
Ingredients

- 1 (2 1/2 to 3-pound) broiler-fryer chicken
- Salt and ground black pepper to taste
- 4 garlic cloves, finely minced
- 1 teaspoon dried rosemary
- 1/4 cup dry white wine
- 1/4 cup chicken broth

Directions

1. Preheat broiler.
2. Season chicken with salt and pepper. Place in broiler pan. Broil 5 minutes preside.
3. Situate chicken, garlic, rosemary, wine and broth in a Dutch oven. Cook, covered, at medium heat about 30 minutes, turning once.

Nutrition: 176 Calories|1g Carb|1g Fat

Pepper Chicken Skillet

Preparation Time: 10 minutes
Cooking Time: 35 minutes

Serving: 4
Ingredients

- 1 tablespoon vegetable oil
- 12 ounces skinless, boneless chicken breasts
- 2 garlic cloves, finely minced
- 3 bell peppers (red, green and yellow)
- 2 medium onions, sliced
- 1 teaspoon ground cumin
- 1 1/2 teaspoon dried oregano leaves
- 2 teaspoons chopped fresh jalapeño peppers
- 3 tablespoons fresh lemon juice
- 2 tablespoons chopped fresh parsley
- 1/4 teaspoon salt

Directions

1. In a big non-stick skillet, heat oil at medium-high heat; stir-fry chicken for 4 minutes.
2. Cook garlic for 15 seconds, stirring constantly. Fry bell pepper strips, sliced onion, cumin, oregano, and chilies for 2 to 3 minutes.
3. Toss lemon juice, parsley, salt and pepper and serve.

Nutrition: 174 Calories |6g Carb 21g Protein

Dijon Salmon

Preparation Time: 8 minutes
Cooking Time: 26 minutes Serving: 3
Ingredients

- 1 tablespoon olive oil
- 1 1/2 pounds salmon fillets, cut into 6 pieces
- 1/4 cup lemon juice
- 2 tablespoons Equal (sugar substitute)
- 2 tablespoons Dijon mustard
- 1 tablespoon stick butter or margarine
- 1 tablespoon capers
- 1 clove garlic, minced
- 2 tablespoons chopped fresh dill

Directions

1. Heat up olive oil in huge non-stick skillet over medium heat. Add salmon and cook 5 minutes, turning once. Reduce heat to medium-low, cover. Cook 6 to 8 minutes or until salmon flakes easily with a fork.
2. Remove salmon from skillet to serving plate; keep warm.
3. Add lemon juice, Equal, mustard, butter, capers and garlic to skillet. Cook at medium heat 3 minutes, stirring frequently.
4. To serve, spoon sauce over salmon. Sprinkle with dill.

Nutrition: 252 Calories|2g Carb|23g Protein

Pulled Pork

Preparation Time: 10 minutes
Cooking Time: 35 minutes
Serving: 6
Ingredients

- 1 whole pork tenderloin
- 1 tsp chili powder
- 1/2 tsp garlic powder
- 1/2 cup onion
- 1 1/2 teaspoons garlic
- 1 (14.5-ounce) can tomatoes
- 1 tablespoon cider vinegar
- 1 tablespoon prepared mustard
- 1 to 2 teaspoons chili powder
- 1/4 teaspoon maple extract
- 1/4 teaspoon liquid smoke
- 1/3 cup Equal (sugar substitute)
- 6 multigrain hamburger buns

Direction

1. Season pork with 1 teaspoon chili powder and garlic powder; situate in baking pan. Bake in preheated 220°C oven 30 to 40 minutes. Set aside for 15 minutes. Slice into 2 to 3-inch slices; shred slices into bite-size pieces with a fork.
2. Coat medium saucepan with cooking spray. Cook onion and garlic for 5 minutes. Cook tomatoes, vinegar, mustard, chili powder, maple extract, and liquid smoke to saucepan. Allow to boil; decrease heat.
3. Simmer, uncovered, 10 to 15 minutes. Sprinkle Equal.

4. Season. Stir in pork into sauce. Cook 2 to 3 minutes. Spoon mixture into buns.

Nutrition: 252 Calories|29g Carb|21g Protein

Herb Lemon Salmon

Preparation Time: 10 minutes
Cooking Time: 27 minutes
Serving: 2
Ingredients

- 2 cups water
- 2/3 cup farro
- 1 medium eggplant
- 1 red bell pepper
- 1 summer squash
- 1 small onion
- 1½ cups cherry tomatoes
- 3 tablespoons extra-virgin olive oil
- ¾ teaspoon salt, divided
- ½ teaspoon ground pepper
- 2 tablespoons capers
- 1 tablespoon red-wine vinegar
- 2 teaspoons honey
- 1¼ pounds salmon cut into 4 portions
- 1 teaspoon lemon zest
- ½ teaspoon Italian seasoning
- Lemon wedges for serving

Directions

1. Situate racks in upper and lower thirds of oven; set to 450°F. Prep 2 rimmed baking sheets with foil and coat with cooking spray.
2. Boil water and farro. Adjust heat to low, cover and simmer for 30 minutes. Drain if necessary.
3. Mix eggplant, bell pepper, squash, onion and tomatoes with oil, ½ teaspoon salt and ¼ teaspoon pepper.
4. Portion between the baking sheets. Roast on the upper and lower racks, stir once halfway, for 25 minutes. Put them back to the bowl. Mix in capers, vinegar and honey.
5. Rub salmon with lemon zest, Italian seasoning and the remaining ¼ teaspoon each salt and pepper and situate on one of the baking sheets.
6. Roast on the lower rack for 12 minutes, depending on thickness. Serve with farro, vegetable caponata and lemon wedges.

Nutrition: 450 Calories|17g fat|41g Carb

Ginger Chicken

Preparation Time: 10 minutes
Cooking Time: 25 minutes
Serving: 5
Ingredients

- 2 tablespoons vegetable oil - divided use
- 1-pound boneless, skinless chicken breasts
- 1 cup red bell pepper strips
- 1 cup sliced fresh mushrooms
- 16 fresh pea pods, cut in half crosswise
- 1/2 cup sliced water chestnuts
- 1/4 cup sliced green onions
- 1 tablespoon grated fresh ginger root
- 1 large clove garlic, crushed
- 2/3 cup reduced-fat, reduced-sodium chicken broth
- 2 tablespoons Equal (sugar substitute)
- 2 tablespoons light soy sauce
- 4 teaspoons cornstarch
- 2 teaspoons dark sesame oil

Directions

1. Heat up 1 tablespoon vegetable oil in huge skillet over medium-high heat. Stir fry chicken until no longer pink. Remove chicken from skillet.
2. Heat remaining 1 tablespoon vegetable oil in skillet. Add red peppers, mushrooms, pea pods, water chestnuts, green onion, ginger and garlic. Stir fry mixture 3 to 4 minutes until vegetables are crisp tender.
3. Meanwhile, combine chicken broth, Equal, soy sauce, cornstarch and sesame oil until smooth. Stir into skillet mixture. Cook at medium heat until thick and clear. Stir in chicken, heat through. Season with salt and pepper to taste, if desired.
4. Serve over hot cooked rice, if desired.

Nutrition: 263 Calories|11g fat|11g Carb

Teriyaki Chicken

Preparation Time: 7 minutes
Cooking Time: 26 minutes
Serving: 6
Ingredients

- 1 tablespoon cornstarch
- 1 tablespoon cold water
- 1/2 cup Splenda
- 1/2 cup soy sauce
- 1/4 cup cider vinegar
- 1 clove garlic, minced
- 1/2 teaspoon ground ginger
- 1/4 teaspoon ground black pepper
- 12 skinless, boneless chicken breast halves

Directions

1. In a small saucepan in low heat, mix cornstarch, cold water, Splenda, soy sauce, vinegar, garlic, ginger and ground black pepper. Let simmer, stirring frequently, until sauce thickens and bubbles.
2. Preheat oven to 425°F (220°C).
3. Position chicken pieces in a lightly greased 9x13 inch baking dish. Brush chicken with the sauce. Turn pieces over, and brush again.
4. Bake in the prepared oven for 30 minutes. Turn pieces over and bake for another 30 minutes. Brush with sauce every 10 minutes during cooking.

Nutrition: 140 Calories|3g Carb| 25g Protein

Roasted Garlic Salmon

Preparation Time: 8 minutes Cooking Time: 45 minutes Serving: 6
Ingredients

- 14 large cloves garlic
- ¼ cup olive oil
- 2 tablespoons fresh oregano
- 1 teaspoon salt
- ¾ teaspoon pepper
- 6 cups Brussels sprouts
- ¾ cup white wine, preferably Chardonnay
- 2 pounds wild-caught salmon fillet

Direction

1. Prep oven at 450°F.
2. Finely chopped 2 garlic cloves and combine in a small bowl with oil, 1 tablespoon oregano, ½ teaspoon salt and ¼ teaspoon pepper. Slice remaining garlic and mix in Brussels sprouts and 3 tablespoons of the seasoned oil in a big roasting pan. Roast, stir once, for 15 minutes.
3. Pour in wine to the remaining oil mixture. Remove from oven, stir the vegetables and situate salmon on top. Dash with the wine mixture. Sprinkle with the remaining 1 tablespoon oregano and ½ teaspoon each salt and pepper.
4. Bake for 10 minutes more. Serve with lemon wedges.

Nutrition: 334 Calories|10g Carb| 33g Protein

Lemon Sesame Halibut

Preparation Time: 9 minutes
Cooking Time: 29 minutes
Serving: 4
Ingredients

- 2 tablespoons lemon juice
- 2 tablespoons extra-virgin olive oil
- 1 clove garlic, minced
- Freshly ground pepper, to taste
- 2 tablespoons sesame seeds
- 1¼ pounds halibut, or mahi-mahi, cut into 4 portions
- 1½-2 teaspoons dried thyme leaves
- ¼ teaspoon coarse sea salt, or kosher salt
- Lemon wedges

Directions

1. Preheat oven to 450°F. Line a baking sheet with foil.
2. Scourge lemon juice, oil, garlic and pepper in a shallow glass dish. Add fish and turn to coat. Wrap and marinate for 15 minutes.
3. Fry sesame seeds in a small dry skillet over medium-low heat, stirring constantly, for 3 minutes. Set aside to cool. Mix in thyme.

4. Season the fish with salt and coat evenly with the sesame seed mixture, covering the sides as well as the top. Transfer the fish to the prepared baking sheet and roast until just opaque in the center, 10 to 14 minutes. Serve with lemon wedges.

Nutrition: 225 Calories |11g fat|2g Carb

Turkey Sausage Casserole

Preparation Time: 12 minutes
Cooking Time: 32 minutes Serving: 4
Ingredients

- 5 ounces turkey breakfast sausage, casings removed
- 1 teaspoon canola oil
- 1 onion, chopped
- 1 red bell pepper, chopped
- 4 large eggs
- 4 large egg whites
- 2½ cups low-fat milk
- 1 teaspoon dry mustard
- ½ teaspoon salt
- ¼ teaspoon freshly ground pepper
- 2/3 cup low fat cheddar cheese, divided
- 10 slices white bread, crusts removed

Directions

1. Grease 9-by-13-inch baking dish with cooking spray.
2. Fry sausage in a skillet over medium heat, crumbling with a fork, until browned. Transfer to a bowl.
3. Cook oil, onion and bell pepper to skillet, stirring occasionally, for 5 minutes. Fry sausage for 5 minutes more. Remove from heat and set aside.
4. Scourge eggs and egg whites in a large bowl until blended. Whisk in milk, mustard, salt and pepper. Stir in 1/3 cup cheddar.
5. Arrange bread in a single layer in prepared baking dish. Pour egg mixture over bread and top with reserved vegetables and sausage. Sprinkle with remaining 1/3 cup cheddar. Seal with plastic wrap and chill for at least 5 hours or overnight.
6. Preheat oven to 350°F. Bake casserole, uncovered, until set and puffed, 40 to 50 minutes. Serve hot.

Nutrition: 141 Calories|10g Carb|10g protein

Spinach Curry

Preparation Time: 10 minutes
Cooking Time: 22 minutes
Serving: 4
Ingredients

- ¾ cup cooked whole-wheat angel hair pasta
- ½ cup baby spinach
- 1/3 cup chopped red bell pepper
- ¼ cup grated carrot
- ¼ cup chopped fresh cilantro
- 2 cups low-sodium chicken broth
- 1 tablespoon green curry paste

Directions

1. Combine pasta, spinach, bell pepper, carrot and cilantro in a heatproof bowl.
2. Bring chicken broth to a boil. Stir in curry paste. Pour the broth over the pasta mixture. Serve hot.

Nutrition: 273 calories |6g Fiber| 45g Carb

Zucchini Herb

Preparation Time: 12 minutes
Cooking Time: 34 minutes
Serving: 5
Ingredients

- 3 cups reduced-sodium chicken broth
- 1½ pounds zucchini,
- 1 tablespoon chopped fresh tarragon
- ¾ cup shredded reduced-fat Cheddar cheese
- ¼ teaspoon salt
- ¼ teaspoon freshly ground pepper

Directions

1. Boil broth, zucchini and tarragon in a medium saucepan over high heat. Decrease heat to simmer and cook, uncovered, for 10 minutes. Puree in a blender until smooth.

2. Place soup back to the pan and heat over medium-high, slowly stirring in cheese until it is incorporated.
3. Remove from heat and season. Serve hot or chilled.

Nutrition: 110 Calories|2g fiber|7g Carb

Kamut Burgers

Preparation Time: 20 minutes
Cooking Time: 20 minutes Serving: 6
Ingredients:

- 3 cups cooked kamut cereal
- 1 cup spelt flour
- ½ cup unsweetened hemp milk
- 1 cup green bell peppers, seeded and chopped
- 1 cup red onions, chopped
- 1 tablespoon fresh oregano, chopped
- 1 tablespoon fresh basil, chopped
- 1 teaspoon onion powder
- 1 teaspoon sea salt
- ½ teaspoon cayenne powder
- 4 tablespoons grapeseed oil
- 8 cups fresh baby kale

Directions:

1. In a bowl, add all the ingredients except for oil and kale and mix until well combined. Make 12 equal-sized patties from the mixture. Cook 2 tablespoons of oil over medium-high heat in a skillet and cook 6 patties for 10 minutes both sides. Do with the rest of oil and patties. Portion the kale and top each with 2 burgers.
2. Serve immediately.

Nutrition: 459 Calories|12.5g Fat|16.4g Protein

Chickpeas & Mushroom Burgers

Preparation Time: 20 minutes |Cooking Time: 20 minutes |Serving: 4
Ingredients:

- 2 Portobello mushrooms, chopped roughly
- ½ cup green bell peppers
- ½ cup white onion, chopped roughly
- 2 cups cooked chickpeas
- ½ cup fresh cilantro
- 2 teaspoons fresh oregano, chopped
- 2 teaspoons onion powder
- ½ teaspoon cayenne powder
- Sea salt, as required
- ¼ cup chickpea flour
- 3 tablespoons grapeseed oil
- 6 cups fresh baby arugula

Directions:

1. Transfer all of ingredients in a food processor and pulse for about 3 seconds. Make 8 equal-sized patties from mixture.
2. In a large skillet, heat half of the oil over medium-high heat and cook 4 patties for 4 minutes per side. Repeat it. Split the arugula and garnish each with 2 burgers.

Nutrition:278 Calories|12.2g Fat|11.2g Protein

Veggie Burgers

Preparation Time: 5 minutes
Cooking Time: 6 minutes
Serving: 2
Ingredients:

- ½ cup fresh kale, tough ribs removed
- ½ cup green bell peppers, seeded and chopped
- ½ cup onions, chopped
- 1 plum tomato, chopped
- 2 teaspoons fresh oregano, chopped
- 2 teaspoons fresh basil, chopped
- 1 teaspoon dried dill
- 1 teaspoon onion powder
- ½ teaspoon ginger powder
- ½ teaspoon cayenne powder
- Sea salt, as required
- 1 cup chickpeas flour
- ¼-½ cup spring water
- 2 tablespoons grapeseed oil
- 3 cups fresh arugula

Directions:

1. Mix in the vegetables, herbs, spices and salt in a bowl. Add the flour and mix well. Gradually, add in the water until a thick mixture is formed. Make desired-sized patties from the mixture.

2. Cook the oil over medium-high heat and cook the patties for about 2-3 minutes per side. Divide the arugula onto serving plates and top each with 2 burgers.

Nutrition: 354 Calories|17.8g Fat|13g Protein

Falafel with Tzatziki Sauce

Preparation Time: 20 minutes
Cooking Time: 12 minutes
Serving: 8
Ingredients:
For Falafel

- 1-pound dry chickpeas
- 1 small onion
- ¼ cup fresh parsley, chopped
- 4 garlic cloves, peeled
- 1½ tablespoons chickpea flour
- Sea salt, as required
- ½ teaspoon cayenne powder
- ½ cup grapeseed oil

For Tzatziki Sauce

- ½ cup Brazil nuts
- ½ cup spring water
- ¼ cup cucumber, chopped
- 1 tablespoon fresh key lime juice
- 1 garlic clove, minced
- 1 teaspoon fresh dill
- Pinch of sea salt
- 12 cups fresh arugula

Directions:

1. For falafel: in a food processor, add all the ingredients and pulse until well combined and coarse meal like mixture forms. Transfer the falafel mixture into a bowl.
2. With a plastic wrap, cover the bowl and refrigerate for about 1-2 hours. With 2 tablespoons of the mixture, make balls.
3. Cook the oil at 375 degrees in a skillet. Add the falafels in 2 batches and cook for about 5-6 minutes or until golden brown from all aides. Meanwhile, for tzatziki: in a blender, add all the ingredients and pulse until smooth. With a slotted spoon, transfer the falafels onto a paper towel-lined plate to drain. Divide the arugula and falafels onto serving plates evenly.
4. Serve alongside the tzatziki.

Nutrition: 283 Calories |9.6g Fat |13.3g Protein

Veggie Balls in Tomato Sauce

Preparation Time: 20 minutes
Cooking Time: 15 minutes Serving: 8
Ingredients

- 1½ cups cooked chickpeas
- 2 cups fresh button mushrooms
- ½ cup onions, chopped
- ¼ cup green bell peppers, seeded and chopped
- 2 teaspoons oregano
- 2 teaspoons fresh basil
- 1 teaspoon savory
- 1 teaspoon dried sage
- 1 teaspoon dried dill
- 1 tablespoon onion powder
- ½ teaspoon cayenne powder
- ½ teaspoon ginger powder
- Sea salt, as required
- ½-1 cup chickpea flour
- 6 cups homemade tomato sauce
- 2 tablespoons grapeseed oil

Directions:

1. In a food processor, add the chickpeas, veggies, herbs and spices and pulse until well combined. Transfer the mixture into a large bowl with flour and mix until well combined.
2. Make desired-sized balls from the mixture.
3. Cook the oil over medium-high heat and let the balls cook in 2 batches for about 4-5 minutes or until golden brown from all sides. In a large pan, add the tomato sauce and veggie balls over medium heat and simmer for about 5 minutes. Serve hot.

Nutrition: 159 Calories|4.8g Fat|7.2g Protein

Air Fryer Breaded Pork Chops

Preparation Time: 10 minutes
Cooking Time: 12 minutes Serving: 4

Ingredients

- Whole-wheat breadcrumbs: 1 cup
- Salt: ¼ teaspoon
- Pork chops: 2-4 pieces (center cut and boneless)
- Chili powder: half teaspoon
- Parmesan cheese: 1 tablespoon
- Paprika: 1½ teaspoons
- One egg beaten
- Onion powder: half teaspoon
- Granulated garlic: half teaspoon
- Pepper, to taste

Direction

1. Let the air fryer preheat to 400 F
2. Rub kosher salt on each side of pork chops, let it rest
3. Add beaten egg in a big bowl
4. Add Parmesan cheese, breadcrumbs, garlic, pepper, paprika, chili powder, and onion powder in a bowl and mix well
5. Dip pork chop in egg, then in breadcrumb mixture
6. Put it in the air fryer and spray with oil.
7. Let it cook for 12 minutes at 400 F. flip it over halfway through. Cook for another six minutes. Serve with a side of salad.

Nutrition: 425 calories|20 g fat|31 g protein

Pork Taquitos in Air Fryer

Preparation Time: 10 minutes

Cooking Time: 20 minutes Serving: 10

Ingredients

- Pork tenderloin: 3 cups, cooked & shredded
- Cooking spray
- Shredded mozzarella: 2 and 1/2 cups, fat-free
- 10 small tortillas
- Salsa for dipping
- One juice of a lime

Direction

1. Let the air fryer preheat to 380 F
2. Add lime juice to pork and mix well
3. With a damp towel over the tortilla, microwave for ten seconds to soften
4. Add pork filling and cheese on top, in a tortilla, roll up the tortilla tightly.
5. Place tortillas on a greased foil pan
6. Spray oil over tortillas. Cook for 7-10 minutes or until tortillas is golden brown, flip halfway through.
7. Serve with fresh salad.

Nutrition: Calories 253|Fat: 18g|Protein: 20g

Air Fryer Tasty Egg Rolls

Preparation Time: 10 minutes

Cooking Time: 21 minutes

Serving: 3

Ingredients

- Coleslaw mix: half bag
- Half onion
- Salt: 1/2 teaspoon
- Half cups of mushrooms
- Lean ground pork: 2 cups
- One stalk of celery
- Wrappers (egg roll)

Direction

1. Put a skillet over medium flame, add onion and lean ground pork and cook for 5-7 minutes.
2. Add coleslaw mixture, salt, mushrooms, and celery to skillet and cook for almost five minutes.
3. Lay egg roll wrapper flat and add filling (1/3 cup), roll it up, seal with water.
4. Spray with oil the rolls.
5. Put in the air fryer for 6-8 minutes at 400F, flipping once halfway through.
6. Serve hot.

Nutrition: Calories 245|Fat: 10g|Protein: 11g

Pork Dumplings in Air Fryer

Preparation Time: 30 minutes

Cooking Time: 20 minutes

Serving: 6

Ingredients

- 18 dumpling wrappers
- One teaspoon olive oil
- Bok choy: 4 cups (chopped)

- Rice vinegar: 2 tablespoons
- Diced ginger: 1 tablespoon
- Crushed red pepper: 1/4 teaspoon
- Diced garlic: 1 tablespoon
- Lean ground pork: half cup
- Cooking spray
- Lite soy sauce: 2 teaspoons
- Honey: half tsp.
- Toasted sesame oil: 1 teaspoon
- Finely chopped scallions

Direction

1. In a large skillet, heat olive oil, add bok choy, cook for 6 minutes, and add garlic, ginger, and cook for one minute. Move this mixture on a paper towel and pat dry the excess oil
2. In a bowl, add bok choy mixture, crushed red pepper, and lean ground pork and mix well.
3. Lay a dumpling wrapper on a plate and add one tbsp. of filling in the wrapper's middle. With water, seal the edges and crimp it.
4. Air spray the air fryer basket, add dumplings in the air fryer basket and cook at 375 F for 12 minutes or until browned.
5. In the meantime, to make the sauce, add sesame oil, rice vinegar, scallions, soy sauce, and honey in a bowl mix together.
6. Serve the dumplings with sauce.

Nutrition: Calories 140 |Fat 5g|Protein 12g

Air Fryer Pork Chop & Broccoli

Preparation Time: 20 minutes
Cooking Time: 22 minutes | Serving: 2
Ingredients

- Broccoli florets: 2 cups
- Bone-in pork chop: 2 pieces
- Paprika: half tsp.
- Avocado oil: 2 tbsp.
- Garlic powder: half tsp.
- Onion powder: half tsp.
- Two cloves of crushed garlic
- Salt: 1 teaspoon divided

Direction

1. Let the air fryer preheat to 350 degrees. Spray the basket with cooking oil
2. Add one tbsp. Oil, onion powder, half tsp. of salt, garlic powder, and paprika in a bowl mix well, rub this spice mix to the pork chop's sides
3. Add pork chops to air fryer basket and let it cook for five minutes
4. In the meantime, add one tsp. oil, garlic, half tsp of salt, and broccoli to a bowl and coat well
5. Flip the pork chop and add the broccoli, let it cook for five more minutes.
6. Take out from the air fryer and serve.

Nutrition: Calories 483|Fat 20g|protein 23g

Cheesy Pork Chops in Air Fryer

Preparation Time: 5 minutes
Cooking Time: 8 minutes
Serving: 2
Ingredients

- 4 lean pork chops
- Salt: half tsp.
- Garlic powder: half tsp.
- Shredded cheese: 4 tbsp.
- Chopped cilantro

Direction

1. Let the air fryer preheat to 350 degrees.
2. With garlic, cilantro, and salt, rub the pork chops. Put in the air fryer. Let it cook for four minutes. Flip them and cook for two minutes more.
3. Add cheese on top of them and cook for another two minutes or until the cheese is melted.
4. Serve with salad greens.

Nutrition: Calories: 467|Protein: 61g|Fat: 22g

Pork Rind Nachos

Preparation Time: 6 minutes
Cooking Time: 5 minutes
Serving: 2
Ingredients

- 2 tbsp. of pork rinds
- 1/4 cup shredded cooked chicken
- 1/2 cup shredded Monterey jack cheese

- 1/4 cup sliced pickled jalapeños
- 1/4 cup guacamole
- 1/4 cup full-fat sour cream

Direction

1. Put pork rinds in a 6 "round baking pan. Fill with grilled chicken and Monterey cheese jack. Place the pan in the basket with the air fryer.
2. Set the temperature to 370 ° F and set the timer for 5 minutes or until the cheese has been melted.
3. Eat right away with jalapeños, guacamole, and sour cream.

Nutrition: Calories 295 |Protein 30g| Fat: 27.5g

Jamaican Jerk Pork in Air Fryer

Preparation Time: 10 minutes
Cooking Time: 20 minutes Serving: 4
Ingredients

- Pork, cut into three-inch pieces
- Jerk paste: ¼ cup

Direction

1. Rub jerk paste all over the pork pieces.
2. Let it marinate for four hours, at least, in the refrigerator. Or for more time.
3. Let the air fryer preheat to 390 F. spray with olive oil
4. Before putting in the air fryer, let the meat sit for 20 minutes at room temperature.
5. Cook for 20 minutes at 390 F in the air fryer, flip halfway through.
6. Take out from the air fryer let it rest for ten minutes before slicing.
7. Serve with microgreens.

Nutrition: Calories 234 |Protein 31g |Fat 9g

Pork Tenderloin with Mustard Glazed

Preparation Time: 10 minutes
Cooking Time: 18 minutes
Serving: 4
Ingredients

- Yellow mustard: ¼ cup
- One pork tenderloin
- Salt: ¼ tsp
- Honey: 3 Tbsp.
- Freshly ground black pepper: 1/8 tsp
- Minced garlic: 1 Tbsp.
- Dried rosemary: 1 tsp
- Italian seasoning: 1 tsp

Direction

1. With a knife, cut the top of pork tenderloin. Add garlic (minced) in the cuts. Then sprinkle with kosher salt and pepper.
2. In a bowl, add honey, mustard, rosemary, and Italian seasoning mix until combined. Rub this mustard mix all over pork.
3. Let it marinate in the refrigerator for at least two hours.
4. Put pork tenderloin in the air fryer basket. Cook for 18-20 minutes at 400 F. with an instant-read thermometer internal temperature of pork should be 145 F
5. Take out from the air fryer and serve with a side of salad.

Nutrition: Calories 390 |Protein 59g|Fat 11g

Air Fried Beef Schnitzel *

Preparation Time: 10 minutes
Cooking Time: 15 minutes
Serving: 1
Ingredients

- One lean beef schnitzel
- Olive oil: 2 tablespoons
- Breadcrumbs: ¼ cup
- One egg
- One lemon, to serve

Direction

1. Let the air fryer heat to 180 C.
2. In a big bowl, add breadcrumbs and oil, mix well until forms a crumbly mixture
3. Dip beef steak in whisked egg and coat in breadcrumbs mixture.
4. Place the breaded beef in the air fryer and cook at 180C for 15 minutes or more until fully cooked through.
5. Take out from the air fryer and serve with the side of salad greens and lemon.

Nutrition: Calories 340|Proteins 20g |Fat 10g

Air Fryer Meatloaf

Preparation Time: 10 minutes

Cooking Time: 40 minutes
Serving: 8
Ingredients

- Ground lean beef: 4 cups
- Breadcrumbs: 1 cup (soft and fresh)
- Chopped mushrooms: ½ cup
- Cloves of minced garlic
- Shredded carrots: ½ cup
- Beef broth: ¼ cup
- Chopped onions: ½ cup
- Two eggs beaten
- Ketchup: 3 Tbsp.
- Worcestershire sauce: 1 Tbsp.
- Dijon mustard: 1 Tbsp.

For Glaze

- Honey: ¼ cup
- Ketchup: half cup
- Dijon mustard: 2 tsp

Direction

1. In a big bowl, add beef broth and breadcrumbs, stir well. And set it aside in a food processor, add garlic, onions, mushrooms, and carrots, and pulse on high until finely chopped
2. In a separate bowl, add soaked breadcrumbs, Dijon mustard, Worcestershire sauce, eggs, lean ground beef, ketchup, and salt. With your hands, combine well and make it into a loaf.
3. Let the air fryer preheat to 390 F.
4. Put Meatloaf in the Air Fryer and let it cook for 45 minutes.
5. In the meantime, add Dijon mustard, ketchup, and brown sugar in a bowl and mix. Glaze this mix over Meatloaf when five minutes are left.
6. Rest the Meatloaf for ten minutes before serving.

Nutrition: Calories 330|Proteins 19g|Fat 9.9 g

Air Fried Steak with Asparagus Bundles

Preparation Time: 20 minutes Cooking Time: 31 minutes |Serving: 2
Ingredients

- Olive oil spray
- Flank steak (2 pounds)- cut into 6 pieces
- Kosher salt and black pepper
- Two cloves of minced garlic
- Asparagus: 4 cups
- Tamari sauce: half cup
- Three bell peppers: sliced thinly
- Beef broth: 1/3 cup
- 1 Tbsp. of unsalted butter
- Balsamic vinegar: 1/4 cup

Direction

1. Sprinkle salt and pepper on steak and rub.
2. In a Ziploc bag, add garlic and Tamari sauce, then add steak, toss well and seal the bag.
3. Let it marinate for one hour to overnight.
4. Equally, place bell peppers and asparagus in the center of the steak.
5. Roll the steak around the vegetables and secure well with toothpicks.
6. Preheat the air fryer.
7. Spray the steak with olive oil spray. And place steaks in the air fryer.
8. Cook for 15 minutes at 400 degrees or more till steaks are cooked
9. Take the steak out from the air fryer and let it rest for five minutes
10. Remove steak bundles and allow them to rest for 5 minutes before serving/slicing.
11. In the meantime, add butter, balsamic vinegar, and broth over medium flame. Mix well and reduce it by half. Add salt and pepper to taste.
12. Pour over steaks right before serving.

Nutrition: Calories 471|Proteins 29g |Fat 15g

Air Fryer Hamburgers

Preparation Time: 5 minutes
Cooking Time: 16 minutes
Serving: 4
Ingredients

- Buns:4
- Lean ground beef chuck: 4 cups
- Salt to taste
- Slices of any cheese: 4 slices
- Black Pepper, to taste

Direction

1. Let the air fryer preheat to 350 F.

2. In a bowl, add lean ground beef, pepper, and salt. Mix well and form patties.
3. Put them in the air fryer in one layer only, cook for 6 minutes, flip them halfway through. One minute before you take out the patties, add cheese on top.
4. When cheese is melted, take out from the air fryer.
5. Add ketchup, any dressing to your buns, add tomatoes and lettuce and patties.
6. Serve hot.

Nutrition: Calories: 520|Protein 31g |Fat: 34g

Air Fryer Beef Steak Kabobs with Vegetables

Preparation Time: 30 minutes
Cooking Time: 10 minutes
Serving: 4
Ingredients

- Light Soy sauce: 2 tbsp.
- Lean beef chuck ribs: 4 cups, cut into one-inch pieces
- Low-fat sour cream: 1/3 cup
- Half onion
- 8 skewers: 6 inches
- One bell pepper

Direction

1. In a mixing bowl, add soy sauce and sour cream, mix well. Add the lean beef chunks, coat well, and let it marinate for half an hour or more.
2. Cut onion, bell pepper into one-inch pieces. In water, soak skewers for ten minutes.
3. Add onions, bell peppers, and beef on skewers; alternatively, sprinkle with Black Pepper
4. Let it cook for 10 minutes in a preheated air fryer at 400F, flip halfway through.
5. Serve with yogurt dipping sauce.

Nutrition: Calories 268|Proteins 20g |Fat 10g

Air Fried Empanadas

Preparation Time: 10 minutes
Cooking Time: 21 minutes
Serving: 2
Ingredients

- Square gyoza wrappers: eight pieces
- Olive oil: 1 tablespoon
- White onion: 1/4 cup, finely diced
- Mushrooms: 1/4 cup, finely diced
- Half cup lean ground beef
- Chopped garlic: 2 teaspoons
- Paprika: 1/4 teaspoon
- Ground cumin: 1/4 teaspoon
- Six green olives, diced
- Ground cinnamon: 1/8 teaspoon
- Diced tomatoes: half cup
- One egg, lightly beaten

Direction

1. In a skillet, over a medium flame, add oil, onions, and beef and cook for 3 minutes, until beef turns brown.
2. Add mushrooms and cook for six minutes until it starts to brown. Then add paprika, cinnamon, olives, cumin, and garlic and cook for 3 minutes or more.
3. Add in the chopped tomatoes and cook for a minute. Turn off the heat; let it cool for five minutes.
4. Lay gyoza wrappers on a flat surface add one and a half tbsp. of beef filling in each wrapper. Brush edges with water or egg, fold wrappers, pinch edges.
5. Put four empanadas in an even layer in an air fryer basket and cook for 7 minutes at 400°F until nicely browned.
6. Serve with sauce and salad greens.

Nutrition: Calories 343|Fat 19g |Protein 18g

Air Fry Rib-Eye Steak *

Preparation Time: 5 minutes
Cooking Time: 14 minutes
Serving: 1
Ingredients

- Lean rib eye steaks: 1medium-sized
- Salt & freshly ground black pepper, to taste

Direction

1. Let the air fry preheat at 400 F. pat dry steaks with paper towels.
2. Use any spice blend or just salt and pepper on steaks.

3. Generously on both sides of the steak.
4. Put steaks in the air fryer basket. Cook according to the rareness you want. Or cook for 14 minutes and flip after half time.
5. Take out from the air fryer and let it rest for about 5 minutes.
6. Serve with microgreen salad.

Nutrition: Calories 470 |Protein45g |Fat: 31g

Breaded Chicken Tenderloins

Preparation Time: 10 minutes Cooking Time: 13 minutes |Serving: 4

Ingredients

- Eight chicken tenderloins
- Olive oil: 2 tablespoons
- One egg whisked
- 1/4 cup breadcrumbs

Direction

1. Let the air fryer heat to 180 C.
2. In a big bowl, add breadcrumbs and oil, mix well until forms a crumbly mixture
3. Dip chicken tenderloin in whisked egg and coat in breadcrumbs mixture.
4. Place the breaded chicken in the air fryer and cook at 180C for 12 minutes or more.
5. Take out from the air fryer and serve with your favorite green salad.

Nutrition: Calories 206|Proteins 20g|Fat 10g

Parmesan Chicken Meatballs *

Preparation Time: 10 minutes Cooking Time: 13 minutes |Serving: 1

Ingredients

- Pork rinds: half cup, ground
- Ground chicken: 4 cups
- Parmesan cheese: half cup grated
- Kosher salt: 1 tsp.
- Garlic powder: 1/2 tsp.
- One egg beaten
- Paprika: 1/2 tsp.
- Pepper: half tsp.

Breading

- Whole wheat breadcrumbs: half cup ground

Direction

1. Let the Air Fryer pre-heat to 400°F.
2. Add cheese, chicken, egg, pepper, half cup of pork rinds, garlic, salt, and paprika in a big mixing ball. Mix well into a dough, make into 1and half-inch balls.
3. Coat the meatballs in whole wheat breadcrumbs. Spray the oil in the air fry basket and add meatballs in one even layer.
4. Let it cook for 12 minutes at 400°F, flipping once halfway through. Serve with salad greens.

Nutrition: Calories 240 |Fat 10g |Protein 19.9g

Lemon Rosemary Chicken

Preparation Time: 30 minutes

Cooking Time: 21 minutes Serving: 2

Ingredients

For marinade

- Chicken: 2 and ½ cups
- Ginger: 1 tsp, minced
- Olive oil: 1/2 tbsp.
- Soy sauce: 1 tbsp.

For the sauce

- Half lemon
- Honey: 3 tbsp.
- Oyster sauce: 1 tbsp.
- Fresh rosemary: half cup, chopped

Direction

1. In a big mixing bowl, add the marinade ingredients with chicken, and mix well.
2. Keep in the refrigerator for at least half an hour. Let the oven preheat to 200 C for three minutes.
3. Place the marinated chicken in the air fryer in a single layer.
4. Cook for 6 minutes at 200 degrees.
5. Meanwhile, add all the sauces ingredients in a bowl and mix well except for lemon wedges.
6. Brush the sauce generously over half-baked chicken adds lemon juice on top.
7. Cook for another 13 minutes at 200 C. flip the chicken halfway through. Let the chicken evenly brown.
8. Serve right away and enjoy.

Nutrition: Calories 308 |Proteins 25g |Fat 12g

Air Fryer Chicken & Broccoli

Preparation Time: 10 minutes
Cooking Time: 15 minutes
Serving: 4
Ingredients

- Olive oil: 2 Tablespoons
- Chicken breast: 4 cups, bone and skinless (cut into cubes)
- Half medium onion, roughly sliced
- Low sodium soy sauce: 1 Tbsp.
- Garlic powder: half teaspoon
- Rice vinegar: 2 teaspoons
- Broccoli: 1-2 cups, cut into florets
- Hot sauce: 2 teaspoons
- Fresh minced ginger: 1 Tbsp.
- Sesame seed oil: 1 teaspoon
- Salt & black pepper, to taste

Direction

1. In a bowl, add chicken breast, onion, and broccoli. Combine them well.
2. In another bowl, add ginger, oil, sesame oil, rice vinegar, hot sauce, garlic powder, and soy sauce mix it well. Then add the broccoli, chicken, and onions to marinade.
3. Coat well the chicken with sauces. And let it rest in the refrigerator for 15 minutes
4. Place chicken mix in one even layer in air fryer basket and cook for 16-20 minutes, at 380 F. halfway through, toss the basket gently and cook the chicken evenly
5. Add five minutes more, if required.
6. Add salt and pepper, if needed. Serve

Nutrition: Calories 191|Fat 7g|Protein 25g

Dessert

Tiramisu Shots

Preparation Time: 5 minutes
Cooking Time: 10 minutes
Servings: 4
Ingredients:

- 1 pack silken tofu
- 1 oz. dark chocolate, finely chopped
- ¼ cup sugar substitute
- 1 teaspoon lemon juice
- ¼ cup brewed espresso
- Pinch salt
- 24 slices angel food cake
- Cocoa powder (unsweetened)

Directions:

1. Add tofu, chocolate, sugar substitute, lemon juice, espresso and salt in a food processor.
2. Pulse until smooth.
3. Add angel food cake pieces into shot glasses.
4. Drizzle with the cocoa powder.
5. Pour the tofu mixture on top.
6. Top with the remaining angel food cake pieces.
7. Chill for 30 minutes and serve.

Nutrition:
75 Calories
12g Carbohydrate
2.9g Protein

Ice Cream Brownie Cake

Preparation Time: 5 minutes
Cooking Time: 10 minutes
Servings: 4
Ingredients:

- Cooking spray
- 12 oz. no-sugar brownie mix
- ¼ cup oil
- 2 egg whites
- 3 tablespoons water
- 2 cups sugar-free ice cream

Directions:

1. Preheat your oven to 325 degrees F.
2. Spray your baking pan with oil.
3. Mix brownie mix, oil, egg whites and water in a bowl.
4. Pour into the baking pan.
5. Bake for 25 minutes.
6. Let cool.
7. Freeze brownie for 2 hours.

8. Spread ice cream over the brownie.
9. Freeze for 8 hours.

Nutrition:
198 Calories 33g Carbohydrate 3g Protein

Peanut Butter Cups

Preparation Time: 5 minutes
Cooking Time: 10 minutes
Servings: 4
Ingredients:

- 1 packet plain gelatin
- ¼ cup sugar substitute
- 2 cups nonfat cream
- ½ teaspoon vanilla
- ¼ cup low-fat peanut butter
- 2 tablespoons unsalted peanuts, chopped

Directions:

1. Mix gelatin, sugar substitute and cream in a pan.
2. Let sit for 5 minutes.
3. Place over medium heat and cook until gelatin has been dissolved.
4. Stir in vanilla and peanut butter.
5. Pour into custard cups. Chill for 3 hours. Top with the peanuts and serve.

Nutrition: 171 Calories |21g Carb|6g Protein

Fruit Pizza

Preparation Time: 5 minutes
Cooking Time: 10 minutes Servings: 4
Ingredients:

- 1 teaspoon maple syrup
- ¼ teaspoon vanilla extract
- ½ cup coconut milk yogurt
- 2 round slices watermelon
- ½ cup blackberries, sliced
- ½ cup strawberries, sliced
- 2 tablespoons coconut flakes (unsweetened)

Directions:

1. Mix maple syrup, vanilla and yogurt in a bowl.
2. Spread the mixture on top of the watermelon slice.
3. Top with the berries and coconut flakes.

Nutrition:
70 Calories 14.6g Carbohydrate
1.2g Protein

Choco Peppermint Cake

Preparation Time: 5 minutes
Cooking Time: 10 minutes
Servings: 4
Ingredients:

- Cooking spray
- 1/3 cup oil
- 15 oz. package chocolate cake mix
- 3 eggs, beaten
- 1 cup water
- ¼ teaspoon peppermint extract

Directions:

1. Spray slow cooker with oil.
2. Mix all the ingredients in a bowl.
3. Use an electric mixer on medium speed setting to mix ingredients for 2 minutes.
4. Pour mixture into the slow cooker.
5. Cover the pot and cook on low for 3 hours.
6. Let cool before slicing and serving.

Nutrition:
185 Calories 27g Carbohydrate
3.8g Protein

Roasted Mango

Preparation Time: 5 minutes
Cooking Time: 10 minutes Servings: 4
Ingredients:

- 2 mangoes, sliced
- 2 teaspoons crystallized ginger, chopped
- 2 teaspoons orange zest
- 2 tablespoons coconut flakes (unsweetened)

Directions:

1. Preheat your oven to 350 degrees F.
2. Add mango slices in custard cups.
3. Top with the ginger, orange zest and coconut flakes.
4. Bake in the oven for 10 minutes.

Nutrition:
89 Calories 20g Carbohydrate
0.8g Protein

Pumpkin & Banana Ice Cream

Preparation Time: 5 minutes
Cooking Time: 10 minutes Servings: 4
Ingredients:

- 15 oz. pumpkin puree
- 4 bananas, sliced and frozen
- 1 teaspoon pumpkin pie spice
- Chopped pecans

Directions:

1. Add pumpkin puree, bananas and pumpkin pie spice in a food processor.
2. Pulse until smooth.
3. Chill in the refrigerator.
4. Garnish with pecans.

Nutrition:
71 Calories 18g Carbohydrate
1.2g Protein

Brulee Oranges

Preparation Time: 5 minutes
Cooking Time: 10 minutes
Servings: 4
Ingredients:

- 4 oranges, sliced into segments
- 1 teaspoon ground cardamom
- 6 teaspoons brown sugar
- 1 cup nonfat Greek yogurt

Directions:

1. Preheat your broiler.
2. Arrange orange slices in a baking pan.
3. In a bowl, mix the cardamom and sugar.
4. Sprinkle mixture on top of the oranges. Broil for 5 minutes.
5. Serve oranges with yogurt.

Nutrition:
168 Calories
26.9g Carbohydrate
6.8g Protein

Frozen Lemon & Blueberry

Preparation Time: 5 minutes
Cooking Time: 10 minutes Servings: 4
Ingredients:

- 6 cup fresh blueberries
- 8 sprigs fresh thyme
- ¾ cup light brown sugar
- 1 teaspoon lemon zest
- ¼ cup lemon juice
- 2 cups water

Directions:

1. Add blueberries, thyme and sugar in a pan over medium heat.
2. Cook for 6 to 8 minutes.
3. Transfer mixture to a blender.
4. Remove thyme sprigs.
5. Stir in the remaining ingredients.
6. Pulse until smooth.
7. Strain mixture and freeze for 1 hour.

Nutrition:
78 Calories 20g Carbohydrate
3g Protein

Peanut Butter Choco Chip Cookies

Preparation Time: 5 minutes
Cooking Time: 10 minutes
Servings: 4
Ingredients:

- 1 egg
- ½ cup light brown sugar
- 1 cup natural unsweetened peanut butter
- Pinch salt
- ¼ cup dark chocolate chips

Directions:

1. Preheat your oven to 375 degrees F.
2. Mix egg, sugar, peanut butter, salt and chocolate chips in a bowl.
3. Form into cookies and place in a baking pan.
4. Bake the cookie for 10 minutes.
5. Let cool before serving.

Nutrition:
159 Calories
12g Carbohydrate
4.3g Protein

Watermelon Sherbet

Preparation Time: 5 minutes
Cooking Time: 3 minutes Servings: 4
Ingredients:

- 6 cups watermelon, sliced into cubes
- 14 oz. almond milk

- 1 tablespoon honey
- ¼ cup lime juice
- Salt to taste

Directions:

1. Freeze watermelon for 4 hours.
2. Add frozen watermelon and other ingredients in a blender.
3. Blend until smooth.
4. Transfer to a container with seal.
5. Seal and freeze for 4 hours.

Nutrition:

132 Calories 24.5g Carbohydrate
3.1g Protein

Strawberry & Mango Ice Cream

Preparation Time: 5 minutes
Cooking Time: 10 minutes
Servings: 4
Ingredients:

- 8 oz. strawberries, sliced
- 12 oz. mango, sliced into cubes
- 1 tablespoon lime juice

Directions:

1. Add all ingredients in a food processor.
2. Pulse for 2 minutes.
3. Chill before serving.

Nutrition:

70 Calories
17.4g Carbohydrate
1.1g Protein

Sparkling Fruit Drink

Preparation Time: 5 minutes
Cooking Time: 10 minutes Servings: 4
Ingredients:

- 8 oz. unsweetened grape juice
- 8 oz. unsweetened apple juice
- 8 oz. unsweetened orange juice
- 1 qt. homemade ginger ale
- Ice

Directions:

1. Makes 7 servings. Mix first 4 ingredients together in a pitcher. Stir in ice cubes and 9 ounces of the beverage to each glass. Serve immediately.

Nutrition:

60 Calories 1.1g Protein

Roasted Plums

Preparation Time: 5 minutes
Cooking Time: 10 minutes Servings: 4
Ingredients:

- Cooking spray
- 6 plums, sliced
- ½ cup pineapple juice (unsweetened)
- 1 tablespoon brown sugar
- 2 tablespoons brown sugar
- ¼ teaspoon ground cardamom
- ½ teaspoon ground cinnamon
- 1/8 teaspoon ground cumin

Directions:

1. Combine all the ingredients in a baking pan.
2. Roast in the oven at 450 degrees F for 20 minutes.

Nutrition: 102 Calories |18g Carb|2g Protein

Figs with Honey & Yogurt

Preparation Time: 5 minutes
Cooking Time: 10 minutes Servings: 4
Ingredients:

- ½ teaspoon vanilla
- 8 oz. nonfat yogurt
- 2 figs, sliced
- 1 tablespoon walnuts, chopped and toasted
- 2 teaspoons honey

Directions:

1. Stir vanilla into yogurt.
2. Mix well.
3. Top with the figs and sprinkle with walnuts.
4. Drizzle with honey and serve.

Nutrition:

157 Calories 24g Carbohydrate 7g Protein

Flourless Chocolate Cake

Preparation Time: 10 minutes
Cooking Time: 45 minutes Servings: 6
Ingredients:

- ½ Cup of stevia

- 12 Ounces of unsweetened baking chocolate
- 2/3 Cup of ghee
- 1/3 Cup of warm water
- ¼ Teaspoon of salt
- 4 Large pastured eggs
- 2 Cups of boiling water

Directions:

1. Line the bottom of a 9-inch pan of a spring form with a parchment paper.
2. Heat the water in a small pot; then add the salt and the stevia over the water until wait until the mixture becomes completely dissolved.
3. Melt the baking chocolate into a double boiler or simply microwave it for about 30 seconds. Mix the melted chocolate and the butter in a large bowl with an electric mixer.
4. Beat in your hot mixture; then crack in the egg and whisk after adding each of the eggs.
5. Pour the obtained mixture into your prepared spring form tray.
6. Wrap the spring form tray with a foil paper.
7. Place the spring form tray in a large cake tray and add boiling water right to the outside; make sure the depth doesn't exceed 1 inch.
8. Bake the cake into the water bath for about 45 minutes at a temperature of about 350 F.
9. Remove the tray from the boiling water and transfer to a wire to cool.
10. Let the cake chill for an overnight in the refrigerator.

Nutrition

295 Calories6g Carbohydrates4g Fiber

Raspberry Cake with White Chocolate Sauce

Preparation Time: 15 minutes

Cooking Time: 60 minutes Servings: 5

Ingredients:

- 5 Ounces of melted cacao butter
- 2 Ounces of grass-fed ghee
- ½ Cup of coconut cream
- 1 Cup of green banana flour
- 3 Teaspoons of pure vanilla
- 4 Large eggs
- ½ Cup of as Lakanto Monk Fruit
- 1 Teaspoon of baking powder
- 2 Teaspoons of apple cider vinegar
- 2 Cup of raspberries

For white chocolate sauce:

- 3 and ½ ounces of cacao butter
- ½ Cup of coconut cream
- 2 Teaspoons of pure vanilla extract
- 1 Pinch of salt

Directions:

1. Preheat your oven to a temperature of about 280 degrees Fahrenheit.
2. Combine the green banana flour with the pure vanilla extract, the baking powder, the coconut cream, the eggs, the cider vinegar and the monk fruit and mix very well.
3. Leave the raspberries aside and line a cake loaf tin with a baking paper.
4. Pour in the batter into the baking tray and scatter the raspberries over the top of the cake.
5. Place the tray in your oven and bake it for about 60 minutes; in the meantime, prepare the sauce by
6. Directions for sauce:
7. Combine the cacao cream, the vanilla extract, the cacao butter and the salt in a saucepan over a low heat.
8. Mix all your ingredients with a fork to make sure the cacao butter mixes very well with the cream.
9. Remove from the heat and set aside to cool a little bit; but don't let it harden.
10. Drizzle with the chocolate sauce.
11. Scatter the cake with more raspberries.
12. Slice your cake; then serve and enjoy it!

Nutrition

323 Calories9.9g Carbohydrates4g Fiber

Lava Cake

Preparation Time: 10 minutes
Cooking Time: 10 minutes Servings: 2
Ingredients:

- 2 Oz of dark chocolate; you should at least use chocolate of 85% cocoa solids
- 1 Tablespoon of super-fine almond flour
- 2 Oz of unsalted almond butter
- 2 Large eggs

Directions:

1. Heat your oven to a temperature of about 350 Fahrenheit.
2. Grease 2 heat proof ramekins with almond butter.
3. Now, melt the chocolate and the almond butter and stir very well.
4. Beat the eggs very well with a mixer.
5. Add the eggs to the chocolate and the butter mixture and mix very well with almond flour and the swerve; then stir.
6. Pour the dough into 2 ramekins.
7. Bake for about 9 to 10 minutes.
8. Turn the cakes over plates and serve with pomegranate seeds!

Nutrition
459 Calories3.5g Carbohydrates0.8g Fiber

Cheesecake

Preparation Time: 15 minutes
Cooking Time: 50 minutes
Servings: 6
Ingredients:
For Almond Flour Cheesecake Crust:

- 2 Cups of Blanched almond flour
- 1/3 Cup of almond Butter
- 3 Tablespoons of Erythritol (powdered or granular)
- 1 Teaspoon of Vanilla extract

For Keto Cheesecake Filling:

- 32 Oz of softened Cream cheese
- 1 and ¼ cups of powdered erythritol
- 3 Large Eggs
- 1 Tablespoon of Lemon juice
- 1 Teaspoon of Vanilla extract

Directions:

1. Preheat your oven to a temperature of about 350 degrees F.
2. Grease a spring form pan of 9¨ with cooking spray or just line its bottom with a parchment paper.
3. In order to make the cheesecake rust, stir in the melted butter, the almond flour, the vanilla extract and the erythritol in a large bowl.
4. The dough will get will be a bit crumbly; so, press it into the bottom of your prepared tray.
5. Bake for about 12 minutes; then let cool for about 10 minutes.
6. In the meantime, beat the softened cream cheese and the powdered sweetener at a low speed until it becomes smooth.
7. Crack in the eggs and beat them in at a low to medium speed until it becomes fluffy. Make sure to add one a time.
8. Add in the lemon juice and the vanilla extract and mix at a low to medium speed with a mixer.
9. Pour your filling into your pan right on top of the crust. You can use a spatula to smooth the top of the cake.
10. Bake for about 45 to 50 minutes.
11. Remove the baked cheesecake from your oven and run a knife around its edge. Let the cake cool for about 4 hours in the refrigerator. Serve and enjoy your delicious cheesecake!

Nutrition
325 Calories6g Carbohydrates1g Fiber

Cake with Whipped Cream Icing

Preparation Time: 20 minutes
Cooking Time: 25 minutes
Servings: 7
Ingredients:

- ¾ Cup Coconut flour
- ¾ Cup of Swerve Sweetener
- ½ Cup of Cocoa powder
- 2 Teaspoons of Baking powder
- 6 Large Eggs
- 2/3 Cup of Heavy Whipping Cream

- ½ Cup of Melted almond Butter

For whipped Cream Icing:

- 1 Cup of Heavy Whipping Cream
- ¼ Cup of Swerve Sweetener
- 1 Teaspoon of Vanilla extract
- 1/3 Cup of Sifted Cocoa Powder

Directions:

1. Pre-heat your oven to a temperature of about 350 F.
2. Grease an 8x8 cake tray with cooking spray.
3. Add the coconut flour, the Swerve sweetener; the cocoa powder, the baking powder, the eggs, the melted butter; and combine very well with an electric or a hand mixer.
4. Pour your batter into the cake tray and bake for about 25 minutes.
5. Remove the cake tray from the oven and let cool for about 5 minutes.

For the Icing

6. Whip the cream until it becomes fluffy; then add in the Swerve, the vanilla and the cocoa powder.
7. Add the Swerve, the vanilla and the cocoa powder; then continue mixing until your ingredients are very well combined.
8. Frost your baked cake with the icing!

Nutrition

357 Calories11g Carbohydrates2g Fiber

Walnut-Fruit Cake

Preparation Time: 15 minutes
Cooking Time: 20 minutes
Servings: 7
Ingredients:

- 1/2 Cup of almond butter (softened)
- ¼ Cup of so Nourished granulated erythritol
- 1 Tablespoon of ground cinnamon
- ½ Teaspoon of ground nutmeg
- ¼ Teaspoon of ground cloves
- 4 Large pastured eggs
- 1 Teaspoon of vanilla extract
- ½ Teaspoon of almond extract
- 2 Cups of almond flour
- ½ Cup of chopped walnuts
- ¼ Cup of dried of unsweetened cranberries
- ¼ Cup of seedless raisins

Directions:

1. Preheat your oven to a temperature of about 350 F and grease an 8-inch baking tin of round shape with coconut oil.
2. Beat the granulated erythritol on a high speed until it becomes fluffy.
3. Add the cinnamon, the nutmeg, and the cloves; then blend your ingredients until they become smooth.
4. Crack in the eggs and beat very well by adding one at a time, plus the almond extract and the vanilla.
5. Whisk in the almond flour until it forms a smooth batter then fold in the nuts and the fruit. Spread your mixture into your prepared baking pan and bake it for about 20 minutes. Remove the cake from the oven and let cool for about 5 minutes.
6. Dust the cake with the powdered erythritol.

Nutrition

250 Calories12g Carbohydrates2g Fiber

Ginger Cake

Preparation Time: 15 minutes
Cooking Time: 20 minutes Servings: 9
Ingredients:

- ½ Tablespoon of unsalted almond butter to grease the pan
- 4 Large eggs
- ¼ Cup coconut milk
- 2 Tablespoons of unsalted almond butter
- 1 and ½ teaspoons of stevia
- 1 Tablespoon of ground cinnamon
- 1 Tablespoon of natural cocoa powder
- 1 Tablespoon of fresh ground ginger
- ½ Teaspoon of kosher salt
- 1 and ½ cups of blanched almond flour
- ½ Teaspoon of baking soda

Directions:

1. Preheat your oven to a temperature of 325 F.
2. Grease a glass baking tray of about 8X8 inches generously with almond butter.
3. In a large bowl, whisk all together the coconut milk, the eggs, the melted almond butter, the stevia, the cinnamon, the cocoa powder, the ginger and the kosher salt.
4. Whisk in the almond flour, then the baking soda and mix very well.
5. Pour the batter into the prepared pan and bake for about 20 to 25 minutes.
6. Let the cake cool for about 5 minutes.

Nutrition

175 Calories5g Carbohydrates1.9g Fiber

Orange Cake

Preparation Time: 10 minutes

Cooking Time: 50minutes Servings: 8

Ingredients:

- 2 and ½ cups of almond flour
- 2 Unwaxed washed oranges
- 5 Large separated eggs
- 1 Teaspoon of baking powder
- 2 Teaspoons of orange extract
- 1 Teaspoon of vanilla bean powder
- 6 Seeds of cardamom pods crushed
- 16 drops of liquid stevia; about 3 teaspoons
- 1 Handful of flaked almonds to decorate

Directions:

1. Preheat your oven to a temperature of about 350 Fahrenheit.
2. Line a rectangular bread baking tray with a parchment paper.
3. Place the oranges into a pan filled with cold water and cover it with a lid.
4. Bring the saucepan to a boil, then let simmer for about 1 hour and make sure the oranges are totally submerged.
5. Make sure the oranges are always submerged to remove any taste of bitterness. Cut the oranges into halves; then remove any seeds; and drain the water and set the oranges aside to cool down. Cut the oranges in half and remove any seeds, then puree it with a blender or a food processor.
6. Separate the eggs; then whisk the egg whites until you see stiff peaks forming.
7. Add all your ingredients except for the egg whites to the orange mixture and add in the egg whites; then mix.
8. Pour the batter into the cake tin and sprinkle with the flaked almonds right on top. Bake your cake for about 50 minutes. Remove the cake from the oven and set aside to cool for 5 minutes.

Nutrition

164 Calories

7.1g Carbohydrates2.7g Fiber

Lemon Cake

Preparation Time: 20 minutes

Cooking Time: 20minutes Servings: 9

Ingredients:

- 2 Medium lemons
- 4 Large eggs
- 2 Tablespoons of almond butter
- 2 Tablespoons of avocado oil
- 1/3 cup of coconut flour
- 4-5 tablespoons of honey (or another sweetener of your choice)
- ½ tablespoon of baking soda

Directions:

1. Preheat your oven to a temperature of about 350 F.
2. Crack the eggs in a large bowl and set two egg whites aside.
3. Whisk the 2 whites of eggs with the egg yolks, the honey, the oil, the almond butter, the lemon zest and the juice and whisk very well together.
4. Combine the baking soda with the coconut flour and gradually add this dry mixture to the wet ingredients and keep whisking for a couple of minutes.
5. Beat the two eggs with a hand mixer and beat the egg into foam.
6. Add the white egg foam gradually to the mixture with a silicone spatula.

7. Transfer your obtained batter to tray covered with a baking paper.
8. Bake your cake for about 20 to 22 minutes.
9. Let the cake cool for 5 minutes; then slice your cake.

Nutrition

164 Calories7.1g Carbohydrates2.7g Fiber

Cinnamon Cake

Preparation Time: 15 minutes

Cooking Time: 35minutes

Servings: 8

Ingredients

For Cinnamon Filling:

- 3 Tablespoons of Swerve Sweetener
- 2 Teaspoons of ground cinnamon

For the Cake:

- 3 Cups of almond flour
- ¾ Cup of Swerve Sweetener
- ¼ Cup of unflavored whey protein powder
- 2 Teaspoon of baking powder
- ½ Teaspoon of salt
- 3 large, pastured eggs
- ½ Cup of melted coconut oil
- ½ Teaspoon of vanilla extract
- ½ Cup of almond milk
- 1 Tablespoon of melted coconut oil

For cream cheese Frosting:

- 3 Tablespoons of softened cream cheese
- 2 Tablespoons of powdered Swerve Sweetener
- 1 Tablespoon of coconut heavy whipping cream
- ½ Teaspoon of vanilla extract

Directions:

1. Preheat your oven to a temperature of about 325 F and grease a baking tray of 8x8 inch.
2. For the filling, mix the Swerve and the cinnamon in a mixing bowl and mix very well; then set it aside.
3. For the preparation of the cake, whisk all together the almond flour, the sweetener, the protein powder, the baking powder, and the salt in a mixing bowl.
4. Add in the eggs, the melted coconut oil and the vanilla extract and mix very well.
5. Add in the almond milk and keep stirring until your ingredients are very well combined.
6. Spread about half of the batter in the prepared pan; then sprinkle with about two thirds of the filling mixture.
7. Spread the remaining mixture of the batter over the filling and smooth it with a spatula.
8. Bake for about 35 minutes in the oven.
9. Brush with the melted coconut oil and sprinkle with the remaining cinnamon filling. Prepare the frosting by beating the cream cheese, the powdered erythritol, the cream and the vanilla extract in a mixing bowl until it becomes smooth.
10. Drizzle frost over the cooled cake.

Nutrition

222 Calories5.4g Carbohydrates 1.5g Fiber

Madeleine

Preparation Time: 10 minutes

Cooking Time: 15 minutes Servings: 12

Ingredients

- 2 Large pastured eggs
- ¾ Cup of almond flour
- 1 and ½ Tablespoons of Swerve
- ¼ Cup of cooled, melted coconut oil
- 1 Teaspoon of vanilla extract
- 1 Teaspoon of almond extract
- 1 Teaspoon of lemon zest
- ¼ Teaspoon of salt

Directions

1. Preheat your oven to a temperature of about 350 F.
2. Combine the eggs with the salt and whisk on a high speed for about 5 minutes.
3. Slowly add in the Swerve and keep mixing on high for 2 additional minutes.

4. Stir in the almond flour until it is very well-incorporated; then add in the vanilla and the almond extracts.
5. Add in the melted coconut oil and stir all your ingredients together.
6. Pour the obtained batter into equal parts in a greased Madeleine tray.
7. Bake your Ketogenic Madeleine for about 13 minutes or until the edges start to have a brown color.
8. Flip the Madeleines out of the baking tray.

Nutrition

87 Calories 3g Carbohydrates 3g Fiber

Waffles

Preparation Time: 20 minutes

Cooking Time: 30 minutes Servings: 3

Ingredients:

For Ketogenic waffles:

- 8 Oz of cream cheese
- 5 Large pastured eggs
- 1/3 Cup of coconut flour
- ½ Teaspoon of Xanthan gum
- 1 Pinch of salt
- ½ Teaspoon of vanilla extract
- 2 Tablespoons of Swerve
- ¼ Teaspoon of baking soda
- 1/3 Cup of almond milk

Optional ingredients:

- ½ Teaspoon of cinnamon pie spice
- ¼ Teaspoon of almond extract

For low-carb Maple Syrup:

- 1 Cup of water
- 1 Tablespoon of Maple flavor
- ¾ Cup of powdered Swerve
- 1 Tablespoon of almond butter
- ½ Teaspoon of Xanthan gum

Directions

For the waffles:

1. Make sure all your ingredients are exactly at room temperature.
2. Place all your ingredients for the waffles from cream cheese to pastured eggs, coconut flour, Xanthan gum, salt, vanilla extract, the Swerve, the baking soda and the almond milk except for the almond milk with the help of a processor. Blend your ingredients until it becomes smooth and creamy; then transfer the batter to a bowl.
3. Add the almond milk and mix your ingredients with a spatula.
4. Heat a waffle maker to a temperature of high.
5. Spray your waffle maker with coconut oil and add about ¼ of the batter in it evenly with a spatula into your waffle iron.
6. Close your waffle and cook until you get the color you want. Carefully remove the waffles to a platter.

For the Ketogenic Maple Syrup:

1. Place 1 and ¼ cups of water, the swerve and the maple in a small pan and bring to a boil over a low heat; then let simmer for about 10 minutes.
2. Add the coconut oil. Sprinkle the Xanthan gum over the top of the waffle and use an immersion blender to blend smoothly.
3. Serve and enjoy your delicious waffles!

Nutrition: 316 Calories 7g Carb 3g Fiber

Pretzels

Preparation Time: 10 minutes

Cooking Time: 20 minutes Servings: 8

Ingredients:

- 1 and ½ cups of pre-shredded mozzarella
- 2 Tablespoons of full fat cream cheese
- 1 Large egg
- ¾ Cup of almond flour+ 2 tablespoons of ground almonds or almond meal
- ½ Teaspoon of baking powder
- 1 Pinch of coarse sea salt

Directions:

1. Heat your oven to a temperature of about 180 C/356 F.
2. Melt the cream cheese and the mozzarella cheese and stir over a low heat until the cheeses are perfectly

melted. If you choose to microwave the cheese, just do that for about 1 minute no more and if you want to do it on the stove, turn off the heat as soon as the cheese is completely melted.

3. Add the large egg to the prepared warm dough; then stir until your ingredients are very well combined. If the egg is cold; you will need to gently heat it.
4. Add in the ground almonds or the almond flour and the baking powder and stir until your ingredients are very well combined.
5. Take one pinch of the dough of cheese and toll it or stretch it in your hands until it is about 18 to 20 cm of length; if your dough is sticky, you can oil your hands to avoid that. Now, form pretzels from the cheese dough and nicely shape it; then place it over a baking sheet.
6. Sprinkle with a little bit of salt and bake for about 17 minutes.

Nutrition
113 Calories 2.5g Carbohydrates 0.8g Fiber

Cheesy Taco Bites

Preparation Time: 5 minutes
Cooking Time: 10minutes Serving: 12
Ingredients

- 2 Cups of Packaged Shredded Cheddar Cheese
- 2 Tablespoon of Chili Powder
- 2 Tablespoons of Cumin
- 1 Teaspoon of Salt
- 8 Teaspoons of coconut cream for garnishing
- Use Pico de Gallo for garnishing as well

Directions:

1. Preheat your oven to a temperature of about 350 F. Over a baking sheet lined with a parchment paper, place 1 tablespoon piles of cheese and make sure to a space of 2 inches between each. Place the baking sheet in your oven and bake for about 5 minutes.
2. Remove from the oven and let the cheese cool down for about 1 minute; then carefully lift up and press each into the cups of a mini muffin tin.
3. Make sure to press the edges of the cheese to form the shape of muffins mini. Let the cheese cool completely; then remove it. While you continue to bake the cheese and create your cups.
4. Fill the cheese cups with the coconut cream, then top with the Pico de Gallo.

Nutrition73 Calories3g Carbohydrates
4g Protein

Seed and Nut Squares

Preparation Time: 30 minutes
Cooking Time: 10 minutes
Serving: 10
Ingredients:

- 2 Cups of almonds, pumpkin seeds, sunflower seeds and walnuts
- ½ Cup of desiccated coconut
- 1 Tablespoon of chia seeds
- ¼ Teaspoon of salt
- 2 Tablespoons of coconut oil
- 1 Teaspoon of vanilla extract
- 3 Tablespoons of almond or peanut butter
- 1/3 Cup of Sukrin Gold Fiber Syrup

Directions:

1. Line a square baking tin with a baking paper; then lightly grease it with cooking spray
2. Chop all the nuts roughly; then slightly grease it too, you can also leave them as whole
3. Mix the nuts in a large bowl; then combine them in a large bowl with the coconut, the chia seeds and the salt
4. In a microwave-proof bowl; add the coconut oil; then add the vanilla, the coconut butter or oil, the almond butter and the fiber syrup and microwave the mixture for about 30 seconds
5. Stir your ingredients together very well; then pour the melted mixture right on top of the nuts

6. Press the mixture into your prepared baking tin with the help of the back of a measuring cup and push very well
7. Freeze your treat for about 1 hour before cutting it
8. Cut your frozen nut batter into small cubes or squares of the same size

Nutrition
268 Calories
14g Carbohydrates
1g Fiber

Ketogenic Cheesecake

Preparation time: 15 minutes
Cooking time: 50 minutes
Serving: 6
Ingredients:
For the Almond Flour Cheesecake Crust:

- 2 Cups of Blanched almond flour
- 1/3 Cup of almond Butter
- 3 Tablespoons of Erythritol (powdered or granular)
- 1 Teaspoon of Vanilla extract

For the Keto Cheesecake Filling:

- 32 Oz of softened Cream cheese
- 1 and ¼ cups of powdered erythritol
- 3 Large Eggs
- 1 Tablespoon of Lemon juice
- 1 Teaspoon of Vanilla extract

Directions:

1. Preheat your oven to a temperature of about 350 degrees F.
2. Grease a spring form pan of 9¨ with cooking spray or just line its bottom with a parchment paper.
3. In order to make the cheesecake rust, stir in the melted butter, the almond flour, the vanilla extract and the erythritol in a large bowl.
4. The dough will get will be a bit crumbly; so, press it into the bottom of your prepared tray.
5. Bake for about 12 minutes; then let cool for about 10 minutes.
6. In the meantime, beat the softened cream cheese and the powdered sweetener at a low speed until it becomes smooth.
7. Crack in the eggs and beat them in at a low to medium speed until it becomes fluffy. Make sure to add one a time.
8. Add in the lemon juice and the vanilla extract and mix at a low to medium speed with a mixer.
9. Pour your filling into your pan right on top of the crust. You can use a spatula to smooth the top of the cake.
10. Bake for about 45 to 50 minutes.
11. Remove the baked cheesecake from your oven and run a knife around its edge.
12. Let the cake cool for about 4 hours in the refrigerator.
13. Serve and enjoy your delicious cheesecake!

Nutrition
Calories: 325
Fat: 29g
Protein: 7g

Coconut Snack Bars

Preparation time: 30 minutes
Cooking time: 0 minutes
Serving: 13
Ingredients:

- 2 Cups of coconut flakes
- ¾ Cup of melted coconut oil
- 1 and ½ cups of macadamia nuts
- 1 large scoop of vanilla protein powder
- ¼ Cup of unsweetened dark chocolate chips

Directions:

1. Gather the coconut flakes with the melted coconut oil, the macadamia nuts, the vanilla protein powder and the dark chocolate chips in a large bowl and mix very well.
2. Line an 8×8 baking tray with a parchment paper.
3. Process the macadamia nuts with the coconut oil in a food processor until it becomes smooth.

4. Pour the batter into a pan and freeze it for about 30 minutes.
5. Cut the frozen batter into bars with a sharp knife into your preferred size.
6. Serve and enjoy your Ketogenic treat or store it and serve it whenever you want.

Nutrition
Calories: 213.7
Fat: 20g
Protein: 4g

Flax Seed Crackers

Preparation time: 8 minutes
Cooking time: 10 minutes Serving: 25
Ingredients:

- 2 and 1/2 cups of almond flour
- ½ Cup of coconut flour
- 1 Teaspoon of ground flaxseed meal
- ½ Teaspoon of dried rosemary, chopped
- ½ Teaspoon of onion powder
- ¼ Teaspoon of kosher salt
- 3 large organic eggs
- 1 Tablespoon of extra-virgin olive oil

Directions:

1. Preheat your oven to a temperature of about 325 F.
2. Line a baking sheet with a parchment paper.
3. In a large bowl, combine the flours with the rosemary, the flax meal, the salt and the onion powder and mix.
4. Crack in the eggs and add the oil; then mix very well and combine your ingredients very well.
5. Keep mixing until you get the shape of a large ball for about 1 minute.
6. Cut the dough into the 2 pieces of parchment paper and roll it to a thickness of about ¼ inch
7. Cut the dough into squares and transfer it to the prepared baking sheet.
8. Bake your dough for about 13 to 15 minutes; then let cool for about 15 minutes.
9. Serve and enjoy your crackers or store in a container.

Nutrition
Calories: 150.2Fat: 13g Protein: 7g

Crackers

Preparation time: 7 minutes
Cooking time: 12 minutes Serving: 15
Ingredients:

- 2 Cups of Blanched almond flour
- ½ Teaspoon of sea salt
- 1 Beaten large Egg

Directions:

1. Preheat your oven to a temperature of about 350 F.
2. Line a baking sheet with a parchment paper; then combine the almond flour and the salt in a large bowl; then crack in the egg and mix very well until you form a large ball of dough.
3. Place your dough between two large pieces of prepared parchment paper; then use a rolling pin to roll the dough into a rectangular shape.
4. Cut the dough into rectangles; then prick it with a fork and place it over the prepared and lined baking sheet.
5. Bake your crackers for about 8 to 12 minutes.
6. Let the crackers cool for about 10 minutes.
7. Store the crackers in a container; or serve and enjoy them right away!

Nutrition
Calories: 120
Fat: 6g
Protein: 3g

Keto Sugar Free Candies

Preparation time: 30 minutes
Cooking time: 0 minutes
Serving: 12
Ingredients:

- 4 Oz of Coconut Oil, melted
- 4.5 Oz of Shredded, unsweetened Coconut
- 1 Teaspoon of Stevia
- 3 Oz of Erythritol powder

- 1 Large egg white
- 1 Teaspoon of vanilla extract
- 3 Drops of Red Food Coloring
- ½ Teaspoon of Strawberry Extract

Directions:

1. In a large bowl, mix all together the erythritol, the shredded coconut, the stevia and the vanilla with a hand blender on a low heat.
2. Melt the coconut oil in a small saucepan over a low heat.
3. Add the oil to the shredded coconut mixture and combine very well.
4. Add in the egg white and mix; then combine half of the mixture into a square dish of about 8 squares and set it aside.
5. Add the strawberry essence and the food coloring and strawberry essence to the remaining mixture and mix very well.
6. Press the mixture right top of the white mixture into the square dish and set it aside in the fridge for about 1 hour.
7. When your coconut ice is perfectly set, cut it into 16 pieces.
8. Serve and enjoy!

Nutrition Calories: 119|Fat: 12g |Protein: 3g

Coconut Fat Bombs

Preparation time: 15 minutes
Cooking time: 0 minutes
Serving: 14
Ingredients:

- 1 and ½ cups of walnuts or any type of nuts of your choice
- ½ Cup of shredded coconut
- ¼ Cup of coconut butter + 1 additional tablespoon of extra coconut butter
- 2 Tablespoons of almond butter
- 2 Tablespoons of chia seeds
- 2 Tablespoons of flax meal
- 2 Tablespoons of hemp seeds
- 1 Teaspoon of cinnamon
- ½ Teaspoon of vanilla bean powder
- ¼ Teaspoon of kosher salt
- 2 Tablespoons of cacao nibs

For the chocolate drizzle

- 1 Oz of unsweetened chocolate, chopped
- ½ Teaspoon of coconut oil

Directions:

1. In the mixing bowl of your food processor, combine the walnuts with the coconut butter; the almond butter, the chia seeds, the flax meal, the hemp seeds, the cinnamon, the vanilla bean powder, the shredded coconut and the chopped; then drizzle with the coconut oil. Pulse your ingredients for about 1 to 2 minutes or until the mixture starts breaking down. Keep processing your mixture until it starts to stick together; but just be careful not to over mix. Add in the cacao nibs and pulse until your ingredients. With a small cookie scoop or simply with a tablespoon, divide the mixture into pieces of equal size. Use both your hands to toll the mixture into balls; then arrange it over a platter. Store the balls in an airtight container or place it in the freezer for about 15 minutes.
2. Serve and enjoy your delicious balls!

Nutrition: Calories 164|Fat 14g| Protein 4g

Nut and Raspberry Balls

Preparation time: 15 minutes
Cooking time: 0 minutes Serving: 14
Ingredients:

- 1 1/3Cup of raw cashews or almonds
- ¼ Cup of cashew or almond butter
- 2 Tablespoons of coconut oil
- 2 Pitted Medjool dates, pre-soaked into hot water for about 10 minutes
- ½ Teaspoon of vanilla extract
- ¼ Teaspoon of kosher salt
- ½ Cup of freeze-dried and lightly crashed raspberries
- 1/3 Cup of chopped dark chocolate

Directions:

1. In a high-powered blender or a Vitamix, combine the cashews or almonds with the butter, the coconut oil, the Medjool dates, the vanilla extract and the salt and pulse on a high speed for about 1 to 2 minutes or until the batter starts sticking together.
2. Pulse in the dried raspberries and the dark chocolate until your get a thick mixture.
3. With a tablespoon or a small cookie scoop, divide the mixture into balls of equal size.
4. Arrange the balls in a container or a zip-top bag in a refrigerator for about 2 weeks or just serve and enjoy your delicious cashew balls!

Nutrition
Calories: 108.2
Fat: 7.4 g
Protein: 3 g

Cocoa and Coconut Balls

Preparation time: 90 minutes
Cooking time: 0 minutes
Serving: 9
Ingredients:

- 1 Cup of almond butter
- 1 Cup of coconut oil, at room temperature
- ½ Cup of unsweetened cocoa powder
- 1/3 Cup of coconut flour
- ¼ Teaspoon of powdered stevia
- 1/16 tsp of pink Himalayan salt

Directions:

1. In a small pot and over a medium high heat, melt the almond butter and combine it with the coconut oil.
2. Add the coconut flour, the cocoa powder and the Himalayan salt and stir.
3. Add the stevia and mix again; then let your mixture cool.
4. Pour the mixture in a large bowl and transfer it to the freezer to solidify for about 60 to 90 minutes.
5. Once solidified, remove the bowl from the freezer and form it into balls.
6. Form balls from the batter and arrange the balls over a tray lined with a parchment paper.
7. Refrigerate the balls for about 15 minutes.
8. Serve and enjoy your delicious Ketogenic bombs!

Nutrition:
Calories: 157
Fat: 12.6 g
Protein: 3.7 g

Pine Nut Cookies

Preparation time: 10 minutes
Cooking time: 12 minutes
Serving: 20
Ingredients:

- 1 Large egg
- 1 Teaspoon of almond extract
- 1 Pinch of salt
- 1 Cup of stevia
- 2 Cups of superfine blanched almond flour
- 1/3 Cup of pine nuts

Directions:

1. Preheat your oven to a temperature of about 325 degrees Fahrenheit.
2. Mix the eggs with the almond extract, the salt and the sweetener in a bowl of a medium.
3. Beat your ingredients with a mixer for about 2 minutes or until the mixture becomes glossy.
4. Add in the almond flour and beat your ingredients until it becomes fluffy.
5. If the dough gets too dry, add about tablespoon of water in a way that it holds up very well together.
6. Place the nuts over a small platter.
7. Take a pinch of the dough and roll it into one piece of about 1 inch in its diameter.
8. Press the top of the ball dough into the nut with the side up.

9. Place the cookie over a parchment paper lined cookie sheet lined with a parchment paper.
10. Repeat the same process with the remaining dough; you can get about 20 cookies.
11. Bake your cookies in the oven for about 12 minutes.
12. Remove the cookies from the oven and let cool for about 6 minutes.
13. Serve and enjoy your cookies.

Nutrition

Calories: 83Fat: 7.5 g Protein: 4 g

Oreo Cookies with Cream Cheese Filling

Preparation time: 15 minutes

Cooking time: 12 minutes Serving: 25

Ingredients:

- 2 and ¼ cups of hazelnut or almond flour
- 3 Tablespoons of coconut flour
- 4 Tablespoons of cocoa powder
- 1 Teaspoons of baking powder
- ½ Teaspoon of xanthan gum
- ¼ Teaspoon of salt
- ½ Cup of softened butter
- ½ Cup of stevia
- 1 Large egg
- 1 Teaspoon of vanilla extract

For the Cream Filling:

- 4 Oz of softened cream cheese
- 2 Tablespoons of almond butter
- ½ Teaspoons of pure vanilla extract
- ½ Cup of powdered of Swerve, you can just grind it in a spice grinder

Directions:

1. Preheat your oven to a temperature of about 350 degrees Fahrenheit.
2. Combine the hazelnut or the almond flour with the cocoa powder, the baking powder, the xanthan gum, the salt, the stevia, the egg and the vanilla extract in a large bowl and mix very well. Add the almond butter and mix again. In a separate medium bowl, cream all together the Swerve and the butter until it become light and extremely fluffy for 2 to 3 minutes.
3. Add the egg and the vanilla and mix until your ingredients are fully combined.
4. Add your already mixed dry ingredients and mix it until it is very well combined.
5. Roll out the obtained dough between two rectangular waxed paper sheets; make sure the thickness is about 1/8.
6. Place the dough over a cookie sheet lined with a parchment paper.
7. Roll the cookie dough again until the end.
8. Bake the cookies for about 12 minutes; then let cool completely before starting to fill.
9. To make the filling:
10. Cream the cream cheese with the butter; then cream all together and add the vanilla extract.
11. Gradually add in the powdered swerve.
12. Fill the Oreo cookies with the cream.
13. Serve and enjoy your delicious cookies!

Nutrition

Calories: 136Fat: 12.3 g Protein: 4.6 g

Whipped Cream Icing Cake

Preparation time: 20 minutes

Cooking time: 25 minutes Serving: 7

Ingredients:

- ¾ Cup Coconut flour
- ¾ Cup of Swerve Sweetener
- ½ Cup of Cocoa powder
- 2 Teaspoons of Baking powder
- 6 Large Eggs
- 2/3 Cup of Heavy Whipping Cream
- ½ Cup of Melted almond Butter

For the whipped Cream Icing:

- 1 Cup of Heavy Whipping Cream
- ¼ Cup of Swerve Sweetener
- 1 Teaspoon of Vanilla extract
- 1/3 Cup of Sifted Cocoa Powder

Directions:

1. Pre-heat your oven to a temperature of about 350 F.
2. Grease an 8x8 cake tray with cooking spray.
3. Add the coconut flour, the Swerve sweetener; the cocoa powder, the baking powder, the eggs, the melted butter; and combine very well with an electric or a hand mixer.
4. Pour your batter into the cake tray and bake for about 25 minutes.
5. Remove the cake tray from the oven and let cool for about 5 minutes.
6. For the Icing
7. Whip the cream until it becomes fluffy; then add in the Swerve, the vanilla and the cocoa powder.
8. Add the Swerve, the vanilla and the cocoa powder; then continue mixing until your ingredients are very well combined.
9. Frost your baked cake with the icing; then slice it; serve and enjoy your delicious cake!

Nutrition

Calories: 357Fat: 33gProtein: 8g

Fruit Cake with Walnuts

Preparation time: 15 minutes

Cooking time: 20 minutes Serving: 6

Ingredients:

- 1/2 Cup of almond butter (softened)
- ¼ Cup of so Nourished granulated erythritol
- 1 Tablespoon of ground cinnamon
- ½ Teaspoon of ground nutmeg
- ¼ Teaspoon of ground cloves
- 4 Large pastured eggs
- 1 Teaspoon of vanilla extract
- ½ Teaspoon of almond extract
- 2 Cups of almond flour
- ½ Cup of chopped walnuts
- ¼ Cup of dried of unsweetened cranberries
- ¼ Cup of seedless raisins

Directions:

1. Preheat your oven to a temperature of about 350 F and grease an 8-inch baking tin of round shape with coconut oil.
2. Beat the granulated erythritol on a high speed until it becomes fluffy.
3. Add the cinnamon, the nutmeg, and the cloves; then blend your ingredients until they become smooth.
4. Crack in the eggs and beat very well by adding one at a time, plus the almond extract and the vanilla.
5. Whisk in the almond flour until it forms a smooth batter then fold in the nuts and the fruit.
6. Spread your mixture into your prepared baking pan and bake it for about 20 minutes.
7. Remove the cake from the oven and let cool for about 5 minutes.
8. Dust the cake with the powdered erythritol.
9. Serve and enjoy your cake!

Nutrition

Calories: 250Fat: 11gProtein: 7g

Cinnamon and Ginger Cake

Preparation time: 15 minutes

Cooking time: 20 minutes Serving: 9

Ingredients:

- ½ Tablespoon of unsalted almond butter to grease the pan
- 4 Large eggs
- ¼ Cup coconut milk
- 2 Tablespoons of unsalted almond butter
- 1 and ½ teaspoons of stevia
- 1 Tablespoon of ground cinnamon
- 1 Tablespoon of natural cocoa powder
- 1 Tablespoon of fresh ground ginger
- ½ Teaspoon of kosher salt
- 1 and ½ cups of blanched almond flour
- ½ Teaspoon of baking soda

Directions:

1. Preheat your oven to a temperature of 325 F.
2. Grease a glass baking tray of about 8X8 inches generously with almond butter.

3. In a large bowl, whisk all together the coconut milk, the eggs, the melted almond butter, the stevia, the cinnamon, the cocoa powder, the ginger and the kosher salt.
4. Whisk in the almond flour, then the baking soda and mix very well.
5. Pour the batter into the prepared pan and bake for about 20 to 25 minutes.
6. Let the cake cool for about 5 minutes; then slice; serve and enjoy your delicious cake.

Nutrition

Calories: 175Fat: 15g Protein: 5g

Keto Orange Cake

Preparation time: 10 minutes

Cooking time: 50minutes

Serving: 8

Ingredients:

- 2 and ½ cups of almond flour
- 2 Unwaxed washed oranges
- 5 Large separated eggs
- 1 Teaspoon of baking powder
- 2 Teaspoons of orange extract
- 1 Teaspoon of vanilla bean powder
- 6 Seeds of cardamom pods crushed
- 16 drops of liquid stevia; about 3 teaspoons
- 1 Handful of flaked almonds to decorate

Directions:

1. Preheat your oven to a temperature of about 350 Fahrenheit.
2. Line a rectangular bread baking tray with a parchment paper.
3. Place the oranges into a pan filled with cold water and cover it with a lid.
4. Bring the saucepan to a boil, then let simmer for about 1 hour and make sure the oranges are totally submerged.
5. Make sure the oranges are always submerged to remove any taste of bitterness.
6. Cut the oranges into halves; then remove any seeds; and drain the water and set the oranges aside to cool down.
7. Cut the oranges in half and remove any seeds, then puree it with a blender or a food processor.
8. Separate the eggs; then whisk the egg whites until you see stiff peaks forming.
9. Add all your ingredients except for the egg whites to the orange mixture and add in the egg whites; then mix.
10. Pour the batter into the cake tin and sprinkle with the flaked almonds right on top.
11. Bake your cake for about 50 minutes.
12. Remove the cake from the oven and set aside to cool for 5 minutes.
13. Slice your cake; then serve and enjoy its incredible taste!

Nutrition

Calories: 164Fat: 12g Protein: 10.9g

Keto Donuts

Preparation time: 5 minutes

Cooking time: 0 minutes Serving: 4

Ingredients:

For the donut ingredients:

- ½ Cup of sifted almond flour
- 3 to 4 tablespoons of coconut milk
- 2 Large eggs
- 2 to 3 tablespoons granulated of stevia
- 1 Teaspoon of Keto-friendly baking powder
- 1 Heap teaspoon of apple cider vinegar
- 1 Pinch of salt
- 1 and ½ Tablespoon of sifted cacao powder
- 3 Teaspoons of Ceylon cinnamon
- 1 Teaspoon of powdered vanilla bean
- 1 Tablespoon of grass-fed ghee
- 2 Tablespoons of Coconut oil for greasing

For the Icing Ingredients:

- 4 Tablespoons of melted coconut butter with 1 to 2 teaspoons of coconut oil
- Optional garnishing ingredients: edible rose petals, or shredded cacao

Directions:

1. Preheat the oven to a temperature of about 350 degrees.
2. Grease a donut tray with the coconut oil.
3. Stir all together the sifted almond flour with the coconut milk, eggs, the granulated of stevia, the Keto-friendly baking powder, the apple cider vinegar, the salt, the sifted cocoa powder, the Ceylon cinnamon, the powdered vanilla bean and the grass-fed ghee.
4. Mix your donut ingredients until they are evenly combined.
5. Divide the obtained batter into the donut molds making sure to fill each to ¾ full.
6. Bake for about 8 minutes; then remove the tray from the oven and carefully transfer it to a wire rack.
7. Serve and enjoy your donut or top it with the icing and the garnish of your choice.
8. Serve and enjoy your delicious treat!

Nutrition

Calories: 122Fat: 6.8g Protein: 3g

Coconut Milk Pear Shake

Preparation time: 2 minutes

Cooking time: 0 minutes Serving: 4

Ingredients:

- 4 Ripe chopped pears
- 4 lettuce leaves finely torn into pieces
- ¼ Cup of unsweetened coconut milk
- 5 Dried and toasted Almonds
- 4 Leaves of mint
- 2 Tablespoons of unsweetened orange juice
- ½ Tablespoon of apple sauce
- 5 ice cubes

Direction

1. Place the chopped pears in the blender.
2. Add the lettuce leaves.
3. Pour in the almond milk and the rest of the ingredients with the ice cubes.
4. Blend all of your ingredients for around 3 minutes.
5. Serve and enjoy!

Nutrition

Calories: 60Fat: 3g Protein: 3g

Chocolate Pudding

Preparation time: 5 minutes

Cooking time: 0 minutes Serving: 3

Ingredients:

- 1 Avocado
- ¼ Cup of apple sauce
- ¼ Cup of organic raw unsweetened cacao powder
- 2 Organic Medjool dates
- 1 Tablespoon of organic coconut oil
- 1 Tablespoon of homemade almond milk
- For the crust:
- 1 Cup of organic walnuts
- 2 Organic Medjool dates
- 2 Tablespoons of organic raw cacao powder
- 1 Tablespoon of coconut oil

Directions

1. Start by preparing the crust.
2. Add all of your ingredients into a food processor and then process it until you obtain a sticky mixture.
3. Divide your mixture into halves and then press it into the bottom of 2 cavities of tart molds and set it aside.
4. Prepare your pudding by combining all of your ingredients into a blender and keep blending until you obtain a creamy mixture.
5. Transfer your smooth mixture to the mound you have prepared on the crust and make sure to spread it evenly.
6. Top with pistachios, walnuts, raw cacao nibs or hemp seeds.
7. Serve and enjoy!

Nutrition

Calories: 227 Fat: 22g Protein: 3.5g

Raspberry Smoothie

Preparation time: 5 minutes

Cooking time: 0 minutes Serving: 3

Ingredients

- 1 Cup of water

- 2 Cups of chopped lettuce
- 1 Cup of fresh or frozen raspberries
- 1 Tablespoon of flax seeds
- 1 Teaspoon of chia seeds
- A little bit of unsweetened apple sauce
- 1 Teaspoon of coconut oil

Directions

1. Place your ingredients into your blender.
2. Blend your ingredients at high speed for around 1 minute.
3. Check on the thickness of the smoothie, if it is creamy and smooth, serve and enjoy!

Nutrition

Calories 344 Fat 34gProtein 19g

Cocoa Mousse

Preparation time: 3 minutes
Cooking time: 0 minutes
Serving: 2
Ingredients

- 1 Cup of Heavy Whipping coconut Cream
- ¼ Cup of sifted, unsweetened cocoa powder
- ¼ Cup of Swerve
- 1 Teaspoon of Vanilla extract
- ¼ Teaspoon of kosher salt

Directions:

1. Start by whisking the cream until it starts stiffening.
2. Add in the stevia, the vanilla and the salt and whisk your ingredients very well.
3. Add the cocoa powder to your ingredients and whisk again.
4. Serve and enjoy your Cocoa mousse!

Nutrition

Calories: 218Fat: 23g Protein: 3g

Coconut Ice Cream

Preparation time: 3 minutes
Cooking time: 0 minutes
Serving: 2
Ingredients:

- 2 Cups of canned coconut milk
- 1/3 Cup of stevia
- 1/8 Teaspoon of salt
- 1 1/2 tsp pure vanilla extract or vanilla bean paste
- optional ingredients for desired flavor

Directions:

1. Make sure to use full-fat canned coconut milk.
2. You can also use the seeds of a vanilla bean instead of the extract.
3. Now, to make the ice cream, mix the milk with the Swerve the salt and the vanilla extract.
4. If you own an ice cream machine, you can simply churn by following the manufacturer's instructions.
5. Freeze the obtained mixture into ice cube trays then blend in a blender on a high-speed; you can use a Vitamix for example.
6. Freeze the ice cream for about 30 minutes.
7. Serve and enjoy your ice cream!

Nutrition

Calories: 283Fat: 21.5g Protein: 3.2g

Choco-Nut Milkshake

Preparation Time: 10 minutes
Cooking Time: 0 minute
Serving: 2
Ingredients

- 2 cups unsweetened coconut, almond
- 1 banana, sliced and frozen
- ¼ cup unsweetened coconut flakes
- 1 cup ice cubes
- ¼ cup macadamia nuts, chopped
- 3 tablespoons sugar-free sweetener
- 2 tablespoons raw unsweetened cocoa powder
- Whipped coconut cream

Directions

1. Place all ingredients into a blender and blend on high until smooth and creamy.
2. Divide evenly between 4 "mocktail" glasses and top with whipped coconut cream, if desired.

3. Add a cocktail umbrella and toasted coconut for added flair.
4. Enjoy your delicious Choco-nut smoothie!

Nutrition

12g Carbohydrates 3g Protein 199 Calories

Pineapple & Strawberry Smoothie

Preparation Time: 7 minutes

Cooking Time: 0-minute Serving: 2

Ingredients:

- 1 cup strawberries
- 1 cup pineapple, chopped
- ¾ cup almond milk
- 1 tablespoon almond butter

Directions:

1. Add all ingredients to a blender.
2. Blend until smooth.
3. Add more almond milk until it reaches your desired consistency.
4. Chill before serving.

Nutrition:

255 Calories39g Carbohydrate 5.6g Protein

Cantaloupe Smoothie

Preparation Time: 11 minutes

Cooking Time: 0 minute

Serving: 2

Ingredients:

- ¾ cup carrot juice
- 4 cups cantaloupe, sliced into cubes
- Pinch of salt
- Frozen melon balls
- Fresh basil

Directions:

1. Add the carrot juice and cantaloupe cubes to a blender. Sprinkle with salt.
2. Process until smooth.
3. Transfer to a bowl.
4. Chill in the refrigerator for at least 30 minutes.
5. Top with the frozen melon balls and basil before serving.

Nutrition:

135 Calories 31g Carbohydrate3.4g Protein

Berry Smoothie with Mint

Preparation Time: 7 minutes

Cooking Time: 0 minute

Serving: 2

Ingredients:

- ¼ cup orange juice
- ½ cup blueberries
- ½ cup blackberries
- 1 cup reduced-fat plain kefir
- 1 tablespoon honey
- 2 tablespoons fresh mint leaves

Directions:

1. Add all the ingredients to a blender.
2. Blend until smooth.

Nutrition:

137 Calories 27g Carbohydrate 6g Protein

Green Smoothie

Preparation Time: 12 minutes

Cooking Time: 0 minute

Serving: 2

Ingredients:

- 1 cup vanilla almond milk (unsweetened)
- ¼ ripe avocado, chopped
- 1 cup kale, chopped
- 1 banana
- 2 teaspoons honey
- 1 tablespoon chia seeds
- 1 cup ice cubes

Directions:

1. Combine all the ingredients in a blender.
2. Process until creamy.

Nutrition:

343 Calories 14.7g Carbohydrate 5.9g Protein

Banana, Cauliflower & Berry Smoothie

Preparation Time: 9 minutes

Cooking Time: 0 minute

Serving: 2

Ingredients:

- 2 cups almond milk (unsweetened)
- 1 cup banana, sliced
- ½ cup blueberries

- ½ cup blackberries
- 1 cup cauliflower rice
- 2 teaspoons maple syrup

Directions:
1. Pour almond milk into a blender.
2. Stir in the rest of the ingredients.
3. Process until smooth.
4. Chill before serving.

Nutrition:
149 Calories 29g Carbohydrate 3g Protein

Berry & Spinach Smoothie

Preparation Time: 11 minutes
Cooking Time: 0-minute Serving: 2
Ingredients:
- 2 cups strawberries
- 1 cup raspberries
- 1 cup blueberries
- 1 cup fresh baby spinach leaves
- 1 cup pomegranate juice
- 3 tablespoons milk powder (unsweetened)

Directions:
1. Mix all the ingredients in a blender.
2. Blend until smooth.
3. Chill before serving.

Nutrition:
118 Calories 25.7g Carbohydrate4.6g Protein

Peanut Butter Smoothie with Blueberries

Preparation Time: 12 minutes
Cooking Time: 0-minute Serving: 2
Ingredients:
- 2 tablespoons creamy peanut butter
- 1 cup vanilla almond milk (unsweetened)
- 6 oz. soft silken tofu
- ½ cup grape juice
- 1 cup blueberries
- Crushed ice

Directions:
1. Mix all the ingredients in a blender.
2. Process until smooth.

Nutrition: 247 Calories |30g Carb|10g Protein

Peach & Apricot Smoothie

Preparation Time: 11 minutes
Cooking Time: 0-minute Serving: 2
Ingredients:
- 1 cup almond milk (unsweetened)
- 1 teaspoon honey
- ½ cup apricots, sliced
- ½ cup peaches, sliced
- ½ cup carrot, chopped
- 1 teaspoon vanilla extract

Directions:
1. Mix milk and honey.
2. Pour into a blender.
3. Add the apricots, peaches and carrots.
4. Stir in the vanilla.
5. Blend until smooth.

Nutrition:
153 Calories 30g Carbohydrate 32.6g Protein

Tropical Smoothie

Preparation Time: 8 minutes
Cooking Time: 0 minute
Serving: 2
Ingredients:
- 1 banana, sliced
- 1 cup mango, sliced
- 1 cup pineapple, sliced
- 1 cup peaches, sliced
- 6 oz. nonfat coconut yogurt
- Pineapple wedges

Directions:
1. Freeze the fruit slices for 1 hour.
2. Transfer to a blender.
3. Stir in the rest of the ingredients except pineapple wedges.
4. Process until smooth.
5. Garnish with pineapple wedges.

Nutrition: 102 Calories |22g Carb|2g Protein

Energy-Booting Green Smoothie

Preparation Time: 15 minutes
Cooking Time: 0 minutes
Serving: 4
Ingredients:

- 2 handfuls of greens
- ½ seeded cucumber
- 1 apple
- 1 burro banana
- ½ tsp. Bromide Plus Powder
- 1 tbsp. walnuts
- ½ lb. soft-jelly coconut milk

Directions:

1. To prepare your green smoothie, first mix all the ingredients in a food processor. Pour into a glass and enjoy.

Nutrition:
16.5g Fat 2.9g Protein 222 Calories

Zucchini Relaxing Smoothie

Preparation Time: 15 minutes
Cooking Time: 10 minutes
Serving: 4
Ingredients:

- 1 zucchini, chopped
- 0.2 lb. herbal tea
- ½ lb. soft jelly coconut water

Directions:

1. To make your smoothie relaxed, first brew the tea according to the instructions and let it cool. Combine all ingredients in a blender. Blend well. Pour into serving glasses and enjoy!

Nutrition:
0.4g Fat 1.1g Protein 52 Calories

Magnesium-Boosting Smoothie

Preparation Time: 10 minutes
Cooking Time: 0 minutes
Serving: 2
Ingredients:

- ½ lb. fresh spring water
- 0.7 lb. Brazil nuts
- ½ burro banana
- 2 strawberries
- ½ lb. figs

Directions:

1. Mix all the ingredients using high-speed mixer. Enjoy.

Nutrition:
182 Calories 3g Fat 2.8g Protein

Detox Smoothie

Preparation Time: 20 minutes
Cooking Time: 0 minutes
Serving: 4
Ingredients:

- ½ avocado
- ½ lb. homemade soft-jelly coconut milk
- 1 handful of "approved" greens, such as callaloo, watercress, or dandelion greens
- 1 squeeze of key lime
- 1 tsp. of Dr. Sebi's Bromide Plus Powder

Directions:

1. Mix all the ingredients in a high-speed mixer. Fill in more water if the mixture is too concentrated. Enjoy.

Nutrition:
202 Calories 19.4g Fat 2.4g Protein

Immunity-Boosting Smoothie

Preparation Time: 35 minutes
Cooking Time: 20 minutes
Serving: 2
Ingredients:

- 1 mango
- 1 Seville orange
- ½ lb. brewed Dr. Sebi's Immune Support Herbal Tea
- 1 tbsp. coconut oil
- 1 tbsp. date sugar or agave syrup
- 1 lime, juiced

Directions:

1. Boil distilled water and pour 1 half tsp. of Dr. Sebi's Immune Support Herbal Tea.
2. Cook for about 15 minutes. Let cool, strain. Seville orange peel and mango cut into pieces. Mix all ingredients in a

high-speed mixer. Add to serving glasses and enjoy!

Nutrition: 97 Calories 3.7g Fat 9g Protein

Blueberry and Strawberry Smoothie

Preparation Time: 5 minutes

Cooking Time: 0 minutes Serving: 2

Ingredients:

- 6-7 strawberries, sliced
- ½ lb. blueberries
- ½ pint of almond milk

Directions:

1. Add all ingredients to a blender jar. Blend until smooth. Add to serving glasses. Serve and enjoy.

Nutrition: 107 Calories 7g Fat 4g Protein

Blueberry and Apple Smoothie

Preparation Time: 25 minutes

Cooking Time: 15 minutes Serving: 4

Ingredients:

- Brae burn apple, or another kind of organic apple
- ½-1 lb. of Brazil nuts
- ½ lb. homemade walnut milk
- ½ lb. blueberries
- ½ lb. of approved greens (dandelion greens, turnip greens, watercress, etc.)
- ½ tbsp. of date sugar or agave syrup

Directions:

1. Incorporate all the ingredients in a high-speed mixer. Stir more water if the mixture is too concentrated.

Nutrition:

181 Calories 5.8g Fat 3.8g Protein

Blueberry Pie Smoothie

Preparation Time: 20 minutes

Cooking Time: 0 minutes Serving: 2

Ingredients:

- 1 oz. fresh blueberries
- 1 burro banana
- 1 glass coconut milk
- ½ lb. cooked amaranth
- 1 tsp. Bromide Plus Powder
- 1 tbsp. homemade walnut butter
- 1 tbsp. date sugar

Directions:

1. Combine all the ingredients in a high-speed mixer. Fill in more water if too concentrated.

Nutrition: 413 Calories 31.9g Fat 5.8g Protein

Cucumber and Carley Green Smoothie

Preparation Time: 10 minutes

Cooking Time: 0 minutes Serving: 4

Ingredients:

- 1 lb. soft jelly coconut water
- 4 seeded cucumbers
- 2-3 key limes
- 1 bunch basil or sweet basil leaves
- ½ tsp. Bromide Plus Powder

Directions:

1. Mix cucumbers, basil, and lime. If you don't have a juicer, treat them in a grinder with sweet coconut jelly.
2. Transfer in a tall glass and stir in coconut water to make it smooth and add powdered bromide. Mix well and enjoy.

Nutrition: 141 Calories 7.4g Fat 5g Protein

Fruity and Green Smoothie

Preparation Time: 10 minutes

Cooking Time: 0-minute Serving: 2

Ingredients

- ½ cup of lettuce
- 1 cup of water
- 3 medium size bananas
- 2 teaspoons of lime juice
- ½ cup of raspberries
- ¼ teaspoon of ginger

Directions:

1. Mash the banana and blend all ingredients for 30 seconds at a time.
2. Serve in a cup and add some ice cubes or place in a refrigerator.

Nutrition:98 calories16g protein9.7g fiber

Banana & Strawberry Smoothie

Preparation Time: 7 minutes

Cooking Time: 0-minute Serving: 2
Ingredients:

- 1 banana, sliced
- 4 cups fresh strawberries, sliced
- 1 cup ice cubes
- 6 oz. yogurt
- 1 kiwi fruit, sliced

Directions:

1. Add banana, strawberries, ice cubes and yogurt in a blender.
2. Blend until smooth.
3. Garnish with kiwi fruit slices and serve.

Nutrition: 54 Calories 11.8g Carb 1.7g Protein

Cantaloupe & Papaya Smoothie

Preparation Time: 9 minutes
Cooking Time: 0-minute Serving: 2
Ingredients:

- ¾ cup low-fat milk
- ½ cup papaya, chopped
- ½ cup cantaloupe, chopped
- ½ cup mango, cubed
- 4 ice cubes - Lime zest

Directions:

1. Pour milk into a blender.
2. Add the chopped fruits and ice cubes.
3. Blend until smooth.
4. Garnish with lime zest and serve.

Nutrition: 207 Calories|18.4g Carb 7g Protein

Watermelon & Cantaloupe Smoothie

Preparation Time: 10 minutes
Cooking Time: 0-minute Serving: 2
Ingredients:

- 2 cups watermelon, sliced
- 1 cup cantaloupe, sliced
- ½ cup nonfat yogurt
- ¼ cup orange juice

Directions:

1. Add all the ingredients to a blender.
2. Blend until creamy and smooth. Chill before serving.

Nutrition: 114 Calories 13g Carb .8g Protein

Raspberry and Peanut Butter Smoothie

Preparation Time: 10 minutes
Cooking Time: 0-minute Serving: 2
Ingredients:

- Peanut butter, smooth and natural [2 tbsp]
- Skim milk [2 tbsp]
- Raspberries, fresh [1 or 1 ½ cups]
- Ice cubes [1 cup]
- Stevia [2 tsp]

Directions:

1. Situate all the ingredients in your blender. Set the mixer to puree. Serve.

Nutrition:170 Calories 8.6g Fat 20g Carbohydrate

Strawberry, Kale and Ginger Smoothie

Preparation Time: 13 minutes
Cooking Time: 0-minute Serving: 2
Ingredients:

- Curly kale leaves, fresh and large with stems removed [6 pcs]
- Grated ginger, raw and peeled [2 tsp]
- Water, cold [½ cup]
- Lime juice [3 tbsp] - Honey [2 tsp]
- Strawberries, fresh and trimmed [1 or 1 ½ cups]
- Ice cubes [1 cup]

Directions:

1. Position all the ingredients in your blender. Set to puree. Serve.

Nutrition:205 Calories 2.9g Fat 42.4g Carbohydrates

Green Detox Smoothie

Preparation time: 10 minutes
Cooking time: 0 minutes Servings: 4
Ingredients

- Baby spinach – 2 cups
- Baby kale – 2 cups
- Celery – 2 ribs, chopped
- Green apple – 1, medium, chopped
- Frozen sliced banana – 1 cup
- Almond milk -1 cup

- Grated fresh ginger -1 Tbsp.
- Chia seeds – 1 Tbsp.
- Honey – 1 Tbsp.

Direction

1. Combine everything in a blender and blend until smooth. Serve.

Nutrition 136 Calories 1g Fat 1g Protein

Cucumber Ginger Detox

Preparation time: 5 minutes
Cooking time: 0 minutes
Servings: 2
Ingredients

- Spinach – 1 ½ oz.
- Orange – 1, peeled
- Ginger – ½ inch, peeled
- Water – 1 cup
- Cucumber – 1, chopped
- Avocado – ½ chopped
- Ice – 1 cup
- Rosehips – 1 tsp.

Direction

1. Combine everything in the blender and blend until smooth. Serve.

Nutrition
144 Calories 8g Fat 3g Protein: 3g

Green Protein Smoothie

Preparation time: 5 minutes
Cooking time: 0-minute Servings: 2
Ingredients

- Kale – 1 oz.
- Pineapple – 4 oz.
- Pea protein – 1 Tbsp.
- Water – 1 cup
- Tangerine – 1, peeled
- Avocado – ½
- Almonds – 3 Tbsp.
- Ice – 1 cup

Direction

1. Except for the almonds, blend everything in the blender.
2. Top with almonds and serve.

Nutrition227 Calories 15g Fat 7g Protein

Ginger Detox Twist

Preparation time: 5 minutes
Cooking time: 0-minute Servings: 2
Ingredients

- Collard greens – 1 ½ oz.
- Apple – 1 chopped
- Ginger – ½ inch
- Water – 1 cup
- Persian cucumbers – 2, chopped
- Meyer lemon – 1, peeled
- Chlorella – ½ tsp.
- Ice – 1 cup

Direction

1. Blend everything in a blender and serve.

Nutrition 114 Calories 1g Fat 5g Protein

Classic Apple Detox Smoothie

Preparation time: 5 minutes
Cooking time: 0-minute Servings: 2
Ingredients

- Baby spinach – 1 ½ oz.
- Celery – 2 oz. chopped
- Lemon – 1, juiced
- Water – 1 cup
- Apple – 1 chopped
- Mini cucumber – 1, chopped
- Ginger – ½ inch, peeled and chopped
- Ice – 1 cup

Direction

1. Blend everything in a blender and enjoy.

Nutrition
66 Calories
0.1g Fat
1g Protein

30 Days Meal Plan

Day	Breakfast	Lunch	Snack	Dinner	Dessert
1	Beef Fajitas	Brunswick Stew	Almond Butter Cinnamon Bars	Spicy Chicken Cacciatore	Keto Orange Cake
2	Keto Salad	Chicken Vera Cruz	Ginger Patties	Veggies Casserole	Cocoa Mousse
3	Rolls with Spinach	Coleslaw	Cheesy Pita Crisps	Sweet & Spicy Chickpeas	Green Smoothie
4	Cheese Yogurt	Tomato and Guaca Salad	Coconut Keto Bombs	Italian Pork Chops	Banana & Strawberry Smoothie
5	Breakfast Egg and Ham Burrito	Chicken Tortilla Soup	Almond Coconut BIscotti	Mushrooms with Bell Peppers	Crackers
6	Berry Avocado Smoothie	Gazpacho	Macadamia Cookies	Ginger Citrus Chicken Thighs	Pretzels
7	Omelet with Chickpea Flour	Carnitas Tacos	Simple Appetizer Meatballs	Coffee-and-Herb-Marinated Steak	Cake with Whipped Cream Icing
8	Huevos Rancheros	Barbecue Brisket	Cheese Crisp Crackers	Homestyle Herb Meatballs	Madeleine
9	Tex-Mex Migas	Roasted Carrot and Leek Soup	Blueberry Fat Bombs	Orange-Marinated Pork Tenderloin	Fruit Cake with Walnuts
10	Bulgur Porridge Breakfast	Lemon-Tarragon Soup	Garlicky Hummus	Chipotle Chili Pork Chops	Tropical Smoothie
11	Barley Breakfast with Banana & Sunflower Seeds	Beef Goulash	Almond Flour Crackers	Pork Chop Diane	Ginger Detox Twist
12	Greek-Yogurt Style	Chicken Cordon Bleu	Pistachio Muffins	Mediterranean Steak Sandwiches	Cantaloupe & Papaya Smoothie
13	Muffins of Savory Egg	Cajun Beef & Rice Skillet	Raspberry and Cashew Balls	Chicken with Creamy Thyme Sauce	Raspberry Smoothie
14	Instant Pot Chicken Chili	Thai Pork Salad	Peppermint and Chocolate	Almond-Crusted Salmon	Peanut Butter Smoothie with Blueberries

15	Balanced Turkey Meatballs	Vegetarian Club Salad	Asian Chicken Wings	Beef Steak Fajitas	Pine Nut Cookies
16	Breakfast Quesadilla	Pita Pizza	Easy Cauliflower Hush	Chickpeas & Veggie Stew	Nut and Raspberry Balls
17	Breakfast Salad	Lemon Garlic Shrimp Pasta	Banana Nut Cookies	Spicy Turkey Tacos	Keto Sugar Free Candies
18	Black Bean Tacos Breakfast	Egg Salad Stuffed Avocado	Cheesy Onion Dip	Quick and Easy Shrimp Stir-Fry	Cheesy Taco Bites
19	Quinoa Burrito	Smoky Carrot & Black Bean Stew	Cocoa Balls	Nori-Burritos	Coconut Fat Bombs
20	Veggie Breakfast Wrap	Corn Tortillas & Spinach Salad	Almond Cheescake Bites	Rosemary Chicken	Seed and Nut Squares
21	Niçoise Salad Tuna	Chicken Thighs	Apple Leather	Air Fryer Meatloaf	Cinnamon Cake
22	Chicken and Egg Salad	Fettuccine Chicken Alfredo	Bean Salad with Balsamic	Dijon Salmon	Waffles
23	White Sandwich Bread	Beef Pizza	Almond Oreo Cookies	Zucchini Herb	Oreo Cookies with Cream Cheese Filling
24	Bagel Hummus Toast	Bell Pepper Basil Pizza	BLT Stuffed Cucumbers	Veggie Burgers	Cinnamon and Ginger Cake
25	Paleo Breakfast Hash	Nacho Steak in the Skillet	Salted Macadamia Keto	Spinach Curry	Keto Donuts
26	Strawberry Coconut Bake	Portobello Bun Cheeseburgers	Taco Cheese Bites	Pork Rind Nachos	Ketogenic Cheesecake
27	Healthy Avocado Toast	Balsamic Beef Pot Roast	Pistachio and Cocoa Sqares	Air Fryer Hamburgers	Lemon Cake
28	Scramble for Lox, Eggs and Onion	Cumin Spiced Beef Wraps	Pesto Veggie Pizza	Air Fried Beef Schnitzel	Walnut-Fruit Cake
29	Strawberry Coconut Bake	Quinoa Fruit Salad	Cheesy Taco Chips	Troute Bake	Cocoa Mousse
30	Breakfast Bowl of Yogurt	Broccoli and hot Sauce	Chocolate Chip Blondies	Coconut Shrimp	Green Smoothie

Conclusion

I hope that this book marks the start of the road to long-term wellbeing and lively life. Many of the tips might be different from something you've done previously, and we recognize that you and others around you may need to make drastic lifestyle changes. It isn't often easy to alter, but it can be highly satisfying. It would be a wonderful feeling to see your diabetes reversing and maybe vanish, particularly knowing that you provided the chance by giving your body the nutrients it requires to do its job.

Remember to prepare for your future as you continue your path to healthier health and perceive each difficulty as a rewarding task to conquer. You should conquer Mount Everest and triumphantly raise your weapons. This is your ability to shine and radiate confidence while you encourage your body to radiate wellbeing.

Hire your support team and inspire them to accompany you in your journey, not simply to cheer you on. After all, the nutrition tips in this book are largely the same ones we will send to someone trying to lose weight, boost their wellbeing, or live longer. Best wishes on your journey.

If you found this helpful book, I invite you to leave a positive review directly on the Amazon page. To do this, just scan the QR code on the next page with your smartphone.

If you have any other requests or particular questions, you can freely contact me at my email address.

scarrett.diet@outlook.com

Remember to also look at my site, which I maintain every day.

www.suzannescarrett.com

You can also find me on Facebook and if you wish, put a like on my personal page.

Good cooking. I wish you much joy and serenity.

Printed in Great Britain
by Amazon

11750036R00133